STAND WITH TED

STAND WITH TED

A Clarion Call From Ted Cruz
Delivered to the United States Senate,
September 24th and 25th, 2013

(Also featuring Senators Mike Lee, Utah; David Vitter,
Louisiana; Rand Paul, Kentucky; Pat Roberts, Kansas;
Jeff Sessions, Alabama; Marco Rubio, Florida; Mike
Enzi, Wyoming; Jim Inhofe, Oklahoma; Dick Durbin,
Illinois; Tim Kaine, Virginia)

Shining City Press

The text, "A Clarion Call," is from the Congressional Record.

This Shining City edition copyright © 2016

Printed in the United States of America

ISBN 13: 978-099115459-3

Shining City Press books are distributed to the trade by
National Book Network.

For bulk sales please contact the publisher:
Shining City Press
PO Box 29502, Dept. 31733
Las Vegas, NV 89126

INTRODUCTION

I've spoken of the shining city all my political life, but I don't know if I ever quite communicated what I saw when I said it. But in my mind it was a tall proud city built on rocks stronger than oceans, wind-swept, God-blessed, and teeming with people of all kinds living in harmony and peace, a city with free ports that hummed with commerce and creativity, and if there had to be city walls, the walls had doors and the doors were open to anyone with the will and the heart to get here. That's how I saw it and see it still.

—President Ronald Reagan

The concept, passage, implementation, and cost to the economy of ObamaCare is at the center of Republican disaffection with President Obama and the agenda of the Democratic Party. The opponents of this law believed it would dim the Shining City. . . .

The voters who gave Republicans control of the House in 2010 expected them to "repeal and replace" ObamaCare, but despite voting often to do so in the House nothing changed. Frustrated conservatives and Tea Partiers found a voice and a champion when Ted Cruz took the Senate floor on September 24, 2013, to speak against ObamaCare and urged voters to "Make DC Listen."

Ted's marathon speech features tales of constituent dissatisfaction with ObamaCare, praise of and lectures on the finer points of

American democracy, and substantial questions and comments from ten senators who stood with him. There are flashes of humor and poignancy typical of a filibuster, such as, when Senator Mike Lee wishes for a Letter of Marque and Reprisal—"effectively a hall pass issued by the U.S. Congress . . . that entitles the bearer of that hall pass to be a pirate on the high seas." (He confesses he longed to be a pirate as a child.) Ted Cruz read *Green Eggs and Ham* by Dr. Seuss (not included here for reasons of copyright), and bantered with Mike Lee about how "things are not always as they seem"—the Hundred Years Way actually went on for 116 years; black boxes are actually orange; Panama hats come from Ecuador, and more.

Though technically not a filibuster (which by definition blocks or delays action on a bill), Senator Cruz's speech was the 4th longest in the history of the United States Senate (after Strom Thurmond: 24 hours, 18 minutes, against the Civil Rights Bill, 1957; Alphonse D'Amato, 23:30 to stall a military appropriations bill in 1986; and Wayne Morse, 22:26 on the Tidelands oil legislation in 1953). It is a clarion call to those who think that President Obama's agenda has taken the country in the wrong direction.

A CLARION CALL

The PRESIDING OFFICER. The Senator from Texas.

Mr. CRUZ. Madam President, I rise today in opposition to ObamaCare. I rise today in an effort to speak for 26 million Texans and for 300 million Americans.

All across this country Americans are suffering because of ObamaCare. ObamaCare isn't working. Yet fundamentally there are politicians in this body who are not listening to the people. They are not listening to the concerns of their constituents, they are not listening to the jobs lost or the people forced into part-time work, to the people losing their health insurance, to the people who are struggling.

A great many Texans, a great many Americans feel they don't have a voice. I hope to play some very small part in helping provide that voice for them. I intend to speak in opposition to ObamaCare, I intend to speak in support of defunding ObamaCare, until I am no longer able to stand, to do everything I can to help Americans stand together and recognize this grand experiment 3½ years ago is, quite simply, not working.

I also say at the outset that I am particularly honored to be standing side by side with my friend and colleague Senator MIKE LEE from Utah. Senator LEE has shown visionary leadership in standing and taking the mantle of leading the effort to defund ObamaCare and to challenge this train wreck of a law, and Senator LEE has been repaid at times with vilification from official Washington.

In my judgment there is no Senator in this body, Republican or Democrat, who is more principled, who is more dedicated, who is more fearless and willing to fight for the principles that make this Nation great than is Senator MIKE LEE. It is a singular privilege to serve with him and to stand side by side with him and so many others in this body, and, even more importantly, so many millions of Americans all across this country.

There is a problem in Washington, and the problem is bigger than a continuing resolution. It is bigger than ObamaCare. It is even bigger than the budget. The most fundamental problem and the frustration is that the men and women in Washington aren't listening. If you talk to the man and woman on the street, that is the message you hear over and over again: Why don't they listen to me? Why don't they hear what we have to say? They aren't listening to the millions of people, Democrats, Republicans, Independents, Libertarians, across the spectrum who say our elected officials get to Washington and they stop listening to the people.

We just had a 6-week recess during August where a substantial percentage of Members of Congress chose not to hold townhalls during the 6 weeks we had to be back in our home States, not even to give their constituents a chance to say their views, because it is very easy when those of us who are in elected office have been here for a long time to believe Washington knows better; to believe that all the solutions are found in Washington, DC, and the rest of the country is better—as they say of small children—seen but not heard.

We need millions of people to get an answer. Millions of people are asking for accountability, for responsibility, for truth from their elected officials, truth about how ObamaCare is failing the men and women of America. It is time, quite simply, to make DC listen. That is a point I intend to make over and over, because it is fundamentally what we are trying to do. We are trying to gather the American people to make DC listen.

The whole debate we are having is not over strategy. It is not about process. It is not about procedure. If you read the papers it looks like it is. If you read the papers it is all sorts of confusing cloture on the motions to the what-the, to the which-the. To anyone outside of DC, their eyes glaze over. Even to anyone in Washington, DC, their eyes glaze over.

This is also not about pollsters. It is not about pundits or consultants or those who are making money back and forth on the political process. They have always been with us, and I am confident they will remain with us for all time. The problem is DC is not listening. The problem is our elected leaders are not listening to their constituents.

Everyone in America understands ObamaCare is destroying jobs. It is driving up health care costs. It is killing health benefits. It is shattering the economy. All across the country in all 50 States—it doesn't matter what State you go to, you can go to any State in the Union, it doesn't matter if you are talking to Republicans or Democrats or Independents or Libertarians—Americans understand this thing is not working.

Yet Washington is pretending not to know. Washington is pretending to have no awareness. Instead we have politicians giving speeches about how wonderful ObamaCare is. At the same time they go to the President and ask for an exemption from ObamaCare for Members of Congress.

If ObamaCare is so wonderful, why is it that its loudest advocates don't want to be subject to it? I will confess that is a very difficult one to figure out.

DC is using a rigged process to keep ObamaCare funded, to keep this job-killing bill funded. What they want to do fundamentally is ignore the men and women of America and keep up with business as usual. People wonder why Congress has such low approval ratings. I remember when all 100 of us were in the historic Senate Chamber for a bipartisan meeting. Multiple Senators stood and expressed frustrationwiththelowapprovalratingsthatCongresshas.Itvaries—sometimes, 10, 12, 14 percent—but it is always abysmal.

Some suggested the reason was that we are not legislating enough. We just need to pass some more laws and the American people will be happy. I have to admit, that does not comport with just about anything I have ever heard in the State of Texas. That doesn't comport with anything I have ever heard from constituents. I am going to suggest the most fundamental reason Congress remains in the low teens in approval ratings is because Congress is not listening to the American people.

Every poll that has been done for years, when we ask the American people what is their top priority, the answer is consistently jobs and the economy—over and over, jobs and the economy. That is national. That is in your State, my State. That is in all 50 States. Jobs and the economy is the answer you get. It is also not partisan. You can ask Republicans, ask Democrats, you can ask Independents. They say we need jobs, we need economic growth back.

Yet I will tell you, Madam President—you and I have both served in this institution some 9 months, not very long, but in the time we have been here we have spent virtually zero time even talking about jobs and the economy. It doesn't make the agenda. It apparently is not important enough for this body's time. We spent 6 weeks talking about guns, talking about taking away law-abiding citizens' Second Amendment rights, and we spend virtually no time talking about fundamental tax reform, about regulatory reform, about getting the economy going. And politicians wonder why it is that Congress is held in such low esteem. This is unfortunately a bipartisan issue, on both sides.

We need to do a better job of listening to the people. If the top priority of the American people is jobs and the economy, I am going to suggest the top priority of Congress should be jobs and the economy.

Madam President, you and I should both be scratching our heads, trying to think about a time when we weren't talking about jobs and the economy because, I tell you, we certainly have not gotten it taken care of yet. The American people are frustrated because their elected officials do not listen.

When we are home on the campaign trail, we say we listen. Yet something about this Senate floor, something about Washington, DC—I don't know if it is the water, something in the air, the cherry blossoms, but people get here and they stop listening to the American people.

As I traveled throughout the State of Texas—I spent the month of August and the beginning of September traveling virtually every day on the road throughout Texas and across the country listening, hearing the stories. The American people are hurting. This is a difficult time. The very rich, they are doing fine. In fact, they are doing better under President Obama than they were before. But hard-working American families are struggling and their life has become harder and harder and harder.

ObamaCare is the biggest job killer in this country. The American people want to stop this madness, and so do I. In Washington, we pass million-dollar bills, billion-dollar bills no one has ever read, often without even voting on them. We call it unanimous consent. It is only unanimous because they don't let anyone know.

In Washington, we spend $2 trillion more than last year and then tell voters we saved money. The system is deliberately designed to hide what we are actually doing.

In this debate right now over ObamaCare and the continuing resolution, voting to pass bills is called procedure, as if it doesn't matter. We pretend it doesn't matter. It does matter. Our leaders right now demand approval for bills before they are amended: Everyone come to the floor, vote for the bill. Then we will amend it to make it say the opposite of what it says right now, but you have already voted so don't worry about it. We are told to agree to the bills without even knowing what the final product will be and that is what is happening right now. Our leaders in both parties are asking us to support a bill, to cut off debate on a bill without even knowing what is in it.

It is as the former Speaker of the House NANCY PELOSI once observed: Pass it to find out what is in it. That is how Washington does business.

Let me tell you how this is likely to unfold. Senate majority leader HARRY REID has said he intends to offer an amendment to determine the future of our health care system and based on the public press reports— and I would note you have to rely on the public press reports because this body doesn't know, but based on the public press reports, that amendment is going to fully fund ObamaCare. It is going to strip the language the House of Representatives passed to defund ObamaCare and listen to the American people.

The central vote the Senate will take on this fight will not occur today and it will not occur tomorrow. The first vote we are going to take on this is a vote on what is called cloture on the motion to proceed. Very few people not on this floor have any idea what that means and even, I suspect, a fair number of people on this floor are not quite sure what that means. That will simply be a vote whether to take up this bill and to begin debating this bill. I expect that vote to pass overwhelmingly, if not unanimously. Everyone agrees we ought to take this up, we ought to start this conversation.

The next vote we take will occur on Friday or Saturday and it will be on what is called cloture on the bill. That is the vote that matters. Cloture on the bill, the vote Friday or Saturday, is the vote that matters.

Why is that? Because that vote is subject to a 60-vote threshold. If Republicans vote with Democrats, then this body will cut off debate on the bill. Cloture is simply cutting off debate. It is saying we are not going to talk about it anymore, we are silencing the voice of the Senate, we are silencing the voice of the people, and we are cutting off debate.

Why does that matter? Because once cloture is invoked, the rules of the Senate allow the majority leader to introduce the amendment to fund ObamaCare and then to have it pass with just 51 votes, not 60—51. As the Presiding Officer is well aware, there are more than 51 Democrats in this body. Postcloture, after this body has voted to cut off debate, the Democrats can vote on a straight party-line vote to fund ObamaCare. Madam President, I am going to let you in on a dirty little secret. When that happens, every Republican, if we get to that point, will vote against it and every Republican will then go home to his or her State and say: Look, I voted against ObamaCare.

That is actually the preferred outcome, to have a vote but yet to have the result be business as usual continue in Washington. It is a little bit akin to the World Wrestling Federation, wrestling matches where it is all rigged. The outcome is predetermined. They know in advance who is going to win and lose and it is all for show. There are some Members of this body, if we could have 100 show votes, saying here is what we are for, but mind you, none of them are actually going to change the law, none of them are actually going to occur, none of them are going to make one iota of difference to the American people because they will never become law, but we will get to vote over and over again in proving how committed we are to principle A, B, C, D or E, that curiously would make a significant number of Senators happy.

Our constituents deserve more—no more fake fights, no more hiding our votes, no more games, no more trying to fool the American people. We need to make DC listen—make DC listen. I want to stand and fight for the more than 1.6 million Americans who signed a national petition against ObamaCare and to the millions more who did not because they were told by a politician it is not possible—don't even try to fight because it is not possible.

I am reminded of a children's story. My wife Heidi and I are blessed to have two little girls, Caroline and Catherine, ages 5 and 2, and one of their favorite children's stories, actually from when I was a kid, is "The Little Engine That Could"—the train going up that said over and over again, "I think I can. I think I can."

I have to say, if we listen to a lot of Members of this body, the message would be simple. That little engine can't. What they say to that train when it starts at the bottom of the hill is, no, you can't.

I think I can. I think I can.

No, you can't. No, you can't. We can't win. You can't stop ObamaCare. It cannot be done. It is impossible. There is nothing we can do.

Are millions of Americans out of work? Yes. Are millions of Americans struggling? Yes. Are millions of Americans seeing their health insurance premiums skyrocket? Yes. Are millions of Americans at risk of losing their health insurance because of ObamaCare? Yes.

But Washington tells our constituents: No, no, never mind. It can't be done. It cannot be done. It is impossible. The rules of Washington say this cannot be done.

And we wonder why this body has such low approval among the people. When we go out and tell the American people it cannot be done, there is nothing that can be done to stop ObamaCare, what we are saying is we are not willing to do it. We are not willing to stand and fight.

We are willing to give speeches. Oh, yes, if we want to have a speech contest, we can line up and fall over backward who can give the best speech against ObamaCare. But when it comes to actually standing and fighting, when it comes to actually having the opportunity to listen to the American people, an awful lot of Members of this body, at least so far, have not shown up to battle.

There are a lot of folks in the Washington establishment who do not want to hear from us. The chattering class is quick to discipline anyone who refuses to blindly fall in line. That is the way Washington plays. There are rules. We are not supposed to speak for the people. There is a way things are done in Washington and make no mistake, DC depends upon Americans not paying attention.

They know most Americans are quite reasonably working too hard to provide for their family. They are too busy spending time with their friends and family. They are too busy working to try to make sure their family is provided for. They are going to church. They are dealing with the day-to-day burdens of life. You know what they have learned? The American people have learned when we get involved, even then it seems as though Washington politicians rarely listen.

I believe that can change. I am standing here today to salute, to celebrate the American democratic system. I am standing here today to suggest that if Senators listen to their constituents, if we listen to the American people, the vote would be 100 to 0 to defund ObamaCare. Even those Senators who voted for it who might have believed it would work. Many of us would have disagreed. Had I been here, not surprisingly, I would have voted against ObamaCare 3½ years ago. A number of Members in this body voted in favor of it. Regardless of how Members voted 3½ years ago, one of the great virtues of life is learning, looking at the evidence, looking at the facts, and seeing when something is not working.

Look at the labor unions. Three-and-a-half years ago the labor unions were enthusiastically supporting ObamaCare. Why? Because they heard the promises. They heard it was going to work, and that it would be a bonanza for all. They believed the promises, and that is understandable. Yet one of the things we have seen this year is one labor union after another after another saying: Whoa. This thing isn't working. This thing is hurting us. This thing is hurting our Members.

(Mr. MANCHIN assumed the Chair.)

By the way, the people whom it is hurting are hard-working men and women and hard-working American families. They are the ones getting hammered.

James Hoffa, the president of the Teamsters, has said ObamaCare is destroying the 40-hour workweek. It is destroying the backbone of the American middle class. That is not me saying that, that is not any politician from Washington saying that, that is the Teamsters.

We should submit the question to the American people: Do the American people want to destroy the 40-hour workweek that is the backbone of the American middle class? That is not a close question. People talk about how we are a 50–50 Nation and how there is a tight partisan divide. I don't believe it. I think on questions such as that there is an overwhelming majority of Americans who say of course we should not destroy the 40-hour workweek. Of course we shouldn't break the backbone of the American middle class.

If more politicians listened to the people, we would respond and avert this train wreck. Yet the politicians of Washington tell us: Don't worry about it. ObamaCare is going to be peachy keen. The Senate is too busy to do anything to avert this train wreck.

Mind you, the Senate is not too busy to exempt ourselves from it. We know enough to say: We don't want to be a part of this thing. The American people know it can't be done. Nothing can be done. We need to accept it.

Americans have never been people who accept failure. Americans have never been people who accept impossibility. If we look to a rag-tag bunch of colonists in the 18th century, the idea that we would stand up to Great Britain, the British Army—the most mighty military force on the face of the planet—was impossible. It can't be done. I guarantee that all of the pundits we see going on TV and intoning in deep baritone voices: This cannot be done—if we were back in the 18th century, they would be writing messages in dark ink and sending it by carrier pigeon, saying: This cannot be done. You can't stand up to the British Army. It can't be done. It is impossible. Accept your subjugation. Accept your taxation without representation. Accept that this is impossible.

If we fast forward to the Civil War—a time of enormous pain, anguish, and bloodshed in the United States—there were a lot of voices then who said the Union cannot be saved. It cannot be done. Accept defeat. I suspect those same pundits, had they been around in the mid-19th century, would have written the same columns: This cannot be done.

If we go to the 1940s, Nazi Germany—look, we saw it in Britain. Neville Chamberlain told the British people: Accept the Nazis. Yes, they will dominate the continent of Europe, but that is not our problem. Let's appease them. Why? Because it can't be done. We cannot possibly stand against them.

In America there were voices who listened to that; I suspect the same pundits who said it couldn't be done. If this had happened in the 1940s, we would have been listening to them. Even then they would have made television. They would have gotten beyond the carrier pigeons and letters and they would have been on TV saying: You cannot defeat the Germans.

If we go to the late 1960s when a President, John F. Kennedy, told this country: We are going to send a man to the Moon—when John F. Kennedy told this country we are going to send a man to the Moon, there were a lot of people who said: It cannot be done. It is impossible. It cannot be done. Yet John F. Kennedy had the vision to say Americans can do things—whatever we set our minds to.

If we go to the late 1970s and 1980s, we were in the midst of the Cold War. I remember growing up in the Cold War. I remember being told the Soviet Union cannot be defeated. It cannot be done. We have to accept malaise. We have to accept second-class citizenship. They have a lot of weapons. We cannot possibly stand up to the Soviet Union.

There was a President—a President whom I admired deeply, President Ronald Reagan—who had the temerity to say: What is your strategy on the Cold War? Answer: We win, they lose.

At the time those same Washington founts of wisdom said: It can't be done. No, no, no, we can't win. Winning is a two-dimensional strategy. We need to be much more nuanced than that. We need to push for detente, whatever that means. We need to push for something short of actually winning.

So we get to ObamaCare, and what do all of those voices say? It cannot be stopped. It can't be done. We cannot defund it. By any measure ObamaCare is a far less intimidating foe than those I have discussed, with the possible exception of the Moon. The Moon might be as intimidating as ObamaCare. Yet those same voices of Washington give the same message that they have said over and over and over again, which is the opposite of the message of the little engine that could: No, you can't. It can't be done. No, we can't.

What should we have instead of you know what? We hear echoes from the past battles. We ought to have a vote where we can go to our constituents and say: By golly, we really, really, really dislike ObamaCare. Can we add a couple of more reallys? I want to make it clear that it is really, really, really.

We wonder why our constituents look at us and say: What on Earth are you doing? Do you actually care that we are losing our jobs? Do you actually care that we can't find a job? Do you care that our small businesses are not growing? Do you care that health insurance premiums for people who are struggling are skyrocketing? Do you care that more and more Americans are losing their health insurance?

We don't need fake fights. We don't need fake votes. We need real change. We need a better economy. We need more jobs. We need more freedom. And what is critical in doing that is stopping ObamaCare because Americans should not have to worry about what Washington is doing to them, what Washington is doing to make their life harder, what Washington is doing to take away their job, what Washington is doing to drive up their health insurance premiums, what Washington is doing to jeopardize the health insurance they have now.

I cannot tell the Presiding Officer how many times across the State of Texas I have had men and women come up to me—some with disabilities and some in wheelchairs—and say: Please, stop this bill. Stop

ObamaCare because I don't want to lose my health insurance. It is jeopardizing the health insurance coverage I have now.

We all remember when President Obama told the American people: If you like your health insurance, you can keep it. Now at the time that sounded good. Any of us who liked our health insurance wanted to keep it. We liked that promise. That is the kind of promise we like from our candidates and our officeholders.

Yet as I mentioned earlier, one of the great faculties of higher reason is the ability to learn—the ability to learn from evidence and facts. We have learned that promise did not, in fact, meet reality because the reality is millions of Americans are at risk of losing their health insurance.

A few weeks ago UPS sent a letter to 15,000 employees and it said: We are terminating spousal health insurance because of ObamaCare. Their husbands and wives were told: Sorry, your health insurance is gone. Remember, the promise was: If you like your health insurance, you can keep it. For those 15,000 UPS employees—for their husbands and wives—that promise has been disproved by reality. This body would step up and stop ObamaCare if we did just one thing: if we listened to our constituents. So together that is what we have to do: Make DC listen.

A lot of folks in Washington are angry we are even having this fight. A lot of folks in Washington are angry—it is fascinating how many politicians in Washington think this isn't even worth our time. I will point out, as is usually the case—almost always the case—the Senate floor is largely empty. Everyone's schedules are apparently busy enough that standing and coming together to stop ObamaCare doesn't make it onto the priority list. We ought to have all 100 Senators on this floor around the clock until we come together and stop ObamaCare. If they talked to their constituents, that is what they would like. If they would talk to their constituents, their constituents would say: What possibly do you have to do that is more important than getting the economy moving again and bringing back jobs? What possibly do you have to do that is more important than stopping me from losing my health insurance or stopping me from losing my health care? That is what I hear from my constituents over and over again. I am confident the Presiding Officer hears it from his constituents. Every one of us hears it from our constituents because that is what Americans are saying in all 50 States. We should not have to worry about what the next rule, the next regulation, or the next tax is that is going to be handed down from the DC ruling class.

ObamaCare alone has produced over 20,000 pages of regulation. I am confident the Presiding Officer has not read 20,000 pages of ObamaCare regulations. I can tell the Presiding Officer I have not read 20,000 pages of ObamaCare regulations. I would wager all the money in my bank account there is no Member in this body who has read 20,000 pages of ObamaCare regulation.

Yet what is Washington telling small businesses all across the country? You are bound by 20,000 pages of ObamaCare regulation, and more and more is coming. There is another 3,000 pages added every 6 months. So it is going to keep coming and coming and coming.

I remember doing a tele-townhall several months ago, and a woman who owns a small business asked: How do I comply with all of these regulations? How do I comply with the burdens of ObamaCare? It was quite striking. She said: I don't even know where to start. I will confess that I felt embarrassed because I said: Ma'am, I don't know how to tell you that.

The complexity is so much that it is causing more and more small businesses to stay small—avoid ObamaCare altogether. They can't decipher the rules and regulations so they don't. If they have under 50 employees, they can get out from under it.

I cannot tell you how many small businesses are not hiring right now. If they have 30 or 40 employees, they are not subject to ObamaCare, but if they get the fiftieth employee, that fiftieth employee better be one heck of an employee, because the instant he or she shows up on the payroll, boom, the entire business is subject to 20,000 pages of regulations and crushing costs.

To the men and women at home today who are out of a job, I point out to you that if it were not for ObamaCare, every small business that has an opportunity to expand right now and is not expanding because of ObamaCare—that is a job you are not able to get.

Do you want to know why the job economy is so bad, why there are so few jobs, why we have the lowest workforce participation in decades in the United States? Small businesses generate two-thirds of all new jobs in the economy, and small businesses have been hammered under ObamaCare unlike ever before.

If we listened to our constituents, we would step forward and act to avert this train wreck. The only way that will happen is if the American people demand it, if together we make DC listen. That is what this fight is about. It is about ensuring that the American people have a voice, ensuring that those who are struggling, those who are without a job, those who are afraid of losing their health insurance—that Washington listens to them, that Washington acts on their needs.

Anyone who wants to know why this body is held in low esteem only has to look out to the empty chairs. If you are out of a job, wondering what the Senate is doing to get our economy moving, to help small businesses create new jobs so you can go to work and provide for your family, the answer is displayed right in front of you.

If you are concerned about the health care for yourself, for your family, if you are seeing more and more people losing their health insurance and you are saying: "What about my family? What if I lose my health insurance because of ObamaCare?" and you ask what the Senate is doing to listen to you, the answer, right now, is an empty Chamber.

Our system was based on a profound notion: that sovereignty resides with the American people, that every one of us—sometimes people in the Senate behave as if they have no bosses, as if they are autonomous rulers. And Washington is a little bit of a town that treats the people in Washington—they behave like kings and queens of their own fiefdoms. Yet every one of us has a whole lot of bosses. In my instance, I have 26 million bosses back home in Texas. Who are the 26 million Texans whom I work to represent? Those who supported me and those who did not. It is my job to represent every one of them, to fight for every one of them. The most fundamental problem, bigger than ObamaCare, is the problem that Washington has stopped listening to the American people.

It is quite striking that in discussions about ObamaCare among elected officials, we hear more complaints about "I don't like all the phone calls I am getting from my constituents" than we do about ObamaCare. It is apparently an imposition on some Members of this body for their constituents to pick up the phone and express their views. It is viewed as somehow illegitimate. How dare they? Apparently, standing on those steps and taking the oath of office invests 100 people with somehow greater wisdom, greater insight, more brain cells. Our constituents—there is a tendency in this town, particularly as time goes on, to view our constituents as an annoyance.

Today—just today—I have heard multiple Senators complaining: too many phone calls from my constituents. What a remarkable complaint. What a remarkable complaint.

Mr. President, you and I have both worked in the private sector. In the private sector, if your boss picked up the phone and called, I suspect neither you nor I sat at our computer playing Solitaire when our boss picked up the phone and called. Neither one of us said: Boss, I am too busy. Boss, I don't want to listen. You may have some priorities for the business but not me. I know better than you.

None of us did that. Because in the private sector, there is a quick and immediate response. If you tell your boss in the private sector: Hey, boss, my time is too important for you; I don't care about your priorities; I am not going to listen to you, I suspect that will be your last day at that place of employment.

Why is Washington broken? Because you have 100 people, a significant number of whom, on a daily basis, tell their boss, tell their constituents: I am too busy for you.

Don't even bother to call my office because it just ties up my staff. It is annoying. I know better than you do. I know the priorities better than you do.

What a broken system. What a broken system. We work for the people. Why are the people unhappy with Washington? Why are they disgusted with Washington? Because Washington is not listening to them. There is a game instead that is focused on maintaining the status quo. Staying in office—that is what is important because it is apparently very important to be invited to all the right cocktail parties in town. I will confess, I do not go to a whole lot of cocktail parties in town. I am pretty sure you do not either. But there are Members of this body for whom that is very important.

At the end of the day, we do not work for those holding cocktail parties in Washington, DC. We do not work for the intelligentsia in the big cities who write newspaper editorials. We work for the American people. We work for single moms. We work for young people. We work for seniors who are struggling. We work for Hispanics, for African Americans. We work for every American who believes in the American dream.

This body is not listening to the people. Indeed, the very fact that over 1.6 million Americans have signed a petition, have picked up the phone, have been calling offices in this great Chamber is viewed as an inappropriate imposition. What an indictment of this body that we think it is somehow illegitimate that the American people would ask us not to focus on irrelevant priorities. It is not like the American people are calling, saying focus on some parochial issue. By the way, phone calls are not coming from our districts saying: Senator, please take more of the American people's tax money and send it back to our district. We would like some more pork.

Those are not the calls. Those are not the calls we are getting. The calls are from people who are saying: Listen, jobs and the economy is my No. 1 priority. Why isn't it Congress's? Jobs and the economy matter. Why? Because if you are working, if you are working in a good job, you are providing for your family. It makes it easier for families to stay together. Moms and dads—it makes it easier for them to raise their kids, raise them with good values. It makes it easier for them to provide a good education for their kids.

When you have one job, it lets you begin to climb the economic ladder to a better job and a better job and a better job. That is the American spirit. Yet we have tens of millions of people in this country out of work. Every month we get the reports from the Bureau of Labor Statistics that say even more people have given up looking for work.

The odd way our unemployment statistics work, that makes the number the newspapers report go down. Because when a few hundred thousand people say: All right, I give up, it is so hopeless, I will never find a job, that, curiously, results in the unemployment number going down because the number that gets reported in the papers is a measure of a percentage of how many of the people looking for work are unable to find it.

I am going to suggest that people giving up is even worse. What a sad testament, given the American spirit, the American spirit that we can do anything we set our minds to, that anyone—the great blessings of this Nation have been fundamentally that it does not matter who you are, it does not matter who your daddy was, it does not matter whether you were born into great wealth and privilege and advantage or whether you were born into humble means, anyone in this country can achieve anything based on hard work, perseverance, and based on the content of your character. What a tremendous, unique blessing that is in the United States of America. The reason this ObamaCare fight matters so much is that is imperiled right now. In order for anyone with nothing to achieve anything, they have to be able to get a job to start. They have to get on to the first rung of the economic ladder to have a chance of getting to the second or the third or the fourth or the fifth.

Just a week ago the *Wall Street Journal* had a long article about the "lost generation," about young people coming out of school in the last few years who have not gotten their first job or who have gotten a part-time job. Because of ObamaCare, their employer does not want to hire them for 40 hours a week, so they get hired for 29 hours a week.

Think about young people. If they do not get that first job, they are not going to get the second, they are not going to get the third. The impact for young people right now that ObamaCare is having is absolutely devastating. What this *Wall Street Journal* article was saying is that the economic data shows that impact will be with them their entire lives; that when they start off their career not gaining skills, not working, not climbing the economic ladder, that delay will stick with them forever.

What a travesty. Where is the outrage? Where is the outrage? Where are the Senators standing here saying: What a travesty that young people are being denied a fair shot at the American dream because of what we have wrought because of ObamaCare. That should unite all of us. If we were listening to the American people, that would be where our attention would lie.

Fundamentally, what this week is about is that we need to make DC listen, make them listen to the single mom working at a diner, struggling to feed her kids, who has just been told she is being reduced to 29 hours a week. Who is speaking for that single mom right now? Who is talking about how ObamaCare is forcing more and more people into part-time employment? And, by the way, she does not get health insurance. Instead, forced into 29 hours a week, what does that single mom do? She gets a second job. So now she is working two jobs, with 29 hours a week for both of them. Now she is away from her kids even more. She does not have health insurance at either job now. But she has to travel from one to the other. She has to deal with two conflicting schedules because one job wants her to work Tuesday, and the other job wants her to work at that same time on Tuesday. She has to go to both of her bosses. Both of them say: You need to be there Tuesday afternoon. Who is speaking for that single mom right now?

On Friday or Saturday of this week we will vote on cloture. Anyone who votes yes for cloture, anyone who votes to cut off debate on this bill, is voting to allow Senate majority leader HARRY REID to fully fund ObamaCare. That is a vote that I think is a profound mistake. It is a vote that I hope all 46 Republicans will stand united against. It is a vote that, in time, I hope more than a few Democrats will stand against.

To fix the problems in this country, this does not have to be a partisan issue. Many of the President's most vocal supporters have started coming out against ObamaCare. Why? Because the facts show it is not working, because if you get beyond the team mentality in Washington, if you get beyond the partisan focus in Washington and you ask, is this thing good for the American people, it is very hard on the merits to make the case that it is.

It is very hard. It is quite interesting that in the course of this debate there have been more than a few newspaper articles, more than a few attacks from our friends on the Democratic side of the aisle and also from our friends on the Republican side of the aisle.

I told my wife that I now pick up the newspaper each day to learn just what a scoundrel I am and just what attacks have come, some on the record and some—actually the ones that are often even better are the anonymous ones. I have to say there is no courage like the courage in Washington of the anonymous congressional staffers. I have chuckled at more than a few of them. You know, it says something when Members of this body, the congressional staffers, and members of the media want to make this about personalities. They want to make this about a battle of this Senator versus that Senator, this person versus that person, so it is all personal. It is like reading the Hollywood gossip pages. That is how this issue is covered. It is not by accident because one of the ways Washington has discovered for not listening to the people is distraction. Distract the voters with smoke and mirrors.

This fight is not about any Member of this body. This fight is not about personality. Look, most Americans could not give a flying flip about a bunch of politicians in Washington. Who cares? You know, almost all of us are in cheap suits and have bad haircuts. Who cares? What the American people care about is their own lives. What the American people care about is giving their kids a better future. What the American people care about is having a job with a future, not a job where they are working 29 hours a week, where they are punching a clock, where they feel as though they are just going through the motions, but a job where they say: Hey, I have a career. I can see the next step. I can see the future for my family. That is what the American people care about.

So regardless of the rocks that will be thrown—and they will continue to be thrown—I have no intention of engaging in that game, no intention of speaking ill of any Senator, Republican or Democratic, because it is not about us. Anyone who is trying to make this a battle of personalities is trying to change the topic from the topic that should matter: whether ObamaCare is helping the American people.

If we focus on the substance, the evidence is overwhelming. This law is a train wreck. Every day the headlines come in: more jobs lost, more people losing their health insurance, more premiums going up, more people pushed into part-time work. Yet every day the

Senate goes about its business and says: We are too busy to listen to the American people.

There are different games, to be sure, that go on on both sides of the aisle. Many of our friends on the Democratic side of the aisle right now endeavor to convince the American people: Pay no attention to your lying eyes; ObamaCare really is terrific. That is not going terribly well. But on the Republican side of the aisle, there is a lot of energy and attention focused on saying: Well, yes, ObamaCare is terrible, but under no circumstances could we ever do anything about it. That is beyond us. We are destined to lose. So what we are interested in on the Republican side of the aisle is let's cast a show vote—2, 3, 10—as many votes as possible to say: ObamaCare is really bad. We cannot fix it.

You know, that problem—it crosses that middle line. Whether you are telling your constituents it is really working out well despite the objective facts to the contrary or whether you are telling your constituents: I agree, it is a terrible thing, but I cannot do anything to fix it, in both cases you are not listening to the people. That is something we need to correct. All of us, all 100 of us—we need to listen to the people. Together, we need to make DC listen. If we do not, the frustration will grow. If we do not, the disillusion with Washington will grow. If we do not, the approval rating of Congress will keep going down, keep going down, keep going down. The only way to fix this problem is to demonstrate that we understand—we understand the fact that we are not driven by partisan ideology; that we are driven by doing our jobs and listening to the American people.

It is my fervent hope that over the course of this week, over the course of this debate, that all 46 Senators on the Republican side will unite and that more and more Democrats will come together and say: Listen, we have an obligation to our constituents. That is an obligation we are going to honor.

Mr. LEE. Will the Senator yield for a question?

Mr. CRUZ. I am happy to yield for a question without yielding the floor.

Mr. LEE. I would ask my distinguished colleague, the Senator from Texas, a series of questions with regard to this concept to make

DC listen. It is interesting that we are having this discussion right now at a time in our history when never has it been easier for so many people throughout the country with so few resources to be heard by so many.

In the past, you had to own a newspaper or perhaps in more recent years you had to own a radio station or a television company or something like that to be heard by a lot of people. But these days pretty much anyone can gain access to a telephone or the Internet, they can send an e-mail, they can submit a post. It is one of the things that have made possible a groundswell of people—just a few minutes ago the Senator mentioned 1.6 million Americans just in the last few weeks signing a petition asking for Congress to make a decision to protect the American people from the harmful effects of ObamaCare.

They want government funded, just as we want government funded. They want government to be able to continue to do the things government does. They want people to be able to rely on government to protect them, to protect our borders, to protect our sovereignty, protect our homeland against those who would harm us. They want government to be able to carry out its basic functions and its responsibility. They want their government funded. But they do not want that held hostage by something else. They do not want that funding tied to the funding of ObamaCare in the sense that they want to keep government funded but they want us to defund ObamaCare.

The House of Representatives shows that at least that side of DC, that side of the Capitol was listening. I applaud the Speaker of the House and the other leaders in the House of Representatives who did that. That suggests to me that they were listening on that side of the Capitol. They had many millions of Americans calling out on the telephone, through mail, e-mail, every conceivable medium for relief from this bill. They listened. They listened because they understand that the American people are being hurt by this. They ask the same questions the Senator from Texas and I and others have asked: How many more Americans will have to lose their jobs because of ObamaCare before Congress acts? How many more Americans will have to see their wages or their hours cut as a result of this ill-conceived law before we do something about this? How many more people will have to lose access to health coverage before Congress does something?

Just last Friday we saw Home Depot—one of America's great companies, one of America's great success stories, one of America's great employers—announce that 20,000 employees will be losing their health coverage. How many more stories like this will we have to hear before Congress does something to protect Americans from the harmful effects of this law—a law that was passed a few years ago without a single Republican vote in the House of Representatives; a law that was passed a few years ago without a single Republican vote in the Senate; a law that was passed—all 2,700 pages as it was then constituted—without, as far as I know, many, if any, Members of this body or the other body in the Capitol having had the opportunity fully to read it. Since then, of course, it has expanded. We have had an additional 20,000 pages of regulations promulgated, increasing rather exponentially the impact of this law. The popularity of the law has not improved with time, just as the complexity of the law has not become less problematic in the intervening 3½-year period.

So as we look at this, we think about the fact that it is important for Congress to listen to the American people. Again, today it has never been so easy for so many Americans with so few resources at their disposal to make sure that they are, in fact, heard. So we have to ask ourselves the question—I have to ask the Senator the question: How long will it be before Congress acts?

I am pleased that the Senator referred to the opportunity crisis, the economic opportunity crisis in America. He referred to the economic ladder in this country. You know, I think it is an interesting fact and we need to consider that—according to one recent study published I believe just in the last few weeks—for the first time in American history, 40 percent of those born in America, into the bottom quintile of the American economy, the bottom 20 percent of income earners in this country—40 percent of the bottom 20 percent will remain in the bottom 20 percent throughout the duration of their lifetime. To my knowledge, that has never happened in this country. To my knowledge, this undercuts what has long been a very distinguishing, enviable characteristic of the United States. It is what has made this the greatest civilization the world has ever known—the fact that this is a country where regardless of where you were born on the economic ladder, regardless of the circumstances in which you came into this world or came into this country, you could make it. In fact, your chances of doing so were relatively strong. Yet 40 percent of those people, we now understand, will stay there throughout the duration of their lives.

Another study came out, also a few weeks ago, indicating that in 34 States and the District of Colombia, an individual or a family is actually likely to see a dip in their well-being, a dip in their standard of living if, instead of receiving welfare benefits, they decide instead to shed those benefits and go on to an entry level job. That is sad. That is sad because that suggests that our government—as well-intentioned as many of those programs might be, they will have set in place a series of conditions that trap people, especially parents, into a vulnerable, poor condition.

If there is one thing that I think parents feel somewhat universally, it is a degree of risk aversion. People do not like to take risks that could jeopardize their ability to provide for their children. If we set up a set of conditions in which people, in order to maintain their level of certainty that they might have while surviving under a system of welfare benefits provided by the Federal Government—if they become locked into that, locked into poverty in perpetuity because of that, that is disconcerting because the risk is always too high to make that jump to an entry level job. Without the entry level job, there will never be the secondary job, there will never be the first raise or the second raise or the first, second, or third promotion. Without those things, there is no ladder. Without those things, there is an opportunity lost and people remain on the bottom rungs of that very ladder.

We see at the top rung a system of crony capitalism that sometimes has the impact of keeping some people and some big businesses artificially held in place at the top of the economic ladder at the expense of others, at the expense of would-be competitors who are driven out or held out from the beginning from the competitive marketplace through the oppressive intervention of the government, through the government's favoritism, and through the government's ability sometimes, regrettably, to choose winners and losers in the marketplace.

You see where most Americans are, right in the middle of the ladder. On the middle rungs you see people working, trying to get by from day to day. They are able to survive, able to provide for the basic needs of their families. But they would like to do better. They would like to be able to provide a more comfortable living for their families.

They find very often that no sooner do they find an increase in their income than that same increase has been gobbled up by a combination of oppressive taxes, oppressive regulations, and a devastating impact of inflation. When those things happen, we find people are unable to make their way up that economic ladder.

We find ourselves at a precipice of sorts. We find ourselves about to embark on a very bold experiment in which we rather dramatically expand the role of the Federal Government, injecting it more directly, more completely, more dangerously into one of the most personal aspects of most people's lives, into the health care industry. This is an industry that comprises a very significant portion of our Nation's economy in an area in which people feel strongly about their own right, about their own innate, inherent need and desire to maintain a degree of control that is not subject to the will and whim of government bureaucrats in Washington.

At the same time the government is doing that, the government will be consuming an increasingly large share of the resources moving through our economy, making it even harder for people who are trying to get by to do so and to do so without undue interference from the government.

This is an issue that is important to so many people. This is an issue that reminds people of the fact that whenever government acts, it does so at the expense of our own individual liberty. It does so at the expense of our ability to live our lives as we would live them. It does so very often at the expense of the American economy. It does so very often at the expense of economic opportunity for Americans, you see, because when we expand government, we expand its cost.

We make ourselves as a country less free. We leave ourselves with fewer alternatives.

Is there a role for government to play in health care? Absolutely. Of course there is. No one disputes that. Are there improvements that can be made to our health care system? Certainly there are.

But a 2,700-page law that was passed after Members of Congress were told they had to pass it in order to find out what is in it, that has expanded since then to include within its penumbra 20,000 pages of regulatory text, a law that has become less and less popular as time has gone on—this has become very difficult. We find this becomes less and less something that the American people support.

I would ask if Senator CRUZ feels that the American people have every right to speak out on this. Specifically does the Senator feel the American people have every right to expect that those of us serving in the Senate will do everything we possibly can, even casting difficult votes, even casting procedural votes that might be difficult to cast or difficult to explain? Do they have every right to do that even if it causes great inconvenience for them and for us in the process of complying with their wishes?

Mr. CRUZ. I thank my friend from Utah for that very good question. The answer is absolutely yes. That is the foundation of our Nation. If you look at the history of government in the world, it hasn't been pretty. The history of government for most of the existence of mankind has been a story of oppression, a story of rulers imposing their will on their subjects. For millennia, we were told that rights come from government. They come from kings and queens, and they are to be given to the people by grace, to be taken away by the whim of the ruler. That has been the state of affairs for most of the history of humanity.

The founding of our Nation embodied many revolutions.

The first revolution was a revolution that was a bloody revolution fought with guns and bayonets. But even more important than that revolution was the revolution of ideas that occurred. The revolution of ideas that began this Nation was twofold.

First, America began from the presupposition that our rights come from God. It is for that reason the Declaration Of Independence begins: "We hold these truths to be self-evident, that all men are created equal," that we are endowed—not by a king, not by a queen, not even by a President—but "endowed by their Creator with certain unalienable Rights, that among these are Life, Liberty and the pursuit of Happiness."

That is and was a revolutionary idea, and it led to the second revolutionary aspect of the founding of our Nation which was that we inverted the concept of sovereignty. For millennia sovereignty began at the top. It was the ruler who was called the sovereign. The word sovereignty derives from that notion. Of course, the sovereign is where sovereignty resides.

The American Framers turned that notion on its head. We said: There is no sovereign. Sovereignty resides with we the people. That is why our Constitution begins "We the People," because this Nation wasn't founded by rulers, it wasn't founded by elected officials, it wasn't even founded by States. It was founded by we the people, the American people. That is the only place sovereignty has ever resided in the United States of America.

The Constitution, in turn, was created to lend power to government, not to give it, to lend it and to lend it, I would suggest, only in good behavior. Thomas Jefferson referred to the Constitution as chains that bind the mischief of government, that sovereignty is an idea we need to get back to.

I am going to suggest that for some time now the Senate has not behaved as if we the people are sovereign. For some time the Senate has not behaved as if each of us collectively has 3 million bosses. For a long time the Senate has behaved as if the rules that matter are the rules in Washington, DC. That is why the most important objective of this week is to make DC listen. The most important objective of this week is to reassert that sovereignty is with we the people, that calls from our constituents and townhalls are not a pesky annoyance. It is the core of our job. It is the core of our job to listen to the sovereign, which is we the people.

Right now we the people are hurting. If you get outside Washington, DC, you ask them about ObamaCare over and over, and the answer you get is: This thing isn't working.

A few weeks ago I hosted a small business roundtable in Kerrville, TX. Kerrville is a delightful town in central Texas. It is in the beautiful hill country. If anyone wants to come to Texas, I would encourage you. Kerrville is a great destination in Texas.

This was a small gathering in a restaurant, about 20 small business owners. I asked each of them and I said: Let's go around the room. If each of you could introduce yourself, share a little bit about yourself, and then share a concern that is weighing on your heart. Share something you are praying about, share something you are worried about, share something you are focused on right now.

It was a totally open-ended question. They could have talked about any issue under the Sun. They could have talked about Syria, guns, they could have talked about anything.

We went around the table one after the other after the other. Over half of the small business owners around that table said to me: TED, the single biggest obstacle I face in my business is ObamaCare. Hands down, not even close, there is nothing that comes close.

It was striking. Of those 20, there were probably 4 or 5 of them who relayed some version of this same story. One was the fellow who owned the restaurant we were meeting in. He said: You know, we have a great opportunity to expand our business. I have an opportunity to make the restaurant even bigger, expand it, and from a business perspective, this opportunity looks good. But he said: You know, we have got between 20 and 30 employees. If we expand the business we will go over 50. And if we go over 50, we are subject to ObamaCare. If that happens, I will go out of business. So you know what. I am not pursuing the expansion. I am not going to do it. We are going to stay the size we are.

One person after another around the table said the same thing. They had 30 employees, 35, 40 employees. They had great opportunities to go open another location, expand into a new aspect. One after the other said: We will not do it, because if we get over 50 employees, ObamaCare will bankrupt us.

I want you to think about each of those 4 or 5 businesses and the 10 or 20 jobs that each of them didn't create, isn't creating right now because of ObamaCare. Then I want you to multiply that by thousands or tens of thousands of small businesses all across this country that could be creating jobs. I want you to think about all the people right now who are home wanting to work.

There are, by the way, I will note, some politicians who suggest that some people in this country are lazy and don't want to work. I don't believe that. I think Americans want to work. Americans want the self-respect that comes from going to the office, from working, from providing for your family, from working to achieve the American dream.

Do some people give up? Sure. Can you give in to hopelessness? Yes. When you keep banging your head against a wall over and over again, trying to get a job, and you don't get anywhere, it is only natural for people to feel despair. I want you to think of the millions of jobs we could have but for small businesses that are not growing, not expanding, not creating those jobs.

Another small business owner around that table owned several fast food restaurants. She had a problem. She owned enough fast food restaurants that she had over 50 employees. I will mention the restaurant business and the fast food business side in particular is quite labor dependent. I doubt if there is a sector in this economy that has been hurt more than the labor in the fast food business. But her problem was she had enough stores so she was over 50 employees, so that strategy wouldn't work for her. She described how she has already forcibly reduced the hours of every one of her employees to 29 hours per week.

I will tell you this woman almost began to tear up. She was emotional. She was not happy about this, to put it mildly. She said: Listen, we have been in business a long time. Many of these employees we have known 10 or 20 years. These are single moms. These are people—look, if you are working in a fast food restaurant you are not at the pinnacle of your career. You are struggling to pay the bills. These are single moms who are working hard and they can't feed their kids on 29 hours a week. But, you know, they can't feed their kids if I go out of business either. If we are subject to ObamaCare, we go out of business.

Why 29 hours a week? Well, just like the 50-employee threshold, ObamaCare kicks in and counts an employee if he or she works 30 hours a week. One of the things that is forcing small businesses all over the country to do is to force their employees out of good full-time jobs into 29 hours a week because they don't get hammered with the costs and burdens of ObamaCare.

I will mention another small business owner who I think will particularly hit home with the Presiding Officer because I know the issues that resonate with him. This is an individual who manufactures hunting blinds—actually very interesting. They are hunting blinds that are camouflaged to look like trees. They are really very clever creations. He described how he has been forced to move his manufacturing overseas, to move it to China. So right now he is manufacturing in China.

He said: Listen, I want to manufacture here in the United States. That matters to me. I care about that.

He said this would be 150 to 200 good manufacturing jobs here in the United States.

The Presiding Officer and I both come from States where there are a lot of people who are struggling and who would love to see 200 more manufacturing jobs. Manufacturing used to be a tremendous strength of our economy, but the manufacturing sector has been hammered in recent decades. Yet this small business owner said that because of ObamaCare, if he brought his manufacturing back to the United States, his workers would all be subject to ObamaCare and he couldn't be competitive in the business. It would drive him out of business.

I would ask my colleagues to consider each of those small business owners and multiply it by the millions of small business owners across this country—the millions of small business owners who aren't growing, the millions of small business owners who are forcibly reducing their employees' hours to 29 hours a week, the millions of small business owners who are considering moving operations overseas or have already because of ObamaCare. Why is the economy gasping for breath? Why are people not able to get jobs? Because ObamaCare is killing jobs, and the Senate should listen to the people. We need to make DC listen.

Mr. VITTER. Will the Senator yield for a question?

Mr. CRUZ. I am happy to yield for a question without yielding the floor.

Mr. VITTER. I thank the Senator. Does he acknowledge that he understands, as I do, that as this monstrosity goes into effect October 1 and as it has all of these really devastating impacts on individuals and small businesses, under a special illegal rule from the Obama administration, Congress and Washington get an exemption; they get a special pass; they get a special deal no other American gets under the law?

Mr. CRUZ. I thank the Senator for his question, and he is absolutely right. There are many scandalous aspects of ObamaCare: how it was passed—on a brutal partisan vote rammed through with late-night deals that have earned rather infamous nicknames, such as the "Cornhusker kickback," which has sadly become part of modern political lore; and the "Louisiana purchase," with all due respect to my friend from the great State of Louisiana, who was not involved in that. And one of the most sorry aspects of ObamaCare is the aspect Senator VITTER refers to, which is that President Obama has chosen, at the behest of majority leader HARRY REID, at the behest of Democratic Members of the Senate, to exempt Members of Congress and their staff from the plain language of the statute.

When ObamaCare was being passed, Senator CHUCK GRASSLEY—a towering giant in this body; a strong, principled conservative—introduced a commonsense provision to ObamaCare that said: If you are going to force ObamaCare on the American people, if you are going to create these health insurance exchanges and you are going to force millions of people into these exchanges, then Congress should not operate by better rules than the American people. So he introduced a simple amendment designed to treat Members of Congress just like the American people so that we didn't have this two-class system.

It has been reported—I was not serving in this body at the time—that amendment was voted on and accepted because Democratic Senators believed the bill would go to conference and in the conference committee they could strip it out and it would magically disappear. But then, because of the procedural games it took to pass it, they didn't have the opportunity to do that, and suddenly, horror of all horrors, this bill saying Congress should be bound by the same rules as the American people became the law of the land.

So what happened? Majority leader HARRY REID and Democratic Senators had a closed-door meeting with the President here in the Capitol where they said, according to public news reports: Let us out of ObamaCare. We don't want to be in these exchanges.

One would assume they are reading the same news reports the rest of us are reading—that ObamaCare is a train wreck, that it is not working—and the last thing Members of Congress wanted to do was to have their health care jeopardized. And the President directed his administration to exempt Members of Congress and their staff, ignoring the language of the statute, disregarding the language of the statute and saying: You guys are friends of the administration. We are taking care of you.

I want to take a minute, in response to this question, to commend the Senator from Louisiana. Senator VITTER introduced an amendment to reverse this exemption, and it was a bold amendment. It was an amendment that said we as Members of Congress should be subject to the same rules as the American people. We shouldn't be treated by special or different rules for us. Indeed, the amendment of Senator VITTER said Members of Congress should be subject to ObamaCare, our staff should be subject to ObamaCare, and members of the administration—the political appointees of the Obama administration, who, by the way, are not in the exchanges—should be too. So if the President and Cabinet appointees and his political officials want to go into communities and tell everyone how wonderful ObamaCare is, then let them do so from personal experience. Let them do so not being exempted but subject to the same exchanges and subject to the same rules the American people are.

The reason I wish to commend the Senator from Louisiana is his introducing that amendment prompted a response that, I will suggest, brought disgrace and disrepute on this body. It prompted a political response that targeted the Senator from Louisiana personally.

Now, we have all heard the saying "politics ain't beanbag," but the nastiness with which the Democratic majority responded to Senator

VITTER for daring to say that the Washington ruling class should be subject to the same rules as the rest of America was extraordinary even for Washington, DC. In fact, I would note that the majority leader and the junior Senator from California, as I understand from public news reports, proposed a response to the Vitter amendment that said any Senator who votes for the Vitter amendment—regardless of whether it passes but simply if you cast a vote in favor of it—he or she will lose their health insurance.

I have to admit that when I first heard of this proposed amendment, I shook my head in amazement. I had never heard of such a thing, and I suggested to a friend who is a law professor that that would make a marvelous law school final exam. Imagine this amendment being passed into law and asking your law students to catalog all of the myriad ways in which such a proposal would be unconstitutional. In fact, I made this point to the law professor I was talking to. I said: If you as a private citizen came to any Member of the Senate and said: Senator, if you vote the way I want you to, I am going to pay you thousands of dollars that you can deposit into your personal bank account, you, Mr. Law Professor, Mr. Private Citizen, would promptly and quite rightly be prosecuted for bribery. It is a criminal offense. It is a felony.

If, on the other hand, you or any other American citizen went to a U.S. Senator—went to Senator VITTER—and said: Senator VITTER, if you don't vote the way I want, I am going to take thousands of dollars out of your personal bank account, I am going to extract them forcibly from your personal bank account, well, as I told the law professor, then you would be guilty of extortion and would be charged and no doubt criminally convicted because under the black letter definition, that conduct—threatening to pay someone individually thousands of dollars or take thousands of dollars away from them as a direct quid pro quo for how a Member of Congress votes—constitutes either bribery or extortion.

Now, let me be clear: No Member of this body is guilty of bribery or extortion. Why? The simplest reason is because the Constitution's speech and debate clause protects all of us, such that given their action was proposing an amendment themselves, there is a constitutional immunity. So I am not suggesting that anyone is guilty of bribery or extortion. But I am saying that if any private citizen who didn't happen to be a Member of the Senate did the exact same thing as the suggested content of their amendment, he or she would have committed a felony under the plain text of those definitions.

So I want to commend Senator VITTER for shining a light on basic fairness, for enduring the vilification that was unfairly directed his way, and for making the point that outside of Washington is simple common sense.

I would suggest that if any of us were to get a gathering of our constituents together, if we were to get a gathering of constituents from the opposing party and ask this question at any townhall gathering in our States: Do you believe that Members of Congress should be exempted from ObamaCare, that we should have a special rule, that we should disregard the language of the statute and not be subject to ObamaCare the way the American people are, the answer would be overwhelmingly no. And it doesn't matter where in the country you are or what your party is.

I thank Senator VITTER for having the courage and the principle to highlight this particularly unfortunate aspect of ObamaCare.

Mr. VITTER. Will the Senator yield for a further question?

Mr. CRUZ. I will be happy to yield for a question without yielding the floor.

Mr. VITTER. Will the Senator also acknowledge that given that history on this issue, given that illegal rule to exempt Congress, to have a special bail-out, a special subsidy for Congress that the Obama administration is putting into law without valid authority, and given that we are debating and acting on a spending bill this week, we should be voting on that? We should get a vote on my amendment and the Cruz amendment together to block that illegal rule this week?

The majority leader said he had no problem with a vote on that, in theory. He said that last week. He should allow a vote on this crucial amendment, which will be filed to the bill, which will even be a germane amendment on this spending bill this week, before this illegal congressional exemption rule goes into effect. Would the Senator agree with me?

Mr. CRUZ. I agree enthusiastically.

Senator VITTER highlights one of the many reasons why every Republican in this body should vote against cloture on the bill on Friday or Saturday and why I believe a great many Democrats should vote against cloture as well.

As we understand it, we are told the amendment process on this bill is going to be rigged. The amendment process on this bill is going to be that once debate is cut off, there will be a bill simply to fund ObamaCare in its entirety, to delete the House language, and that other amendments will not be allowed. The amendment of the Senator from Louisiana will not be allowed, the amendment repealing the medical device taxes will not be allowed, and the amendment getting the IRS out of the business of ObamaCare will not be allowed. Instead, it will be a rigged playing field.

The only way to prevent that rigged playing field is for Senators to stand together and vote no on cutting off debate on Friday or Saturday when we have that vote. If we stand together and vote no, that forces this body to deal with the problem; otherwise, we know how the Kabuki dance ends. If cloture is invoked, if debate is cut off on the bill, very shortly thereafter the majority leader has publicly announced he will introduce an amendment to fully fund ObamaCare. That will require just 51 votes. So every Republican will get to vote no and tell his or her constituents they voted no. Yet magically and wonderfully it will pass because it will be a straight party-line, partisan vote, and other Senators will be silenced.

I think Senator VITTER is absolutely correct, we should vote on the Vitter amendment. Indeed, I would like to see the Vitter amendment broadened. Another member of our conference indicated that if the Vitter amendment were brought up, he would offer an amendment to expand it to all Federal employees. I think that is a terrific rule.

Right now, Federal employees earn substantially more than the private sector does. I don't think there is any entitlement to take our tax dollars and to live in a privileged condition being a Federal employee. If Members of this body are going to go on television and tell the American people: ObamaCare is great, it is good, it is terrific, it is so great, then they should be eager to live under it.

You can't have it both ways. Either ObamaCare is a train wreck, in which case we ought to listen to the American people and fix it, or ObamaCare is wonderful and terrific and fantastic and all of the great adjectives the proponents of the bill have used, in which case Members of Congress, staff, and Federal employees should all eagerly embrace it.

I very much agree with Senator VITTER that it is critical we vote on the Vitter amendment, and it is critical we make clear to the American people there are not two sets of rules. There is not a ruling class in Washington that somehow gets treated differently.

Let me talk for a minute about congressional staffers. Behind closed doors this issue generates a lot of passion. There are a great many congressional staff members who are dedicated public servants, who have often taken substantial salary cuts to come to Washington to serve this country, who work brutal hours. Among congressional staff, just like among Members, the idea that they would be subject to ObamaCare deeply concerns them. It concerns them on the money side and it concerns them on the quality of care and health insurance that they will be able to get on the exchanges.

To make it real, I note there are multiple members of my staff who have had very serious, even life-threatening health issues for whom the limited health insurance, the subpar, the poor quality health insurance that many fear will be available on the exchanges is not a passing concern, not an academic concern, not a concern that let's put in talking points, it is very real for a great many congressional staff, including staff in my office. If the Vitter amendment passes and Congress is subject to the same rules as the American people, there may well be quite a few congressional staff who tender their letters of resignation and leave.

I have had one staff member already indicate she would retire after many years of service, and the possibility of being put on ObamaCare was a real factor in that decision.

If we lose some good talent from Congress, that will be a shame and a hardship for every office. But what does that say? If ObamaCare is such a disaster that congressional staffers—and, mind you, a lot of these congressional staffers who may tender their letters of resignation are staffers working for Democratic Senators who drafted ObamaCare, who fight for ObamaCare every day. What does it say that staffers would be willing to quit because the quality of health care under ObamaCare would be so poor that they would rather go somewhere else than be subject to those laws? I think that speaks volumes.

Neither Senator VITTER nor I in the long term has any interest in seeing congressional staff and Federal employees on ObamaCare, but it does have the value of highlighting how bad it is.

If this body is content to leave the American people stuck in ObamaCare, then we ought to be subject to the same rules. If we are not willing to live under those rules, if we say, Wow, ObamaCare scares the heck out of us and we don't want to be subject to it, then the proper answer is not to vilify the Senator from Louisiana or any other Senator in this body. The proper answer is to step in and say to the American people—in fact, let me suggest something that would have a powerful clarifying impact on this body.

If only Senators would behave as if their constituents were at least as important as their congressional staff; if only Senators were to behave as if their constituents were at least as important as they are—to be honest, our constituents are more important. Our constituents are our bosses. They are the reason we are fighting. The fact that this body is so torn apart by the notion that each of us would be subject to ObamaCare and subject to the same rules the American people are highlights how broken Washington is. That shouldn't be controversial. That should be obvious.

Let me suggest to every Member of Congress, to every staffer who is dismayed—and, to be honest, saying they are dismayed is an understatement, to describe the degree of deep concern and even panic about this. Let me suggest to every Member of Congress and every staffer who is feeling that panic, direct that panic not to our own skins; direct that panic to the American people. Direct that panic to the single mom working at the diner, working two 29-hour-a-week jobs who is facing the consequences of ObamaCare.

Under ObamaCare, this President is getting ready to force millions of people onto exchanges where they are very likely to lose their health insurance.

In the privileged corridors of Washington, the risk of losing your health insurance, boy, that gets people worried. And it should. But it should worry us even more for all the people across this country.

The majority leader and Members of Congress can get a sit-down with the President of the United States. But 26 million Texans, most Texans can't get a sitdown with the President of the United States.

If you are powerful, you can get a special exemption. We have seen the President exempting every big corporation in America. Giant corporations, he said, for a year it doesn't apply to you. The language of the law explicitly applies. There is no year delay of the language of the law.

For over 200 years we have operated as a nation of laws, not men. We have operated as a nation that says if that is what the law says, then it kicks in January 1 and not a year from now.

What did the President say? No. Big companies have come to us. My friends in big business, I am going to give you a year-long exemption.

If ObamaCare were so terrific, why would the President be wanting to delay it until after the next election? The year-delay timing is not entirely coincidental. The employer mandate was supposed to kick in January 1 of next year, and the President unilaterally and contrary to law delayed it one whole year until after the November 2014 elections.

If the representations that so many Members of this body make to the American people were true that ObamaCare is terrific, is wonderful, then I would think the President would be eager to have it kick in before the election. If it were a good thing, you would want the good stuff to happen before the election and not after the election. The fact that it was moved for big businesses is an indication of how badly this law has failed.

But it is not just big businesses that have got an exemption. Members of Congress. Senators can get a closed-door meeting with the President of the United States. With much fanfare, the President came to the Capitol, met with the Democratic Caucus, and as was widely reported they asked for a special exemption and they got it. How about the American people? They can't go in.

One of the reasons people are so unhappy with Washington is they get a sense that there are special rules that apply. Wall Street gets special exemptions, the big banks get special exemptions. Dodd-Frank sets up rules that hammer small banks, hammer community banks, hammer the little guy. But what happens to the big guys? They keep getting bigger. Why? Because they get rules made in Washington that favor the big guy over the little guy. And you wonder why there is such dissatisfaction in this country. But if you have political friends in this administration, you too can get an exemption.

Labor unions have more and more been expressing their dismay about ObamaCare as they have realized in practice the thing isn't working. Recently the labor unions came to the Obama administration and said, We want an exemption too. Big businesses got an exemption, Members of Congress got an exemption. Shouldn't labor unions, shouldn't union bosses get an exemption? And with much fanfare the administration reportedly told them, No.

I am going to make a prediction right here and now. If the Congress does not act, if we don't show leadership in defunding ObamaCare, if we don't stand together in imposing cloture on Friday, if we don't act to avert this train wreck for the American people, before the end of this President's term we are going to see him grant an exemption for labor unions. That has been the pattern. Friends, political buddies—they get a slap on the back. They get special treatment.

It wouldn't have been great politics to grant the labor unions an exemption right now, right in the middle of this debate. Right when you have over 1.6 million people signing a national petition, right when Congress is debating it—gosh, it would have looked bad to grant an exemption then.

It is a little reminiscent of the President's remarks regarding Mr. Putin that were caught on tape before the last election—I forget the exact language, but, Tell Vladimir I will be able to work with him a lot more after the election.

I don't think it takes any stretch of the imagination at all to understand that, give it a little time, let the pesky people who are sort of worked up a little bit on ObamaCare dissipate. Then we will quietly do the exemption for labor unions.

Let me note the point "quietly." One of the self-described fact checkers—and we may talk long enough that I talk a little bit about fact checkers, because that is a particularly pernicious bit of yellow journalism that has cropped up that lets journalists be editorial writers and pretend they are talking about objective facts, and basically conclude as a factual matter—not as a matter of opinion—and anyone who disagrees with them is objectively lying.

One point that one of the so-called fact checkers in the *Washington Post* took issue with was an observation I made that President Obama is quietly granting exceptions.

I note that the exception for big business was announced in a blog posting by a midlevel political appointee in the Treasury Department, if I remember right, on a Friday. I may be wrong on the day but I think it was on a Friday. In Washington language, by any measure, when you announce a major policy that impacts the whole country that exempts giant businesses from your rule that you are jamming on the American people and you don't do it from the White House, you don't do it from the President, you don't do it as an announcement, you don't take questions on it, you simply put a blog posting from a midlevel staffer, that counts as "quietly."

It hasn't been quiet since then because everyone happened to notice. So my prediction right now is if we get past this, if the forces in this body who defend the status quo—and, wow, are there a lot of forces that defend the status quo. There are a lot of people with a vested interest in maintaining the status quo. If they prevail, if ObamaCare goes into effect before the end of this President's administration, mark my words, you will see an exemption for labor unions just like the exemption for big business, just like the exemption for Members of Congress.

What are we left with then? We are left with a system where ObamaCare is a rule for, as Leona Helmsley so famously described them, the little people. For everybody who doesn't have power and juice and connections in Washington, for everyone—look for the men and women at home, maybe you have an army of lobbyists working for you. Maybe you have Senators' cell phones on your speed dial. Maybe you can walk the corridors of power. In that case you too get an exemption. But if you are just a hard-working American, if you are just trying to provide for your family, if you are just trying to do an honest day's work, make your community better, raise your kids, set a good example, then the message this President has sent—and sadly the message the Senate has sent—is you don't count. We are going to treat everybody else better than you.

That is exactly backward. It is the hard-working American we work for, not the lobbyists with tassels on their loafers who wander the halls but the single mom in a diner. They are the people who are losing.

I wish to talk about the harm to jobs and economic growth that is coming from ObamaCare. Americans continue to suffer from high unemployment and severe underemployment. Instead of helping job growth, ObamaCare's mandates and costs are causing businesses to stop hiring workers, to cut employees' hours, and they are increasing the costs to operate businesses. Small businesses in particular are being hammered by ObamaCare.

Here are some recent statistics on unemployment and underemployment. According to the Bureau of Labor Statistics report for August of 2013, there are 11.3 million unemployed persons. The unemployment rate, the official unemployment rate is listed at 7.3 percent. Yet college graduates over 25 face just a 3.5-percent unemployment.

Former Democratic Vice-Presidential nominee John Edwards used to talk about two Americas. I didn't agree with a lot of things John Edwards said as a political candidate, but I actually agreed with that notion, and it is a tragic notion, that there are two Americas. There are two Americas, A, between the ruling class in Washington and everyday Americans, but there are also two Americas right now between those of wealth and privilege and power and everybody else. If you are lucky enough to be a college graduate, your unemployment rate is 3.5 percent. That is pretty good. The people who are getting hammered, who are losing under ObamaCare, are the most vulnerable among us. They are young people, Hispanics, African

Americans, single moms. For Black teens the unemployment rate is over 10 times higher than it is for college graduates—38.2 percent.

Let me ask, when small businesses are not hiring, when small businesses are laying off people, when small businesses are forcing employees to work 29 hours a week, whom do you think that is impacting? It doesn't impact titans of industry. The rich and powerful are not losing their jobs. They are not finding themselves forced into part-time work.

We talked about the fast food business. The fast food business, that industry is being hammered. You want to talk about what a tremendous avenue for employment the fast food industry has been, particularly for the first and second job someone has. When we look at the unemployment rate of African-American teens of 38.2 percent, the fast food industry has been such a great avenue for advancement for minority teenagers.

I note I do not view that from the perspective of abstract numbers on a piece of paper. I view that from a very personal perspective, because 55 years ago, when my father came from Cuba, he was 18, he was penniless, and he couldn't speak English. But he was lucky. He was lucky to get to America. He was lucky to be able to apply for a student visa, to be accepted to the University of Texas, to flee the Batista regime, where he had been imprisoned and tortured as a kid. By the time he was a teenager, my father had endured more than the vast majority of Members of Congress will ever experience.

I will note with that background it does make the back-and-forth of Washington pretty mild by comparison. If someone says something mean about you in the newspaper, it may not be altogether pleasant, but it is pretty darned mild compared to being beaten and almost killed in a Cuban jail as my dad was 55 years ago.

When he landed in Austin—if I could, Mr. President, I would ask you to put yourself in his shoes—not literally, because I think your feet are bigger than his, but figuratively. When my dad landed in Austin, he couldn't speak English. He didn't know anybody. Imagine being in a strange land where you cannot speak English, you have $100 sewn into your underwear that my grandmother put there. The first thing he needed was a job, so he went to look for a job.

The problem is if you are an 18-year-old kid from Cuba and you cannot speak English, there are not a lot of jobs you can get. If you can't speak English, it is pretty hard to get a job where you have to deal with customers who are going to expect you to speak English. At that point he didn't have a lot of skills. He was a teenager. So his first job was washing dishes. He made 50 cents an hour.

Why did he get that job? Because you didn't have to speak English. Even though he did not have a lot of skills as an 18-year-old kid, he was perfectly capable of taking a dish, putting it under very hot water, scrubbing it and setting it aside and he did it over and over.

When my father was here, he had no means of support other than washing dishes. So what he did, one of the reasons he wanted to work in a restaurant, is that restaurants would let you eat while you were working. It was one of the perks of working in a restaurant; the employees were able to eat. My father had no money for food. He barely had money to pay for a tiny little apartment. In fact, he started in the dorms, I believe, and tuition. That was it. He didn't have money to buy food, so what my dad did is he ate at work. Since he liked to eat 7 days a week, he worked 7 days a week. He would go in and he only ate during those 8 hours. During the 8 hours he was working washing dishes, he would eat like crazy, I mean he would just feed his face. Because when he left, the next 16 hours he wasn't eating anything, wasn't buying food until the next 16 hours he showed up at work. That was the next time he was going to eat.

Some people may look at a dish-washing job paying 50 cents an hour and turn up their nose at it and say: Who really cares about people in jobs like that? Sometimes this Senate behaves like that. Who cares about people in jobs like that?

But after some time my father learned English. I will tell you how he learned English. He did a couple of things. No. 1, my father signed up for Spanish 101. When he was a freshman at UT, he signed up for Spanish 101. You might say: Why would a native speaker take Spanish 101? That seems a little dumb.

What my father would do is sit in the classroom and basically try to reverse engineer everything. So the professor would say milk is leche, and he would write it down and say leche is milk. He would try to sit and listen, and as the teacher was teaching Spanish he would try to do everything backward and try to figure out what the English was.

The other thing my dad would do, on Saturdays, he would go to movies. In fact, when I was a kid, we would go to movies all the time together. It was one of the things we loved to do together, still do. My dad used to go to movies on Saturday and he would sit there and watch the same movie in English typically three times. He would just sit there and watch it. When he first came there to Austin, he would watch a movie three times and have no idea of what was going on the first, second or third time. But then he would do it again and do it again.

The human brain is a miraculous thing. As he would watch the movie two or three times, by the second time you start picking up context, start picking up what was going on and start following the plot. By the third time he would start following it even more. So relatively quickly my father learned English.

I note he had a pretty exquisite incentive to learn English. His incentive to learn English was if he didn't, he was going to flunk out of school because he was taking his classes in English. He took mostly math classes and math was the sort of thing you did not need as much language as you do in other topics. But if he didn't learn English pretty fast, he was going to flunk out of the University of Texas.

Once he learned English, he managed, at the restaurant he was working at, to get a promotion. He got a promotion to be a cook. Being a cook, that was good. Look, being a cook was a lot better than being a dishwasher. It paid a little bit more. I don't know how much he got paid being a cook, but it paid better than 50 cents an hour. He had to speak enough English, so when someone came in and ordered, let me get a steak and potatoes, he had to know what that was and not give them scrambled eggs. So he learned enough to be a cook and respond to the orders.

The place he cooked was a place called the Toddle House. It was a place where the cooks were in front of the people. It doesn't exist anymore, but my father described it as a sort of Denny's. Imagine Denny's combined with Benihana. The menu was similar to Denny's, but the cook was in front of you so you could see him. So my dad learned to flip pancakes. Let me tell you, as a kid on Saturday or Sunday morning and your dad is making pancakes, it is very cool when he can flip them—you could make him flip them high in the air and catch them. But he could do that.

I will credit my father; he invented—this wasn't for the restaurant, but he did it anyway—he invented green eggs and ham. He did it two ways. No. 1, the easy way, is he put green food coloring in the eggs, chopped up ham in it. *Green Eggs and Ham* was my favorite book when I was a boy. The food coloring is a little bit cheating, but if you take some spinach and mix it into the eggs, the eggs turn green.

My dad worked as a cook to finish his way through the University of Texas. In 1961, my dad graduated, got a math degree. At his next job, he was hired as a teaching assistant. He began taking graduate classes in mathematics at the University of Texas and he got hired as a teaching assistant teaching undergrads math. A teaching assistant was a better job than washing dishes or being a cook. It paid more and it had more forward advancement. So he enjoyed being a teaching assistant.

He had all sorts of clever final exam questions that he would give. He taught college algebra. I remember one of his final exam questions was: You have a triangle with sides 11, 20, and 9. Compute the area.

You get students who would write pages and pages, trying to put all these various equations together, trying to figure out the area. Almost all of them were wrong. It is a basic rule of geometry, for a triangle the sum of any two sides has to be longer than the third side or else they don't actually meet. A triangle with sides of 20, 11, and 9—11 and 9 add up to 20. That is a straight line. The area is zero. So he enjoyed kind of coming up with clever final exam questions. That was one of them.

But from there, after being a teaching assistant, he applied for and got a job with IBM as a computer programmer. This was, I think, 1962, 1963. It was in the early 1960s. From there he got the skills as a computer programmer. He worked in the oil and gas industry. Subsequently, with my mother, he went on to start a small business, a seismic data processing company in the oil and gas business.

So when I was a kid, as I grew up, my parents were small business owners. When I talk about small businesses, similar to a great many Americans, the majority of Americans, it is not a hypothetical. I have grown up as the son of two small business owners, seeing the hard work, the challenges of trying to run a small business. In fact, I saw my parents' business go bankrupt when I was in high school. I saw the up sides and the down sides of being in a small business. It ain't easy.

If my father had not been able to get that first job washing dishes and making 50 cents an hour, he never would have gotten his second job as a cook. If he hadn't gotten his second job, he wouldn't have gotten his third job as a teaching assistant. If he hadn't have gotten that job, he wouldn't have been hired by IBM. If he hadn't been hired by IBM, he wouldn't have started his own business.

Earlier, the Senator from Utah talked about opportunity and the American dream. When we look at a statistic, such as the fact that African-American teenage unemployment is 38.2 percent, we are talking about a generation of young people who are not getting that first job. They are not getting the equivalent today of that job of washing dishes and making 50 cents an hour. They are not getting the job of flipping burgers in the fast food business because the impact of ObamaCare on the fast food business is so devastating that it is not hiring workers. The travesty is that they do not get to flip burgers. Flipping burgers is honorable work. It is not necessarily the fulfill- ment of someone's life's ambition, but it is so frequently a stepping stone to the next job and the next job and the next job.

As a young kid, one of the things you have to learn is basic work skills, such as how to show up on time. A lot of teenagers are not very good at showing up on time. They don't understand how to show up on time. Even some U.S. Senators have not figured that out. Yet, if a young American doesn't get a job or learn to work with his coworkers, customers, their boss, how to show up on time, to be courteous, respectful, diligent, and responsible, he or she can't learn the skills it takes to achieve in any job.

Some time ago I tweeted a speech Ashton Kutcher gave. It was actually a terrific speech. It was a speech at one of those award shows where he talked about the value of hard work. One of the things I remember he said was this: In my life, opportunity looks an awful lot like hard work. That was a great message. It was a great message to young people. Part of the reason I tweeted it out and to salute him—I have watched his TV shows and his movies, but I don't know him personally—was because he can speak to millions of young people who would never listen to me. I salute him for carrying a message about hard work, diligence, and working toward the American dream.

The greatest travesty of what is happening with ObamaCare is a generation of young people are being denied a fair chance at the American dream. If we look at economic growth, according to the Bureau of Economic Affairs, GDP growth over the last four quarters has been an abysmal 1.6 percent. The historic average since World War II is 3.3 percent. Our economy is stagnant, and ObamaCare is a big part of the reason.

So I ask the Presiding Officer, where is the urgency in this body? When the Presiding Officer goes home and talks to the men and women in West Virginia—or the men and women in Texas—he must hear that they are hurting. They understand that 1.6 percent economic growth is unacceptable and it is hurting the American people. Where is the urgency in this body? Where is the urgency to say: We have to stand and do something to turn it around.

Jobs are being lost because of ObamaCare. A U.S. Chamber of Commerce survey of small businesses in 2013 found that 71 percent of small businesses say ObamaCare makes it harder to hire workers. The study also found that two-thirds of small businesses are not ready to comply with ObamaCare rules.

Why do we care about small businesses? Look, on one level, we care about the entrepreneurs—the Horatio Algers and the people working toward the American dream—but even more fundamentally, small businesses produce two-thirds of the new jobs in this country. If small businesses are suffering, jobs are suffering and America suffers.

ObamaCare is an absolute disaster for small businesses. Forty-one percent of small business owners have held off on plans to hire new employees, and 38 percent say they are holding off on plans to grow their businesses in direct response to the law.

By the way, the most egregious parts of ObamaCare still have not kicked in. Forty-eight percent of small business owners say ObamaCare is bad for business. Less than 10 percent say it is good for business.

Jamie Richardson of White Castle explained how ObamaCare is impacting her business: In the 5 years prior to the health care law, we were opening an average of eight new White Castle restaurants each year. In 2013 we plan to just open two new locations. While other factors have slowed our growth, it is the mounting uncertainty surrounding the health care law that brought us to a standstill.

I want the Presiding Officer to think about that for a second. They were opening eight White Castle restaurants a year—I like their little burgers—and that dropped to two. So six a year over the last 4 years amounts to 24 White Castle restaurants. No. 1, just as a consumer—and I am a big fan of eating White Castle burgers—that is 24 places we can't go to get a White Castle burger. But that is not the real hardship. The real hardship is all the jobs that are lost from those 24 restaurants that didn't open. Every one of those stores would have multiple shifts with managers, cashiers, or kids just mopping the floor. All those jobs would have been on the economic ladder toward the American dream.

Even within a fast food restaurant there has been tremendous opportunity for investment. Maybe you get hired mopping a floor because you don't have any other skills or, like my dad, washing dishes because you don't have any other skills. If you work a little while, maybe you can move over to the fries and then to the griddle. You can move to the cashier desk and learn how to count change. A lot of kids don't know how to count change. Sadly, because of the educational challenges we have, a lot of kids don't have the skill to count change yet. They can learn that. Then, if you demonstrate hard work, perseverance, and customer service, maybe you will get promoted to assistant manager, then manager, and then who knows.

Just a few weeks ago I had dinner with a number of franchisees who own fast food restaurants for one particular very well-known hamburger chain. I listened to their stories. I start most meetings, if they are small enough that this is feasible—like the Kerrville small business gathering—by asking them to go around and share an issue that is of a concern to them. I remember one gentleman, an African-American gentleman, who described exactly that path. He described how he got hired in an entry-level position at a fast food restaurant, developed skills, advanced, and then he was hired as an assistant manager and then as a manager. After that, he saved up and bought his own restaurant.

It was interesting. There were people—and some of the franchise owners had pretty extensive backgrounds. I think there was one fellow who had 27 fast food restaurants. So there were some people who were very successful businesspeople.

I remember this African-American gentleman who had relatively recently saved up to buy his first restaurant that he owned and the pride he justifiably felt—and the pride I felt. I mean, what an incredible country. What was interesting is that he described the exact same challenges as the fellow who owned 27 restaurants and was far wealthier and had a far bigger business.

What all of them said as we were going around the table was that ObamaCare is devastating. They didn't say it was sort of a little problem. They didn't say it was making life more difficult. They said: It is devastating. It is going to put us out of business. We don't know what to do. This is a disaster for our business.

A March 2013 Federal Reserve report on current Federal economic conditions explains that employers in several Federal Reserve districts cited the effects of the ObamaCare act as reasons for planned layoffs and reluctance to hire more staff.

In May 2013 Moody's economist Mark Zandi noted a slowdown in small business hiring due to ObamaCare.

The U.S. Chamber of Commerce, in the second quarter of 2013 small business survey, found that Washington policies continue to hamper hiring and growth, with over a quarter of small businesses saying they had lost employees in the last year. They cited health care as the very top concern.

Concern about ObamaCare has increased by 10 points since June of 2011 and by 4 points just last quarter. Seventy-one percent of small businesses say the health care law makes it harder to hire. Only 30 percent say they are prepared for the requirements of the law—including participation in the marketplaces.

Among small businesses that will be impacted by the employer mandate, one-half of small businesses say they will either cut hours to reduce full-time employees or replace full-time employees with part-time workers to avoid the mandate. Twenty-four percent say they will reduce hiring to stay under 50 employees.

I want to repeat those numbers because those numbers are deeply troubling. Among small businesses that will be impacted by the employer mandate, one-half—50 percent—say they will either cut hours to reduce full-time employees or replace full-time employees with part-time workers to avoid the mandate. We are not talking about a few small businesses, we are talking about half of them. Twenty-four percent say they will reduce hiring to stay under 50 employees. That is a disaster for small business, it is a disaster for jobs, and it is a disaster for American families who are struggling.

The outlook for hiring remains grim. The majority—61 percent—of small businesses do not have plans to hire next year.

A Grand Rapids, MI, company reported that they had to lay off over 1,000 people due to the ObamaCare medical device tax. Let's think about that. In Grand Rapids, MI, there are 1,000 people out of a job directly because of ObamaCare. Now let's think of their spouses and their kids. One of the major breadwinners in their family lost his or her job because of ObamaCare.

On September 18, 2013, the world-renowned Cleveland Clinic announced that it would cut jobs and slash 5 to 6 percent of its $6 billion annual budget to prepare for ObamaCare. This is not just impacting fast food restaurants, this is impacting everyone. The Cleveland Clinic has a $6 billion annual budget, and yet they are forced to fire employees. The Cleveland Clinic is Cleveland's largest employer.

Every 4 years during the Presidential election, both parties purport to care passionately about what happens in the great State of Ohio. Both parties focus and descend on Ohio—and a handful of other swing States—as the center of the universe. Yet, as we sit here now in 2013—not a Presidential election—somehow the concern about what is happening to the Cleveland Clinic in Ohio has diminished. The

Cleveland Clinic is Cleveland's largest employer, and it is the second largest employer in the State of Ohio after Walmart.

I would suggest that if all of the folks from this body and the political parties who descend on Ohio every 4 years are genuinely concerned about what is occurring in Ohio in a non-Presidential year we should see the floor of this Senate filled with Senators concerned about the impact ObamaCare is having directly on Cleveland and the State of Ohio.

Cleveland Clinic is responsible for 80 percent of the economic output of northeast Ohio, according to a 2009 study. It is the largest provider in Ohio of Medicaid health coverage for the poor, the program that will expand to cover uninsured Americans under ObamaCare.

The Cleveland Clinic has close to 100 locations around the State. They employ 3,000 doctors. Its main campus is recognized worldwide for its cancer and cardiovascular treatments.

(Ms. WARREN assumed the Chair.)

Madam President, some Members of this body might say: Well, these are hard times. Everyone is struggling, so maybe the Cleveland Clinic is responding to economic challenges. Who is to say what the Cleveland Clinic is doing has anything to do with ObamaCare? Well, the answer to that is, who is to say? The Cleveland Clinic is to say. A spokeswoman for the Cleveland Clinic said: "To prepare for health care reform, Cleveland Clinic is transforming the way care is delivered to patients."

She added that $330 million would be cut from the clinic's annual budget.

You want to talk about direct job losses from ObamaCare, go to Cleveland, OH, go to those working at the Cleveland Clinic, go to those depending on the Cleveland Clinic for health care, and that is one very real manifestation of the train wreck that is ObamaCare. According to the *Star-Ledger*, in a story printed on September 12, 2013, Barnabas Health, which employs over 19,000 people, is laying off employees. Why? Well, according to Barnabas Health, the reason is ObamaCare. According to a spokeswoman for Barnabas Health:

Healthcare reform, in combination with Medicare cuts, more patients seeking out-patient care and decreasing patient volumes—as a result, we have made the difficult decision to reduce our workforce. Decisions like this are never easy and we are working with these employees to help them look for other opportunities within the Barnabas Health system.

This is not us putting words in their mouth. This is people on the ground in the States dealing with the very real struggles and the disaster that is ObamaCare.

The problem we face in Washington is that our elected officials are not listening to us. We need to make DC listen. We need to make elected officials in both parties listen to the very real hardship that is coming from ObamaCare.

I would like to share a number of real constituent letters concerning ObamaCare. So this is not me speaking. As I said at the outset, the reason Congress is held in such disrepute, so little approval, is because for many years now elected officials in both parties have refused to listen to the people, and there is a sense of despair that no matter what the American people say, our elected officials will not listen because they are more interested in themselves, they are more interested in getting an exemption for Members of Congress from ObamaCare than they are on fixing the problem for the American people. And that level of disillusion is not irrational. It is based on a very real problem. Yet I am inspired that if and when the American people stand and make their voices heard, our politicians will have no choice but to listen.

I remember early on—Madam President, you and I are relatively new in this body. We have been here 9 months. I remember early on standing at this very desk along with my friend Senator RAND PAUL in his historic 13-hour filibuster on drones. I remember when Senator PAUL began that filibuster, many Members of this body viewed what he was doing as curious, if not quixotic, as a strange issue that most Members of this body, frankly, were not concerned about. We saw something incredible happen during that time, which is the American people got engaged, got involved, began speaking out, and it

transformed the debate. As a result of the American people's involvement, it transformed the debate.

If you want Washington to listen, the only way that will happen
is if it comes from the American people. So let me read some letters
from American people who do not have the opportunity to come
to the Senate floor. I hope in a very small way to provide a voice
for them.

A small business from Alice, TX, wrote, on August 9, 2013:

> We, the undersigned employees . . . are growing increasingly
> concerned with the apparent disregard for small businesses
> and the middle class that is on display by the United States
> government. We are trying to figure out how we are going to
> cope with the 14% increase in health insurance premiums we
> are facing, despite the fact that we have a lower average
> employee age and loss ratio than we have had at any point
> in our 21-year history. The increase is because of insurance
> companies preparing for new taxes and unreasonable require-
> ments within ObamaCare.
>
> On top of struggling to find the means to cover our own
> group of employees, our government now makes it clear that
> part of the massive amount of taxes we pay a year will be used
> to cover 75% of health insurance costs for Members of Congress
> AND their staffers. As waivers are granted daily, shielding . . .
> big business, unions, government agencies, and various other
> Affordable Care Act supporters, it is clear the burden will rest
> firmly on middle class small businesses like us. . . .
>
> We strongly encourage our elected officials to place a higher
> importance on public service than self-service.

Let me read that sentence again: "We strongly encourage our
elected officials to place a higher importance on public service than
self service."

> We are hurting badly because of this, as are many disillusioned
> businesses with whom we communicate in our industry.

Headlines nationwide report hiring freezes and layoffs due to increased costs on businesses large and small. The weight is too heavy at the worst time, and in result the economy will soon break. We urge Congress to defund or repeal the Affordable Care Act with no further delay. . . .

That is not me speaking. That is from a small business in Alice, TX. I would note, that is not even the CEO speaking. That is a letter signed by the employees of that small business because they are hurting.

But let me note, it is not limited to the State of Texas. I guarantee you, there are people hurting in every one of the 50 States, every one of the States we represent. A commercial real estate broker from Chesapeake City, VA, wrote, on September 20, 2013:

I also wanted to share with you how ObamaCare is affecting my business. I am a commercial real estate broker in Virginia and am already feeling the effects of this disastrous bill. I am currently in the process of analyzing an apartment portfolio for sale for a client and recently the occupancy has dropped dramatically in this class C low-income community. The community is not subsidized as these tenants are paying out of pocket for the rent. Most of the tenants work in fast food, janitorial, and low paying service related jobs. A great deal of them have had their hours cut to 29.5 hours per week and cannot pay the rent. Our occupancy has dropped as well as the income. Our management company has reached into the City of Richmond for rent assistance for these tenants but to no avail. Not only are these people going to be forced into government housing but my client will realize a smaller equity harvest. This is a disaster, and it affects everyone.

As you can see by this scenario, many are affected by this bill. Also, a class A franchisee with a national restaurant chain whom I represent is experiencing the pain from this bill. They are being forced to sell off to a larger franchisee because they cannot afford to comply with the requirements. I wish the American people understood how severely the economy will be impacted. Thank you for fighting the good fight. We are behind you.

Let me read again two sentences from that letter from a commercial real estate broker in Chesapeake City, VA: "Most of the tenants work in fast food, janitorial, and low paying service related jobs. A great deal of them had their hours cut to 29.5 hours per week and cannot pay the rent."

So they are losing their housing. I want you to think for a second about the spiral that comes from this. If you have someone who is working as a janitor, if you have someone who is working flipping burgers, if you have someone washing dishes, as my dad did, and they have their hours forcibly reduced to 29 hours a week, as so many people across this country are having happen because of ObamaCare, they cannot provide for their family on that, so they cannot pay the rent, as these people cannot. But not being able to pay the rent means some of them may move to government housing. And what is the answer? Look, they are losing their hours because of ObamaCare. The answer is not: Well, let's give them a rent subsidy. Let's tax people even more. First let's pass rules and laws and regulations that prevent people from getting decent jobs. Then let's jack up the taxes even more so we can pay them to subsidize their rent and subsidize their housing because they cannot afford to pay their rent, they cannot afford to pay their housing because of a law we passed that forcibly reduced their hours. That is the path to destruction in this country.

Far better that we get back to our founding principles, far better that we get back to what has made America great, which is our free enterprise system—a robust, free enterprise system that encourages small businesses to grow and to prosper, that encourages people working a job as a janitor to work hard and get a promotion and climb that ladder, to pay their own rent, to pay for their own food for their kids, to work and to advance.

These cries are coming from all across the country. Yet Washington is not listening. We need to make DC listen.

A small business owner from Port Clinton, OH, wrote, on September 19, 2013:

I strongly urge you to stand up for the middle class and small business and vote to DEFUND ObamaCare. As a small business owner, we have always offered health insurance. After meeting with our health insurance representative, we learned that the lowest coverage level of ObamaCare offered is estimated to be about $400 a person, twice what we pay now for excellent coverage. . . .

With big business and government being exempted from this policy, again the SMALL BUSINESS OWNER and individual are left with all the costs for everyone else. This could well end up closing our business and then there will be 15 more individuals collecting from the government.

A constituent from Nacogdoches, TX, wrote, on May 29, 2013:

I need a little help here! Can you explain something to me? My health insurance premiums for my wife, three children and myself were $850 or so back in 2010. After ObamaCare was passed my premiums are now $1400 or so. This January, when ObamaCare is implemented it is estimated by Blue Cross Blue Shield I could see a 25% increase in premiums. That will be almost $1,800 a month for premiums plus on my HSA plan my deductible is $10,000. If my calculator is correct, that is $21,600 per year out of my pocket before the insurance company pays a penny.

I also own a small business and have four others on our group plan. If this cost increase is across the board with the others as well, my business will stop the benefit of insurance and each will be on their own to get coverage. I understood this health care overhaul would be a benefit. From where I am sitting it is only a burden. If you can, please repeal this before it gets worse.

We are hearing these voices from Americans all over the country, both Republicans and Democrats in this body. All we need to do is listen to the people. A veterinarian from Montgomery, TX, wrote on February 20, 2013:

> I would like to bring to your attention a troubling development. I am a veterinarian, and in the past had to use a group health care policy offered by the American Veterinary Medical Association. I am currently under my husband's insurance. However, a number of my colleagues use one of the various plans AVMA offers. The AVMA insurance is being canceled at the end of the year. This decision is due directly to ObamaCare. Here is the text of that notification. Group Health and Life Insurance Trust Programs and New York Life attributes the program's demise to regulatory requirements put in place as a result of the Patient Protection and Affordable Care Act signed by President Obama in 2010.
>
> Company officials told trustees that the challenges of complying with provisions of the law that take effect in 2014 are the primary reason New York Life opted to quit the association health insurance market entirely. New York Life has underwritten the American Veterinarian Medical Association Trust medical coverage for the past 20 years.
>
> A number of veterinarians are contract labor, called relief veterinarians. These vets contract out on a daily or weekly basis to fill in for doctors at various clinics when someone takes a vacation or during seasonal business increases. Many of those vets do not have access to health care in any other way. This is a travesty. Perfectly good plans are being discontinued due to a perfectly awful law. This health care law is directly contributing to people losing their health care.
>
> My husband and I made long-term plans to potentially retire early and use an AVMA plan until eligible for Medicare. We also had the safety net of the AVMA insurance if something happened with this job. For me, AVMA's decision is currently an inconvenience. However, it removes an option

for me in the future. My colleagues on the other hand will likely be forced into inferior health care or pay penalties through no fault of their own.

We all remember President Obama told the American people: If you like your health insurance plan, you can keep it. Even in these cynical days of politics, promises should mean something. For this woman and her husband, that promise is a hollow failure. She is losing her health insurance because of ObamaCare. That is not me saying that, not some politician saying that. That is from her own words.

The rules of the Senate will not allow her or any other small business owner to walk onto the Senate floor and speak out, to say: Why am I losing my health insurance? Why am I struggling? Why is my business going under? So I am doing my very best to in some small way help provide a voice for those people who are struggling, those people who are hurting.

But if this body were operating the way it should, there should be 100 voices; 100 of us, Democrats and Republicans, should be standing side by side reading letter after letter like this. You know what. These are our bosses. These are the people we work for. They are struggling.

These letters I am reading are not ideological letters. They are not coming from a partisan perspective. They are people who are seeing on the ground this law is not working.

Yet DC does not listen to them. The Democrats in this body tell America: ObamaCare is great. ObamaCare is terrific. I am sorry you lost your health care, but ObamaCare is terrific. The Republicans in this body, sadly more than a few of them, say: We will take lots and lots of symbolic votes against ObamaCare, but there is nothing we can do. If every Republican Senator stands together and votes no on cloture this Friday or Saturday, there is something we can do. We can stand and say: We are listening to the American people. This law is not working and people are suffering.

They are not interested in political games. They are not interested in show votes. They are not interested in the fact that if the majority leader succeeds in cutting off debate on this bill and there is a 51-vote threshold on an amendment to fund ObamaCare, at that point every

Republican will happily vote no. That may be solicited from the personal political perspectives of the Republicans in this body, but it does not benefit the American people one iota. It does not benefit the American people. It does not stop ObamaCare. It does not fix the problem. That is what we should be doing.

A constituent from Euless, TX, wrote on July 3, 2013:

> I have been disabled since 1997 and on a fixed income. My wife lost her job of 16 years in 2008 and was not able to find a good job so she was forced to take her Social Security last year at age 62. She is 41-year type I diabetic and her medical costs are expensive. Luckily, I was paying for medical and long-term disability insurance when I was working, which allowed me to continue the medical insurance with a company even after I became disabled.
>
> I got a letter in May of this year informing me that I was going to lose that medical coverage come 2014. Since we are both on a fixed income, it will be impossible for us to maintain our mortgage and to start paying for all of our health costs. Repeal ObamaCare.

These are voices from the people. This is a disabled man, a senior couple who is suffering, who is losing their health insurance because of ObamaCare. Every one of us has an obligation to listen to people.

Look, I understand in Washington, in a football game we all cheer for our respective team. I cheer when the Houston Texans win a game. I am not generally thrilled, having grown up in Houston in the 1970s, when the Pittsburgh Steelers win a game, because I remember as a kid year after year seeing the Steelers sadly trounce the Oilers and the great Earl Campbell when the Steelers had one of the greatest football teams ever to play the game. I understand that. It is a good thing to cheer for your team.

In politics sometimes we cheer for our team too. So I understand the great many Democrats who take the view: Well, a Democratic President signed the law, Democrats passed the law on a straight party vote so we have got to cheer for our team. You know, I will note that more than a few Democratic Members of this body privately, when they are behind closed doors, are worried about what is happening to ObamaCare. They are seeing the problems. But yet publicly they are still cheering for their team.

This is not a team sport. This is life and death. There is a fundamental divide between the people and Washington. We need to make DC listen, listen to the people.

Mr. PAUL. Would the Senator yield for a question?

Mr. CRUZ. I am happy to yield for a question without yielding the floor.

Mr. PAUL. You know, Senators do not always ask for advice from other Senators. I thought I would come down and make sure the Senator had comfortable shoes on, make sure he is getting enough to eat—try not to eat on television. That is a little free advice that sometimes shows up.

But my question relates to ObamaCare. I think the Senator has done a good job of bringing attention to something I think is going to be a real tragedy for the country. As we get involved with this, there is so much talk about tactics and this or that, whether now is the right time, when is the right time to do this, but I think the question is, do we need to talk about something that is going to affect 16 percent of our economy, one-sixth of our economy? Do we need to bring up an issue? Do we need to draw attention and try to stop something that could be damaging to the people precisely it is intended to help?

I think it is personally not a good idea to shut down government. I think it is also, though, not a good idea to fund ObamaCare. Can they both go together? Can you do one without the other? Some, like the President, have said: Oh, Republicans, they just want 100 percent of what they want or they are going to shut down government.

Well, can you say something so patently false and get away with it, is my question. The President wants 100 percent of what he wants. He wants ObamaCare as he passed it with only Democrats. He wants it never to be changed. He wants no compromise. He wants what he wants or he is willing to shut down the government. That is what this debate is about.

ObamaCare was passed with only Democrats, no Republican input, no Republican votes. When people are saying there are problems, his own people are saying there are problems. The Teamsters have said there is a problem. Authors of the bill are saying it is a train wreck. The former President came out this week and said: It is going to hurt the people it was intended to help.

So we have got all of these people saying: For goodness sakes, slow this train down. Stop this train. Stop this train wreck of ObamaCare. All everybody cries about is: Oh, somebody wants to shut down the government. The President does not want to compromise.

What we are talking about is, we do not want to spend money on something that is not going to work and hurt the people—precisely the people it was intended to help. But the thing is, how do we fix it? What do we do? Can we scrap the whole thing? Well, the Democrats control one body, we control the other body, they control the Presidency.

Historically what would happen, and what I think the American people would like to see is, we stand up, as the Senator from Texas is, and say what we are for. We are for a different solution. We are for competition. We are for the free markets. We are for bringing health care to everyone with a lower price. We went through this whole debacle of giving people ObamaCare and it is going to be expensive. Everybody is going to pay more.

Many people still will not have insurance. The ones who do have insurance are going to pay more. So what would we like? Why are we here today? Why is the Senator from Texas here today? To say to the President: We need to talk. What does the President say? He says: My way or the highway.

When the American people said they want dialog between Republicans and Democrats, how do we get there? We have to stand for what we believe in so they will come and talk. Does it mean we are going to get 100 percent of what we want? No. But if we do not stand for what we believe, how will we have any dialog? How will we get to compromise? How do we get them to talk to us? We are not asking for 100 percent of what we want, but we are asking for a dialog. How do we get the dialog unless someone is willing to stand and say: Enough is enough. When we look at this, if we want to ever get to the point of getting to compromise, the only way we get there is by standing and saying we believe in this.

It isn't about us demanding 100 percent of what we want. But right now, if you look at this objectively, the President is getting 100 percent of what he wants—ObamaCare passed only by Democrats, not one Republican vote. Really, how do we get to what the American people want, which is dialog and compromise? We have to look at a deadline. We have a deadline.

My question to the Senator from Texas is whether he wants to shut down the government. Is that his intention or is it the President's intention to shut down the government or is it that perhaps when deadlines come forward, that is a good time for dialog because no one ever seems to talk at any other time?

I would ask the Senator from Texas, what are his intentions? Does he want to shut down the government or would he like to find something to make ObamaCare less bad? I know we would both like to repeal it, but would the Senator accept anything in between?

Mr. CRUZ. I thank the Senator from Kentucky for his very fine question. Let me say at the outset before I respond directly to the question that I remember not too many months ago standing on this same Senate floor in the midst of the Senator's historic filibuster. I will say it was one of the proudest moments of my life. Indeed, during that filibuster on drones, that was the first time I had ever spoken on the Senate floor.

I have observed multiple times that I will go to my grave in debt to RAND PAUL, to have the opportunity for the first time—and there will only be one first time that anyone gets to speak on this floor—to have that first time be in support of that tremendous filibuster that mobilized and unified the American people.

I will note that one of the things I remember the Senator shared with me afterward was the advice he just gave a minute ago. I remember asking: What do you think? The Senator was pretty weary at the end. His comment at the time was, well, I wish I had worn more comfortable shoes. I will confess I thought about that. That struck me as pretty good advice.

I am going to make an embarrassing admission right now. I will get to the question in a second, but I wanted to make an embarrassing admission first. For many years, when I was in private practice and when I was solicitor general, I wore a particular pair of boots, my argument boots. They were black ostrich boots. Litigators are kind of superstitious, so anytime I went into court to argue a case I wore my argument boots. I had them resoled four or five times.

When I had the great honor of serving in this body, of being sworn into the Senate, when I was sworn in standing on the steps just in front of us, I wore my argument boots. I have worn them every day since. I don't believe there has been a day on this Senate floor that I haven't worn my argument boots.

I had a choice with which I was confronted, which was do I follow through and wear my argument boots or do I listen to the very sage counsel from my friend from Kentucky and go with more comfortable shoes. I will embarrassingly admit that I took the coward's way out. I went and purchased some black tennis shoes. Actually, I think they are the same model the senior Senator from Utah ORRIN HATCH wears on a regular basis. I am not in my argument boots, and I will confess I do feel pretty embarrassed by that. I am pretty sure, since we are on the Senate floor and C–SPAN is covering it, that this may not be covered by the priest-penitent privilege, but I do feel it is a question of sorts.

The question Senator RAND PAUL asked was an excellent question. His question was whether I or anyone here wishes to shut down the government. The answer is absolutely not. We should not shut down the government. We should fund every bit of the government, every aspect of the government, 100 percent of the government except for ObamaCare. That is what the House of Representatives did. The House of Representatives—232 Members of the House, including 2 Democrats—voted to fund every bit of the Federal Government, 100 percent of it, except for ObamaCare.

I would note that last night on the floor of the Senate, I asked the majority leader to consent to passing the continuing resolution the House passed, passing it into law. Had the majority leader not stood there and said: I object, the continuing resolution would be passed into law and the government would not be shutting down. The majority leader had every opportunity to not shut down the government.

Let me be absolutely clear. We should not shut down the government. I sincerely hope Senator REID and President Obama do not choose to force a government shutdown simply to force ObamaCare on the American people. That would be a mistake. Instead, what we should do is listen to the American people. Make DC listen.

Mr. PAUL. Would the Senator yield for one quick question?

Mr. CRUZ. I am happy to yield for a quick question without yielding the floor.

Mr. PAUL. Since we are making it clear, the Republican message and alternative here is not to shut down the government; our desire is to have no ObamaCare. We desire not to have it. We think he went in the wrong direction. But we don't control the government. We don't control the government. We don't control the Senate. It is controlled by the opposition party. We don't control the Presidency.

My question to the Senator is, If he can't get everything he wants, if he can't defund ObamaCare, which is exactly what he and I both agree on, and millions of people across America want us to get rid of ObamaCare, if the Senator can't, if he stands today and argues and cannot get rid of it, will he accept a compromise? Will he work with the President and will he work with the majority leader if they are willing to come and say: You know, you are right. We messed up on a bunch of this. There are a lot of people who are going to be hurt by ObamaCare. A lot of part-time workers are going to lose their jobs or are going to lose hours. There are going to be real workers who are full time who are going to lose their insurance or lose their jobs. Is the Senator willing to work with us? Is he willing to work with the leader, Senator REID, and with the President to find a compromise?

Mr. CRUZ. I thank the Senator from Kentucky for that question. I think it is a very good question.

This afternoon the Senator and I and all the Republican Members of the conference spent some 2 hours in a closed-door strategy session. I am not going to reveal what anyone else said there, but I certainly feel comfortable revealing what I said there, which is that if we are going to make real progress in solving the problem that is ObamaCare, in listening to the American people and mitigating the job losses, with people losing their health insurance, all of the harms that are coming from ObamaCare, we have to stand and fight right now.

The battle before this body is the cloture vote that will occur on Friday or Saturday of this week. If all 46 Republicans vote together in unity to support the House Republicans and to deny Majority Leader REID the ability to fund ObamaCare on a straight party-line vote, that puts us in a position to address the problem.

The Senator's question was would I vote for something less than defunding ObamaCare. Personally, no. Why? Because I have committed publicly over and over to the American people that I will not vote for a continuing resolution that funds one penny of ObamaCare.

I am reminded of when I first arrived in the Senate. I spent 2 years campaigning for the Senator from Kentucky. Senator PAUL campaigned with me in Texas over and over.

If you want to talk about a rock star, you should see, when RAND PAUL shows up in Texas, the huge number of fans who come out for Senator PAUL and for his dad.

I spent 2 years campaigning in Texas saying: The first bill I will introduce in Congress will be a bill to repeal ObamaCare.

When I showed up, there were lots of reporters. I introduced the bill to repeal ObamaCare.

They immediately said: Well, why did you do that?

My response: Well, I spent 2 years campaigning telling the American people that would be first bill I would introduce.

They were utterly befuddled why anyone would actually do what they said.

In answer to the Senator's question of whether I will vote for something that is a middle ground that funds ObamaCare partially, no. Why? Because, as I have repeatedly told the American people, as I have told Texas, I will not vote for a continuing resolution that funds ObamaCare. But that being said, are there Members of our conference who would like to see a compromise, who would like to see a middle ground that is perhaps not what I very much want and will fight for with every ounce of strength I have but that mitigates some of the damage of ObamaCare, that responds to the people who are suffering from ObamaCare, I think there are quite a few Senators who would like to see that happen.

If Republicans roll over on the cloture vote on Friday or Saturday, if we allow the majority leader to fund ObamaCare with 51 votes, we will get no compromise. There will be no middle ground because there will be no reason to compromise. It is much like a poker game. I know the Senator from Kentucky—many of his libertarian supporters enjoy a good game of poker. As a Texan, I will admit to not being entirely adverse to it myself. In a game of poker, if somebody makes a bet and then says to you "if you raise me, I am going to fold," you will lose 100 percent of your poker games. That is a path to losing.

For those Members of the Republican caucus who were perhaps not as adamant that we should insist on a complete and total defund now, I don't intend to waiver from that position, but there may be others who disagree.

If you want to get to any middle ground that is not a symbolic vote to tell our constituents but that actually changes the law to make things better for the men and women at home, to mitigate the harms of ObamaCare, the only way to do so is for Republicans to stand united and to deny the majority leader the ability to fund ObamaCare on a 51-vote partisan vote.

Mr. ROBERTS. Would the courageous Senator from Texas yield for a question?

Mr. CRUZ. I yield for a question without yielding the floor.

Mr. ROBERTS. Let me ask the Senator a question to cut to the chase. Let's get to the bottom line. Former Speaker of the House NANCY PELOSI, our respected leader of the Senate, HARRY REID, because of his position, Secretary of Health and Human Services Kathleen Sebelius, and President Barack Obama have all said publicly that the Affordable Care Act is the first step to a single-payer system. Listen to the folks on the other side of the aisle, and many of them say the same thing.

We can call it a single-payer system, we can call it national health insurance, but is this not the first step toward socialized health care—socialized health care—and is stopping socialized health care worth pulling out all of the stops and fighting the fight?

Mr. CRUZ. I thank my friend from Kansas for that very fine question. He is exactly right. Socialized medicine is—and has been everywhere it has been implemented in the world—a disaster. ObamaCare—its intended purpose is to lead us unavoidably down that path.

I thank the Senator from Kansas for his good question on that front and for his leadership.

I would note that there are some Republicans, some commentators who have said: Don't fight this fight. Don't fight to defund. Why? Because ObamaCare is going to collapse on its own weight. If we just stay quiet, we don't take any risks. Give it time; it is getting worse and worse. Stay out of the way; it is going to collapse on its own weight. And there is both truth and falsity in that prediction. There is no doubt that ObamaCare is going to collapse. But the problem is that the way it will collapse, if it is implemented, is likely to permanently damage the private health insurance system, which will result in millions of people losing their health insurance and having no ability to go back. That is what enables Majority Leader REID to go on television and say: Fear not, this will lead us to single-payer government health care. Because when ObamaCare collapses in shambles—he doesn't say this, but this is the necessary reasoning that leads him to this—it will take down the private health insurance business with it, so there will be nothing left.

Listen, I commend the majority leader for his candor. I mean, there is a degree of courage in embracing socialized medicine. There are a number of Members of the Democratic caucus who embrace socialized medicine. I think every one of them shows courage and candor. I am very happy to debate in great detail whether socialized medicine would be good or bad for this Nation.

I don't think the American people are conflicted. If you look at the nations that have socialized medicine, everyplace it has been implemented you see low quality, you see scarcity, you see waiting periods, and you see government bureaucrats getting between you and your doctor. If you go in for government treatment, you may be told that you are going to have to wait 6 months, you are going to have to wait a year or, you know what. A bureaucrat in the ministry of whatchamacallit has determined you don't get that treatment. That is what has happened in every socialized medicine country in the world. And so to those on the Republican side, those commentators who say this is a risky fight, I have never once suggested this is an easy fight. But in my 42 years on Earth, I have yet to see any fight that is worthwhile that is easy. In his years as a marine, I would venture to guess that Senator ROBERTS never saw a fight that mattered that was easy. None of us were elected to this body to do easy things.

If the majority leader is right, that leaving ObamaCare alone will necessarily lead us to socialized medicine because private health insurance will collapse—ObamaCare will collapse—and there will be nothing left, what a call to urgency. Indeed, I would say the majority leader, in making that argument, should be one of the most effective spokespersons for saying we ought to have 46 Republicans uniting and voting against cloture on this bill to say: No, we are not going to let a partisan Democrat vote fund ObamaCare because we are not going to be complicit in any way, shape or form with destroying private health insurance and forcing Americans into socialized medicine.

Let me note that in the meantime, even for those who somewhat serenely say: Fear not; this is going to collapse on its own. The process will inevitably be painful. Just a few minutes ago I read a letter from a constituent from Euless, TX, who is disabled and on a fixed income, whose wife has retired and who has lost his insurance because of ObamaCare. There are millions of Americans in Kansas, in Kentucky, in Alabama, in Texas, and in States all over this country who are worried right now because their health insurance is in jeopardy. In my view the decision of some Members of the Senate to say: Well, let ObamaCare collapse—either on the Republican side because when it collapses it will all just magically go away, or on the Democratic side because when it collapses it will lead us all to the perfect utopia of socialized medicine—is easy. It is easy for Members of this body to say such things from the cheap seats, particularly when the President has granted an exemption to Members of Congress from ObamaCare, where they feel that if the system collapses, if millions of Americans are suffering, it is not going to be us. It is not going to be our staff. The President has carved us out for special rules. It is just going to be the American people.

The most fundamental divide that is happening here is this body has stopped listening to the American people. We ought to have the urgency for this man and woman in Euless, TX, who is disabled and on a fixed income and retired and who wants to keep his health insurance, that we have for ourselves and our staffs. We ought to have that kind of urgency. And you know what. If it were our wife or our husband's health insurance, we wouldn't say: Let the system collapse because, in time, there will be a political victory. I guarantee if it were our spouse's, if it were our daughter's or son's health insurance, particularly if they had significant health issues, not one of us would be serene in saying: Let it collapse, because we want to immunize ourselves from the criticism or because we want to ultimately move to socialized medicine.

I think the stakes have never been higher. In my view, the cloture vote we will take on either Friday or Saturday of this week is the most important vote that I will have taken—I think that any Member of the Senate will have taken—in the 9 months I have served in this body because it goes fundamentally to: Will we respond to the suffering ObamaCare is causing? Will we respond to the millions of people who are jobless? Will we respond to the people getting forced into part-time work? Will we respond to the people who are losing their health care or will we continue to say: For me but not for thee. Different rules apply to Washington that apply to the ruling class. The President can grant exemptions to the big corporations and to Members of Congress, but hardworking American families, you guys are left in the cold. I would suggest that is a fundamental abdication of our responsibility. We are here—or we should be here—fighting for the people.

Mr. SESSIONS. Madam President, will the Senator yield for a question?

Mr. CRUZ. I am happy to yield for a question without yielding the floor.

Mr. SESSIONS. By chance, or maybe because of the significance of it, my first question is very similar to what Senator ROBERTS had asked, because I have given a lot of thought to this. I haven't signed letters. I haven't said how I was going to vote on this issue. But it was called to my attention that Senator REID, the majority leader, flatly stated a month ago he believed in a single-payer system.

They asked him: Is it the Senator's goal to move toward a single-payer system? And his answer is: yes, yes, absolutely yes.

I just left the Budget Committee hearing. We have a great team there, on the Republican and Democrat side, and my friend SHELDON WHITEHOUSE and I had a little exchange about the new health care law, and I thought he was suggesting it wasn't much of a change. So I asked him this, I said: The majority leader said he favors a single-payer system. He said: I do too.

It wasn't long ago in the Budget Committee that Senator BERNIE SANDERS also said he favored a single-payer system. And Senator ROBERTS mentioned others. And of course the President did. I checked the President's quote from 2003. He has denied it since, when he was trying to get the votes to pass the new law, but in 2003 he said he was a proponent of a "single-payer universal health system."

I think this is a huge national issue. This new health care law is clearly driven by an agenda: to have a single payer. So I ask Senator CRUZ: If there is a single payer, who will the payer be?

Mr. CRUZ. The payer is always the government, which ultimately means the taxpayer, hardworking American families.

Mr. SESSIONS. In other words, the Federal Government?

Mr. CRUZ. I will continue to yield for a question without yielding the floor.

Mr. SESSIONS. Let me ask this. In other words, the government is going to be the one that pays for everything. In health care in America there will be only one payer, the government, and it would then, since it is a predominant power, be able to dictate health policy, such as in the socialized medical systems that have failed around the world; would it not?

Mr. CRUZ. The Senator is absolutely correct. Once the government is paying for health care, it controls health care. That has proven to be the case in every country in the world.

I agree with the Senator from Alabama that it is commendable that there are some Members of this body who openly embrace socialized medicine. That is commendable for candor. I don't agree with it as a policy matter, but I actually think there is virtue to speaking honestly about what it is you support and not occupying the middle ground, as those—to take a quote from Teddy Roosevelt slightly out of context—cold, timid souls who know neither victory nor defeat.

One of the problems in this debate over ObamaCare is the relatively few who are candid about what ObamaCare is designed to do. It is worth noting, as Senator SESSIONS has, that Majority Leader REID is not a passive observer from the sidelines. He is the man responsible, in his role as majority leader, for passing ObamaCare through this body with only Democratic votes—without a single Republican vote. So when he says it is designed to lead to a single-payer system, when he says it is designed to lead to socialized medicine, we should trust that he knows what he is talking about.

Mr. SESSIONS. Madam President, if the Senator will yield again for a question.

Mr. CRUZ. I am happy to yield for a question without yielding the floor.

Mr. SESSIONS. And is it not true—since Senator REID has made his position crystal clear ideologically, and based on the actions the Senator from Texas and I have observed—that he has steadfastly resisted any change whatsoever in the legislation as passed, certainly any change that would constrict its power and reach?

Mr. CRUZ. I think Senator SESSIONS is exactly correct.

If we look at the way this vote is set up, Republicans are being asked to vote with majority leader HARRY REID to shut off debate on this bill. Any Republican who votes yes on Friday or Saturday to invoke cloture will be voting alongside majority leader HARRY REID to give Leader REID the authority to fund ObamaCare using just 51 votes on a straight party-line vote, which is exactly how ObamaCare passed in the first place.

At the same time the majority leader has made clear he is not going to allow other amendments. He is not going to allow amendments that would improve ObamaCare or fix ObamaCare. He is not going to allow the amendment of Senator VITTER, as we talked about earlier, that would correct or get rid of the congressional exemption and treat Members of Congress the same as the American people, get rid of President Obama's lawless exemption, and stop treating Members of Congress like a privileged ruling class who are different from the American people. Leader REID has said he is not going to allow a vote on that, not going to allow a vote on repealing the medical devices tax that has been crippling the medical devices industry, and that is killing innovation and killing jobs.

If Republicans are complicit in shutting off debate and allowing just a single vote on funding ObamaCare, then we have only ourselves to blame. If we give the majority leader the power to do that, we should not be surprised when he exercises it. It is within the power of the 46 Republicans in this body to say no, to say: No, we will not shut off debate that allows the majority leader to use 51 votes to fund ObamaCare on a straight party-line partisan Democratic vote. We will not be complicit in a process that treats Members of Congress like a privileged ruling class and that ignores the cries for help from the American people. All we have to do to accomplish that is for Republicans to stand together and stand united.

It is my hope, my fervent hope, that the voices of dissension within the Republican conference will stop firing at each other and start firing at the target. And let me be clear who the target is. The target is not Democrats. I don't want us to start firing at Democrats or at the President or at anyone else. It is not about us. The target is ObamaCare. It is fixing this train wreck that is hurting the American people.

If Members of the Republican conference in the Senate could devote one-tenth of the ferocity they have devoted to fighting within the caucus on this issue, to actually stopping ObamaCare—not a symbolic vote, not a press release, not a speech, but actually fixing the problem—I could think of nothing better this Senate could do.

And you know what. If, instead of 100 Senators, this Chamber had 100 citizens picked from our States at random, I guarantee not a one of them would say in discussing this: You know what we need is a bunch of symbolic votes. They wouldn't say that. Regular people who live on planet Earth would know a symbolic vote is not a good thing or bad thing. They would say, if we grabbed any hundred—and I wouldn't even have a partisan screen on it. I would grab 100 people at random, and I guarantee you they would say: We have to fix ObamaCare. This thing is hurting people.

The problem is too many Members of this body are not listening, and we need to make DC listen.

Mr. SESSIONS. Madam President, without yielding the floor, will the Senator yield for a further question?

Mr. CRUZ. I am happy to yield for a question without yielding the floor.

Mr. SESSIONS. I notice a real low number of jobs being created this year. And the reports were that 77 percent of those jobs created this year were part-time, not full-time jobs.

Allan Meltzer, one of the great economists in the last 50 years, a knowledgeable observer of our economy, just testified in a Budget Committee maybe 3 hours ago that ObamaCare was a factor in that occurring.

Would the Senator agree that we have had this extraordinary increase in part-time jobs rather than full-time jobs, and that is hammering working Americans who need full-time work?

Mr. CRUZ. Senator SESSIONS is absolutely right. One of the most devastating consequences of ObamaCare is that it is forcing so many Americans into part-time work. The U.S. Chamber of Commerce 2013 second quarter small business survey found that among small businesses that will be impacted by the employer mandate, 50 percent of small businesses say they will either cut out to reduce full-time employees or replace full-time employees with part-time employees to avoid the mandate, and 24 percent say they will reduce hiring to stay under 50 employees.

As Senator SESSIONS knows, this is not one isolated anecdote here or there. According to the U.S. Chamber of Commerce, this is 50 percent of small businesses reducing employees' hours forcibly or just hiring part-time employees instead. This is an enormous problem.

Who gets hurt? When someone gets their hours reduced to 29 hours a week, it is never the CEO. It is usually not the lawyers. It is usually not the professionals. It is absolutely never Senators and Members of Congress.

The people whose hours get forcibly reduced are almost always, without exception, the vulnerable among us. They are the young, they are the Hispanics, the African Americans, the single mom working in a diner, struggling to feed her kids, to be a good example to her kids, who suddenly finds instead of having one job where she works her fingers to the bones to take care of her kids, she has to get two because 29 hours a week is not enough to provide for her kids. Suddenly she has two jobs, both at 29 hours a week. She has to commute from one to the other. She has to deal with two bosses. Boss No. 1 says: I want you at work Tuesday morning. Boss No. 2 says: I want you at work Tuesday morning. What is a single mom supposed to do?

Earlier this afternoon I read from a constituent's letter talking about low-income housing in Virginia, where a significant percentage of the residents were janitorial or service industry workers and were paying their rent out of their own pocket. Because of ObamaCare, because of having their hours reduced, they weren't able to pay the rent. I will read two sentences from a constituent letter from a commercial real estate broker in Chesapeake City, VA.

> Most of the tenants work in fast food, janitorial, and low-paying service-related jobs. A great deal of them had their hours cut to 29.5 hours per week and cannot pay the rent.

So they are losing their apartments and being forced to live elsewhere. This is a tragedy playing out across this country, and it is incumbent on this body to listen to the people. We need to make DC listen.

Mr. SESSIONS. Madam President, will the Senator yield for a question without yielding the floor?

Mr. CRUZ. I will yield for a question without yielding the floor.

Mr. SESSIONS. I know the Senator is aware that the number of people employed in the workforce today has fallen to the lowest level since 1975 and wages have declined. We learned today in our Budget Committee hearing we have had a surge from around 300,000 people working part-time to 1 million.

These are bad trends, but one place has avoided that; that is, the Washington, DC, area. It has had more job growth, higher income job growth than any place in America.

If this bill becomes entrenched into law, will it not create a huge additional increase of government workers and bureaucrats in and around this city, all riding on the backs of American workers?

Mr. CRUZ. The Senator from Alabama is absolutely correct. One of the disturbing trends we have seen in recent years is the boom business in our economy is government. There are lots of consequences to that; one is that the best and the brightest learn, hey, you want to have success, go into government. The private sector? That is apparently not what America is about.

Look right now at government employees who are paid substantially more than their counterparts in the private sector. It is one of the reasons Senator VITTER's amendment would say that Members of Congress shall be subject to the same rules as the American people and not have the special exemption President Obama has put in place is so important and why I support an even broader amendment that would include all Federal employees on the ObamaCare exchanges.

Our friends on the Democratic side of the aisle routinely say ObamaCare is terrific, it is great. If that is the case, then Members of Congress should be excited about being on those exchanges, which are apparently so great for our constituents, and so should Federal workers. But they are not, indeed, as the Senator from Alabama knows well.

This issue has caused more consternation among Members and congressional staff than probably any other issue because people are quite rightly afraid of losing their health insurance and losing their coverage.

That concern is not irrational. There are many good public servants, congressional staffers who are Federal employees, even who are Members of the Senate. It is not irrational at all for them to be concerned about losing their health insurance and forced onto poor-quality health insurance. But that desire shouldn't push us to say let's exempt them. We don't want to be subject to it. That desire should push us to fight for hard-working American families. That desire should say: If we don't want to be on the exchanges, let's not make anyone else be on them. That divide between Washington—the ruling class—and the American people is the most significant reason for the disillusion we see.

The view from Americans all over this country—and this is true of conservatives and liberals—is that Washington doesn't listen. Politicians don't listen. We just had an August recess. A significant number of Members of this body held no townhalls, didn't go back and listen to their constituents. You can't fault Americans for saying politicians don't listen to us when, in fact, politicians don't listen to us. That is what this fight is about.

If it is just up to Washington, we are not going to have to do anything to stop ObamaCare. For one thing, Members of Congress and their staff are exempted so there is no urgency. But if we listen to the American people, there is urgency. That is why it is so critical that we make DC listen.

Mr. SESSIONS. Madam President, if the Senator would yield for another question.

Mr. CRUZ. I would be happy to yield for a question without yielding the floor.

Mr. SESSIONS. I know the Senator is aware that Senator BAUCUS, the chairman of the Finance Committee, a long-time Senator who I believe has announced he is not going to run again but shepherded this legislation through the Senate and worked in many ways to try to make it better—lost some battles in that time—has referred to this as a "train wreck" because there are so many things going wrong right now. Did the Senator hear that from him?

It seems to me we are at a point where we have to push hard. That is the conclusion I have come to, and I will ask the Senator's opinion. It seems to me we are at a position where we need to push hard to force discussion of this legislation because the majority leader wants to make it even bigger government, to take it even further. He is blocking and going to resist any attempt to have real debate, real amendments being offered. He will not allow votes, and he is going to fill the tree and otherwise dominate the Senate so we can't even have the classic debate and amendments and votes to improve this train wreck of a law.

Is that the way the Senator sees the situation we are in today?

Mr. CRUZ. Senator SESSIONS is absolutely correct. I would note, first of all, the Senate Democrat who is the lead author of ObamaCare has referred to ObamaCare's implementation as "a major train wreck." That is not I speaking. That is not Senator SESSIONS speaking. That is the lead author of ObamaCare, a Democratic Senator.

I commend his candor. It is indeed a major train wreck. I have no doubt that more than a few of his colleagues on that side of the aisle were unhappy with him for speaking the truth on that.

There should be a lot more truth-speaking in this body, not engaging in partisan team politics but speaking the truth for the American people. That was commendable for Senator BAUCUS to speak for the American people and say this is a major train wreck. We need to all acknowledge it is a major train wreck and then step forward to avert the train wreck.

Senator SESSIONS' second point is a very important one. I note Senator SESSIONS is an elder statesman in this body, has served admirably a great many years, fighting for the citizens of Alabama, and is well experienced when a day a time existed when the Senate operated like a deliberative body, where Senators would speak and offer amendments and amendments could be considered. That doesn't occur now.

The practice Senator SESSIONS referred to, and I suspect some folks may not be familiar with, is called filling the tree. Filling the tree has become commonplace. Filling the tree is a procedural and parliamentary tree that only the majority leader can do. The majority leader has a privileged role under the Senate rules in that he has priority of recognition, the ability to insist he is the first Senator on the floor to be recognized.

Filling the tree enables him to do what he has said he is going to do on this bill, which is file an amendment to fund ObamaCare in its entirety and then fill the tree so no other Senator can offer any amendments, so the other 99 Senators are muzzled, we can't offer amendments to improve ObamaCare, we can't offer amendments to fix ObamaCare, and we can't offer amendments to do anything. Indeed, the more liberal Members of the Democratic caucus can't offer amendments to adopt a single-payer socialized medicine system, which some of them openly embrace. That is a sign of a Senate that is not working.

There should be open debate and there should be open amendments. One of the great strengths of this body is that all 100 Senators for most of the history of the Republic could offer any amendment at virtually any time. That has all but disappeared. Why has it disappeared?

For folks who are at home watching this debate, it is easy to let the procedure make your eyes glaze over. When you hear someone talk about invoking cloture on the motion to proceed, it is utterly incomprehensible to virtually anyone in the country. Indeed, I suspect more than a few people on the floor of the Senate right now don't quite understand what it means.

But what is all the procedure about? Why should you care about filling the tree? You should care about it because it is a tool of power, of silencing the people, and using the positions of power to enforce Washington's ideological view on the rest of this country.

If we got out of Washington, DC, if we went to the American people and said what are your top priorities—we actually have. We don't have to hypothesize about that. The American people over and over again say jobs and the economy are their top priorities. The American people want ObamaCare stopped because it is not working, it is killing jobs, it is pushing people into part-time work. Yet this Senate has not been listening to the American people.

We need to make DC listen.

Mr. SESSIONS. Madam President, will the Senator yield for a question?

Mr. CRUZ. I am happy to yield for a question without yielding the floor.

Mr. SESSIONS. I would also observe, and the Senator probably is aware, it does appear there is a budget point of order against this whole continuing resolution. I want to mention a couple of things.

I want to thank the Senator for having the courage to stand here and raise the concerns I am hearing all over my State. I had three separate meetings in August, as I traveled the State, with small business groups. It is difficult to overstate the concerns they have with this law. They tell me without a doubt it is impacting their willingness to hire and the uncertainty in the workplace is damaging business in America, and they are passionate about it.

They are struggling to get by. They are laying off people and they are not happy about it. They say this law alone is the primary thing that is hammering them in this country. I have given a lot of thought to it. I am beginning to see that we have to use the opportunities we have to confront this issue and talk about it and try to force some changes and improvements.

I appreciate the effort, and I am going to support the Senator. I am going to oppose any advancing of the final bill that does not provide some change in ObamaCare.

I did not sign the letter, and have some great friends who see it differently than I do who likewise are totally opposed to the health care law. I want to be sure people who are listening need to know good people, I think, can disagree on this. But the Senator stood up and raised the question and forced us to confront it and talk about it and I think it is good. I intend to support him. I am not going to vote to move a bill where we are sure we are going to be blocked from having any meaningful discussion on one of the most historic, damaging laws in maybe the last hundred years that would basically move us to single-payer, government-run socialized medicine. I think that is where we are heading.

I thank the Senator for his leadership. Hopefully we can begin to force this Senate to act. The House has already acted. They have repeatedly acted to fix this legislation, because it is so damaging. But the Senate, the Democratic Senate, refuses to act. It refuses to listen. That is the problem I have. One way I have to express that is to support the position the Senator has taken.

I thank him very much and wish him good luck.

Mr. CRUZ. I thank the Senator from Alabama for his question and fundamentally for his support. His support is very needed. Senator

Sessions is a man who is respected in this body. He commands the respect of his peers.

If you read the newspapers, the votes have already been decided. If you watch the TV commentators, I read one newspaper article—it was actually styled a news article—that talked about the "effort to defund ObamaCare, which is doomed to fail."

That was the lead, the opening line of what purported to be an objective news article. A lot of folks in official Washington and the Washington establishment have said there is no way this can happen.

Three weeks ago they said there is no way the House is going to vote to defund ObamaCare. Three weeks ago you read it was impossible, cannot happen, will not happen. Yet on Friday the House voted overwhelmingly to defund ObamaCare.

This week it is all the same pundits. A funny thing: Everyone who said it is impossible in the House—apparently there are no consequences for their being proved laughingly, totally, completely wrong. And they all come out with the same certainty, the same deep baritone voices, to say it is impossible that the votes will be there in the Senate. Republicans will not stand together.

Let me point to just a minute ago. Senator JEFF SESSIONS who, as he knows, was not on the letter Senator MIKE LEE circulated, was not initially part of the group—according to all of the press, anyone who was not on the letter was necessarily going to oppose us, and Senator SESSIONS is here, courageously standing, and I appreciate his leadership, his principle, and his courage. I am going to suggest this debate is having exactly the function it is supposed to.

Back when this body was in fact the world's greatest deliberative body, as it was reputed to be, debates were about moving hearts and minds and making the case. How can we best serve the American people? Now, sadly, debates usually occur in an empty Chamber and the Washington establishment tells us this is the result of the vote before it happens.

Let me note for those of you keeping score at home, the momentum has consistently been in favor of defunding ObamaCare. Two months ago everyone said it was impossible, the American people were not behind it, the House was not behind it, the Senate was not behind it, it could not happen. We saw the American people unite. We saw over 1.6 million Americans sign a national petition, we saw the House unite, and now the Senate must unite, and I am grateful to Senator SESSIONS for his leadership and his support.

Mr. RUBIO. I thank the Senator for his efforts here today and in the weeks that led us here. I ask the Senator from Texas—let me preface this by saying so much of the focus—if you read the coverage, all the focus is on what is going to happen, the process, the votes, who is going to vote what. I think that is important and I think we will have a conversation about that in the moments to come.

What I am most enthusiastic about in the last few hours is there is an increasing focus on why. Why are people so passionate about ObamaCare, particularly those who are opposed to it? Why is there a growing number of Americans coming out and saying ObamaCare is a bad idea? Why are Republicans united against ObamaCare?

Let's be clear. We do have a tactical debate going on in the Republican Party about the right way to stop ObamaCare. What there is no debate about among Republicans is this is a bad idea for the country. Why are we so passionate about that? I only speak for myself in what I am about to say, and I think it speaks for others. I will ask the Senator from Texas to comment in a moment about that. I think sometimes when you are born and raised, as I have been, your whole life in this country, speaking for myself, sometimes it is easy to take for granted how special America is because this is all you have known, this is all we have ever been around so we take that for granted a little bit.

I had a blessing, similar to the same one the Senator from Texas had. I actually grew up around people who knew what life was like somewhere else. They knew what America had is special because they lived somewhere else and they knew what the world was like outside of America. It is a reminder that what makes America different and special from the rest of the world is that it is one of the few places in human history where no matter where you start out in life, no matter how poor you were, no matter how poor your parents were, no matter how disconnected they may be from power, if you are willing to work hard and you are willing to sacrifice, you can have a better life.

For us Americans, that seems, of course, right. That is the way it has always been. It is not. In fact, for almost all of human history that has not been the case. In much of the world that is still not the case. For almost all of human history almost everyone who has ever lived is basically trapped by whatever they were born into. If your parents were poor, you were poor. If your parents were farmers, you were a farmer. I want you to think about what that means for a moment. Imagine for a second—because all of us have dreams and hopes, when you are young, especially. Imagine for a second if you are someone with talent and dreams and aspirations and ambitions but knowing that in the society you live in, none of that matters because you are not from the right people. You don't come from the right family. Imagine how frustrating that must be.

That is the story of humanity up until about 200 years ago when the American experiment began, based on something very powerful the Senator from Texas talked about a moment ago, the idea that every single one of us has a God-given right to go as far as our talent and our work will take us.

The result is the most extraordinary story in all of human history. I point that out today because I remember growing up knowing my parents wanted me to clearly understand that I would have a chance to do things they never had a chance to do because I lived in an extraordinary place unlike any that had ever existed before.

Fast forward to today and the challenges we face as a country. The one thing that most worries me as I analyze American politics and the state of our country is there is a growing number of people who are starting to doubt whether that dream is still true; a growing number of people who are starting to wonder is it still true that if you work hard and you sacrifice, you can get ahead. Do you know why they are doubting that? Because they are working hard, they are working harder than they ever have, they are sacrificing, and not only are they not getting ahead, they are struggling to keep from falling behind.

There are a lot of reasons why this is happening. Globalization has changed the nature of our economy. So have advances in information technology. We have an emerging skills gap in this country where unfortunately many Americans have not acquired the skills needed for these new jobs in the 21st century. We have to address these things. Societal breakdown is real. It is having an impact. In fact, it is one of the leading causes of poverty in the United States, and that is troubling too.

But for those of us who are in the Federal Government and in the policy-making branch of government, I think it is time we realize that one of the leading threats to the American dream is the policies that are being pursued at the Federal level, policies that are undermining the free enterprise system. Here is why that is important—because the only economy, the only economic system in human history that rewards hard work, sacrifice, and merit is the American free enterprise system. The evidence is all over the world. Look all over the world at people whose families have lived in poverty for generations, who now have joined the middle class. They live in countries that are trying to copy the American economic example. They don't live in countries that embrace socialism, they don't live in countries that embrace big government. They live in places that are trying to move toward free enterprise. Free enterprise has eradicated more poverty than all the government programs in the world combined. That is the story of free enterprise. That is why it is startling that over the last few decades, Federal policies have contributed steadily to undermining the free enterprise system.

We talk about all those policies, but ObamaCare is an example of that. You ask yourself how does ObamaCare undermine the free enterprise system? There are a few examples. First, because of the disruptive costs and rules created by ObamaCare, there are thousands of middle-class jobs that will not be created. These are jobs that were going to be created that someone wanted to create. I met a restaurant owner. I think he was from Louisiana. He testified before the Small Business Committee. He wants to open new restaurants. He has specific sites in mind. He knows he can make it work. He is not going to do it and he cites ObamaCare as the reason why. Those are jobs that were going to be created that do not now exist because of ObamaCare. That undermines the free enterprise system.

ObamaCare has a mandate. It has already been discussed here on the floor. It says if you have more than 50 fulltime workers, you have to live by a bunch of mandates that it creates. Do you know what the result of that has been? Businesses close to that number are deciding I don't want to have 50 employees, I want to have 48 or 49 so that doesn't apply to me because I can't afford for it to apply to me. Do you know what that means? That means those were jobs that were going to be created or those are jobs that were there but now they are part time. That means you lost money out of your paycheck.

It also has redefined, ObamaCare has redefined what part-time work is. An American economic reality is that part-time work is anything less than 40 hours, except for ObamaCare, anything less than 30 hours. So what is happening? People working part time are losing their hours.

Real world example. Sea World in Florida just announced it is moving over 2,000 of its part-time employees from 32 hours a week to 28 hours a week. That is not just a statistic. These are people who are losing 4 hours' worth of pay a week.

The very people that this bill is supposed to be helping, the working class and middle class—the people who are trying to get ahead—are the people it is directly hurting. That is just one example. There are multiple examples. Senator CRUZ and I could cite examples all night of real people who will be hurt in this way.

I have one more point that has not been talked about enough. Medicare Advantage is a program that gives seniors choices. It has competition. There are different companies that provide Medicare Advantage benefits, and they compete for the business of seniors by offering additional benefits.

My mom is a Medicare Advantage recipient. She is heavily marketed every year because—like all seniors are in that area—they want her business. How do they compete? They offer transportation, free pharmaceuticals, or whatever it may be. Well, guess what. ObamaCare takes money out of Medicare Advantage, not to save Medicare but to fund ObamaCare. Later this year—in early January—these seniors are going to get a letter in the mail saying that their Medicare Advantage plan no longer offers X, Y, or whatever some of these benefits are. That is just another example of who is hurt by this. Why are we passionate? Why are we here about this? Look, we have an ideological objection to the government being involved in such a widespread way in health care, but now it is beyond that. We are passionate about this opportunity that we have to stop ObamaCare because of the impact this is having on real people. At the end of the day, that is what we are fighting for. We are not fighting against ObamaCare, and we are fighting for these people.

By the way, the people we are fighting for includes people who voted for the President. This includes, by the way, people who didn't vote for me or the Senator from Texas or the Senator from Utah. We are fighting for them because they are going to be hurt by this.

If your dream is to open your own business one day and to grow it, ObamaCare will hurt you. It is going to make it harder for you to be able to do that. If your dream is to do what my parents did, which is to work a job so your kids could one day have a career, ObamaCare is hurting you too. It could cost you the insurance you have now that you are happy with. It could cost you hours out of your paycheck. It could cost you your very job.

What about if you are working part time while you go to school at night? If you are paying your way through school as a part-time worker, ObamaCare is going to hurt you. You are going to lose hours at work potentially because of ObamaCare. What if you graduated from college? You finished college and have done everything that has been asked of you.

What do we tell young people in America who go to school, get good grades, a degree, and dream of having a career and better life? What do they want to do? They want to graduate from college, get married, buy a house, and start a family. A lot of people are having to put that off for a lot of reasons. ObamaCare will be one of the reasons. You know why? Because that job or career you wanted to start may not be created now because of ObamaCare.

What if you worked your whole life—like the 3 million seniors who live in Florida—and are living with dignity, security, and stability, and can finally sign up for the Medicare Advantage plan, but now ObamaCare is hurting you? That is the irony in all of this. The very people they said this plan—this bill, this idea—would help are the very people it is hurting the most. That, by the way, is the experience of big government.

I know that big government sounds appealing sometimes when you are hurting and struggling to make ends meet and then a politician comes along and says: I'm going to create a new program called jobs for Americans and health care for everybody. When you are struggling, this stuff sounds enticing. The problem is it never works. Anytime and anywhere it has been tried, it has failed, and it will fail again. It doesn't work.

In fact, big government hurts the people who are trying to make it. If you are a multibillion-dollar corporation or a millionaire or billionaire, you may not like big government, but you can afford to deal with it. If you are a major corporation in America, you can hire the best lawyers in America to navigate whatever complex rules the government throws at you. If you really don't like it, you can hire the best lobbyist in this city to write the laws in your favor or try to get them written in your favor.

However, if you are trying to start a business by using the free wi-fi at Starbucks or you are using the spare bedroom in your home to start a business, you can't navigate all of that big government stuff. You can't afford to hire a lobbyist to get a waiver from ObamaCare. That is the irony of this. The very people that big government promises to help are the people it hurts the most, and we are seeing it again with ObamaCare.

Who is getting waivers from ObamaCare? The people who can afford to influence it. That is the experience of big government. It is the experience of ObamaCare, and that is unfair. That is just not fair. It is not fair that in America the people who are willing to work hard and sacrifice are not able to achieve a better life. That is wrong.

The only way to assure that those opportunities are there is to embrace the free enterprise system, not to undermine it or try to replace it with an expansion of government that in the end will collapse under its own weight. But that is the direction we are headed in right now.

You want to know what the biggest issue facing America politically is? It is not whether Republicans or Democrats win the next election, it is whether we will continue to be an exceptional country where anyone from anywhere can accomplish anything or whether we will become like the rest of the world, just another powerful, rich country with a big economy, but no longer the place where hard work and sacrifice is enough. That is the choice we are being asked to make on issue after issue that comes before this body, and especially on this one.

I will yield back to the Senator from Texas by just saying this: My parents were never rich. I told this story before, but I tell it, not so much to talk about me, but to talk about us, because this is our story, not just mine. My parents were never rich. When they came here, they didn't know anybody. They had no money or connections. They barely spoke the language. When they first came here, they struggled. They were discouraged. Sometimes they wondered if they made a mistake. Sometimes they thought that maybe they should have stayed back in Cuba. Ultimately, they persevered and hung in there.

Ten years after they had been here, my dad was working as a bartender and my mom worked as a maid and a cashier. They bought their first home in 1966. In fact, by 1971, they were so optimistic about the future, that after both of them were over 40 years of age, they had me, and then my sister a year and a half after that. Talk about optimistic about the future. America fundamentally changed their lives because of free enterprise.

My dad had a job at those hotels because someone had access to money and risked it. They took a risk and said: I am going to invest this money into opening up a hotel because I believe in my idea. Because someone took a risk, my dad and my mom had a job. They weren't rich. We never owned multiple homes. We never had a yacht. We never traveled to Europe. There is nothing wrong with any of those things.

My parents lived the American dream. Why? Because they lived a life no one in their family history had ever lived in terms of stability and security, and they were able to provide opportunities for their children they themselves never had. That is the American dream. It is about being able to fulfill your God-given potential, whatever it may be, and it is what is at play right now.

There are millions of people in this country who are trying to achieve their American dream. There are millions of people across America who are trying to do what my parents were able to do for me and what Senator CRUZ's parents were able to do for him. Our job is to make it easier for them to do it, not harder. Our job is to do everything we can to ensure that this is the one country on Earth where that is still possible.

When we pass bills such as ObamaCare, which claims to help people like this, we are not helping them. We are hurting them. If we hurt them, we hurt the country because there cannot be an America without an American dream. We can't be special and exceptional without the American dream, and that is what is being undermined by big government and by ObamaCare.

At the end of the day that is why we are so passionate about this, and that is why this is an issue worth fighting for.

The Senator from Texas was reading stories and cases earlier today that he heard from around the country, and that is what these people are telling us. That is what they are saying to us. They are saying: All we want is a chance to turn our dreams into reality. All we want is a chance to be able to work hard and sacrifice so we can achieve a better life. All we want is for you guys to give us a chance.

I ask the Senator from Texas: Isn't that what this issue is all about?

Mr. CRUZ. The junior Senator from Florida is absolutely correct. I agree entirely. Senator RUBIO is inspiring. Senator MARCO RUBIO is a critical national leader. When Senator MIKE LEE began this fight, MARCO RUBIO was there from day one. He was there from the beginning, despite the protests and despite official Washington saying that he should know better than to stand against the DC establishment and stand for the people.

I don't know if there is anyone more effective, more articulate, or a more persuasive voice for conservative principles than my friend MARCO RUBIO. His race in Florida 2 years ago was supposed to be impossible. I know that because I read it in the paper over and over.

Actually, many of the same people are saying this fight is impossible. They all said it with that same certitude and that same deep baritone voice: This young lad RUBIO has no chance of winning this race. If it were up to official Washington, they would have been right. By every measure of official Washington, the winner of that race that would have been picked was the governor of the State. All of Washington was behind him. The only thing that was standing with MARCO RUBIO was the people.

When he started, he was at 3 percent in the polls. That is a condition I know well because 2 years later I found myself in a similar position. Yet he ran a campaign where he crisscrossed the State of Florida. He listened to the Florida people and got support from the grassroots. His victory in 2010 was a transformational moment in American politics, and it is also emblematic about what this fight is about right here.

If you trust the talking heads on television, if you trust the reporters who tell us what is up and what is down, what is white and what is black, then ObamaCare is here to stay and America has to continue to suffer with it because we can never, ever do anything to change it. As long as this body, the Senate, believes the opinions of these 100 people in this room is more important than the American people, that will remain a true and accurate description. But that is not our job. Our job is to listen to the people.

MARCO RUBIO's parents were Cuban immigrants. His dad was a bartender. It was a family experience that resonates powerfully with me because I came from a similar background. But more important than that, MARCO RUBIO's story is the American story. There is not a Member of this Senate, or a person in this country, who doesn't have a story just like that somewhere in their background.

The most unique aspect of the United States of America, I believe, is that we are all the children of those who risked everything for freedom. I think it is the most fundamental aspect of our DNA and what it means to be an American. What unifies all of us is that as Americans we value liberty and opportunity above all else.

One of the things I admire about Senator RUBIO is how he views issues in this Senate. He doesn't look at it from how it impacts the titans of industry, such as the CEOs, but from how it impacts people such as his dad and my dad, the people who struggled and climbed the economic ladder, seeking the American dream.

If today you are a bartender at a Nevada hotel or if you are washing dishes at a restaurant, like his father and my father, respectively, ObamaCare is hurting you. It is hurting you in a way that all the Senators who have a special exemption from Barack Obama don't have to worry about. It is hurting you because your job is in jeopardy. You may well lose your job or you may not have a job to begin with.

Maybe you would like to be a bartender or wash dishes, but because of ObamaCare, there is no job to hire you. Maybe it is hurting you because what used to be a 40-hour a week job has become a 29-hour a week job and your boss has told you: I don't have any choice. ObamaCare kicks in at 30 hours a week, and it will bankrupt me.

Suddenly you are struggling by either working 29 hours a week and are unable to feed your kids or have to get a second job and work 29 hours a week and have to juggle your schedule, which results in making your life more difficult than it was before—not to mention your concerns about health insurance. Maybe you have a health insurance.

Maybe a person has a health insurance plan they have been struggling to pay, but it is important to them and they want to make sure their kids are covered, they want to make sure their spouse is covered. Yet every year they see their premiums going up and up and up.

We remember when President Obama was defending the ObamaCare bill. He promised the American people that as a result of ObamaCare, the average family's health insurance premium would drop $2,500. He said: That is going to happen by the end of my first term. I would point out that the President's first term ended 9 months ago, and by the end of the President's first term, that promise was proven not just a little off the mark, not just kind of sort of a little bit not entirely accurate; it was proven 100 percent, categorically, objectively false.

Let me suggest to every American, if your health insurance premiums have dropped $2,500, as the President promised the average family—so there would be tens of millions for whom that is true—then I would encourage those Americans to enthusiastically stand and defend ObamaCare. But there is a reason it is so profoundly unpopular, and it is because it hasn't happened. Premiums have gone up, and the American people are hurting as a result. So DC should listen to the people. We should make DC listen.

Mr. LEE. Will the Senator yield for a question?

Mr. CRUZ. I am happy to yield for a question without yielding the floor.

Mr. LEE. I wish to ask the Senator from Texas whether he has received comments similar to those I have received from my constituents and from other concerned citizens from around the country in recent months. I wish to highlight a few and ask whether these are similar to comments the Senator from Texas has heard, concerns he has heard expressed.

Let me start by sharing one expressed by Shawn from Utah, who says:

> I do not like the fact that the President is picking winners and picking and choosing which parts of the law he will enforce. We need the three branches of government to keep freedom alive.

Well, Shawn from Utah, I share your concern. I would add to that, to Shawn from Utah, the fact that this is really what started this effort. In other words, during the first week of July 2013, when the President announced there were several provisions in the law he simply would not be implementing, he simply would not be enforcing, along the lines of what Congress enacted with the Affordable Care Act in 2010, it was at that point that I and several others put our heads together and realized that if the President is saying this law is not ready to implement, if the law objectively is not ready to implement; if, as we now understand it, the law is going to make health care less affordable rather than more affordable for so many Americans, perhaps Congress shouldn't be funding its implementation and enforcement. Perhaps that ought to be telling us something.

So it is important to remember, as Shawn from Utah points out to us, that we do have three branches of government. This is the legislative branch. Our job is to make the laws. The President does not have law-making authority. The President can seek changes in the law just as other citizens can seek them from Congress, but Congress does have to act.

Although the President wields the veto pen, the veto pen is not the legislation pen. He doesn't have the power to legislate on his own without the assistance of Congress. It is one of the reasons we are in this debacle today. It is one of the reasons we have, along with so many millions of Americans, expressed this position that we would like to fund government while defunding ObamaCare. This is something the American people are calling out for. It is something they are requesting. It is something the House of Representatives acted boldly and bravely in doing, in standing behind the American people. This really is what we are doing. This is the whole reason we are concerned about this, because we want to stand with the American people and with the House leadership, Speaker BOEHNER and the other leaders in the other body in Congress, who bravely put forward this legislation to keep government funded while defunding ObamaCare.

One of the things we have been concerned about today and one of the things I think we need to focus on over the next few days is the fact that with the House of Representatives acting last week, passing this legislation, this continuing resolution to keep government funded while defunding ObamaCare, in order for us to stand behind them, we have to monitor the manner in which that legislation is reviewed over here.

Now that the House-passed continuing resolution has reached the Senate, we have a few options. There are a few acceptable ways of treating this legislation now that it has been passed by the House. One very acceptable approach would be for us to say: OK, let's bring up the House-passed continuing resolution—the resolution that funds government but defunds ObamaCare—and let's have an up-or-down vote. Let's vote for it as is, the same way it was crafted in the House of Representatives. That would be an acceptable approach. I would be comfortable with that.

Another acceptable approach would be to say: Instead of just taking it up and passing it or not passing it as is, let's have an amendment process. Let's allow Democrats and Republicans as they may deem fit to offer amendments. Let's debate those amendments, discuss their relative merits, the pros and the cons. Let's put those before the American people in the few days we have left before the existing continuing resolution expires, let's vote on all of those, and then at the end of it we will get to the bill itself as it may have been amended by that point. That would be acceptable as well.

What is not acceptable is what many have suggested will occur. Many have suggested that the majority leader will bring up this bill and instead of saying "let's vote on it as is" or instead of saying "let's have an amendment process," he apparently wants to have his cake and eat it too. He wants to have it both ways. He wants to bring it up and subject it to one and only one amendment—an amendment that would strip out a very critical part of the legislation, a part of the legislation that probably is the "without which not" element for many of the House Members who voted for it: the provision defunding ObamaCare. He wants that amendment and no other. That is not acceptable, and under that circumstance, in my opinion and in the opinions of several of my colleagues, some of whom we have heard from today, the appropriate way to register that concern is to vote against cloture on the bill if, in fact, that is what the majority leader chooses to do.

That is why we are fighting this particular battle today. That is much of what we are discussing today, is why it is that we should not be facilitating the effort of Senate leadership to, in effect, gut the House-passed continuing resolution of an extraordinarily critical element, an element without which it could never have passed in the House of Representatives and an element which, frankly, the American people expect us to take up and discuss and debate. So either way—an open amendment process, fine; an up-or-down vote on the bill as is, fine. What is not fine is an effort to try to have it both ways.

Let me share with the Senator from Texas another comment I received from a man named Michael who is also from Utah:

We are getting a bigger and bigger government. They're telling us what we should have, what we are entitled to instead of protecting a free people paving our own path. Government gets bigger while the job market is getting crushed. I work for a company in the middle of layoffs and more are to follow. We can't continue like this.

This is an acknowledgment that so many people across our great country are making as they discover the impact of this bill—passed into law some 3½ years ago—that has not increased in popularity over the last 3 years.

Time might not have increased its popularity—in fact, it has had quite the opposite effect—but time has had the effect of expanding its volume. It has gone from 2,700 pages when it was passed to more than 20,000 pages now when we add the implementing regulations. That is quite stunning. The length of it is quite stunning. It reminds me of something James Madison wrote—I believe it was in Federalist No. 62. He said, if I may paraphrase him, it will be of little benefit to the American people that their laws may be written by individuals of their own choosing if those laws are so voluminous and complex that they can't reasonably be read and understood by the American people. Well, 2,700 pages is a little too long. It is a lot too long. And I certainly know that 20,000 pages is much, much, much too long.

That brings to mind a comment I received from Marcia, also from Utah, who writes this:

> However well intentioned Obama care may be, I do not feel this is the best solution. I think something "less wordy" and more succinct would be a much better plan. If you can't say it in 5 pages or less, it may be best unsaid! The changes already enacted have made it more difficult for me to get medical care. Not a big help!

Well said, Marcia, very well said.

When we vote on legislation people haven't read, the American people tend to suffer. When we perpetuate a mistake once made embodied in a 2,700-page bill, things go from bad to worse to much, much worse.

What we have right now is an opportunity for us to debate and discuss the merits of something that perhaps was not adequately debated and discussed 3½ years ago when this law was passed, when Members of Congress were told to pass this law to find out what is in it. Well, we know a lot more about what is in it now. The American people have concerns.

It is appropriate to have the discussion now in connection with spending legislation because, after all, Congress does have the power of the purse. Congress is given this power, this responsibility of making decisions regarding taxing and spending. It was for this reason the founding generation wisely put it in the hands of the House of Representatives—the power of the purse—giving the House of Representatives the responsibility to initiate or originate bills relating to this power. It is the House of Representatives that is, after all, the branch of a government and of Congress that is most directly responsive to the needs of the people.

It is appropriate that we have this discussion regarding funding or not funding a piece of legislation that is going to require a lot of money and is going to be proven costly to the American people in many, many ways in the coming years—I say "costly in many ways" to reflect the fact that it is not just the cost of government money; it costs the American people a lot of things as well. It is costing them jobs. It is costing them wages. It is costing them access to health care in many circumstances.

Let me read something I received from Randy. Randy is from my neighboring State of Idaho. Randy writes:

> My wife and I have a small business with about 20 employees. We struggle to stay in business. We feel that if and when Obamacare is implemented, we will not be able to continue to be in business.

Randy, I can't tell you how many people I have heard make very similar comments from one end of my State of Utah to the other and from people across America. You are not alone, Randy. A lot of people out there are concerned as well.

That is one thing people lose in addition to wages or jobs or access to health care—some of them lose the opportunity they have to stay in business. We are not talking about millionaires and billionaires; we are talking about hard-working Americans who put a lot on the line in order to make a decent living, in order to provide jobs for their few employees. This is something we need to look out for. This is something we may not, we must not lightly brush aside.

Here is something else some Americans will sometimes lose—something they were promised they would not lose—access to a doctor they like, access to a doctor they have come to trust over the years.

This one comes from Jack from the State of Texas. Jack says:

> My family doctor of 25 years is talking about an early retirement because of policies Obamacare is going to require him to follow that will compromise the oath he took when he became an M.D.

This is sad, Jack. This is something we were promised would not happen, and it is something that should not happen. This is something that we are told is happening from time to time.

Ryan, also from Texas, writes:

> My mother is a middle-class mortician whose health care coverage is going up by 68 percent for this poorly envisioned law with no other changes. She simply cannot afford to maintain health care coverage without significant changes to her lifestyle, and for what?

Sometimes we have to ask that question: And for what?

Sometimes we have to ask the question, the same question that physicians are required to ask themselves: Are we doing harm? It is my understanding that when a physician becomes licensed, he or she must take an oath, an oath that involves an obligation to first do no harm. We as lawmakers have to ask ourselves that question from

time to time. We as lawmakers have to view ourselves as subject to a
similar obligation to first do no harm.

(Mr. DONNELLY assumed the chair.)

Some have said that when you are carrying around a hammer,
everything starts to look like a nail. I wonder whether that is sometimes true of Congress and the law-making power. Because of the
law-making power we wield, sometimes, when we view problems, we
assume we automatically, necessarily, inevitably have the right solutions. Well, in some cases that may be true. In other cases, it might be
true in part. But that power might be used incorrectly. Sometimes
when legislation is hastily drafted, thrown together in a hurry, rather
than for purposes of making sure it is part of a cohesive whole—
something that will be a coherent mechanism that can be
implemented in a commonsense fashion—sometimes if it is thrown
together too hastily and these cautions are ignored, we can end up
doing a lot of harm, we can find ourselves first doing harm above all
else, and that is not OK.

When we look at this law, and we look at the fact that the American people are funding its implementation, we discover it is much
deeper than something that deals with an individual mandate or an
employer mandate or a set of regulations governing the insurance
industry. It is much more than that. It is much more than what people will have to do with regard to the reporting of some fairly
personal details about their lives to the IRS, an agency that Americans have come to trust substantially less than they already did, as if
that were possible.

It is about the fact that the American people—in addition to being
made less free by this law, and in addition to being made less prosperous by this law—are also required to fund its implementation and its
enforcement against them. That is where the power of the purse must
come into play. That is what makes it so appropriate, so essential, so
vital that we have this discussion right here and right now as we consider spending legislation, spending legislation that may well represent
our last best hope of achieving a degree of delay or defunding of this
legislation before its primary operative provisions take full effect. That
is why it is important for us to have this discussion right now.

Let me emphasize again the importance of the cloture vote and the position we are taking on that. It is grounded fundamentally in the understanding that the House of Representatives acted in a manner consistent with what the American people have been asking. I cannot emphasize enough the fact that House Speaker JOHN BOEHNER and his leadership team in the House—the House Republicans have supported him in this effort. They did great work. They stood valiantly with the American people who were calling out overwhelmingly for them to take this step, to keep government funded but defund ObamaCare. And that is what they did.

Now that they have acted, there are two approaches we could take to this that are perfectly appropriate. We could vote on that legislation as is, up or down, or we could subject it to an amendment process, allow Democrats and Republicans alike to present amendments to make the House-passed resolution better, as they might deem fit. We can debate and discuss and vote on each of those. Sure, it can be time-consuming. Sure, it can be grueling. But that is our job. We took an oath to do that job. We do this all the time—maybe not as much as we should. But a few months ago in connection with the budget resolution, we as Senators stood and sat—a little of both—here all night long. We voted all night long, until 5 o'clock in the morning. People got a little cranky at times, but that is what we are here to do—not to be cranky, but we are here to vote, to cast votes on amendments. That is what we had to do that day because there were a lot of amendments. That is what we should be doing with this if, in fact, we decide we want amendments to the House-passed resolution.

So vote on it up or down as is; fine. Subject it to an open amendment process; fine. Trying to have it both ways, the majority leader telling us this will be subject to one amendment, one amendment only—an amendment that would gut and render nugatory the operative provision that was so important to so many House Members—that is not OK. That is why those who agree with us on this point, those who feel that way, those who feel the American people need us to stand up for them, should vote no on cloture when we get to the cloture vote on the bill later in this week.

I would ask my colleague from Texas, as to these concerns I have expressed, these statements that have been made from people around the country—some of them my constituents in Utah, some of them from other parts of the country, including a couple from Texas—what similarities does the Senator see between these statements I have read today and comments the Senator has heard from his constituents as he has traveled through his great State, a State of great expanse and a State of close to 30 million people? What similarities does the Senator see between these statements and those he has heard around his State?

Mr. CRUZ. I thank my friend from Utah for that very insightful question. Let me note there are many reasons why I love the Senator from Utah. But very near the top of the list is the fact that when he "paraphrases" the Federalist Papers, it is darn near a word-for-word, verbatim quote. MIKE LEE is extraordinary and it is an honor to stand by his side and serve with him. The stories he has read are exactly consonant with the stories I have heard all across Texas and, frankly, all across the country. This thing is not working. It is not political. It is not partisan. It has nothing to do with what team you are on. The facts are clear. There is a reason why the unions are jumping ship. There is a reason why Teamsters President James Hoffa says ObamaCare is destroying the 40-hour workweek that is the backbone of the American middle class. There is a reason why the IRS employees union has asked to be exempted from ObamaCare. These are the guys who are in charge of enforcing it on the rest of us. They have asked to be exempt because it is not working. The facts are clear. It is a train wreck. As the lead author Democratic Senator put it: It is a train wreck.

In fact, let me share some of the tweets that have come in the preceding days. In the preceding days, the American people had a chance to speak out about ObamaCare and in particular there was a hashtag "DefundObamacareBecause." In the last several days, Americans all over this country have tweeted their reason why ObamaCare should be defunded.

I will note to Senator LEE that some months ago, he and I stood on this same Senate floor, side by side with our dear friend Senator RAND

PAUL, supporting him in his historic filibuster on drones. At that time I had the opportunity to read tweets that were supporting RAND's filibuster. To the best of my knowledge, that was the first time tweets had been read on the Senate floor, which I have joked to my wife makes me happy because 20 years from now if there is some obscure political geek trivial pursuit game, I am pretty confident I am going to be an answer as to the first person to have the chance to read tweets on the Senate floor.

I am going to do my best now to be the second person. Now I am reading tweets that concern the hashtag "DefundObamacareBecause," but I will note there has been another hashtag tonight: "MakeDCListen." And that hashtag has been trending higher and higher—"MakeDCListen"—and as the evening goes forward, I fully expect for those of you who have something you want to say, but you are not currently able to come to the Senate floor—maybe in a few years you will be, maybe you will be elected to the Senate and stand at your desk and make your arguments, but right now you are not—let me encourage you to tweet with the hashtag "MakeDCListen," and I expect later in the evening to read a sample of those tweets so we can help provide voice to those millions of Americans who are frustrated that DC is not listening.

But these are some of the tweets in the past few days with the hashtag "DefundObamacareBecause."

It is just another way to gain control over people.

Defund ObamaCare because I don't want the government dictating my health care.

Because I don't trust the government to run my health care.

Because it was sold to us on lies. You can keep your insurance? No. My coverage reduced to nearly nothing, premiums the same.

Because it's too intrusive on our privacy.

Because it's killing jobs and stifling the economy.

Because it's forcing small businesses to lay off full-time workers and replace them with part-time workers to avoid bankrupting mandates.

Because Congress should be representing us, we the people. A majority of Americans don't want ObamaCare.

Because it adds layers of government, inefficiency, centralizes control to ivory-tower bureaucrats. Massive drag on the economy.

Because it will lead to SINGLE-PAYER health "care".

"SINGLE-PAYER" is all caps and "care" is in quotes.

Bad, bad, bad, bad, bad.

Because it's not even implemented yet and it has already raised my insurance rates and reduced the quality of my medical care.

Because cancellation notices from my carrier due to ACA kind of ruined the narrative: Like it, keep it. Bombs away on ACA.

Because I don't want the government deciding my family's health care.

Because the cost of health care will increase with quality decreasing. Empower the free market.

Because it is a threat to jobs and our economy.

Because I got laid off. My chances of finding another job are slim too. None now.

Because it's time people in DC do what's best for this country instead of their political party.

Let me read that one again: "Because it's time for people in DC to do what's best for this country instead of their political party."

If we listened to the people, if we make DC listen, this would not be about party, this would not be about Democrats sticking to the bill they passed, this would not be about Republicans afraid of political blame and repercussions. This would be about 100 Senators listening to people and saying: This bill is not working.

Because it kills jobs and the backbone of the American middle class.

Because it's killing free clinics and reducing access to care.

Because Americans love freedom.

Because it's a job-killing machine, up to and including doctors.

Because I don't want government to control my health care.

Because the free market works and government regulation does not.

Because Americans can't live on part-time wages and pay the outrageously high cost of ObamaCare.

Because it violates Americans' first amendment right to religious liberty. Because we the people don't want it and the government works for us.

Let me repeat that one again: "Because we the people don't want it and the government works for us."

Let me note something, by the way. That hashtag was a simple hashtag: "DefundObamacareBecause." That is the message that is coming from the people. Washington is not listening. It is why tonight "MakeDCListen" is trending higher and higher as a hashtag because that is what this fight is about. Washington is not listening to the people.

Because it has already resulted in great doctors leaving medicine.

Because government is not meant to force me into something they have no business in. Because I'm against force and coercion from government. If it was a great idea, it would be voluntary.

Now that says something.

If it was a great idea, why is the Federal Government forcing you to be a part of it? By the way, why, at the same time, is the President granting exemptions to big corporations and to Members of Congress? If it is a great idea, they would not have to force you to participate. If it was a great idea, Members of Congress would not have asked the President for an exemption so that Members of Congress get a special rule that does not apply to the American people.

Because I do not want bureaucrats involved in my physician's decisions on my health care.

Because I value my freedom.

Because it's ruining the 40-hour work week, according to unions.

Because it is crony capitalism for the health care industrial complex.

Because you don't want a bunch of bureaucrats deciding which medical treatments you can and can't receive. What do they know?

Because the government SHOULD NOT own our medical data.

Because the IRS will be enforcing it.

Now, that is a pair that gives you great comfort. The IRS in charge of it, the IRS employee unions publicly asked them to be exempted from ObamaCare. Right now they are assembling the largest database in the history of our health care records. We have seen the IRS—their willingness to abuse their power. Under ObamaCare right now, they just have access to our health care records so it is not like anyone should be concerned about it.

Because it is a job-killing, economy-destroying, health care-ruining, debt-exploding, out of control government mess.

I like that one.

Because it is a job-killing, economy-destroying, health care ruining, debt-exploding, out of control government mess.

Because ObamaCare is all about socialistic control of we the people and nothing to do with fixing health care.

Because it was rammed through in the dark of the night, and that should matter. Because it has already come between me and my doctors and it is not even fully implemented yet.

Next time you see your physician, do you want your friendly neighborhood Federal bureaucrat sitting down and being part of the physician's meeting? I do not. I know Texans do not either, most Americans do not either.

Because it is a Trojan horse. Once inside it will destroy us.
Because even the unions agree it's not working.
Because we need the IRS to get out of our lives, not make health care decisions for us.
Because it will cost Americans their jobs.
Because it's a red herring being used to move the credit to a single-payer system.

As we noted earlier, that is not—some people dismiss that. Oh, single payer, this is designed to go there. You know that is just crazy, tinfoil hat-wearing stuff. But there is an old saying: Just because you are paranoid doesn't mean they are not out to get you. Yes, there are people worried about single payer. They have every good reason to be, particularly when the majority leader of the Senate goes on television and says: The purpose of ObamaCare is to send people into a single-payer system, government-provided socialized health care.

That is the express purpose from those who voted for ObamaCare, to destroy the private health insurance system and to move to single-payer government socialized medicine.

Because honestly the people do not want it.

Because problems cannot be solved by a larger government than the one that created them.

Because after 3 years, they are still trying to sell it to us.

That is a good point. If it were such a great idea—don't you remember at the time, they said: Gosh, when people get it, they are going to love it. It is going to work. You know what. If it had, we would be having a very different discussion. If it had worked, the American people would support it. We would see the results. We would see the benefits, and we would not have this debate. If it were working well, we would not be having this debate because the American people would support it. The facts are clear. So even those who voted 3 years ago, unless your view of serving in office is: Hey, once I vote, I stick to it no matter what the facts say, no matter how much people are hurting, no matter how big a disaster it is. I ain't changing no matter what.

I cannot believe there are many Senators in this body who want to approach voting like that. That is not a responsible way to approach a job. The facts are clear. This thing is not working. All 100 of us ought to act to avert this train wreck.

> Because it is and will continue to destroy jobs, slow hiring, and move others to part-time status.
>
> Because if you don't, your doctor might just retire early.

How many know a doctor who is retiring early? I know quite a few who are retiring. Do you think that is good for our health care system, seeing doctors retire early? I know older doctors who are advising young students, do not go to med school. Do you think that is good for health care? Do you think that is going to expand our health care if we do not see bright young students going to medical school? That is what ObamaCare is doing.

> Because you do not want an IRS agent deciding if your mom lives or dies.
>
> Because it makes health insurance less affordable. My premiums will be higher to subsidize people who cannot afford insurance.
>
> Because even the unions don't want it.
>
> Because the IRS has shown they are willing to abuse power for political gain.
>
> Because it's not about care, it is about government control.
>
> Because I shouldn't have to pay for the murder of innocent, unborn babies through abortion.
>
> Because if it worked, Democratic Senators would not have needed to be bribed to vote for it.
>
> Because the death panel is an unchecked bureaucracy accountable to no one.
>
> Because I love my current health care and doctors.

Do you like your current health care? Do you like your doctor? Do you want to keep seeing your doctor? I tell you, Americans all over this country are losing their health care because of ObamaCare. They are losing their ability to see their doctors. That is what happens if the Senate does not act to defund ObamaCare.

Because the majority of the country is against it.

Because premiums up 100 percent after dropped off spouse's plan. Elimination of meds coverage, reduction of choices and treatments.

These are real people tweeting. They are sharing their stories of why they do not like ObamaCare. Do you notice these stories are not: Because I am a Republican. Because I am a Democrat. Because I believe in this ideology. It is because: This thing is hurting me and my family. If this body were listening to the people, we would have 100 Senators concerned about all of the Americans being hurt by ObamaCare and here at any hour of the night ready to act to stop it.

Because no one wants to live in their parent's basement forever.

Because Reagan once said, you can't be for big government, big bureaucracy and still be for the little guy.

Boy, ain't that the truth.

Because I don't want to pay more taxes to fund it.

Because it does nothing to reduce costs while hurting many full-time employees who are dropped to part time.

Because it makes health insurance less affordable, my premiums will be higher to subsidize people who cannot afford insurance.

Because it actually does add a dime to the deficit, and a lot of them.

Because—[Three words in all caps.]—INTERNAL REVENUE SERVICE.

Because it is killing full-time jobs and stunting the growth of businesses that want to hire.

Because government should not be in charge of something as important as health care.

Because the devil himself wouldn't put the IRS between you and your doctor.

I like that one too.

Because the more exemptions that are given out, the more ObamaCare won't work.

Because I cannot afford to get two jobs, pay outrageous prices for crappy insurance. I will lose my full time.

Because that time Congress passed the law and then excluded themselves. #healthcarehypocrisy.

Because doctors and hospitals are already becoming limited.

Because it is designed to collapse private insurance and force us all to single payer. Socialism.

Again, I would note that is not hypothetical. That is what majority leader HARRY REID has publicly said on television.

Because insurance isn't very helpful when you can't find a doctor.

Because I don't need to spend a decade of my life filling out government forms.

Because baby-boomer doctors will retire in droves, plus more who won't practice in this environment.

Because if it is not good enough for Congress, it sure as shooting is not good enough for the people.

Those are sentiments we are hearing from all across the country. Those are sentiments that reflect the views of the American people, not just in Texas, in all 50 States, and not just Republicans but Democrats, Independents, Libertarians. The American people understand that when you have a law that is killing jobs, when you have a law that is hammering small businesses, when you have a law that is forcing people into part-time work and to work 29 hours a week, when you have a law that is causing skyrocketing insurance premiums, when you have a law that is causing more and more people to lose their health insurance, you have a law that is not working.

You have a train wreck, as the Democratic Senator who is the lead author of this bill described it. Yet right now the Senate is not listening to the American people. The Democrats in the Senate understandably have circled the wagons. They passed this bill, and even if it is a sinking ship, we have yet to see Democrats come out and say: We tried it. It didn't work. Let's listen to the American people. I hope the time comes this week where we see some courageous Democrats stand—and let me say to any Democratic Senator who does so, he or she will receive withering criticisms from the partisans in your party.

Now I will know, as someone not entirely unfamiliar with receiving withering criticisms from one's own party. There are worse things in life. I promise you that it is, in the order of things to be worried about, quite low. You know I am a lot more concerned about a single mom working in a diner trying to feed her kids than I am about whether some Senator or some congressional staffer wants to run to a newspaper and say something mean about me.

So any Democratic Senator who is thinking about responding to the concerns that I know you are hearing from your citizens, because we are hearing it all over the country, let me suggest a little bit of grief for breaking party discipline is a small price to pay for doing your job, for listening to the American people.

Let me say to the Republicans: There is a lot of concern about political blame. There is a lot of concern about: If we would just get a symbolic vote so we can all say we are opposed to it, but let's not actually do anything to change ObamaCare. Let me suggest to my Republican friends that we should worry a lot less about blame and credit and politics and just worry about fixing the darn thing for the American people.

If we get back to an economy where jobs are booming, where small businesses are thriving, where people who are struggling and want the American dream can get that first job and get that second job and climb that economic ladder and advance, provide for their families, that answers a whole lot of problems.

I have heard some partisan observers say: ObamaCare is not the biggest job killer in the country. No. 1, it is ironic that is the particular debate, about whether it is the biggest job killer or the second biggest job killer. But let me tell you, I do not think there is any debate on that question.

So let me point to a list by *Investor's Business Daily* of 300 cuts to work hours or jobs.

Well, if you don't believe ObamaCare is the biggest job killer in the country, look to the facts. This year report after report has rolled in about employers restricting work hours to less than 30 hours per week—the point where the mandate kicks in. The data also points to record-low workweeks in low-wage industries. It is low-wage industries in particular because the people who get hammered by this are not the CEOs. It is not the rich. The rich have done just fine under President Obama. It is hardworking American families, the people who are struggling. It is young people, Hispanics, African Americans, and single moms. They are the ones who are losing their jobs and being forced to work 29 hours a week.

Investor's Business Daily compiled a list of job actions that provide strong proof that ObamaCare's employer mandate is behind cuts to work or staffing cuts. As of September 18, 2013, their ObamaCare scorecard included 301 employers.

In the State of Alabama, Houston County cut the hours of part-time employees to less than 30 hours per week.

In California, Biola University cut student work hours to a maximum of 25 per week and suspended the limit due to the employer mandate delay. That is interesting. They cut it, and then when the employer mandate delay kicked in, they suspended that. If you want to understand cause and effect, look to the behavior, look to the suffering, look to the job losses that are coming as a direct result of ObamaCare.

In Florida, Bealls department stores restricted part-time hours to less than 30 hours a week.

In Florida, SeaWorld Entertainment—have any of you ever taken your kids to SeaWorld? They cut hours for part-time workers from a maximum of 32 hours to 28 hours a week. That is SeaWorld, which is a big employer.

In Illinois, Palmer Place Restaurant cut hours for some workers below 30 hours a week.

In Kansas, the Salina Family YMCA cut part-time employee schedules to a maximum of 25 hours per week.

In New Jersey, Middletown Township Public Schools cut hours for paraprofessionals to below 30 hours per week.

The great State of Texas—it actually doesn't say "great State" on the list, but I view that as implied—Sam Houston State University limited student work hours to 29 per week, impacting multiple job holders.

In Michigan, Auburn Hills reduced hours for part-time seasonal workers to less than 30 per week.

In Pennsylvania, Friendship Community cut part-time hours to below 30 per week. That, by the way, is a group home for adults with disabilities. Not only are the folks at Friendship Community working to help adults with disabilities, they are also getting their hours cut. That is their penalty for making a difference in their community.

In Michigan, Meridian Public Schools cut schedules of hourly workers to less than 30 hours per week.

In Arizona, Arizona State University limited course loads for non-tenured associate faculty members.

In Maine, Mainesubway, the Subway franchisee, reduced worker hours to no more than 29 per week.

In New York, Finger Lakes Community College capped course loads for adjunct faculty.

In South Carolina, Tsunami Surf Shops—I like that name; that is a surf shop with an attitude—will limit workers to less than 30 hours per week.

In Illinois, Southern Illinois University limited graduate teaching assistants to 20 hours per week.

In Indiana, Vincennes cut the hours of part-timers to 29 per week.

In California, the Mexican American Opportunity Foundation cut the hours of employees working up to 39 hours a week to less than 30. I am talking about a real impact from this law.

In Georgia, Georgia Military College cut the hours of adjunct faculty to below 30 hours per week.

In Illinois, Vcm Inc., the Subway franchisee, reduced hours for hourly wage earners to below 30 per week.

In Indiana, Ball State University limited work hours for graduate assistants.

In New Jersey, Toms River will cut part-time hours to 25 hours per week, effective July 2014.

In North Carolina, Forsyth Community Technical College reduced hours for adjunct faculty to below 30 hours per week. Also in North Carolina, Wilkes Community College reduced teaching loads for adjunct faculty to below 30 hours a week.

Let me go through a few of these that are much the same:

Texas, Consolidated Restaurant Operations and Dave & Buster's; Pennsylvania, Philadelphia University; Virginia, K-VA-T Food Stores; Missouri, Three Rivers College. In Alabama, the University of Alabama capped student work hours at 20 per week. That may, in fact, be justifiable punishment for their having beaten Texas A&M, but it is still not good for the students who would like to work more than 20 hours per week. Florida, Brevard County; Florida, Buca di Beppo restaurant chain; Florida, Hillsborough Community College; Florida, St. Petersburg College; Georgia, Cherokee County School Board; Indiana, Hancock County; Indiana, Morgan County; Michigan, Central Michigan University; New Jersey, NEMF trucking company; North Carolina, Henderson; Ohio, White Castle. We read a letter from White Castle earlier today. They used to open eight new restaurants a year. They have reduced it to two. Think of all the people who won't get jobs because there is no White Castle over there, not to mention all of the hungry college kids who at 3 in the morning are just craving a White Castle and they can't find one. Oregon, Shari's restaurants; Pennsylvania, Carnegie Museum; Tennessee, Oneida Special School District; Tennessee, Scott County School System; Tennessee,

Stewart County School System; Texas, Jim's Restaurant; Virginia, Christopher Savvides Restaurant & catering; Wisconsin, Minocqua-Hazelhurst-Lake Tomahawk School District; Wisconsin, Trig's Supermarkets; Alabama, University of North Alabama; California, Fatburger. Now there is truth in advertising. Iowa, Lee County; Michigan, Delta County; Texas, Bee County; Idaho, Boundary County; North Carolina, Rutherford County; Pennsylvania, Lawrence County; Michigan, Kenowa Hills Public Schools; New Jersey, City of Burlington Public Schools; Texas, the Lion & Rose British Restaurant and Pub; Texas, MTC Inc. Restaurant Management; Utah, Millard School District; Arkansas, Area Agency on Aging of Western Arkansas; Arkansas, Walmart Stores, Inc. Has anyone heard of them? They increased temp share of workforce to "fewer than 10 percent" from 1 to 2 percent before this year. California, CKE Restaurants, Inc.

The list goes on and on.

Every one of those—and I read the first 50 or 75 out of 301—it is all over the country. It is every State. A lot of folks in this body may say: Well, that doesn't impact us. What is the problem? If you serve in the Senate, your salary is guaranteed no matter what. Besides, we are exempted from ObamaCare. So what is the concern?

That is official Washington for you. What is the problem? Government is a boom business. If you look at the counties surrounding Washington, DC, they are booming. Why? Because government is growing, growing, growing, and growing.

At every place I just read, there are men and women working and almost none of them are wealthy. Almost none of them are fat cats. Almost none of them are, as the President likes to invoke so often, millionaires and billionaires. They are 22-year-old kids, some who are recent college graduates and some who dropped out of high school, but they are trying to work. They would like to make a better life. They are not able to do so. They are not able to do so because of ObamaCare.

Every one of those names—and listening to those names, it would be easy to zone out: Oh, another name, another name; those are just empty names. Every one of those names—there are men, women, and their kids who are suffering because of that. If you have a job, working hard, trying to provide for your family, and you are told: Congratulations; you will be working 29 hours a week courtesy of the Senate and ObamaCare—talk about a failed law.

In the last election, young people voted overwhelmingly for the reelection of the President. Indeed, some of my friends on the Democratic side of the aisle believe that a new dawn has arrived, that young people will remain permanently Democrats and thus keep a Democratic majority in the Senate for time immemorial. I am not convinced of that.

I will say it is interesting—you could not design a law to do more damage to young people than ObamaCare if you sat down and tried. If you sat down and said: Let's really pound the living daylights out of young people, you couldn't do it.

We will talk later tonight about premiums that are going up, especially for young people, because one way to understand ObamaCare is it is a massive wealth transfer from young healthy people to everyone else. If you are young and healthy, Congress looked at you, licked their chops, and said: You are for dinner. Not only that, the people who are getting their hours forcibly reduced are overwhelmingly young people. They are people who are starting their climb on the economic ladder. If you don't get that first job, you don't get the second, and you don't get the third. It impacts you for a long, long time.

Just recently, I read an article in the *Wall Street Journal* that I think is relevant for every young person to read because it explains how ObamaCare is impacting you not just today but for decades to come. I think young people have a particularly acute desire to see this Senate act this week to defund ObamaCare because it is young people paying the price. Don't take my word for it, take the *Wall Street Journal*. On September 1, 2013, the *Wall Street Journal* had a major article that was entitled "Wanted: Jobs for the New 'Lost' Generation." If you are a young person, you should feel excited: there is now a title for your generation—the "lost generation." I mentioned that if you were trying to design a law to hurt young people, ObamaCare—you couldn't do better than that. Well, it has produced a lost generation.

Here is what the Wall Street Journal said: [In thefolowing pages, Cruz reads from Ben Casselman and Marcus Walker, "Wanted: Jobs for the New 'Lost' Generation: Five years after the 2008 crisis, younger adults still struggle to find work," *Wall Street Journal*, Sept. 14, 2013. His reading of copyrighted text is abridged here, but the entire article can be found on the *Wall Street Journal* website.]

> Like so many young Americans, Derek Wetherell is stuck. At 23 years old, he has a job, but not a career, and little prospect for advancement. He has tens of thousands of dollars in student debt—

I know what student debt is like. It was only 2 years ago that I paid off my student debt. I had to take out student debt to pay my way through college and law school. There are a lot of young people right now struggling to pay off student debt. I will tell you, if you combine student debt with a dead-end job or not being able to find a job at all, that is a recipe for a lost generation.

Continuing with Derek Wetherell:

> He has tens of thousands of dollars in student debt, but no college degree.

That is becoming more and more common. People take out loans to get a college degree, but they are not finishing. They are not able to finish.

> He says he is more likely to move back in with his parents than to buy a home—

The American dream used to be that everyone wanted to buy their own home, have a white picket fence, have a swing out front on which your kids could play. That was our parents' dreams. That was their parents' dreams. That has been the American dream for generations. I ask young people, how many of you feel that dream is a realistic prospect for you? It was for your parents when they were your age. Let me tell you, the policies this Congress has put in place because we are not listening to the American people are a direct cause of that. ObamaCare is a direct cause of that.

Mr. Wetherell continues:

> He says he is more likely to move back in with his parents than to buy a home, and he doesn't know what he will do if his car—a 2001 Chrysler Sebring with well over 100,000 miles— breaks down.

Is there anyone else in America who has a car that is 12 years old with 100,000 miles and is wondering what happens if they wake up one morning and turn the key and nothing happens? If you have a good job, if you are climbing the economic ladder, if you have career prospects, you can deal with that. If you are stuck in a dead-end job and living paycheck to paycheck, that is a huge problem.

> "I'm kind of spinning my wheels," Mr. Wetherell says. . . .

There are millions of Americans who feel exactly like that.

> Mr. Wetherell is a member of the lost generation. . . .

Young people should feel particularly privileged that they have coined a new term for their generation—the lost generation— because of ObamaCare and the policies of this administration.

> . . . The financial crisis that struck five years ago this month opened up a sinkhole in the U.S. economy that swallowed Americans of all ages and backgrounds. . . . The unemployment rate is down to 7.3 percent amid slow, steady job growth.

Although, as we noted earlier, that 7.3 percent vastly understates it, because so many have given up looking for work altogether.

. . . The official unemployment rate for Americans under age 25 was 15.6 percent in August, down from a peak of nearly 20 percent in 2010 but still more than 2½ times the rate of those 25 and older. . . .

In other words, it has gotten worse for young people during the past few years. . . .

Do any of you know anyone—do any of you, right now, know anyone doing that—going to school because, gosh, jobs are so lousy, maybe, you think, you will try to do something at school and maybe things will get better? If ObamaCare keeps hammering small businesses so they do not hire new workers and they keep reducing hours, the prospects for things getting better are not very bright.

. . . Little more than half are working full time—compared with about 80 percent of the population at large—and 12 percent earn minimum wage or less.

Let me repeat that. For young people who are working, little more than half are working full time. If you are a young person, if you are hoping to start a career, being forced into a parttime job because of ObamaCare is a big problem. . . .

It is getting worse for young people. It is young people who are really getting hit by this. Let me ask young people: What urgency do you see in the Senate? Is the floor of the Senate filled with Senators saying there is a crisis with young people; let's step forward and help them get jobs? Nope. Senators have very busy calendars. There are cocktail parties to go to. Responding to the crisis that young people are facing is not high on the priority of enough Members of this Senate because Washington isn't listening to the people. That is why the hashtag is trending: "MakeDCListen." Because we need to make DC listen.

This generation's struggles have few historical precedents, at least in the U.S.

You all should feel excited. You have made history, although, unfortunately, not for a good reason, because the government has put policies in place that have so hammered small businesses that they have created a job market that makes life incredibly difficult for young people.

The recession of the early 1980s was comparable but was followed by a rapid recovery.

Well, gosh, what happened in the early 1980s? President Ronald Reagan was elected. He implemented policies the exact opposite of this administration's policies. Instead of jacking up taxes by $1.7 trillion, as this Congress and this President has done, President Reagan slashed taxes and simplified the Tax Code. Instead of exploding government spending and the debt, President Reagan restrained the growth of government spending. And instead of unleashing regulators like locusts that destroy small businesses, President Reagan restrained regulation and the result was incredible growth.

For young people who have never known anything other than these abysmal economic conditions, there is another way. Every time we have implemented pro free-enterprise policies of restraining taxes, restraining regulation, reining in out-of-control government spending and debt, the result has been small businesses have prospered and thrived. They have created jobs, and the result has been young people could get jobs, full-time jobs that advance towards a career and towards the American Dream.

The economic legacy of the Great Depression was erased to a large degree by World War II and the boom that followed. No similar rebound looks likely this time around.

What a crying shame. Wouldn't it be nice if this week we forced them to change that sentence. Suppose this week Washington, DC, changed. Suppose this week Senators in this body—Republicans and Democrats—decided we are going to do something we haven't done in a long time. We are going to listen to the people. The American people say their top priority is jobs and the economy. Suppose Members of the Senate said: Hot diggity, our top priority is jobs and the economy. Suppose Members of the Senate came together, and Republicans said we are going to stand together on cloture. On the vote on Friday or Saturday, all 46 of us are going to vote against cloture because ObamaCare is killing jobs. It is the biggest job killer and it is hurting the American people. And suppose Democrats said: You know, even though we supported ObamaCare, we have seen how it is implemented, it is not working, it is a train wreck, the American people are hurting, and we are going to respond. We are going to respond to young people—the young people, by the way, on Twitter and in social media we are reaching out to all the time.

You know, lots of politics is very interesting, but nothing is better for a young person than a growing economy and an opportunity to have a job to work to achieve the American Dream. Yet the *Wall Street Journal* says no similar rebound looks likely this time around. I tell you what. If we act in an historic show of courage to defund ObamaCare, that will change.

What evidence does exist suggests today's young people will suffer long-term consequences.

Now, this is important. You may say: Well, the job I have now is not great, but it will be fine in a few years. Here is part of the problem. When young people are stuck in dead-end jobs, if they don't get opportunity now, it echoes throughout that generation for decades.

. . . Economist Lisa Kahn found that after the 1980s recession, new college graduates lost 6 to 7 percent in initial wages for every one percentage point increase in the unemployment rate. The effects shrank over time, but even 15 years after graduation, those who finished college in bad economic times earned less than similar people who graduated in better times. Some never caught up at all.

So this stagnant economic growth, if you are a young person, I am sorry to tell you, it is not just a problem now. If you don't see the Senate finally listening to the American people, finally working to bring back economic growth, the stagnant economic opportunities we have right now are likely to haunt the lost generation of young people for decades to come. This is an urgency that should have this Senate floor packed.

You know what. A lot of men and women in this body have kids who are in that generation. And we should be horrified, we should be outraged that the future of our young people is jeopardized. . . .

How many young people right now are able to save for retirement? That is something else that will echo for decades. Savings when you are young are most important for retirement because through compounding interest they can grow over the years. . . .

. . . Even more unsettling: Wetherell has noticed that more and more of his coworkers have college degrees, some from well-regarded colleges like Washington University. What he had intended as a job to help pay his way through college has now turned into a destination for college graduates. . . .

What does that say when what used to be a part-time job that would help people pay their way through school becomes a destination for college graduates?

You know, my dad worked his way through the University of Texas as a dishwasher and then as a cook. That job is what let him get the education. How much different would it have been if, after he had gotten his degree, he had shown up and they had said: Let's start washing dishes. . . .

I'm going to pause in this article because it is 8 o'clock right now, and I mentioned before that Heidi and I are blessed to have two little girls, Caroline and Catherine. Caroline is 5 and Catherine is 2. I love my daughters with all my heart. They are the joys of my life. I will tell you the hardest aspect of public service is not someone saying something mean about you—the press. The hardest aspect of public service is being away from those little precious angels and coming up here to DC. I tell you, it breaks your heart on Monday morning when I walk out of the house and one girl grabs one leg and one girl grabs the other and they say: Don't leave, Dad.

Well, right now, Caroline and Catherine are both at home getting ready to go to bed, and they have both turned on the television. They are both watching C–SPAN. Now I'm going to confess that Caroline and Catherine don't usually watch C–SPAN since there are far too few animated features on C–SPAN. But because the girls are watching, and my wife Heidi is watching with them, I wanted to take an opportunity—an opportunity I don't usually have when I am in DC—to read them a couple of bedtime stories. They are watching right now, and if you will forgive me, I want to take the opportunity to read two bedtime stories to my girls.

But there is a point to this also. The point is very simple: The urgency we have and should feel is because of our kids. It is because of the future they are facing. It is because of the limited opportunities they have.

I wish to read first to Caroline and Catherine Bible stories from the Old and New Testaments. We often read similar stories at home. This one is entitled "King Solomon's Wise Words." It is from Proverbs 10, 11, 12, 14, 16, 17, 20, and 21.

So, Caroline and Catherine:

King Solomon had good advice for how people could live a good life and be happy. Here are some of his wise sayings:
Children with good sense make their parents happy, but foolish children make them sad.

Sweetheart, you make your mommy and me very happy.

You will say the wrong thing if you talk too much, so be sensible and watch what you say.

I will have to confess to my colleagues, that is not an encouraging Proverb for someone in the midst of a filibuster.

Kindness is rewarded—but if you are cruel, you hurt yourself.
Try hard to do right, and you will win friends; go looking for trouble, and you will find it.
Good people are kind to their animals, but a mean person is cruel.
We trap ourselves by telling lies, but we stay out of trouble by living right.
It's wrong to hate others, but God blesses everyone who is kind to the poor.
Kind words are like honey—they cheer you up and make you feel strong.
Don't trust violent people. They will mislead you to do the wrong thing.
Even fools seem smart when they are quiet.

I suppose that may counteract the other one.

Good people live right, and God blesses the children who follow their example.
Hearing and seeing are gifts from the Lord.
The food you get by cheating may taste delicious, but it turns to gravel.

And,

If you try to be kind and good, you will be blessed with life and goodness and honor.

So that is the first story for Caroline and Catherine.
The second one is what they know is my favorite story. It was my favorite story when I was a kid and it is a story I love reading to them. I actually don't get to read it to them often because we have a rule at home that they get to pick the books. For whatever reason, they don't

pick Dr. Seuss's *Green Eggs and Ham* all that often. I don't get to read it that often because I tell them, Go pick the books you want to read, and I read to them. But since tonight, girls, you aren't here, you don't get to pick the book, so I got to pick *Green Eggs and Ham*. I love this story, so I am going to read it to you. [At this point, Senator Cruz reads the entire text of *Green Eggs and Ham* by Dr. Seuss (New York: Random House, 1960). The work is protected by the copyright and we are not permitted to print it here.]

I want to say to Caroline and Catherine, my angels, I love you with all my heart. It is bedtime. Give Mommy a hug and a kiss, brush your teeth, say your prayers, and Daddy is going to be home soon to read to you in person.

Let me say more broadly to everyone, *Green Eggs and Ham* has some applicability, as curious as it might sound, to ObamaCare, because 3½ years ago President Obama and Senate Democrats told the American people, Just try ObamaCare. Just try it. There were an awful lot of Republicans who were very skeptical of it, I think for good reasons, but very skeptical. And we were told try it, try it, try it, try it. Unfortunately, through an exercise of brute political force, ObamaCare became the law of the land.

But the difference with *Green Eggs and Ham* is when Americans tried it, they discovered they did not like green eggs and ham and they did not like ObamaCare either. They did not like ObamaCare in a box, with a fox, in a house, or with a mouse. It is not working.

One of the oldest definitions of insanity is continuing to do the same thing over and over expecting different results. I understand why many supported ObamaCare in the beginning. But if you look at the facts, if you look at the evidence, if you look at what is happening when the American people have tried it, it is not working. And if we listen to the people—if we listen to the American people, every one of us will stand together and say, We are going to stop this train wreck. Together, we need to make DC listen.

Mr. ENZI. Through the Chair, would the Senator yield for a question, retaining the floor?

Mr. CRUZ. I am happy to yield for a question without yielding the floor.

Mr. ENZI. I want to thank the Senator for the recitation of *Green Eggs and Ham*. That is as good as I have heard. I loved the different voices in it. One of my favorites was "Hand, Hand, Finger, Thumb" by Dr. Seuss. And another one was "Hop on Pop." I think all of those could have related to the messages here. They might even be simple enough that we could get the message across.

I appreciate all the passion and preparation the Senator has put into explaining this and his careful way with words.

We are on a continuing resolution, and I don't know that people out there understand what continuing resolution is. It means that we failed to do our job on time—that we should have had 12 appropriations bills, one at a time, and been able to go through them with some care.

I think maybe the Senator would agree that perhaps if we had done that, when we got to Health and Human Services we might have had the issue on the individual items of defunding ObamaCare. Had we had those individual ones, I think some of those would have passed and it wouldn't have had to have been an all-or-nothing as we have now.

Would the Senator agree that doing it this way, particularly if we have no debate and no amendments, would be the wrong way, and that all we are doing is delaying some more decisions a little further down the road that again should have been covered by appropriations in a very timely manner? Isn't that the same problem we had with sequester, where we went through two-thirds of the year when there was supposed to be a 2.3-percent sequester, so we only had 4 months left and those agencies had to pack it into the 4 months, and that made it 5.3 percent and that hurt worse? Of course, the President's note to everybody to "make it hurt" was not particularly helpful either.

But aren't we faced again with that when we are doing a 2-month delay on a CR, so that we have to go through this exercise again probably when we would like to be home at Christmas personally reading those stories to kids? I would like to be reading to my grandkids.

We have been kind of put in a box here that the American public doesn't like, I don't like, but it wasn't our doing.

If those bills would have been brought up one at a time, we could
have debated each of them and gotten into some details on them. It
has been a long time since we got into details on trillions of dollars
of spending. Health care is a part of that, and health care deserves
some individual attention. That is what the Senator and I and a
number of people are trying to give it, some individual attention.
But we are being denied that right. We are not being allowed to go
into it in detail so we can show exactly which parts we would
defund, which parts we would dismantle and replace with something better.

I spent a lot of time on this bill because I was here when it was
going through the committee process. In fact, I had a 10-step plan on
my Web site that would have done more than this bill and it would
have been paid for. But that isn't a part of the bill. When they say the
Republicans don't have solutions, they are not willing to look at any
of the solutions even if they would wind up in a better situation.

This was passed with a partisan government. It is a health care that
is failing and we are not getting a chance to change it. Of course, I am
one of those who would have liked to have repealed it and started
over again and gotten it right.

I know of another substitute bill that Senator COBURN and Senator BURR did, and that would have been a better replacement too.
It would have covered more of the things the President, in a joint
session of Congress when he covered it—I was on a committee that
was working on it particularly, and I sat there and took extensive
notes. The next day in our meeting I said, There are 14 things that
he said in that speech we did not cover and I think we should have
covered them.

Instead, we wound up with the bill we have because there were 60
Democrats and that is all it took to pass the bill. They had to make a
few deals in order to get the 60 to stick together, and it is surprising
they did stick together.

I will end on that question. I have one other I would like to ask
too. But I think our failure to do appropriations leads us to this point,
and also gets us to a point where we can't go into the details of the bill.
We have to take an all-or-nothing approach. That is not legislating.

That is deal-making. I think we have an alternate approach and I would like the Senator to comment on it.

Mr. CRUZ. I thank my friend from Wyoming for that very good question. I thank him also for his early support of this fight to defund ObamaCare. When Senator MIKE LEE and I began this endeavor, Senator ENZI was with us from the start. I am grateful for his support and for his leadership.

I note his question is exactly right. We would not be in this mess were it not for the failure of the Senate, the failure of the Senate to do its job, the failure of the Senate to have open debate, to have open amendments, the failure of the Senate to actually pass appropriations bills.

Continuing resolutions exist because Congress has fallen down on the job. Congress has not actually passed appropriations bills into law. One of the things the continuing resolution bill does—a continuing resolution basically says let's keep everything going because we have not actually passed the appropriations bills that would properly make the funding decisions on the various agencies of government. But a continuing resolution enables those who want to keep funding ObamaCare to try to hold everything hostage to it.

For example, you hear some in the Democratic majority suggesting—they often run through a parade of horribles. If there is a government shutdown, if the continuing resolution doesn't pass, here are all of the horrible things that will happen.

Some of the parade of horribles that are suggested are contrary to law. For example, they will sometimes suggest people will not get their Social Security payment or they will not get their Medicare or they won't get their Medicaid or we won't pay interest on the debt. That is not the way the Government works. All of those are paid through mandatory spending. The continuing resolution does not impact those continuing to happen. I note in 1995 when there were two partial temporary shutdowns, Social Security checks continued to go out, the interest on the debt continued to be paid. All that continued.

Another thing those who are trying to force ObamaCare on the American people frequently want to hold hostage is the men and women in the military. My friend from Wyoming noted if we passed appropriations bills that would not be a problem. The House has passed an appropriations bill for the military. Yet the majority leader, Harry REID, the Democratic majority, had not taken that bill up. If we had passed it into law you could quantify the chances of the men and women in the military having their pay suspended to mathematical certainty to 0.000 percent. If we passed the appropriations bill, the issue would be off the table. But the Senate did not do its job; we did not pass the appropriations bill for the military.

That leaves a tiny window for the President to threaten. If Congress listens to the American people and defunds ObamaCare, we may just stop paying the men and women of the military. Let me be absolutely clear. Under no circumstances ever should the United States not pay the men and women of our military who risk their lives on the front lines. Current law gives the President ample authority to continue to pay the military regardless of whether there is a temporary partial shutdown.

What has happened in the past, if and when there has been a temporary partial shutdown, is nonessential government services are temporarily suspended. By any measure, the military of the United States is not nonessential. So if we had done our job, as the Senator from Wyoming puts that forward, if we had passed appropriations bills, we would have taken off the table one after the other after the other of these hostages that are being held as the price to force ObamaCare on the American people.

Part of the reason why the Democratic majority of the Senate does that is because the debate on the merits of ObamaCare is very hard to win. You notice we are, by and large, not engaging in a debate on the merits of ObamaCare, in terms of defunding ObamaCare. You don't see Democratic Senators talking about all the people who are losing their jobs, you don't see Democratic Senators talking about all those people having their hours reduced or all the people seeing skyrocketing health insurance premiums, or who are losing their health insurance. Instead, we see Democratic Senators going on television and saying: Well, if they stick to their guns on this, it is going to shut down the government.

The Senator from Wyoming points out there is no reason for that. We could have passed the appropriations bill or we could do what the

House of Representatives did. The House of Representatives, in an overwhelming vote, 232 Members, including 2 Democrats, voted to fund every aspect of the Federal Government—including, I note, some parts of the Federal Government that I am certain House Republicans are not fans of—yet they voted to fund all of it except for ObamaCare.

I know my friend Congressman LOUIE GOHMERT has come over to the Senate floor in a show of solidarity. I appreciate Congressman GOHMERT joining us.

I note if the Senate wants to avoid a shutdown, it can do so. Indeed, last night I took the opportunity to ask the majority leader, Why don't we avert this whole train wreck right now? Why don't we agree by unanimous consent to pass the continuing resolution the House has passed, take the prospect of a shutdown off the table entirely, and defund ObamaCare because it is hurting the American people? Majority Leader REID objected and said no. No, he wants to keep ObamaCare, he wants to force it on the American people. Critically, he wants to use the threat of a government shutdown to try to do so. That, I suggest, is inconsistent with the obligation that every Senator has.

Mr. ENZI. Mr. President, I ask permission to ask another question through the Chair, with the Senator being allowed to keep the floor.

Mr. CRUZ. I am happy to yield for a question without yielding the floor.

Mr. ENZI. Mr. President, would the Senator agree that there are a number of things in this bill that have been changed because we have recognized that those things would not work? We have changed— not we, the President has changed a number of these things. I am having trouble finding in the law where those changes come from. There is not a lot of waiver authority in the bill, but every time a difficulty is found with the bill, then there appears to be a waiver so that particular part of the bill no longer exists.

I have never seen that done before on legislation. How do they take a piece of the law that is in the bill, that does not have a waiver right, and go ahead and exempt us under that particular part of the law? One particular part of that I am particularly sensitive on because

I worked on it very diligently. As the bill came through committee, that piece was the one where Congress should be under the law that we passed, Congress and the staff.

That got remodeled, as you will recall, a little bit so that the committee staffs did not have to come under it because the committee staffs were actually going to finish up the bill. But we had intended for all of our staffs to be under that bill.

Would the Senator agree that one of the amendments that we have not been able to vote on—it would have only taken 30 minutes to do a 15-minute vote. That is kind of standard around here; it takes us a little longer to do a 15-minute vote. Heck, it takes us 20 minutes to do a 10-minute vote and that has to follow on the heels of a 30-minute 15-minute vote.

We could have had that vote, but we were not allowed to. What that amendment is, as you will recall, what it would have done is put Congress back under the bill. It would have subjected Congress to suffering the same exact thing the American public is going to start experiencing on Tuesday as they go into the exchange or at the very latest by the 1st of January when they are required to do that.

If their company is no longer providing them with insurance, the company will pay a little penalty but they get to come under the exchange. But they do not get to bring the company's tax-free donation to their health care along with them. But that is the way we had envisioned it working for Congress too. They would not get a special dispensation. So we brought up this amendment which would require that not only would Congress come under it, but since the President is the one who exempted this and did not have the right to exempt this from it, we thought perhaps he and the Vice President and the political appointees maybe ought to come under that same bill. I mean, why wouldn't the President want to come under it? After all, it is called ObamaCare. It is named after him.

Apparently there is a tremendous desire not to do that, to explain that the Federal Government is different. That is exactly what the American people are upset about, that we are different. We should not be different. That is one of the things that could have been taken care of if we had taken this all through regular order.

I appreciate efforts of the Senator to be able to do something. I ask if the Senator believes we ought to be exempted under any parts of this law or if these exemptions would be legal for the President to do if it is not written in the law? As a lawyer, my colleague probably has better insight into that than I do—and a constitutionalist. That is why I ask the question. Does the President have the right to do that?

Mr. CRUZ. I thank my colleague for that very good question. The simple answer is no, the President does not have the authority to rewrite the law or alter the law. We operate under a principle that no one is above the law. We are a nation of laws and not of men. There are many disturbing aspects of ObamaCare, but one of the persistent ones is this law has been such a train wreck that the approach of the President has been, over and over, simply to disregard the language of the law, to pretend as if the law of the United States does not exist because as passed it was such a bad law. The way that is manifested, as my friend from Wyoming pointed out so accurately, is to grant exemptions to politically favored classes.

It started out with big business. Giant corporations were all, with the wave of a pen, told don't worry about ObamaCare. It is supposed to kick in for you January 1 of next year, but the President has decided he is going to do a favor for big businesses that he will not do for small businesses, that he will not do for hard-working American families.

The next significant waiver we saw was for Members of Congress. It occurred after a closed-door meeting here in the Capitol where majority leader HARRY REID and all the Senate Democrats, according to the public reports, came to the President and said: We want out of the ObamaCare exchanges.

As my friend from Wyoming pointed out, if the ObamaCare exchanges were a good thing, if ObamaCare was working, why would there be panic among Senate Democrats saying please exempt Members of Congress? Why would there be panic among congressional staffers, as I can assure you there is, in a bipartisan way, about being subjected to these ObamaCare exchanges? Why would there be such opposition to subjecting the political appointees of the Obama administration to the ObamaCare exchanges or, as my friend from Wyoming pointed out so correctly, the President himself?

It is, after all, called popularly ObamaCare. Even the President has embraced that name. You would think, I suspect, if there were a health care plan called EnziCare, the Senator from Wyoming would be happy to be covered by it and he would probably be very careful to draft a plan that he would be willing and excited to be covered by.

What does it say that the people in charge of enforcing ObamaCare on the American people want out? They want a special rule. The IRS employee unions, the men and women who are given the statutory responsibility of going to Americans, going to hard-working Americans and forcing Americans to comply with ObamaCare, have said in writing: Please, let us out of ObamaCare. We don't want to be a part of this thing. This is our health care you are talking about.

The most profound issue we are dealing with here today is not jobs, it is not the economy, it is not health care, it is not ObamaCare. The most profound issue we are dealing with here today is the fundamental divide between Washington and American people. There is a ruling class in Washington, DC; that they are subjected to different rules than the American people; that it is perfectly appropriate for political friends and allies of the President to get exemptions while single moms and young people and Hispanics and African Americans, people struggling, union workers struggling to pay the bills, provide for their kids—they don't get an exemption. Just those who walk the corridors of power. Just those with access to political influence.

You know what that does? It strengthens politicians even more. Look, politicians are in the business of granting dispensations, granting exceptions. That means everybody in the country who wants some exception better come to politicians and support them.

If you want to talk about something corrosive to our system of democracy, why do you think the American people hold this body in low regard? Because we pass laws that treat us better than everybody else. Tonight we are listening to the American people. We need to make DC listen.

By the way, I have been told that during the course of this filibuster, the "#MakeDCListen" has at times been trending No. 1 in the country.

I say to my colleagues who have come to the floor in support of this effort that it is because the American people understand and are frustrated as to why Washington doesn't listen to them, and for at least a brief moment each of us together—the Senator from Wyoming and the Senator from Oklahoma—are trying to serve as a voice for the American people who don't often have a voice in Washington. We need to make DC listen. There is nothing more important we can do than that.

Mr. INHOFE. Will the Senator yield for a question?

Mr. CRUZ. I am happy to yield for a question without yielding the floor.

Mr. INHOFE. A lot of people have forgotten the cost of this. I would like to go over a couple of things if it is all right with the Senator. First, I wonder if the same thing is happening in his State—which is to the south of Oklahoma—of Texas that is happening in my State of Oklahoma. We are just a week away from when people will have to start signing up for ObamaCare. I commend Senator CRUZ for reminding the American people that this law doesn't have to be a new reality. It doesn't have to be that way. We can stop it. There are still lingering questions about exactly what this is all going to look like.

We do know this reform law, as they call it, continues to be expensive and overreaching. When it started out, it didn't sound too bad to the American people. It is estimated that the program will now cost as much as $2.4 trillion over the years.

As I have suggested to my friend from Texas, around here we know what $1 trillion is, but most people don't know what that means. It is hard to understand this as far as what is going on in America. It will cost $2.6 trillion over 10 years once this is fully implemented, assuming they are successful in doing it. The cost estimates have only continued to rise since the law was passed.

Most recently the administration asked for another $5.4 billion in discretionary funds next year for implementation. That is $5.4 billion in discretionary funds. Let's stop and think about that. One of the worst things about the Obama administration—and the Senator from Texas understands this since he is on the Senate Armed Services Committee—is how this President has been disarming America. The discretionary money that would be coming out of this is money that otherwise could be used for our systems and to support our warfighters over there. That is just the cost of the Federal Government. It doesn't include the lost hours, wages, and employees who have lost their jobs and the cost it will be to their families.

Everyone agrees the premiums will rise. In my home State of Oklahoma we have a guy named John Doak. After talking to the insurance companies, he said Oklahomans' insurance will increase by a minimum of 30 percent and up to 100 percent. He also said that one in four insurers in Oklahoma will have their rates vary from $143 a month for a 30-year-old with basic coverage to $673 a month for a 64-year-old who wants the best coverage.

Remember, the President promised to lower the premiums by $2,500. What I want to do, if I could, is share a little bit of good news. I know the Senator from Texas is aware of it, but I don't know how many other people are aware of this. We have a great attorney general in the State of Oklahoma whose name is Scott Pruitt. I suspect the Senator from Texas has met Scott Pruitt. Before we voted on this issue, we had a question on whether some of these subsidies would go any further. Scott Pruitt, through the courts, filed a lawsuit and is leading the charge to dismantle ObamaCare and put an end to it.

Last month the judge overseeing the lawsuit ruled against a motion filed by the Obama administration to dismiss the case, which means the case will proceed. That is huge. If this goes through, this whole thing will be dismantled. That is why we need to go ahead and fight this as best we can, recognizing that there are other areas where the American people are speaking. Certainly Scott Pruitt is doing great things.

I heard the Senator mention Congressman LOUIE GOHMERT. Congressman GOHMERT is a very close friend of mine. We have been together on a lot of things. I was visiting with him. He is in the

Chamber right now and would like to share some of the things that are happening in his district, which is eastern Texas.

These are some of the letters that he gets from constituents. This says:

> To get setup on the software was too expensive. She also didn't want to be limited on the time she felt she needed to spend with her patients. Therefore, she stopped taking Medicare. Had to go on strictly cash basis.

This text says:

> My wife's doctor has just retired because he did not want to deal with ObamaCare.

This is a letter that came from someone whose name is Katy Smith. She goes through quite a bit, and then says:

The explanation from IBM was that they "projected that health care costs under the current IBM Medicare-eligible retiree plan options will nearly triple by 2020."

This is another letter from Riverside Cottages. I guess that is someplace in eastern Texas.

> We were notified July 15, 2013 that my husband's insurance coverage, Blue Cross and Blue Shield of Montana/Montana Comprehensive Health Association will terminate December 31, 2013. When my husband contacted Blue Cross Blue Shield, they told him that this policy will no longer exist due to Obama Care. He will need to find new coverage.

And it goes on and on.

The interesting thing—and the reason I am reading Texas letters right now—is that we receive a lot of them, and they are up in my office someplace. So this hits home and hits home hard.

I ask my friend from Texas if he has received a lot of these anecdotal letters from people who are suffering serious hardships and are now anticipating what will happen when this becomes a reality?

Mr. CRUZ. I thank my friend from Oklahoma for his excellent question. Let me say from the outset that I am grateful for Senator INHOFE's leadership and his courage. From the outset Senator INHOFE has been with me on this fight, fighting to defund ObamaCare.

I want to also note that Senator INHOFE, like some of the other Senators who have come to the floor of the Senate this afternoon—including Senator ROBERTS, Senator SESSIONS, and Senator ENZI—are respected veterans of this institution. They are leaders who have earned the respect of their colleagues.

I am grateful for Senator INHOFE being willing to stand up and be a leader in this fight. That courage is contagious. I hope it will continue to be even more contagious in the Republican Congress. I hope by the time we come to the cloture vote on Saturday that we see all 46 Republicans united in voting against shutting off the debate and against allowing majority leader HARRY REID the ability to fund ObamaCare with a straight 51 party vote.

Mr. INHOFE. Before that happens, I think it is important that the people of this country have to know what this is all about. This is socialized medicine. A lot of them didn't believe that. Last week majority leader HARRY REID was on the PBS "Nevada Week in Review." He was asked whether his goal was to move ObamaCare to a single-payer system. His answer was: Yes, yes. Absolutely yes. Do a lot of the people know what a single-payer system is? That is essentially socialized medicine.

I was around during the Clinton administration when there was a thing called Hillary health care. Does my friend from Texas remember Hillary health care?

Mr. CRUZ. I do indeed. I remember in particular at the time the press and all of the graybeards in Washington at the time saying that Hillary Care was unstoppable. It can't stop it. Republicans need to get together.

If the Senator from Oklahoma will recall, initially the response was described as like Hillary care lite. Back then in the midst of the

Hillary care fight there were a few courageous leaders in the House who stood up against Hillary Care. What changed that battle was the American people rising. At the end of the day, it is the only thing that can win any fights.

Mr. INHOFE. That is exactly what did happen. I can remember going from Washington to my hometown of Tulsa. Normally I have to go through Chicago. Chicago is where the AMA has their headquarters, and it is probably still there. I will always remember this. I was rejoicing. I was coming back after the long fight against Hillary health care or socialized medicine. I remember saying the question on the Senate floor: Try to explain this to me: If socialized medicine doesn't work in Great Britain, Sweden, or Canada, why would it work in this country? They never said it, but what they were thinking was: If I were running it, it would work. We got that point across.

They started way ahead with Hillary health care, and then we started to catch up. Just like now people are realizing this is a failed socialized medicine effort. We had won.

That kind of relates to what is happening today. I was on that plane going through Chicago to Tulsa, and I picked up the *Wall Street Journal*, and there was a full-page ad by the AMA supporting Hillary health care. Of course, when I stopped in Chicago, I went and visited the AMA. This is an organization that represents a lot of real smart doctors and others who were saying that we can't win. We can't win this and therefore let's go ahead with it. We had already won when they ran that ad. I don't know how many days before that they put the ad in, but nonetheless we had won.

I don't know if my friend remembers that because my friend was not in the Senate at that time. That is exactly what happened, and it is very analogous to a lot of things that are happening today.

The other thing I wanted to mention is that anytime desperation starts to set in, there are a lot of things that go around to confuse people. Let me tell everyone what happened in Oklahoma today. This will surprise my friend from Texas. There are 14 people who started this—the Senator from Texas, myself, and 12 other people about 6 weeks ago. During this time we have been in lockstep to see what we could do to stop this from happening to my 20 kids and grandkids and the rest of America.

People realized I was there from the very beginning, as the Senator from Texas mentioned, and yet we have some of the Obama people who are doing robocalls in my State of Oklahoma posing as tea party people and saying to call INHOFE because he is for ObamaCare.

I say to my good friend, I can't believe something like that is happening. It shows a level of desperation where they are trying to get people confused as to what the issue is and want to get to these deadlines so we can get past this and have this thing as a reality. Every liberal in America is probably for it.

Mr. CRUZ. I thank my friend from Oklahoma for that question. I have to say I am not surprised. There is an old adage among courtroom lawyers: If you have the facts, pound the facts. If you have the law, pound the law. If you don't have either, pound the table.

To be honest, the approach by ObamaCare defenders is an awful lot of table pounding. It is an awful lot of "let's discuss anything other than what, in fact, happened." Pick up any newspaper and it is talking about this issue. What will the reporters, the political reporters in Washington, DC, write about? I think some may be frustrated because they wanted to be Hollywood gossip reporters because they covered these issues as a battle of personalities. If you want to get a story on the front page of the paper, find some anonymous congressional staffer to say something scurrilous, ideally include profanity in it, and the political reporters eat it up, because, apparently, the only thing that matters is the personalities bickering back and forth. In many ways, that is not surprising, because if one is trying to defend a law that the lead author calls a train wreck, that the unions who supported it are desperately trying to get out from under, that you and your Democratic Senate colleagues are desperately asking for yourselves to be exempted from it, then you sure as heck don't want to talk about how the law is operating. You sure as heck don't want to talk about all of the people who are losing their jobs because of ObamaCare. You sure as heck don't want to talk about all the people who can't get jobs, all the small businesses that aren't growing because of ObamaCare. You certainly don't want to talk about all of the people forced into part-time work, 29-hours-a-week work. You don't want to talk about the insurance premiums that are going up, pricing people out of the insurance market, and you especially don't want to talk about all the people losing their health insurance.

My colleague read the stories from East Texas of citizens there losing their health insurance. That is happening all over the country.

So it doesn't surprise me that the Senator from Oklahoma is seeing robocalls in the State of Oklahoma because they don't want to debate on the merits of ObamaCare because it is indefensible. So the only strategy is smoke and mirrors. The only strategy is, if we can't talk about the law, let's convince them about something else. Let's distract them. Let's figure out anything to take people's minds off of the underlying issue.

I would note to my friend from Oklahoma, the only way that strategy works is if the American people don't believe Washington will listen to them.

Look, there are a lot of reasons for the American people to believe Washington is not going to listen to them because Washington hasn't been listening to us for a long time. Politicians on both sides of this aisle have lost touch with their constituents. They don't go home, don't go to townhall meetings, and view the desires of their constituents as simply uninformed and not relevant to doing our jobs.

Mr. INHOFE. If the Senator from Texas will yield, because he said something that is so profound.

Mr. CRUZ. I am yielding for a question but not yielding the floor.

Mr. INHOFE. Of course. The Senator from Texas said if you don't have logic on your side or the facts on your side or the public on your side, what do you do? It is not just pounding the table. It is name-calling.

I went through this, I would suggest to my friend, 12 years ago when the Kyoto treaty was up and everyone thought global warming was coming and that was going to be everyone's trip to the White House to support global warming, until we realized what the cost would be. I was the bad guy because I stood and said: No, this isn't true. First of all, it is a hoax; and secondly, even if it is not, we couldn't do it. That is when all the name-calling started. I can remember being called—in writing and by a fairly prominent person—I should be hanged for treason at that time. That is what they get, and that is what my friend is going through right now with a lot of people who don't agree with him.

Twelve years later, what has happened? People realize I was right. I am not suggesting it is going to be 12 years before they realize the Senator from Texas is right on this, but it means the behavior of people today is something that has happened many times in the past.

So I would just ask my friend to remember that and to realize that quite often, when a person is right on a controversial issue, they are going to be the subject of a lot of criticism, a lot of cussing, a lot of name-calling, and a lot of violence. So this isn't the first time.

Mr. CRUZ. I thank my friend from Oklahoma for his very kind remarks of support and encouragement and for his friendship from day one since I arrived in the Senate. I do hope other colleagues in this body don't listen to all of the remarks of the Senator from Oklahoma and suddenly discover that hanging for treason is an option because that may not work out terribly well for me. I hope that becomes purely fictional.

I will know that at the end of the day—listen, the Senator from Oklahoma and I, and all 100 of us, are incredibly fortunate. We have lived lives in this country of relative privilege. We, everyone in the Senate, enjoys a good home, has a soft bed, I suspect, has air-conditioning, has food on the table. I feel blessed to have a wife who is my best friend in the world and whom I love with all my heart, to have two precious little girls who are the joy of my life. To be able to come to work every day, to walk on this Senate floor, there is not a day when that doesn't take my breath away. The idea that the son of a Cuban immigrant with nothing, who finds himself suddenly elected to the Senate, to have the opportunity to come in every day, it is truly awesome, in the real sense of the word. There was a time when the word "awesome" was a Valley girl phrase for everything, but awesome, in its real sense of inspiring awe—I will tell my colleague I find it awesome every day to walk into this Capitol and to have the amazing privilege to serve, as the Senator from Oklahoma and I do, as do all

100 of us. The slings and arrows one deals with serving in public office, to be perfectly candid, are all chickenfeed. The old phrase about sticks and stones—listen, someone saying something mean about another is nothing compared to the suffering that so many people across this country are experiencing.

I sat down with one single mom who is working her heart out to provide for her kids because she wants her kids to have a good home, she wants her kids to have an education, she wants her kids to have a future. Her hours have been reduced to 29 hours a week and she doesn't know what is coming next. That is hard work. That is suffering. This ain't nothing.

The Senator from Oklahoma speaks with disabled veterans, as I know he has done many times, and he is worried about the impact of ObamaCare on our economy, of jobs drying up. He is worried about his grandson who is just coming out of school right now but who can't get a job. That is a lot more important than the political bickering back and forth. That was my point about all of the press coverage dealing with—it is not about any personality here; it is about listening to the American people.

The American people do not give a flying flip about any Member of the Senate—none of the 100 of us. What the American people are interested in is what we have always been interested in, which is freedom, our families, providing for our kids, being a good example to our kids, working for a better world and working so our kids and their kids have an even better future and opportunity than we have had. If we go back centuries, we see that every generation of Americans has been able to give to the next generation a brighter future, greater prosperity, greater opportunity. We are on the verge of being the first generation of Americans not to do so. If we want to put our fingers on the discontent so many Americans feel, that goes right to the heart of it: What we are doing in Washington isn't working.

The economic malaise. I refer to the last 5 years as the "great stagnation" because for 4 consecutive years our economy has grown on average 0.9 percent a year. It is not working. Intelligent, rational people looking at a set of policies that aren't working would do the intelligent, rational thing. We would correct course. We would say, OK, this isn't working. What has worked? But that is not happening. It is not happening because even though it is not working, the failures aren't visited on Congress. The failures are visited on the American people. Congress exempts itself from ObamaCare. It doesn't even do it in the law. The law says we are covered by it, but, instead, Democratic Senators go to the President and say: We want a special exemption for us that doesn't apply to the American people. So the fundamental problem is that elected officials are not listening to the people.

Earlier, I was reading the article about the lost generation of young people from the *Wall Street Journal* that ran on September 19. I made it about halfway through. Let me finish that article because I think it raises some very important issues. The last thing I read was about the young man, 23 years old, working a job where he says his job at the grocery store—he doesn't have a college degree, but he is seeing more and more college degrees getting in, and he is saying: Gosh, I thought this was a job that helped me pay my way through school. If this is the end job after you get a degree, what does it say about opportunity?

The last quote I read was:

I think a lot about whether I am ahead or behind. I really hope I'm not ahead. . . .

The article continues:

Americans aren't the only ones asking such questions. . . .

Let me move forward beyond the Europeans, back to where it discusses American young people again:

But there are signs that the weak economy is leading to deep societal changes. An entire generation is putting off the rituals of early adulthood: . . . The marriage rate among young people, long in decline, fell even faster during the recession, and the birth rate for women in their early 20s fell to an all-time low in 2012.

Why do we think it is that young people are putting off marriage and putting off kids? . . .

Fifty-six percent of 18- to 24-yearolds lived with their parents in 2012— . . .

Moreover, many young people are losing hopes of matching the prosperity of their parents' generation.

I talked a minute ago about the hope of all of us that our kids have greater opportunity. What does it say that young people are losing hope of even matching where we are, much less having greater prosperity?

Just 11 percent of employed young people in a recent Pew survey said they had a career as opposed to "just a job"; fewer than half said they were even on track for one.

John Connelly thought he was on the right track in life. The son of a New Jersey auto mechanic, he was the first in his family to go to college when he enrolled in Rutgers in 2009.

I will note as an aside, my uncle went to Rutgers. I went to college, to Princeton in New Jersey, and my uncle was often fond of reminding me that the very first collegiate football game that ever was played in the United States was played between Rutgers and Princeton. At every Thanksgiving, my uncle would then remind me who won and it was Rutgers who won. Princeton got whipped in that Princeton game. I am sure John Connelly is quite aware that Rutgers won the first collegiate football game in the United States. . . .

I am still reading from the *Wall Street Journal*:

The costs of a "lost generation" go beyond the impact on young people themselves. A 2012 analysis commissioned by the Corporation for National and Community Service, a federal agency, estimated that the 6.7 million American youth who are disconnected from both school and work could ultimately cost taxpayers $1.6 trillion in lost tax receipts, increased reliance on government benefits and other expenses. . . .

Mr. DURBIN. Will the Senator yield for a question?

The PRESIDING OFFICER (Mr. KAINE). Will the Senator yield?

Mr. CRUZ. I am happy to yield for a question without yielding the floor.

The PRESIDING OFFICER. The Senator from Illinois.

Mr. DURBIN. My understanding is that the Senator's position is, if we do not defund ObamaCare, as he has characterized it—the health care reform act—that he believes we should shut down the government on October 1. Is that the Senator's position?

Mr. CRUZ. I thank the Senator from Illinois for that question. That most assuredly is not my position, so I thank the Senator for the opportunity to clarify it.

Let me be very clear. I do not believe we should shut down the Federal Government. The only reason we might shut down the Federal Government is if President Obama and Majority Leader REID decide they want to force a government shutdown.

What I believe we should do is the same thing the House of Representatives did, the same thing the House courageously did, which was last Friday the House of Representatives voted to fund every aspect of the Federal Government—every bit of it, including parts they disagree with—except for ObamaCare. I would note to my friend from Illinois, they did so in response to the American people because the American people are hurting under ObamaCare.

Mr. DURBIN. Will the Senator yield for a further question?

Mr. CRUZ. I am happy to yield for a question without yielding the floor.

Mr. DURBIN. The Senator has spoken at length many times, including today, about his education. I respect him. He has gone to some very famous schools. Certainly, the Senator understands it takes 60 votes to achieve the goal he is trying to achieve, which means the Senator believes he has at least all the votes on his side of the aisle and another 14 votes on the Democratic side of the aisle to repeal ObamaCare. Does the Senator have that belief?

Mr. CRUZ. I thank the Senator for that question, and I thank the Senator for the comment he has made in public, noting that having attended the schools I have that perhaps I had not learned to count to 60. I will note that I am quite familiar with what is necessary to defund ObamaCare. What I have said for months is this is a long process. I am not remotely Pollyannaish. I am not remotely under the illusion that this is going to be a short, quick process, that suddenly ObamaCare will be defunded.

I am getting to the answer to the Senator's question, but it is a detailed answer, so if he will forgive me, I will take a few moments to lay it out.

In my view, the first step to this process was unifying and motivating the American people. This process was never going to work unless the American people became engaged in historic numbers. So I spent much of the month of August and September during our recess traveling the State of Texas, traveling the country, doing everything I could to go directly to the American people, to go around the lobbyists, to go around the entrenched interests in Washington, and go straight to the American people.

I will tell the Senator, the response was incredible. Everywhere I would go, I would see 1,000, 2,000 people show up. We have seen over 1.6 million Americans sign a national petition to defund ObamaCare.

That was the first step. That was not going to be enough, but it was a critical first step.

The second step was what happened last week. It was the House of Representatives voting to defund ObamaCare.

I would note, as the Senator from Illinois is well aware, that as recently as a couple weeks ago, every learned observer, every pundit, everyone in Washington said: It is impossible that the House is going to pass a continuing resolution that defunds ObamaCare. It is not going to happen. Yet on Friday it did. Why did it pass? Because the House of Representatives listened to the American people, because the Speaker of the House and House conservatives stood and did the right thing and made a courageous vote. I will note, two Democrats joined the House Republicans in that vote.

Mr. DURBIN. Will the Senator yield further for a question?

Mr. CRUZ. I would like to finish answering the Senator's last question, and I am happy to yield for another. But let me finish answering the Senator's question.

The third step is where we are now as the Senate. In the Senate, we are going to have to do two things. The first thing we are going to have to do in order to successfully defund ObamaCare is to unify Republicans, to bring together all 46 Republicans, opposing cloture, opposing HARRY REID being able to fund ObamaCare on a straight 51-vote partisan vote. I believe every Republican should be unified in that. Right now we are not. Right now there are divisions in the Republican caucus. I am hopeful Republicans will listen to our constituents. I cannot convince my colleagues. The only people who can convince my colleagues on this side of the aisle or that side of the aisle are the people all of us work for, the American people.

If we are able to unify Republicans, the next step—the Senator asked me: How do we ultimately get to 60? I assume the predicate of that question is that the first thing we would have to do is to get to 51—so if we got 46 Republicans and we initially got five Democrats. How would we get five Democrats? As the Senator from Illinois is well aware, there are quite a few Democrats who are up for election in red States, States where their citizens understand ObamaCare is a train wreck. It is not working. I believe if those Democratic Senators, particularly in red States, begin hearing from their constituents in overwhelming numbers, that will change their calculus.

Let me readily admit, as long as Republicans are divided, as long as we are shooting at each other, there is not a lot of incentive for Democrats to come join us. But if we can unify Republicans, then I believe we will start with red State Democrats who will potentially lose their jobs if they continue not listening to their people.

Mr. DURBIN. Will the Senator yield for a further question?

Mr. CRUZ. Sure.

Mr. DURBIN. I might question the Senator's premise as to whether the House was going to vote the way it did. Since it has voted 42 times to abolish ObamaCare, it came as no surprise.

But let me ask a specific question. One of the reasons I voted for health care reform—and I am proud that I did—was illustrated by a woman whom I met in southern Illinois. The Senator has spoken today about hard-working people, including members of his own family, and I do not doubt that.

This woman's name is Judy. Judy is a housekeeper at a motel that I often go to, and we have become friends. Judy has worked her whole life in manual labor. She has been everything you can imagine—a cook, a waitress, a housekeeper, all of these things. She is 62 years old. Judy told me that she had never had health insurance one day in her life, ever. She worked every single day she could, but she never had health insurance. It turns out Judy was diabetic, and we found some doctors and hospitals locally in her area to give her some care.

We have just had an announcement in Illinois that is going to be officially released tomorrow about what this new health insurance marketplace in Illinois means for people such as Judy. It means we are going to offer 165 different health insurance plans in Illinois by eight different insurers. The premiums at the lowest level of health insurance, for those who are not under Medicaid, will be in the range of $84 a month. But the good news for Judy is that her income is so low she now qualifies for Medicaid for the first time in her life. For the first time in her life, Judy who would be turned down because of the pre-existing condition of diabetes, is going to have the peace of mind of health insurance.

The Senator and I are blessed to have the best health insurance in America as Members of the Senate. So when the Senator says he wants to disband and stop ObamaCare, does he want to deny the opportunity for Judy and millions more just like her for the first time in their lives to have the protection of health insurance they can afford?

Mr. CRUZ. I thank the Senator from Illinois for that question. I will say, I respect his sincerity and passion in believing that government solutions from Washington can fix this problem. I do not know if the Senator from Illinois shares the views that Majority Leader REID expressed on television. I do not know if his objective is as Majority Leader REID said his was: to move to single-payer, government-provided, socialized health care. But it may be. I do not want to put words in the Senator's mouth. Certainly, I do not know one way or the other what his view would be.

Mr. DURBIN. Thank you.

Mr. CRUZ. But I will say this. The Senator tells the story of Judy. The best way for Judy or anyone to have health insurance is to have an economy that is booming where people can get jobs and have opportunities. Indeed, let me respond with two things.

No. 1, before the Senator from Illinois came to the floor of the Senate, I read a number of letters that have come from people all over the country. Let me just read the next one in my stack because it happens to actually be a counterpart to his story about Judy. This is a constituent from Brackettville, TX, who wrote earlier this year:

> Since the passage of what is known as Obama Care, my insurance premiums have gone up three times. That doesn't count the increases in my Medicare Part A and B that have also risen. I was also informed prior to passage that certain retirees from one group would see their company support terminated after 2013 and my support will terminate after 2018. In the meantime, I've lost two family doctors who have left the practice . . . and must settle for nurse practitioners and physician assistants. I am fortunate to have good coverage, for which I pay dearly, that is accepted everywhere; but I fear the day I can no longer afford it. I am paying for Obama's train wreck ever since the bill was passed. Surely, there must be some way to defund or repeal the bill. . . . Please help.

I would note for the Senator from Illinois, these pleas for help are coming from all across the country.

Mr. DURBIN. Will the Senator yield for another question?

Mr. CRUZ. I am happy to yield for a question without yielding the floor.

Mr. DURBIN. I think the Senator's answer to Judy is: You need a better job. After working a lifetime—62 years, hard work, the best she can do; she has never had health insurance—and I think the Senator's answer was: Judy, get a better job.

So let me ask another question.

When I voted for ObamaCare, health care reform, one of the things that motivated me was the fact that health insurance companies would no longer be able to discriminate against Americans with preexisting conditions.

I have had a situation in my family, a child who had a serious physical problem, who could not have qualified but for group health insurance that was available to me as a Member of Congress. If I had gone in the open market to buy a policy, I am not sure I would have bought one for my family to cover my child.

So when the Senator says he wants to abolish ObamaCare, does he want to abolish that part of ObamaCare which says you cannot discriminate against people with preexisting conditions when it comes to health insurance? If those people are victims of asthma, diabetes, cancer treatment, mental illness, does the Senator want to abolish ObamaCare and that protection?

Mr. CRUZ. I thank the Senator from Illinois for that question.

Let me answer it in two different ways. Let me talk generally about what the Senator talked about, about his health insurance and my health insurance as a Member of the Senate and let me talk about preexisting conditions separately.

The first point I will make is that the Senator from Illinois is passionate and has been quite eloquent describing what he perceives to be the benefits from ObamaCare. Yet I think it speaks volumes that the Senator from Illinois and I and every other Member of Congress have been exempted by President Obama from the plain text of the statute.

The statute provided—and it was inserted quite deliberately—if we are going to impose rules on the American people, we should be subject to the same rules, we should be put in the exchanges similar to millions of other Americans. The Senator just talked about the wonderful exchange. The text of ObamaCare provides that he and I should be in those exchanges. It also provides that, just like the other people in the exchange, our employers cannot subsidize it once we get in that exchange.

Once it passed into law, the Democratic caucus met with President Obama. Obviously, I was not in that meeting. But I read the public reports of what occurred there. I read the press accounts. The press accounts all indicated that the majority leader and the Democratic Members of the Senate asked President Obama: Please get us out from under this. We do not want to be in the exchanges.

I see my friend from Illinois is shaking his head. I was not in the room. The press reports all say that is what occurred. But regardless, that is what happened.

So that message was heard by the President because shortly there-after the administration issued a ruling that exempted Members of Congress and exempted our staff.

I am curious, if the Senator from Illinois is such a fan of the exchanges, is such a fan of the health care that has been provided to Judy, would the Senator from Illinois then support Senator VITTER's amendment to provide that every Member of Congress, every one of our staffs, every political appointee in the Obama administration— and, frankly, I would like to see every Federal employee all put under the exchanges—so if we are going to make the rules for the American people, that we be subject to those same rules, those same plans, so that when we go on television and say the exchanges are very good, we are not talking about something someone else is experiencing, we are talking about our own health care.

Mr. DURBIN. If the Senator would yield, I would like to respond and ask a question.

Mr. CRUZ. I am happy to yield for a question without yielding the floor.

Mr. DURBIN. The point I would like to make is that the Senator is just plain wrong. What he has stated is just plain wrong. Here is the state of the situation: The health insurance that you enjoy and the Senator from Alabama and I enjoy, as well as the Senator from Virginia, is the Federal Employees Health Benefits Program. It cov-ers 8 million Federal employees and their families, including Members of Congress and our staff. The premiums we pay for the health insurance we choose—the Federal Government as our employer pays 72 percent of the premiums. This is not an unusual situation—150 million Americans, which is half of our population, have exactly the same arrangement. These are employer-sponsored employer contributions to the health care of their employees.

What the President did was to say, No. 1, that you, Senator CRUZ, I, and others will now have to buy our health insurance through the insurance exchanges that we created in ObamaCare. With it, we will get the employer contribution, as we do now—as you enjoy now personally and I enjoy—for that purchase of health insurance.

My wife and I will be choosing a policy from the health insurance marketplace in the State of Illinois. We will have 8 different insurance companies and 165 choices. That is our insurance.

What you quarrel with is the employer contribution to health insurance. If that is now your position and the position of Senator VITTER and the Republican Party, that it is a Federal subsidy which should be stopped, you are affecting the health insurance not just of Members of Congress and their staff but 150 million Americans. You better think twice about this. If you want to stop employer contributions to health insurance, that will be the headline for tomorrow morning. I do not support that. My question is, Do you?

Mr. CRUZ. I thank the Senator from Illinois for his certainly genuine political advice and counsel. I would note that the experience Democratic Senators found under ObamaCare of suddenly facing the prospect of losing their health insurance, of being forced into the exchanges, health insurance that had been employer provided—being forced into the exchanges with no employer subsidy, is a disconcerting experience. It is an experience nobody liked. It is an experience that is lousy. There is a reason why Democratic Senators were so upset. There is a reason why congressional staff were so upset.

What my friend from Illinois is not focusing on is that right now there are Americans all over this country who are experiencing that same exact sentiment because of ObamaCare. Just a few weeks ago UPS sent a letter to some 15,000 employees saying: We are dropping spousal health insurance because of ObamaCare. That is 15,000 UPS employees who had insurance for their husbands and wives, and suddenly those husbands and wives are left without health insurance and being told: Go on an exchange with no employer subsidy. Senator DURBIN just made a passionate case for why that is a terrible thing to tell people. I agree.

Listen, my preferred outcome is not to subject Members of Congress, congressional staff, political appointees of the administration, and Federal employees to the exchanges and ObamaCare. My preference is to subject nobody to that. But the reason Senator GRASSLEY inserted that amendment is because we have a problem of a ruling class in Washington—in both parties; this is a bipartisan affliction—that believes the rules that govern working Americans do not govern us.

So if we are going to set up a system, if ObamaCare is going to force Americans all over this country to lose their employer-provided health insurance, to be forced into the exchanges with no subsidies, then the men and women who serve in this body should feel that pain exactly the same. So when we go on television and say "this is great," we should know of which we speak because we got skin in the game and we are not being treated better. I think under no circumstance should Members of Congress be treated better than hard-working Americans. That is what President Obama did. He did so, by all reports, at the request of Democratic Senators in this body.

Mr. DURBIN. Would the Senator yield for one last question?

Mr. SESSIONS. Would the Senator yield?

Mr. DURBIN. I would like to ask one last question.

Mr. CRUZ. I am going to yield to the Senator from Alabama. I am happy to return to the Senator from Illinois if he would like to remain, but I want to be fair because the Senator from Alabama has been waiting for some time. So I am happy to yield for a question without yielding the floor.

Mr. SESSIONS. I thank the Senator.

An econometric firm and others have studied what is likely to happen in our economy. As I understand it, they predict that far more people will be dumped from coverage into the exchanges than they have today. So people who are under health care coverage today—it is being paid for by their employer. The employer discovers it would be less expensive to quit providing health care coverage and let those individuals go into the exchange, and they may or may not provide any subsidy to them.

So I do think the extent to which we as Senators go into the exchange and are guaranteed the full subsidy we have been getting— that is different from what is going to happen to millions of Americans. I guess the Senator maybe has heard that argument and how it is possible that if businesses decide to drop health care, individuals can then be forced to go into the exchange without any subsidy at all. I would ask Senator CRUZ if he understands that is possibly what could happen to large numbers of Americans.

Mr. CRUZ. I think the Senator from Alabama is exactly right. We are seeing Americans all over this country hurt by ObamaCare.

I want to suggest that the problem we are debating today is bigger than this continuing resolution, it is bigger than ObamaCare, and it is bigger even than the Federal budget. The problem is that the men and women of DC are not listening. They are not listening to the millions of Americans who are asking for more accountability, more responsibility, and more truth from their elected officials. It is time to make DC listen.

I would observe that during the course of this afternoon, the hashtag "MakeDCListen" has been trending No. 1 because the American people are frustrated. They are frustrated that the Democratic Senate is not listening to them. They are frustrated that the Republican Senators are not listening to them. The whole debate we are having right now is not about strategy, it is not about process, it is not about procedures, and it is not about all of the pundits and pollsters and consultants. The problem is that DC is not listening.

Everyone in America knows that ObamaCare is destroying jobs. What the Senator from Alabama so eloquently talked about, the econometric predictions—you have to get outside the beltway to any of the 50 States and actually talk to people who are trying to find jobs and talk to small business owners who are struggling under the 20,000 pages of regulations. Everyone in America knows ObamaCare is destroying jobs and driving up health care costs.

Let me encourage right now everyone in America—President Obama 3½ years ago promised the average American that by the end of his first term, by the end of last year, the average American family's premiums would drop $2,500. Let me encourage everyone in America whose premiums dropped $2,500 to go online and tweet "ObamaCare cut my premium." You know what. I am willing to venture that in every one of these States, if all of the Democratic Senators who support ObamaCare are willing to say "I will take only the votes of those of you whose premiums have gone down," I can tell you right now on the Republican side that I will happily take the votes of everybody else because I am going to predict that is not going to be a 50/50 election, it is not even going to be a 60/40 election. Everyone knows this thing is not working, and Washington is pretending it does not know. This process is rigged. That is why we have to make DC listen.

In traveling across Texas, just like the Senator traveling across Alabama, I hear the stories everywhere I go. It does not matter what town I am in, it does not matter whom I am talking about, I hear the stories. I see people with disabilities saying: Please stop ObamaCare before I lose my health insurance. I see young people who would like to be working toward a career saying: Please, I would like a job.

I met with a whole bunch of service men and women who had just come back from Afghanistan at a military base in Texas. I asked them, as I try do in any gathering that is a small enough group that I can do this: Go around, share an issue that is weighing on your heart, that you pray about, that you are concerned about.

I remember one young soldier said: I am most worried about jobs. When I come out of the military, am I going to have a job? All of my buddies, when they come out, they cannot find jobs.

Everyone nodded and said: That is exactly right.

The American people want to stop this madness. So do I.

Here in Washington we pass million-dollar bills and billion-dollar bills no one has ever read, without even voting on them. We call it unanimous consent. It is only unanimous because we do not let the American people know. It would be very interesting to bring 100 of our constituents in on any unanimous consent that is spending $1 billion here, $1 billion there, and see what our constituents think about that. The system is designed deliberately to hide what we are doing.

In this debate right now there are many Members of this body who are happy that the debate is covered with obscurity over pressure, obscurity over a motion for cloture on a motion to proceed. Nobody knows what that is. You know what. That benefits Members of this body because it lets all 100 go back to their citizens and say: What were you for? Yeah, yeah, I was for that because I was for the motion to whatchamacallit.

No one understands what that is.

You know, one of the things we see is our leaders demand approval for bills before they are amended. So we are being asked this Friday or Saturday to vote to shut off debate on this bill before we know what the bill will be. We do not know what amendment HARRY REID is going to file, but we are asked to cut off debate nonetheless. It is like former Speaker of the House NANCY PELOSI when she said: Pass it to find out what is in it. You wonder why the American people are disgusted with what happens in Washington. That is business as usual in this town.

Listen, the way this is planning to unfold is very simple. Majority Leader REID has said that if he succeeds in cloture, if he succeeds in shutting off debate on Friday or Saturday, that he is going to introduce one amendment—and by all appearances only one amendment—to fund ObamaCare in its entirety. That will be subject to a straight 51-vote threshold.

There are a couple of dynamics going on. No. 1, Republicans are actively debating among ourselves: Should Republicans vote with HARRY REID and Senate Democrats to allow HARRY REID and Senate Democrats to fund ObamaCare with a straight 51-vote partisan majority? I do not find that a difficult question. I think that should unify all 46 Republicans to say no. We should not enable ObamaCare to be funded, and a vote for cloture on Friday or Saturday is a vote to fund ObamaCare. They are one in the same. They are identical.

If you vote to give that power to HARRY REID to fund ObamaCare, then you are responsible for it being funded—and, by the way, for it being funded in the same broken process where there are no amendments, there is no opportunity to change it, there is no opportunity to offer anything. The Presiding Officer will not have an opportunity to offer an amendment, and I will not have an opportunity to offer an amendment. Instead, it is brute political force.

But I will tell of an upside—an upside, frankly, from some Members of the Republican caucus. If debate is cut off, they can tell their constituents: I voted for the House bill. That is not true, but they can tell them that. But even better, a 51-vote threshold—here is the dirty little secret people do not want to admit: There are more than a few Republicans on this side who affirmatively want a 51-vote threshold on funding ObamaCare. Why? Because they want two outcomes. No. 1, if we have a 51-vote threshold on funding ObamaCare, I promise you all 46 Republicans will vote against it. It will be a straight party-line vote, which means every Republican can go back to their district and say: Mr. and Mrs. America, when I had the opportunity to vote against ObamaCare, I did it. I did what you wanted.

I did what you want. The rest of it is kind of hidden in the procedural mumbo jumbo. But the beautiful outcome—and the reason why some Republicans want a 51-vote threshold—is if it is 51 votes we will lose. The President is well aware there are more than 51 Democrats in this body. It will be a partisan party-line Democratic vote, exactly how ObamaCare got passed into law.

I am going to suggest that Republicans going along and saying we want a symbolic vote is not listening to the people. Look, the dysfunction is on both sides. The Democratic Members of this Chamber—I understand, look, ObamaCare is a Democratic law passed and signed into law by a Democratic President, passed into law with only Democratic votes.

It is hard, if you are a political party, to admit, gosh, this thing that we put a lot of political capital in, it ain't working. That is a difficult, risky thing for anyone to say.

I am going to encourage—and my hope is that by the end of this process we will see some Democrats, Senate Democrats, listen to their voters and say: Listen, I thought this thing would work, I hoped it would work, but it hasn't. That is what the unions have said. The labor unions that publicly, vocally supported ObamaCare—and many of them were active proponents of getting it passed—have looked at it and said: Do you know what, we thought it would work and it hasn't.

There is no shame in admitting you tried something and it didn't work. I very much hope over the course of this debate we will see some Democratic Senators doing so. I would note that the fact that Senate Democrats are not participating, are not here, makes it less likely. But on the Republican side, the game is the same.

Washington, DC, is a strange place in many regards, one of which is symbolic votes are treated as tremendously important. I am told of a conversation that Senator LEE had with a Member of the House when early on the House had not yet voted to defund ObamaCare, but there was discussion about casting a symbolic vote to do so. The American people were quite unhappy with that and expressed that view.

Both Senator LEE and I expressed the view that we shouldn't be engaging in procedural games; we should actually be defunding ObamaCare. One particular House Member who will remain unnamed called Senator LEE and made a comment that I thought was particularly revealing. He said: You guys should be grateful. We gave you your vote.

I remember thinking what a curious turn of phrase, "grateful." What an odd, Washington view of things. Why should we feel gratitude for getting a vote that is 100 percent destined to lose because it is offered in such a way that HARRY REID, on a party-line vote, can fund ObamaCare, and yet we can all have a symbolic vote. The reason, frankly, is that this is a town where for a long time neither side has listened to the team. This is the town where for a long time there have been elected politicians who want symbolic votes.

Let me be very clear. I don't want any symbolic votes on anything. I think everyone—our constituents should know what we believe.

Whether or not we get a vote on it to demonstrate it shouldn't matter, because if we are standing and fighting, and if we are walking the walk, our beliefs should be self-evident.

DC responds, the DC establishment responds, if anybody tries to tell the truth—look, I promise you, my observations right now that there are some Republicans that would like a symbolic vote and then would like to lose so that they don't have any risk of it actually being defunded, I promise you those comments are not getting me invited to any cocktail parties in Washington anytime soon. That is perfectly fine. I don't particularly enjoy cocktail parties anyway.

This town needs a lot more truth telling. It is absolutely true. Everyone here knows it, but we are not supposed to say it out loud. There is a custom where we kind of wink at each other and say, listen, you are telling your constituents one thing, I am telling my constituents one thing. Let's not bother to give them the opportunity to know the truth.

If we got 100 of your constituents or mine, if we got 100 citizens from any of the 50 States and we put them in this room instead of 100 Senators, I promise you, No. 1, our constituents would not care about a symbolic vote. If you got 100 people, why would you want a symbolic vote? What is the point of that?

It is only the politicians who make a living staying in office that want symbolic votes. Symbolic votes are useful for getting reelected. They don't actually change the country. They don't make the lives of people better. But they do help politicians who want to get reelected and want to run a campaign ad saying, here is what I voted to do.

If you have 100 citizens in the Commonwealth of Virginia, the great State of Texas, the great State of Alabama, what they would say on ObamaCare is, we have to fix this. We have to get people back to work. We have to deal with all the young people that are stuck in dead-end jobs because they can't get a job coming out of school. We have to deal with all the people, all single moms working in diners who are finding themselves working 29 hours a week because of ObamaCare. We have to deal with all of the people who are struggling because their health insurance premiums are skyrocketing under ObamaCare. We have to deal with all of the people who are losing their health insurance under ObamaCare.

This is why I am speaking out today and why so many others have come here speaking out because we have to make DC listen. That is what this fight is about, to make DC listen to the American people. I very much hope that the debate over the course of this week has a real effect changing the culture. That is why this body has held 10, 12, 14 percent approval ratings.

I remember a few months ago when all of us were in the Old Senate Chamber, all 100 Senators. It was a bipartisan meeting, and it was actually a very interesting, productive conversation. I remember a number of Senators commenting about the low approval ratings that Congress has and saying something to the effect that it is because we are not more efficient, that we don't pass more laws.

I have to say I think that gets it exactly backwards. I have never once found any constituent in the State of Texas—and I suspect there are not many in your State, in my State, or in anyone else's State—who says the problem is you guys aren't passing enough laws. That is not what I hear from people.

It is what you hear from politicians in Washington who would like to pass as many laws as possible so they can take credit for them. But it is not what you hear from people. The people at home say: You guys have done enough damage already. I will tell you why I think we are held in such low esteem. It is because we don't listen to the American people.

In every poll that has been done for years of the American people, in any State, whether your State, my State, any State, even bright blue States, Democratic States, if you ask the American people what is their top priority, jobs and the economy is the overwhelming answer. This is true if you ask Republicans, even if you ask only Democrats. If you ask only Democrats in bright blue States, jobs and the economy are still the top priority—or independents, Libertarians, anyone in the United States.

Yet the Presiding Officer and I have both served in this body 9 months. I would note the 9 months we have been here the Senate has spent virtually zero time talking about jobs and the economy. It is not on the agenda. We don't talk about it. We spent 6 weeks talking about guns, talking about taking away people's Second Amendment right, and no time talking about fundamental tax reform, fundamental regulatory reform. Today we are talking about defunding ObamaCare, the biggest job killer in the country. If you want to get jobs and the economy going, there is nothing we could do that is more important than defunding ObamaCare.

What is the case? There are right now three Members of the Senate on the floor of the Senate and two Members of the House of Representatives. Ask the American people, how many Senators should be here in the debate over defunding ObamaCare, the biggest job killer in this country? Because the American people's top priority is jobs and the economy, the people would say to all 100 Senators, what possibly do you have that is more important to do?

I expect some of my colleagues are at a fundraising dinner. Some of our colleagues are at home with their families.

Do you want to know why Congress is held in such low esteem? It is not that we don't pass enough laws; it is that the priorities of the men and women in this body are not the priorities of the men and women in America. We are not listening to America.

The most important objective, what I hope will come of this week, more important than the continuing resolution and the budget, more important than ObamaCare, is that we make some real progress to changing the culture of this place so that both Democrats and Republicans start listening to the people. That is the way our democratic republic is supposed to work. Right now, unfortunately, it is not how it is working.

Mr. SESSIONS. Will the Senator yield for a question?

Mr. CRUZ. I yield for a question without yielding the floor.

Mr. SESSIONS. The Senator made an important point about too often what goes on around here is that we have to obscure the reality of what is happening. I think that is important. I wish to ask about it. The Senator asked Senator DURBIN—I didn't see exactly how he answered. I think the Senator asked him whether or not he believed in a single payer. I don't think he answered. We know for a fact, though, that Senator REID in August said, when squarely asked: Do you believe in a single payer, he said: Yes, yes, absolutely yes.

What we have learned since then is that others are making the same statement. This spring, Senator SANDERS of Vermont, a nice and able Senator in the Budget Committee, said this bill is not going to work; really, in my view, it is not going to work; It needs to be a single payer.

Senator SANDERS is one of our more liberal Members—and I think it was how he identified himself, as a socialist, but he is an honest, able advocate. He said the truth: this bill, as written, will not work. It has to be a single payer.

Only this afternoon in the Budget Committee, one of our esteemed Members of the Democratic Party, when asked—when I made a comment about Senator REID, that the majority leader of the Senate said he wanted a single payer—he said, this ought to be a single payer system.

I don't know how many others have. The President said, in 2003, when he was running, he flat out said he wanted to have a single payer. Then he backed off and began to obscure that position, it seems to me. It seems to me that they realize that the American people were nowhere ready to have their government take over health care. So what did they do? It seemed to me that they obscured what the reality of this legislation was. They began to move away from it, and they began to say that it was something that it wasn't.

In the last few days it is almost like they have come out here in the open and begun to say that is what should happen. I understand the Democratic leader in the House, NANCY PELOSI, has said that she favors a single-payer system.

I think I will say to Senator CRUZ that I feel you are doing important work because the American people may not yet fully know how huge an issue it is before this Congress. This is huge.

Let me ask again, when we say there is a single payer—hair begins to stand up on my neck—I think I know who the payer is. Who would be the single payer for all health care in America if that kind of agenda took place?

Mr. CRUZ. I thank Senator SESSIONS for that very important question. The payer would be the U.S. Government, which means the payer would be the U.S. taxpayer, which means the payer would be hard-working Americans, once the Federal Government starts paying for all health care in all of America, which has been the stated position of the far left for a long, long time.

The Senator from Alabama made reference to Senator BERNIE SANDERS. I agree. I respect Senator SANDERS's commitment to his principles. As you know, he previously ran as a socialist. That is correct. I respect that degree of candor. Quite frankly, I would be very happy if this body had 10 more BERNIE SANDERS and 10 more MIKE LEES, because I think there would be far more truth in advertising and then we could have real debate about what the role of government should be in our lives.

Should we have socialized medicine? That is a very good debate to have, especially because—and I know the Senator from Alabama agrees with me on this—the facts are on our side. In every country on Earth where socialized medicine has been implemented it hasn't worked. We know what the results are. If you implement socialized medicine, you inevitably see poor quality. You see rationing, you see scarcity. You see the government getting between you and your doctor, the government deciding you want a health treatment, your mother wants a health treatment, your child needs a health treatment. And you have a government bureaucrat deciding whether you get one. Maybe the bureaucrat tells you: Well, you can get that hip replacement you want in 6 months, in 1 year. But they may turn to Senator LEE and say: You know what. Your mom can't get that treatment. We have determined in our tables it doesn't make sense to give her that treatment. I guess she is at the end of her road.

That is what happens. It is the government that decides who gets health care and who doesn't. And you know what. Americans over-whelmingly don't want that. This is another point that is critical. It is not just that Majority Leader REID said he likes single-payer socialized health care; it is that he says, and a number of others have, that ObamaCare is designed to lead to that. I think it is very important to ask the question: Why? How does it lead to that? Because that goes to both sides of the aisle.

There are many Republicans who have said: We shouldn't fight this fight. It is risky. We will get political blame. All of the DC pundits say we shouldn't do this. Let's sit quietly and let ObamaCare collapse. It is collapsing of its own weight, it is not working. If we sit quietly, it will collapse and the Democrats will take the blame. I am suggesting there is far too much worry about blame and credit. Who cares? I don't care if Democrats take the blame. I would prefer to avoid the collapse and spare the Democrats the blame. Who cares?

But if it collapses, why is it that Majority Leader REID says ObamaCare will lead to single payer? Because in the process of the collapse, it will take our private health insurance system with it. Yes, it will collapse, but it will leave a wreckage. It will leave millions of people losing their health insurance, being pushed more and more into the exchanges, with one insurer after the other pushed out of the market. So when it collapses, there is no private health insurance market to go back to. That is why Majority Leader REID can tell the American people: Hey, I want the single-payer socialized medicine. And relax, ObamaCare will take us to that.

But that is also a real message to all the Republicans who right now have not yet announced they are going to oppose cloture on this bill. Because if we wait for ObamaCare to collapse—yes, it will collapse—with it will go the private health insurance system, and we may find ourselves in single payer. I think instead of worrying about blame, instead of trying to play the politics and think through it— and, listen, I am not nearly smart enough to play through all the political angles and everything else—it is a lot simpler to stand and do the right thing. One of the easiest ways to do the right thing is to listen to the American people.

You want to know what the American people are worried about. Go home and listen to your constituents. Their concerns are: I am trying to get a job and I can't get a job. I am trying to grow my small business and ObamaCare is driving us out of business. I am afraid of losing my health insurance and ObamaCare is taking away health insurance.

Look, we have read, and I have stack after stack that I am going to keep reading, from individual constituents—constituents in Texas and Virginia and Utah and Alabama and all over the country—who are losing their health insurance because of ObamaCare, who are losing their jobs and being forced into part-time work. We need to listen to the people.

I told the men and women who are watching tonight if they were to tweet the hashtag "MakeDCListen," which has been, over the course of this, trending No. 1, that I would share some of the tweets they sent. So with your indulgence, I would like to do so to help give them a voice.

Many of these folks right now presumably cannot walk on to the Senate Floor and give a speech. Maybe in a few years some of them might. Maybe in a few years, if enough politicians in this body don't listen to the American people we may get quite a few of these tweeters who show up as new Senators committed to listening to the American people. But in the meantime—

Mr. SESSIONS. Mr. President, will the Senator yield for one question?

The PRESIDING OFFICER. Will the Senator from Texas yield?

Mr. CRUZ. I am happy to yield for a question without yielding the floor.

Mr. SESSIONS. When the Senator thinks about those people who have tweeted and e-mailed and called and have written, most know something about the American system. If you were in Illinois or Alabama or Texas or Utah and you talked about this and said: This law has got real problems and it can't work the way it is, wouldn't the Senator think they would think the Senate would be able to take up this legislation and actually discuss it in a grownup way; that amendments could be offered that could fix it and be voted on up or down?

Doesn't the Senator think the fact we are in this situation—the Senator called it a steamroller—where the majority leader is blocking all amendments, all ability to attempt to fix this legislation and make something that would actually work, even though the House has passed repeatedly changing this law and ending this law, that the average American would be shocked to think we are incapable in this

Senate of bringing up legislation and having it voted on in order to fix this bill?

Mr. CRUZ. I think Senator SESSIONS is absolutely right. The Senate isn't trying to fix this bill. The Senate isn't trying to respond to the needs of the American people. It isn't trying to respond to the jobs that have been lost, to the people who have been forced into part-time work, to the people who have lost their health insurance. Instead, it is responding to political power.

I will note that any Republican—on Friday or Saturday when we have the cloture vote—who votes to cut off debate is voting to give majority leader HARRY REID the ability to force funding for ObamaCare with no changes—no amendments, shutting off amendments. The Senator from Alabama can't offer amendments, I can't offer amendments, and we can't do anything. It is a pure exercise of political power on a straight party-line vote. That will make many Republicans happy because they will get to symbolically vote against it, and then we will be certain to lose if it is a 51-vote threshold.

Part of the reason, I would suggest—and one can understand why the majority leader wants to do that. Listen, if you are defending a law such as ObamaCare, that is a train wreck, in the words of the Democrat who wrote the bill, you don't want to debate the substance of it. When the esteemed Senator from Illinois was down on the floor—and I appreciate his coming—he sure didn't want to debate why there is a congressional exemption, why Members of Congress are treated better than average Americans, why President Obama has said Members of Congress are going to be exempted from ObamaCare but hard-working American families are not.

Look, I understand. If I were the Democratic majority leader and I were defending that position, I wouldn't want to defend it either. Because I have to tell you there is not a State in the Union where our constituents wouldn't just about tar and feather us if we stood in front of them and defended that, yes, there should be a special exemption for Members of Congress but not for you. And for big business. President Obama granted a special exemption for big business, but not for you, not for hard-working Americans.

Look, what a perfect example of the broken system, of the disconnect between DC and the American people. It is indefensible on the merits, and so this whole process is designed not to debate on the merits. It is designed never to have that debate because, as I observed earlier, the old adage in the courtroom—and my friend Senator Lee will recognize this from his days as a litigator, as will the Chair—if you have the facts, pound the facts; if you have the law, pound the law; and if you don't have either, pound the table.

So if you are defending ObamaCare, if you are defending exemptions for giant corporations and Members of Congress that don't go to the average American family, you don't want to talk about the facts and you don't want to talk about the law, so you want to pound the table. You want to talk about shutting down the government. You want to scare people. You want to threaten cutting off the funding of the men and women in the military, which is grossly irresponsible. I think Congress should never ever imperil the salaries of the men and women who risk their lives to protect us.

This body should immediately take up the Defense authorization bill the House passed so that we can make sure the men and women in the military are always paid. And, by the way, even without that—if there were a partial shutdown—the President has all the authority he needs in existing law to pay the men and women in the military.

But if you don't want to debate the merits, you have to distract people. So it is a game. If you talk to a professional magician, magicians are good at banter and they are good at smoke and mirrors and distraction. Sometimes when they raise their hand and they have a shiny object over here and they want everyone to look over here, it is because they are pulling a card out of the deck with this hand. There are a lot of professional magicians in this Senate. There is a purpose to all of the discussion about shutdown and, for that matter, all of the personal politics—all of the attacks, more than a few of which have occurred within the Republican conference, more than a few of which have been directed at Senator Lee, more than a few of which have been directed at myself, and more than a few have been directed at the courageous House conservatives who led the fight in the

House to get the House of Representatives to do the right thing and defund ObamaCare. It is not even the purpose that appears on the face of it. One would think the purpose is as it appears on the face. One would think the purpose for leaking nasty quotes, trying to beat up people, sending congressional staffers to get anonymous quotes—a little bit of profanity, a sort of mean, wicked sense of humor is because they are trying to pound somebody. It is not that, although that is an added side benefit. It is all about distraction. Make it about the personalities, make it about the people, make it about anything, anything, anything other than ObamaCare.

If we were actually talking about ObamaCare, if we were listening to the people—listen, if we were listening to the people, the people don't give a flip about any of the hundred of us. They don't care about politicians. And for good reason. There are very few people in America who say, when asked what do you want to do on the Fourth of July, they want to pal around with a bunch of elected politicians. Most people want to be in their backyard grilling burgers with their kids. God bless them. That is why America is the greatest country on Earth, because we have families and it is not about government. You know, in a totalitarian regime, everyone thinks about government almost all the time. Because when you have a jackboot on the back of your neck, it is hard to think about anything else.

The game in Washington is smoke and mirrors. The game in Washington is distract from anything, anything, anything, except the thing the American people care about—fixing the jobs and the American economy. That is not what is happening.

All right, let me read some tweets.

Mr. SESSIONS. Mr. President, will the Senator yield one more time for a question?

The PRESIDING OFFICER. Will the Senator yield?

Mr. CRUZ. I am happy to yield for a question. I would note my friend from Alabama seems bound and determined to stop the tweets. God bless him.

Mr. SESSIONS. I am interested in those tweets. I just wanted to thank the Senator for what he has done, because I think he is alerting all of us to the critical importance of the health care issue.

This is a plan, it seems to me, and the Senator has expressed it, I believe, to take over health care by the U.S. Government. We can all disagree. I was here when everybody on the Republican side fought this legislation until Christmas Eve, when it was finally rammed through shortly before Scott Brown from Massachusetts could take office and kill it. That is how close it was. I know people disagree about how to deal with it, and I understand and respect people with differing visions, but I wanted to say the Senator's leadership has served a valuable purpose tonight, and I am pleased to be able to support his effort. I wish him every success in those efforts, and I hope, as the Senator continues tonight, he will drive home the critical importance of this issue as we go forward. It is a matter this entire Nation cannot look away from. It is a matter we need to consider fixing because the legislation, as presently written, will not work.

We have two choices, it seems to me. We move forward to a single payer, as Senator SANDERS said we must do because this legislation won't work as written or will we move back to the classical American view of insurance and private health care and our own personal physicians.

I thank the Senator from Texas and would be pleased to hear some of those great tweets I know he has.

Mr. CRUZ. I thank the Senator from Alabama, and I thank him for his perseverance, his leadership, and his courage. I will say there have been more than a few legislative fights, and even a few while I have served in this body, on which JEFF SESSIONS and I have been fighting side by side, and I appreciate his friendship and wisdom, and it matters in this body.

Let's hear from the American people some of the tweets that were sent this afternoon during this discussion:

Already got a second job again because taxes are squeezing me dry. Make D.C. listen.

Congress passes laws that they don't follow, lives large off our money, and has contempt for those they represent. Make D.C. listen.

2700 pages when it was passed, over 20,000 pages now to
implement. Make D.C. listen.

Vote no on cloture. A vote for cloture is a vote to fund
ObamaCare. Defund ObamaCare. Make D.C. listen.

We will not go quietly into this disaster called ObamaCare.
Make it cover everyone or no one. Make D.C. listen.

What a great point. If ObamaCare is such a terrific thing, as its
defenders say, then all of us should be subject to it—big businesses,
Members of Congress, our staffs, President Obama, every political
appointee in the government, every Federal employee.

If that is a burden—and I believe it would be a huge burden—
I would not be eager about that personally, but if that is a burden,
then it shouldn't cover anyone. If there is some reason why that
would be unacceptable—I actually think, of all of those, our friends
on the Democratic side of the aisle would probably get the most
pushback from having it apply to all Federal employees because Federal employees would push back mightily for good reason. But the
right thing to take from that is not, well, all these guys should be
exempt. It is, why would they push back?

If Members of Congress and their staff, Federal employees, the President, and the executive branch employees all found themselves subject
to the same exchanges, the same rules that hard-working Americans
find themselves subject to and they would be really, really dismayed,
that should motivate every one of us to say: Hey, I am a lot more worried about the single mom working in a diner than I am about the IRS
tax agent making $125,000 a year who is dismayed about being subject to
the same rules as that single mom. And if we wouldn't be willing to
make it apply to everyone, then it shouldn't apply to anyone.

Make D.C. listen. Do the right thing and defund this abomination of an unfair tax.

Listen up, America. This is your wake-up call. Make
D.C. listen.

Defund ObamaCare now. We do not need this injurious
legislation to be enacted. Make D.C. listen.

Stay strong. Vote no on cloture. ObamaCare must be stopped. The will of the majority of Americans is to defund ObamaCare. Make D.C. listen.

Sick of our employees deluding themselves into believing they are our bosses. Make D.C. listen.

For those who didn't follow it, we are the employees, the elected representatives who work for the American people, and yet an awful lot of people in this body think we are the bosses. That is exactly backward.

We don't want ObamaCare. We never did. Defund it. Make D.C. listen.

Just finished college. Can't get a full-time job. Thanks, ObamaCare. Make D.C. listen.

There should be no law that exempts a few and burdens the citizens. We, the people, do NOT want ObamaCare. Make D.C. listen.

D.C. a leader out of touch. IRS has no business being involved with health care. Make D.C. listen.

Make D.C. listen, because ObamaCare and its tax will damage the opportunity of Americans to choose the course of their own lives.

My insurance premiums went from $450 in 2010 to $880 in 2013 with $1500 deductible. Make D.C. listen. ObamaCare is a job killer, will ruin health care.

Let's look at those numbers again. Two thousand ten was just a few years ago, and $450 was that individual's health insurance premium. Now it is $880 in 2013. That is the impact ObamaCare is having.

Here is a nice one:

Thank you for reading tweets so the American people can be heard. Make D.C. listen.

You are welcome. It is a privilege to have a chance to in some small way help provide a voice for the American people.

IRS bureaucrats don't want ObamaCare, either, but they are happy to force everyone else to conform to it. Make D.C. listen.

ObamaCare has turned America into a part-time nation. People are losing their homes. They can't feed their children properly. Make D.C. listen.

I wish to think about that last tweet for a second. ObamaCare has turned America into a part-time nation, and people are losing their homes. They can't feed their children properly. If any Member of this body was forced to work part-time, was losing his or her home, couldn't feed his or her children properly, it would be a crisis. Talk about getting our attention—it would be a crisis. If it was a family member, if it was our parents, if our kids were facing that, we would move Heaven and Earth to address it. Yet here it is our boss, the American people who are experiencing that, and most Members of this Senate are doing something else other than being here.

I will note that we have Congressman LOUIE GOHMERT, Congressman PAUL BROUN, and Congressman RICHARD HUDSON was here earlier. But where is the Senate?

We don't feel the pain of the American people like it is ours, like it is us. It is not surprising because President Obama has exempted Congress from ObamaCare, so we are not feeling the pain. That is the problem.

ObamaCare has turned America into a part-time nation and people are losing their homes. They can't feed their children properly. Make D.C. listen.

Three years and they still can't get it going. Make D.C. listen.

Make D.C. listen, because D.C. is not listening to the American people. HELP US.

Defund ACA. It is job killing and not affordable and we won't get care, and our politicians act like it is good for us.

Well, that is true. A lot of politicians do act as though this is really good for you. Mind you, we don't want to be subject to it, but trust us, it is good for you. Different rules apply to the Washington, DC, ruling class than apply to the American people. That is the problem.

Help revive the economy. Make D.C. listen and defund ObamaCare. Fight for real reform.

ObamaCare is a disaster. Make D.C. listen.

Letters saying your plan is cancelled due to the ACA ruins the "like it, keep it" narrative. Make D.C. listen.

By the way, that is from an individual who is @demcalal Makes me wonder if that is a Democrat in California named Al. I don't know if it is, but it would be interesting if it were.

What is interesting about this is that if you get outside of Washington, it is not just Republicans who understand ObamaCare isn't working; it is Democrats, Independents, libertarians.

I feel quite confident that James Hoffa, the president of the Teamsters, is not a Republican. I really have no doubts on that. Yet Mr. Hoffa in a public letter has said that ObamaCare is destroying the 40 hour workweek that is the backbone of the American middle class.

Those are just the facts. That is what is happening. If we were listening to the American people, every one of us would be here doing everything we could to turn it around now. We wouldn't be happy to wait until the end of the week. We would say: Now, let's stop this job killer.

Defund ObamaCare, because I know what is best for my health care, not some bureaucrat. Make D.C. listen.

Defund ObamaCare. The majority of America is against this intrusion into our private relationship with our doctor. Make D.C. listen.

Make D.C. listen because ObamaCare is killing full-time jobs.

Make D.C. listen. Defund ObamaCare because it takes our freedom away.

If you love your country, value freedom and choice, oppose tyranny-style government laws, then make D.C. listen to you.

Tired of Senators who won't listen. Make D.C. listen.

Make D.C. listen. Please stop ObamaCare. It is killing this country.

We need the government to listen to the people and do what is best for the country. I support defunding ObamaCare 100 percent. Make D.C. listen.

Make D.C. listen. We don't want government intrusion into our health care.

D.C. isn't listening. Everyone in America understands that ObamaCare isn't working. Make D.C. listen.

The health care reform that the President sold America isn't the health care reform that America is getting. Make D.C. listen.

ObamaCare. AIN'T NOBODY GOT TIME FOR THAT!!! Make D.C. listen.

Way to go. Make D.C. listen to our voices calling for individual liberty.

Make D.C. listen. We don't get an exception, so you shouldn't either.

I agree. I think all of us should get an exception. Every American should get an exception. And there is no world in which Congress should be treated better than hard-working American families.

I don't want more government. Make D.C. listen.

I wish the Senate would listen to us. Please listen to the people. We don't want this bill. We want freedom. Make D.C. listen.

Make D.C. listen. ObamaCare is turning us into a part-time economy.

Government is designed to go by the will of the people, not the other way around. Make D.C. listen.

We don't want it, don't need it, can't afford it. Please tell them to listen to its citizens. Make D.C. listen.

Ronald Reagan warned us about government-run health care. Bad. Bad. Bad. Make D.C. listen.

Make D.C. listen. Analysts, experts, and business people agree that the ACA will hurt our economy.

Americans are fed up with our elected officials not listening. WE don't want ObamaCare. Make D.C. listen.

Let the free market make health care more affordable by allowing sales across state lines. Make D.C. listen.

Let me say, by the way, that is a terrific proposal. Once we defund ObamaCare, there will be a lot we will need to do on health insurance. There is a lot we need to do on health care reform to make it more affordable, to make policies personal and portable so they go with you regardless of what job you are in.

One of the best things we can do is allow interstate competition. Right now it is illegal to purchase health insurance across State lines. Why does that matter? Well, the biggest barrier to access for people who don't have health insurance is the cost. You get government regulators who drive the cost up and up because they mandate this bell and this whistle, and you have to cover everything they want. It is a great thing for politicians because if you mandate that every health insurance policy has to cover this procedure, it lets politicians come to the people and say: I am giving you free what-have-yous. But one of the simplest principles of government is that there ain't no such thing as a free lunch. Every time you mandate that a health insurance plan must include whatever benefit it is that politicians want to give away to the people, it drives the cost up. Every time the cost goes up, there are more and more people who can't afford it. So you can have a lot of politicians giving away free stuff, and when you do that, it will mean there will be a whole bunch of people who get no coverage at all because they can't afford it.

If we were to allow purchases across State lines, we would see a true 50–State national marketplace, true competition. There would be real choice.

By the way, the people who may be the biggest losers of all under ObamaCare are the young. It is difficult to design a bill to do more damage to young people. The "lost generation" is what economists are now dubbing young people, in significant part because of the consequences of ObamaCare. If you are a young healthy person, it may well make sense to purchase catastrophic health insurance—health insurance that if, God forbid, you get hit by a truck tomorrow or you get diagnosed with some horrible life-threatening disease.

The odds are relatively small that is going to happen to any of us, but if it does, it is very bad, and that is when we want health insurance. If you could purchase insurance across State lines, there would be a 50–State market and you could get low-cost, inexpensive catastrophic health insurance.

If you think about health insurance right now, it doesn't work like insurance. I wish to compare it to an insurance market that works. Most of us are familiar with car insurance. Most of us who have cars have car insurance. With car insurance, if you need to change the oil in your car, you do not call Allstate and say: Change the oil in my car. If you get a flat tire, you typically do not call Allstate and say: Hey, I have a flat tire, change the tire on my car. God forbid, if you get hit by an 18-wheeler and your car gets totaled, then you call your insurance company and say this catastrophic event happened; that is why I have insurance. A lot of people when it comes to health insurance though, right now the system is treated as just a third-party payer instead of dealing with catastrophic, unlikely events. That is a reform that would make a real difference.

If you want access to low-cost health insurance, allowing people to purchase it across State lines after we defund ObamaCare would make a real difference, and if we added to that reforms that expanded health savings accounts so you could save in a tax-advantaged way to meet routine prevention and maintenance, to take care of the equivalent, in the auto context, of changing the tire, that would go even further; and if we changed the tax law right now—most people do not know that employer-provided health care is an historical anomaly. It actually arose during World War II. Shortly thereafter, when wage and price controls were in effect, employers had a challenge. They wanted to recruit employees, but they could not raise wages. It was against the law. So they began offering health insurance as a way to attract people, to say come work for my company, we will give you health insurance.

Right now the Federal tax laws heavily favor employer health insurance. The problem is, we don't live in 1950s America now. There was a time when people would get a job in a big company and work 30, 40, 50 years, retire, get a gold watch, and that would be it. We don't live in that kind of world anymore.

Most people will work for one company, then another company, then another company—relatively unlikely that American workers are going to stay with one company their entire life. They are going to switch jobs, possibly a lot, sometimes voluntarily and sometimes not voluntarily.

When you and I were in the private sector, Mr. President, if we lost our jobs and got fired, you didn't lose your life insurance. You didn't lose your car insurance. You didn't lose your house insurance. The only insurance you would lose if you lost your job was your health insurance. That doesn't make any sense. Of all of them it is the worst one to lose.

The Senator from Illinois asked about preexisting conditions. If we could change the law so health insurance plans were personal and portable, just like your car insurance, regardless of where you happen to work it goes with you, it travels with you, that goes a long way to solving the problem of preexisting conditions, because where preexisting conditions have such a big impact is when somebody loses one job and is trying to get coverage for the next job. If you could take your personal portable plan with you, that goes a long way to mitigating it. Let me point out all of those reforms have a fundamentally different philosophy than ObamaCare. ObamaCare has a philosophy—empower government over your life, put a government bureaucrat between you and your doctor. The reforms I laid out are all about empowering you, the American people, empowering you, the patient, to make a choice, empowering you to make decisions about your health care with your doctor, with no government bureaucrat anywhere near you. I am going to suggest the difference is those plans come from listening to the people. ObamaCare is the opposite of listening to the people.

Mr. LEE. Will the Senator from Texas yield for a question?

Mr. CRUZ. I am happy to yield to my friend from Utah for a question, and I will return with yet more tweets at a later point.

Mr. LEE. I say to Senator CRUZ I have come with some updates from the outside world, updates based on what I am hearing from my constituents at home. You may be interested in learning, I say to Senator CRUZ, that just today in the last 12 hours or so my office has received nearly 1,100 e-mails, 1,093 to be precise. Almost every single one of those is asking us to do whatever we can, do whatever it takes, to defund ObamaCare. People are asking us to fund government, keep government functioning, but to defund ObamaCare.

I also have some news from a local paper in the State of Utah. This is from the *Box Elder News Journal* in the northern part of my State. In an article written by Mike Nelson, an associated editor with the *Box Elder News Journal*, we read about Brigham City moving to adjust its pay, to cut its payroll, in order to avoid certain ObamaCare provisions. I am going to quote just from part of it here. It says:

> Changes are coming for paid on-call employees at Brigham City Emergency Services Department in an effort by the department and the city to avoid employee eligibility for health care under the Affordable Care Act. "Back in February it became apparent the ACA—

Or for those of you who see the newspapers, ObamaCare—

> was going to dramatically impact the way we manage our fire and ambulance crews," said emergency services director Jim Buchanan, while addressing the issue at an August 1 city council meeting.

This is one of many examples of not just businesses but also local governments that are having to make cuts in their payroll in order to adjust for this law. This is having a real impact on real people.

It is having an impact also on students. I received a message from a student in Utah named Sarah. Sarah, today, a college student, writes:

> I am a student facing a shrinking job market with fewer options. Now it seems ObamaCare is going to force me as a healthy young person to pay more to keep the President's health plan functioning. How is that fair?

She asks rhetorically. Sarah, it is not fair. Sarah, I would add to that, we have this health care law called the Patient Protection and Affordable Care Act. The idea of it is it is supposed to make health care more affordable. What we have found in recent months is that it is going to make health care less affordable, with premium hikes expected around the country. What we are seeing is that this law will make health care not only less affordable, it is also fundamentally unfair. It is unfair in that it is forcing a lot of people to have cuts made to their wages, cuts made to their hours. In many cases, people are losing access to health care plans that they have enjoyed for years. In some cases, they are even seeing that they will no longer have access to the same physician or other health care provider that they have enjoyed for years.

This is a law that while touted as making health care somehow more affordable is actually making it less affordable. It is also being implemented in a manner that will make our health care system fundamentally unfair. Within my State, the State of Utah, we have no fewer than five school districts and three universities that have been announcing cuts in their hours, cuts in their number of employees, all in response to this law. It is interesting that what we are discussing, much of what we have been discussing, has been on the upcoming cloture vote. There have been those who have argued that if you want to support the continuing resolution passed by the House of Representatives—remember, this is the continuing resolution that will keep our Federal Government funded while defunding ObamaCare—that if you want to support that, that you must vote yes on the cloture vote on the bill.

That is an interesting take on it because not withstanding the fact that some in my party have been making that suggestion, it is anticipated that Mr. HARRY REID—the Senator from Nevada who is currently serving as the Senate majority leader—that HARRY REID and 53 Democratic allies will, as I understand it, all be voting for cloture on that bill. That begs the question, are those same people who are suggesting that if you support the House-passed continuing resolution, the one that funds government, keeps government funded while defunding ObamaCare, that you have to vote yes on cloture on the bill, does that mean that HARRY REID and the 53 Democrats who are likely to follow him are also supporting the House-passed continuing resolution, the one that keeps government funded while defunding ObamaCare?

I find that a little strange. I find that a little counterintuitive. I think it is important that we remember, and we continually remind ourselves, what this is about. When this continuing resolution passed by the House last week—heroically in my opinion. It showed a real strong sense of leadership by Speaker JOHN BOEHNER and by the other Republican leaders in the House of Representatives and by the rank-and-file Members of the House who voted for this legislation. When they voted for this legislation to keep government funded while defunding ObamaCare they stood with the American people who asked them for relief from this bill.

American people had been telling them: Look, we need help. They have been asking: How many of us will have to see our hours cut? How many of us will have to experience wage cuts? How many of us will have to lose access to the health care we have enjoyed for many years before Congress acts?

The House of Representatives did act. The body within our government, the branch within Congress that is most responsive to the American people, acted to protect the American people from this harmful law while simultaneously keeping the Federal Government operating.

Now that that has happened and that bill is moving over to the Senate, the ball is in our court, we have a couple of possible responses to that. The first would be we could take it up and we could vote on it as is. We could vote on it just as it was passed by the House. We could vote on it, up or down, as is without any amendment. That would be fine. I would be fine with that. If that is what we were doing, I would be voting yes on the cloture vote. Of course I would. I suspect my friend, the junior Senator from Texas, would as well.

There is another option. We could say rather than vote on it as is, let's make adjustments to it. Let's invite amendments. Let's have an open amendment process whereby Senators, whether Democrats or Republicans or the couple of Independents we have, could submit amendments as they deem fit, have those amendments not just proposed but debated, discussed, and ultimately voted upon. That would be an acceptable alternative.

People around here often call this, the Senate, the world's greatest deliberative body. They call it that because this is a place where, in theory, we are supposed to have access to an open amendment process; theoretically unlimited debate. Is it time consuming? Yes. Is it cumbersome? Absolutely. Can it be frustrating? Without question. But it is one of the things that distinguishes this body. It is one of the things that makes this the Senate.

So if we were to have an open amendment process, it would take a lot of time and it might even require another all-night session just like we had a few months ago in connection with the budget resolution, but it would be worth it. It would be entirely acceptable, and I would be voting yes on cloture on the bill if that is what we were faced with. But what we are faced with, what we are told is going to happen, what we are told is being prepared to accept is neither of those options; not being given the opportunity to vote yes or no, up or down on the resolution passed by the House of Representatives nor would we be given the opportunity to have an open amendment process, one that allows individual Senators to propose amendments and have those amendment considered, voted on in this body.

What we are being told instead is that what we will have is a single amendment brought forward by the Senate majority leader, one amendment and one amendment only, and that amendment, by the way, would strip out the defunding language, it would gut the House-passed continuing resolution of a provision that many would consider the "without which not" part of the House-passed bill, meaning the part without which the House of Representatives could not and would not have gotten the necessary 218 votes to pass a continuing resolution. That is a problem. That is a problem indeed because that suggests that by voting for cloture in that posture, where Senator REID is contemplating allowing neither an open amendment process nor an up-or-down vote on the House-passed resolution in as-is condition—in either of those circumstances, we would be fine. But we are not getting that. We are getting stuck with something else. He wants to gut the House-passed continuing resolution with the defunding language without any open amendment process and without the opportunity for an up-or-down vote.

So in that circumstance, I don't understand why it would be the case that Republicans would feel that voting yes would be supporting the House of Representatives and voting no would be voting against the House of Representatives. In fact, it seems to me, I say to Senator CRUZ, that would be quite the opposite of that. It seems to me that if, in fact, one wanted to stand behind the House of Representatives and stand behind their willingness to defend the American people and protect them from this harmful law, at the end of the day that would entail that anyone who wanted to stand with the House of Representatives on that point would necessarily need to vote no if, in fact, Senator REID does what we expect him to do later this week.

Would the Senator agree that is what one could expect in that circumstance? And would the Senator also agree that Senator REID is likely to have 53 Democrats going along with him, and if Senator REID has 53 Democrats going along with him, doesn't that rather undercut the argument that in order to support the House-passed bill one must vote yes on the cloture vote on cloture on the bill?

Mr. CRUZ. I thank Senator LEE for his very good question. I think the answer is absolutely yes. If the objective of any Senate Republican is to support the House Republicans, the bill they passed to defund ObamaCare, then one obviously would not vote to allow Majority Leader HARRY REID to strip out all of the operative language and to fund ObamaCare with a 51-vote pure-partisan Democratic majority. That is not complicated. To be honest, it is something every Senator in this body understands. All the Democrats understand it. It is why HARRY REID is voting yes on cloture. It is why, presumably, every Democrat will vote yes on cloture. Why? It is the reason some of our colleagues have used as well: A "yes" vote on cloture says that they support the House of Representatives' bill and support defunding ObamaCare.

I suppose that means, then, that HARRY REID suddenly supports defunding ObamaCare and that every Democrat supports defunding ObamaCare. I say to my friend Senator LEE that I would be very happy if that were the case. If that interpretation were right and suddenly HARRY REID and every Democrat supported defunding ObamaCare, that would be terrific. We know for a fact it is not the case. We know for a fact it is not the case because they publicly said it. We know for a fact it is not the case because just yesterday I asked for unanimous consent to simply pass the House bill. If every Democrat and HARRY REID supported defunding ObamaCare, he wouldn't have objected.

Everyone understands that the cloture vote on Friday or Saturday will be a vote to allow HARRY REID to fully fund ObamaCare using only a 51-vote majority that allows it to be done on a straight partisan line. There is no confusion on that. Every Democrat understands that, and every Republican understands that.

However, there is some confusion, but not in this body, and it is so Senators believe with the American people because Senators think, well, the politics and procedural mumbo-jumbo is confusing enough that I can vote yes, give HARRY REID the ability to fund ObamaCare, and at the same time I can run paid advertisements—as more than a few of our colleagues may well be doing right now—that say: I want to defund ObamaCare. They can't do both. They can't hand HARRY REID the ability to fund ObamaCare and claim they want to defund it. Pick a side. Pick a position and stand by your beliefs.

I will give an analogy. The House of Representatives passed a bill that cut taxes, and then it came over to the Senate. Majority leader HARRY REID announced that he wanted to file for cloture on that bill, and then after that happened, he would file an amendment to erase all the tax cuts and to jack up taxes by $1 trillion. Let's suppose he announced this publicly and told everyone: This is what I plan to do—and by the way, it is going to be the only amendment. I will totally gut the House bill and turn a tax cut into a tax increase. I am absolutely certain if that were the case all 46 Republicans would vote against cloture. We get the game.

Voting to cut off debate is voting to allow the majority leader to gut the House bill. So any Senator who votes for cloture is saying: I want the majority leader to be able to gut the House bill. But it is even better than that. What was it that P.T. Barnum said? You can fool some of the people all the time, and all the people some of the time, but you can't fool all of the people all of the time. [This was actually first said by Abraham Lincoln.] There are a lot of Members of this body who think: Some of the people all of the time will be just good enough for me. If I can vote to give HARRY REID the ability to fund ObamaCare, and then, beauty of all beauty, when we get to a 51-vote threshold on ObamaCare, I can vote against funding ObamaCare, I can go home and say: Hey, I voted twice the right way. Of course, I did it in a way that guaranteed 100 percent that we are going to lose. It guaranteed that ObamaCare would be funded.

Now, for that strategy to work, it depends upon voters being really gullible and confused.

I was reading tweets earlier. Earlier we talked about how we are not living in the 1950s. In many respects we are not living in the 1950s. One of those respects is we no longer have three big networks that control all the news and limited avenues for the American people to find out what is going on. We have seen a democratization of information. We now have cable TV and more channels, it seems, than one could possibly imagine. We have avenues such as FOX News that get out content that the mainstream media won't cover in an effort to provide fair and balanced news. We have talk radio. God bless talk radio. It is an avenue to reach out to millions of Americans, and it is able to go right around the media gatekeepers. We have the Internet. We have social media. We have Facebook and Twitter. We can disseminate information directly.

In the 1950s one could do some procedural smoke-and-mirrors. One could hide an obfuscation, and people wouldn't know. One of the fascinating things—and I suspect the Presiding Officer has done this as well as an avid student of history—is listening to the old L.B.J. tapes. L.B.J. would be talking to one group on tape and say: I am totally with you. And then he would be on tape talking to the other side saying: I am totally with you. He would tell different groups things that were 180 degrees opposite of each other. He would say one thing to one group and another thing to another group. They were so different, they would never get a chance to reconcile.

I would suggest that in 2013 that is a lot harder to do. In 2013, if they tell one group they are totally with them, you better believe the other group will find out about them.

In 2013, if a Member votes—I hope they don't, but some Republicans might—to give HARRY REID the power to fund ObamaCare on a straight partisan 51-vote threshold, then that Member is voting to fund ObamaCare and their constituents are going to know about it. It is not anything any of us are going to do because our constituents are now engaged and following this debate directly. So the ad that says "I am for defunding ObamaCare" while at the same time fighting to keep funding ObamaCare doesn't work in the Internet age. It doesn't work.

What is the old line? I try not to lie. I try to tell the truth because it is so hard to keep track of the lies. Instead of telling people multiple positions, just stand and fight for what you believe in.

Earlier we were talking about BERNIE SANDERS. I respect the heck out of BERNIE SANDERS. Actually—and this is a comment that often surprises our friends in the media and even some Democrats— I respect President Obama. I respect the man a great deal because I think he is deeply committed to his principles. I think he has taken political risks for his principles, I think he has fought for them, and I think he is a true believer. Everything I have seen about his entire course of life—I think he believes genuinely, earnestly, and with all of his heart in government solutions, government control of the economy and our lives, and in redistribution of wealth. I have no reason to doubt that the President sleeps like a babe at night believing that he is fighting to better America. At the same time, I believe the ideas the President believes in and the policies he has advanced are profoundly harmful—not a little bit wrong but profoundly harmful to this country.

You know what. That is a debate we can have. That is a policy debate I welcome. Has it been good or bad for Americans to implement ObamaCare? Has it been good or bad for Americans to see jobs drying up? Has it been good or bad for Americans to see small businesses not grow anymore? Has it been good or bad for Americans to see health insurance premiums skyrocketing? Has it been good or bad for Americans to see more and more people losing their health insurance? That is a debate I am happy to have on the substance. That is an honest debate. The President embraces that policy.

I will confess that what produces more of the cynicism and skepticism toward Washington are the politicians who don't have the honest debates and don't say: You know what. I am not all that fond of ObamaCare, but it doesn't matter enough to me to risk anything on it. I care more about staying in office than I do, actually, about fighting a fight. So I want to take some symbolic votes, and I don't want to risk any chance of anyone blaming me for the downside.

I get why voters are frustrated with that. I get why voters are frustrated with politicians saying one thing and doing another. It shouldn't be complicated. Do what you say. It shouldn't be complicated. Stand for your principles. If you don't believe ObamaCare should be funded and that Obamacare is hurting Americans, then stand and say: Let's defund ObamaCare.

I have made it very clear that we could end this debate right now if the majority leader would come down and say—look, the best way to end this debate would be if he would agree to pass the House continuing resolution to fund all of government except for ObamaCare. I recognize that is not likely to happen anytime soon, but it would be the best way, and it would be the way that is most responsive to the

American people. But the second way to end this debate—and, by the way, to expedite this whole process—is to simply have the majority leader agree to have open amendments and have those amendments subject to a 60-vote threshold.

The Presiding Officer and I have both been here the same number of months—9 months. During the time we have been here, we have seen vote after vote after vote with a 60-vote threshold. That is very common.

The Presiding Officer will remember the guns debate we had. Guns are an emotional and passionate issue. It is an issue people on both sides care a lot about. I get that. The Presiding Officer will remember that when we voted on the floor of this Senate, every single amendment was subject to a 60-vote threshold.

In the course of that debate, I introduced, along with Senator CHUCK GRASSLEY, the Grassley-Cruz bill. It was a law enforcement alternative. Instead of restricting the Second Amendment rights of law-abiding citizens, it was targeting violent criminals. It was going after felons and fugitives who tried to illegally buy guns. It was going after those who commit violent crimes with guns. It was going after States that don't report mental health records to the background check system.

We just saw a horrific shooting in Washington, DC. All of us are mourning for the victims and the families there. The individual, it appears, had significant mental health issues. The Grassley-Cruz bill would have mandated significant incentives and penalties for States to get them to report mental health records, because our background mental health system doesn't work if we don't have the mental health records in them. As of a date relatively recently—I don't recall the date off the top of my head but relatively recently this year—I believe there were 18 States that reported 100 or fewer records.

The Presiding Officer will recall what happened with that bill, and every amendment. We got a majority. A majority of Senators voted for the Grassley-Cruz bill. Indeed, nine Democrats voted for the Grassley-Cruz bill. It was the most bipartisan of any of the comprehensive gun legislation that was considered by this body. There was no other comprehensive bill that had anywhere close to that level of bipartisan support across the aisle. Yet the Grassley-Cruz bill did not pass into law. It didn't even get sent over to the House. Why? Because there was a 60-vote threshold because, effectively, Majority Leader REID filibustered it.

As important as guns are, I think restoring jobs and the economy, restoring economic growth, dealing with the train wreck that is ObamaCare, is at least as important to the American people. The idea that somehow a 60-vote threshold was OK there but here there has to be a partisan exercise in brute power in my view is completely inconsistent with the traditions of this great body. But I will note it serves the purposes of politicians on both sides of the aisle. It serves the purposes of Democrats because most Democrats right now still want to preserve ObamaCare.

Most Democrats, in my view, are privately getting more and more nervous about the train wreck that this is. They are seeing—we can't go home and talk to our constituents without seeing the job loss and the health insurance premiums going up and people losing their health insurance. I think most Democratic Senators are nervous about it but not yet ready to abandon ship. On the Republican side, there is not a Republican here who doesn't enjoy giving speeches about ObamaCare. We can give speeches, humdingers sometimes. But there are more than a few Republicans who are nervous about actually doing anything that has a real chance of happening, because anytime we take a stand that has risk, there is downside to risk. If we hold our ground, if the House holds their ground, it is entirely possible that majority leader HARRY REID and President Obama will force a government shutdown. I don't think they should. I think it will be a mistake. But they have said they are willing to shut the government down in order to force ObamaCare on the American people. That has a lot of people on the Republican side in the conference nervous because they think, Well, if President Obama and HARRY REID shut the government down, they will blame it on Republicans and the media will all repeat that attack. The mainstream media, every one of them, will repeat word for word the talking points. It will get to the point that the stories we read in the major newspapers will read as if they were written by the White House Press Office.

But that has been the way of the world for a long time. So there are Republicans nervous about, Well, even if the President and HARRY REID force a shutdown, Republicans will get blamed and we don't want the political blame so we don't want to fight this fight. In fact, a lot of Republicans have gone out to the press and said, We can't win, we can't win, we can't win. When we have a lot of Republicans saying we can't win, that is one way to make it less likely we are going to win.

It is true if Republicans don't stand together on this, we can't win. Some have asked, Why haven't Democrats come over to join us? Listen, the Presiding Officer and I both know no Democrat is going to come join us as long as half the Republican conference is split and throwing rocks at us. There is no incentive for anyone to do that now. The only hope of bringing Democrats over to join us is if we first unify Republicans. If we get all 46 Republicans to stand together opposing cloture and to say, No, we are not going to let HARRY REID shut down all amendments; we are not going to let HARRY REID fund ObamaCare on a straight partisan party-line vote; and then, if those Democrats elected in red States begin hearing from their constituents in incredible numbers—listen, I will tell my colleagues, the people of Arkansas, the people of Louisiana, the people of North Carolina, they understand ObamaCare is a train wreck. They would like their Senators to listen to them. The Presiding Officer and I both know, when we start to hear from 5,000, 10,000, 20,000, 50,000 of our constituents, it changes our calculus. If there is one thing the men and women of this body like, it is to get reelected. The only way this fight is going to be won is if the American people speak so loudly that the politicians in this body have no choice but to listen to the people.

Let me give an example, an example the Presiding Officer and I spoke about at the time. About a month ago, we all remember that President Obama publicly announced his intention to launch a unilateral military attack on the nation of Syria. When that happened, bipartisan leaders in both the House and the Senate fairly quickly came out in support of that plan. Just about every commentator— just about every talking head in Washington—said there was no chance of stopping it. It was going to happen. It was a done deal. It was going to happen. In fact, they were the same voices who are saying now, with regard to defunding ObamaCare, it can't be done, accept it, accept it, it can't be done, it can't be done. All of those exact voices said about Syria: He is going to attack, there is nothing we can do, it will be done.

The Presiding Officer and I both spoke out loudly, saying the President should bring the issue to Congress, and I commend the President for listening to bipartisan calls. That was not easy. I have no doubt there was significant dissension among his advisers who didn't want him to do so, and I commend the President for listening to those bipartisan calls. It was the right thing to do. Once he submitted it to Congress, what happened next the Presiding Officer and I both know because we both went home to our respective States. People in our States were not evenly divided on the question of Syria. It wasn't a close call. I can tell my colleagues in my office the calls literally went 100 to 1 against the United States launching a unilateral military attack against Syria and getting involved in that sectarian civil war in a way that didn't further our national security. We had over 5,000 calls from Texans opposing getting us in the middle of that Syrian civil war. We had roughly 50 in support of it. I think the percentage in our office at one point was 99.13 percent of the calls were against military intervention.

We saw something even more incredible. Everyone said it was a done deal and the Senate was going to vote to approve it. The more the American people spoke up, the more people in this body began listening, the more some of those who early on were fans of the military intervention suddenly began listening to their constituents and saying, I am not so sure this makes sense.

And then astonishingly, remarkably—and I give him credit for this—the President of the United States listened, and the President went before this Nation and asked this body, do not vote on this. I am glad he did, because if we had voted, I think at that point it was very clear he would have lost the vote, that Congress would not have voted to authorize military force. The House clearly would have voted against it and I think there is a good chance the Senate would have also, although the Senate is a little harder to predict. I am glad the President asked us to call off that vote, because I don't think it is good for this country, for Congress to vote against the Commander in Chief on issues of national security and defending this Nation, so I am glad we didn't have that vote. But I am glad he listened to the American people.

I want to point out, for everyone who says defunding ObamaCare is impossible, they are the same voices who said stopping the attack on Syria was impossible—the exact same voices, graybeards—all of the media.

The only thing that is going to change the dynamic in this body, the only thing that is going to unite 41 Republicans against cloture, against ObamaCare, and to defund ObamaCare, is if the voice of the people becomes so loud it can't be ignored. The only thing that is going to start moving red State Democrats is if the voice of the people in their States becomes so loud they cannot be ignored. Ultimately, that is how we win this fight. It comes down to the people.

I would also like to have a bit of a discussion on an issue that I would note the Presiding Officer and Senator LEE both care about and are quite expert in, which is constitutional law and the separation of powers. We have often seen pundits go on television and they use a phrase that I think is particularly asinine. They say, Republicans cannot expect to—fill in the blank here—defund ObamaCare, cut taxes, push tax reform, have regulatory reform—do anything— Republicans cannot expect to X because we control just one-half of one-third of the government. The only thing the Republicans have in Washington is a majority in the House, and they can't do anything from one-half of one-third of the government. There is a technical legal term for that argument: It is poppycock. It is complete and utter nonsense. That is not the way our constitutional system works.

It is true that Democrats currently have a majority in the Senate and that a Democrat sits in the White House. That is true. But the Constitution gives different branches different responsibilities and in their respective spheres each branch has exceptional power. So when it comes to ordering our military troops into battle, to selecting targets, to making direct decisions of military conflict, the President of the United States is Commander in Chief, and it does not matter if the President is a Democrat or whether 535 Members of Congress are

Republicans. When it comes to being Commander in Chief, when it comes to ordering our troops into battle, to making decisions in the midst of conducting war, the Constitution gives the President preeminent authority on that under article II.

When it comes to adjudicating the constitutionality of law—one could make arguments about whether this is right—but as a practical matter, the Constitution and modern acceptance gives the Supreme Court preeminence in adjudicating whether a law comports with the Constitution. I would note that is true even if five Justices of the Court are appointed by a different political party, the party that controls both Houses of Congress and the Presidency. We could have five Justices appointed by a Democratic President and 535 Republican Members of Congress and a Republican President. Yet on the questions of adjudicating the constitutionality of the law, the Supreme Court would still have preeminence and very significant authority.

When it comes to appropriations, when it comes to the power of the purse, when it comes to spending, article I of the Constitution gives Congress preeminence and, in particular, the House of Representatives. So I will be perfectly honest. If I were to pick one thing for Republicans to have control over, particularly when it comes to funding or defunding something, it would be the House of Representatives. Every pundit who goes on television and says, Well, we just control one-half of one-third of the government—what complete and utter nonsense. Not a single law can pass into law without the House of Representatives. It is a necessary but-for. And on questions of spending, the House of Representatives has preeminence. So this notion that it can't be done—and a related point. There are some on the Democratic side of the aisle who make the argument this is the settled law of the land. Accept it already. You guys are bitter enders. We passed it into law. We won a Presidential election again. Game over. You lose.

I understand the political virtue of making that argument. It is always good to convince those who disagree with you to give up their beliefs. Sometimes those on this side of the aisle oblige by doing so. But it is not an argument that has any basis in the Constitution. Is

ObamaCare currently the law of the land? Of course. It was passed into law, it is in the statute. It is on the books.

No one on this side of the aisle has argued it is not. We are arguing it should not be. That is a very different thing than saying it is not.

Congress has the power of the purse. Congress has the power—let me finish this point, and then I am happy to yield for a question. Congress has the power to appropriate. There is no obligation for Congress to appropriate, to fund a law that is not working, that evidence and experience—that what the American people are experiencing has demonstrated it is not working.

So the House of Representatives in voting to defund ObamaCare, while funding the rest of government, is fulfilling its constitutional function. If this body took up that same gauntlet, kept government funded, never shut down government, funded every aspect of government except ObamaCare because it is not working, it is hurting the American people, we would be fulfilling our constitutional function as well.

(Mr. MURPHY assumed the Chair.)

I would note the Senator from Virginia rose for a question. I am happy to yield for a question without yielding the floor.

Mr. KAINE. I thank the Senator.

I would ask the Senator to yield for a series of questions around two issues—first, comments the Senator made earlier about helpful reforms that could be made to the health care system and, second, the Senator's comments about the need for Members of this body to listen to their constituents. Being in the chair and hearing the Senator, I could not resist but to follow up on those two items.

On the issue of reforms, I understood one of the Senator's points to be that a helpful reform might be for Congress to take up and potentially eliminate the current prohibition of purchasing insurance across State lines. Did I hear that correctly?

Mr. CRUZ. Yes, that is correct.

I am happy to yield for a second question without yielding the floor.

Mr. KAINE. In addition, I think I understood, and I agree with a comment the Senator made about potential reforms—that even the whole notion of health care provided through employers is a little bit of a historical anomaly that came up in the aftermath of World War II.

I was not sure if the Senator was suggesting that as part of a health care reform he would want to alter that norm of employers providing at least some health care provision for their employees.

Mr. CRUZ. I thank the Senator for that question.

What I was suggesting is we should do tax reform that encourages policies to be personal and affordable. Right now, Federal tax laws, Federal laws heavily favor employer-provided health insurance, and that creates some real failures in the market where when someone loses their job, they lose their health insurance. We would be better serving, I believe, our constituents if health insurance became like car insurance, something that went with you regardless of what job you were in.

Mr. KAINE. I say to the Senator, you engaged in a colloquy with the Senator from Illinois about a provision that I wanted to follow up on.

Prior to the passage of the Affordable Care Act, it was completely lawful and, in fact, common for insurance companies to turn down individuals for insurance because of preexisting health conditions. I do not think—but I want to make sure about this—I do not think the Senator was arguing that we should go back to that day and that we should go back to a status quo where children would be turned down for health insurance because of preexisting health care conditions.

Mr. CRUZ. I thank the Senator for that question.

Let me point out that preexisting conditions and the individual mandate of ObamaCare are integrally connected because the way the insurance market works—let me take an example that does not deal with health care. Let's talk about fire insurance, fire insurance on your home.

I suspect both our homes have fire insurance. Imagine if Congress were to pass a law that says fire insurance companies cannot take into account preexisting conditions, such as whether the home has already burned down in a fire.

If that were the law, what any rational person would do—we would both cancel our fire insurance policies because our house had not burned down, and if it did burn down, we could then buy a fire insurance policy and say: Please pay for my house.

Under that rule, the whole insurance regime collapses because the entire basis of insurance is you get people whose homes have not burned down to pay relatively small premiums to create a pool of capital that will be used to compensate—we do not know who, but somebody's home is going to burn down. If enough people whose homes have not burned down put in money in premiums, there will be a pool to pay for whichever unlucky soul faces their home burning down.

The health insurance market works quite similarly. If the rule is simply that for anyone, regardless of their medical condition, any insurance company has to cover them, no matter what, then the incentive is the same as with fire insurance; that if the Senator and I are healthy, it is, frankly, irrational to get health insurance, if the rule is, if I get sick, then I can get health insurance and they have to cover me. What you end up with is insurance that consists only of people who have sicknesses, who have grave diseases, and that bankrupts every insurance plan. If you have a mandate that you cannot take into account whether someone is already sick before giving them insurance, it means the insurance companies go out of business, and what it leads to is what Majority Leader REID has argued for—it leads ultimately to single-payer government health insurance.

· Mr. KAINE. Does the Affordable Care Act require that insurance be provided to folks despite preexisting conditions at the same rate across the board?

Mr. CRUZ. It restricts the terms at which the rates are given.

Mr. KAINE. So then, to make sure I understand, the Senator is opposed to the provision in the current Affordable Care Act that requires insurance companies to write insurance to individuals within those limitations, regardless of preexisting conditions.

Mr. CRUZ. Let me finish my explanation on that. I will answer the Senator's question, but I wish to finish the explanation. That is the reason ObamaCare includes the individual mandate. Because, to use the fire example again, it would be the equivalent of, if you are saying you have to issue a fire policy to anyone regardless of whether their house has already burned down, it would be the equivalent of saying we are requiring everyone who has a house to buy a policy. Because that is the only way you prevent the insurance market from being bankrupt.

So the individual mandate, the reason ObamaCare says we are forcing everyone to buy insurance—whether you want to or not—is because of the preexisting condition.

Now listen, my view on preexisting conditions is we ought to reform the market to deal with that problem. I do not think ObamaCare is the right solution. I think ObamaCare is the wrong solution. I think we ought to defund it all now. I think we ultimately ought to repeal it in its entirety.

But on preexisting conditions, I will point out, No. 1, if you have an issue—and there have been issues with insurance companies acting in bad faith, with insurance companies dropping someone when they get sick, and I think there the legal system should work to prevent that. If you have purchased insurance, if you have paid your premiums, your company should not be dropping you when you become sick. I think there is a vital role for State insurance regulators to be involved there and for our contract and tort system—the legal system—to be involved.

I think if we move toward changing the Federal tax laws to make health insurance policies portable, personal, it will go a long way to solving the problem of preexisting conditions. I am not maintaining it will solve it in every instance 100 percent of the time. It is very difficult to come up with a Federal rule that will address 100 percent of the inequitable circumstances one could come up with, and if we tried to the unintended consequences could be staggering.

ObamaCare was justified in terms of wanting to provide insurance for those without insurance. Listen, I would like to see those without insurance get health insurance. I would like to see a competitive market where low-cost catastrophic policies were attractive to people and they chose to purchase it. But one of the best ways for someone to get health insurance is for them to get a good job, for them to actually start making real money, have some disposable income, start climbing the economic ladder.

The unintended consequence of ObamaCare is it has ended up hammering economic growth, hammering small businesses. So a lot of the people the law was trying to help have been made worse off.

Mr. KAINE. If I could, let me ask: A reform in the Senator's view that might encompass a different solution for the preexisting condition or an ending of the ban on interstate purchasing of insurance, if we get through this week and we are into next week and ObamaCare has not been defunded and we have funded government operations going forward, the Senator could introduce a reform bill proposing to do just those things, could he not?

Mr. CRUZ. I thank the Senator for that question.

I could. I will confess, our policy team is working on a number of affirmative health insurance reform policies.

I will confess—and for some reason we are kind of going with the home fire analogy, so let's stick with it right now. There are some who, in the course of health care matters, argue that the heavy focus of those of us who are opposed to ObamaCare should be what is the alternative, that should be the heavy focus. Listen, I absolutely think the health care system needs reforms to change real problems in it. I am a strong believer in that.

But an analogy I have used before is, if your home is on fire, you put out the fire first before building an addition to the house. Likewise, with ObamaCare, I think ObamaCare is such a train wreck, is such a disaster that the first imperative is to stop the damage from ObamaCare. Then I think we should work, and I would like it to be in a bipartisan way. The Senator and I have talked many times about how we could work together. We have yet to find a great opportunity to do so. But I am hopeful that will change because I would like to see us listen to our constituents and work constructively to fix the problems that hard-working Americans are struggling with.

When it comes to introducing affirmative health care legislation, I fully anticipate our team will do so, and we are working on proposals now. As the Senator knows well, our having been here just 9 months, it has not been a quiet 9 months.

Mr. KAINE. I say to the Senator, if we get to that point and he introduces affirmative legislation to reform the health care system—after we get through this debate—that would be legislation that would not be connected to the question, the existential question, of whether the government would continue to operate on October 1. So it would not be integrally wrapped up with sort of a threat to the economy that would be posed by a potential government shutdown, and it could be analyzed just on its own merits: Is this a good reform or a bad reform, without being wrapped around the question of whether we would shut down the government and do we lay off or put on some kind of furlough the nurses at Fort Belvoir Hospital who are taking care of wounded warriors every day. That would be a reform bill where we could dig into the reform and talk about the reform and analyze what is good and what is bad and what should be fixed and maybe what should not be, without it being wrapped around the question of a government shutdown.

Would the Senator not agree with that?

Mr. CRUZ. I thank the Senator from Virginia.

I would certainly agree that this body should spend considerable time working, and working together, on positive, proactive health care reforms, to expand competition, to empower patients.

I also agree with something else the Senator from Virginia said, which is that we should not be threatening a government shutdown. I do not want a government shutdown. I want the government to continue.

I salute the House of Representatives for passing a continuing resolution that keeps the government funded. But it also defunds ObamaCare. In my view, that is responsive to the suffering that so many millions of Americans are experiencing—to the loss of jobs, to being forced into part-time work, to facing higher health insurance premiums, to losing their health insurance.

Mr. KAINE. I ask the Senator, would he not agree that the best way to avoid a government shutdown or threats of a government shutdown or talking about the consequences of a government shutdown would be to separate out his question of what are the right reforms of the health care system from the funding of government operations?

Mr. CRUZ. I certainly agree with the Senator from Virginia that we should stop holding hostages. So an ideal way—and I had an earlier exchange with Senator ENZI from Wyoming, who pointed out that the entire reason we are having this continuing resolution battle is because Congress failed in its job to pass appropriations bills.

For example, the House of Representatives has passed a Defense appropriations bill. It is sitting here in the Senate. Majority Leader REID has not taken it up. I think we should take it up and pass it immediately so that any discussion of government shutdowns does not in any way, shape or form even remotely threaten the salary of the men and women of our military. I am confident the Senator and I agree, under no circumstances should anyone who is risking his or her life to defend the rest of us find their compensation, their salary threatened.

In my view, existing law allows and even requires the President to fund the military regardless of what happens on the continuing resolution, regardless of if we had a partial temporary shutdown.

Mr. KAINE. In the Senator's view, is it acceptable for the discussion of a government shutdown to threaten the nonmilitary priorities that are important to the American public?

Mr. CRUZ. I appreciate the question from the Senator from Virginia. I would note, I do not think we should shut anything down except ObamaCare. I think we should fund it all. Indeed, I have indicated a willingness—the Senator from Virginia knows well that I think we have a deep spending problem in this country and Congress has abdicated its responsibility and built a record debt.

It has gone from $10 trillion when the President was elected to now nearly $17 trillion—over a 60-percent increase. So if you ask me, do I like a continuing resolution that funds everything the Federal Government is doing without significant spending cuts, no. I would much rather have real spending cuts, roll up our sleeves and address the out-of-control spending and debt.

But I am perfectly willing to vote for a continuing resolution that maintains the status quo on everything, except for ObamaCare, because I view the gravity of ObamaCare, the threat of ObamaCare to hard-working American men and women so grave. As you know, in politics and in life you have got to pick your battles. We have to pick our battles one at a time.

So over time, I would prefer for us to work to have real spending cuts. But I do not think the avenue to doing that is that we should shut down the government. In my view, we should not shut down the government. The only way a government shutdown will happen—it may happen—is if majority leader HARRY REID and President Obama decide they want to shut down the government in order to force ObamaCare on the American people.

Mr. KAINE. So the Senator will not vote to continue government operations unless ObamaCare is defunded?

Mr. CRUZ. The Senator from Virginia is correct, and I have stated that I will not vote for a continuing resolution that funds ObamaCare. I believe this body should not vote for a continuing resolution that funds ObamaCare. Why? Because the facts show it is not working.

That is why the unions that used to support it are, one after the other, coming out against it.

Mr. KAINE. I want to switch and ask the Senator a question about "MakeWashingtonListen." That is the second piece. If the Senator will let me get back into a little bit of campaigning activity, he and I were candidates at the same time in 2012, and I gather that he told his constituents that he was opposed to ObamaCare and that he would vote to repeal or defund it if he were elected to office. Is that correct?

Mr. CRUZ. That is most assuredly correct.

Mr. KAINE. I believe I am correct that the Senator won his election not by a small margin but by a large margin. Is that correct?

Mr. CRUZ. Thanks to the work of a whole lot of Texas men and women across the State who really worked their hearts out. Yes, we were privileged to win the primary by 14 points and to win the general election by 15 points.

Mr. KAINE. Would it be fair to say that part of the Senator's mission here is he told his voters what he would do. They knew what the Senator would do and chose him to do the job. One of the things the Senator is doing today on the floor with this effort is to basically live up to the promise that he made to them, and the mandate that they gave to him?

Mr. CRUZ. I would agree with all of that.

Mr. KAINE. Let me offer a hypothetical situation. Contemplate another State and another race between two candidates, where one candidate took the strong position that ObamaCare should be repealed and the other candidate took the strong position that ObamaCare should not be repealed. In that State, the candidate that won by a sizable margin was the candidate who said ObamaCare should not be repealed, having been plain about it with the voters, and the voters having heard the choices and made a choice. Does the Senator think it is also the case that a Senator in that hypothetical State should come to the body and do what he said he was going to do for his voters?

Mr. CRUZ. I appreciate the question from the Senator from Virginia. He raises a very good and a fair point. I think that point is particularly valid for those Senators—I would note that all three of the Senators in the Chamber right now were elected in 2012. I think the point that he raises is particularly valid for those of us who were ruining in 2012, when this was an issue before the voters.

Now, in the hypothetical given, which I am not sure is entirely hypothetical, what I do not know is the exact representation that candidate made to the voters in his or her State, the exact statements that candidate made. I absolutely agree that he should honor the commitments made to the people. I would also note that all of us have an obligation to take note of changed circumstances, to take note of new facts that come to light, and even honoring your commitments does not mean that you ignore changed circumstances.

To give an example, prior to World War II, there were quite a few Members of this body and in the House of Representatives who campaigned and said they would keep America out of the war. Following Pearl Harbor, it was a different circumstance. It was a changed circumstance. I think, quite reasonably, people change their views. Constituents change their views and representatives change their views based on changed circumstances. So I would submit—listen,

198 STAND WITH TED

the argument the Senator makes is a serious one. I would not encourage any Member of this body to disregard the commitments they made to their constituents.

But I would, at the same time, encourage every Member not just to keep in mind the promises made on the campaign trail but the ongoing views of their constituents, because as circumstances change all of us respond to changed circumstances including our constituents. So one must certainly respect the promises made, but at the same time in the 9 months we have been here, in the year since the 3 of us were active candidates, the situation on ObamaCare has changed.

Look, I very much was opposed to ObamaCare a year ago, 2 years ago, and 3 years ago. At the time it passed, I thought it was a bad idea. But a year ago, the unions did not oppose it. A year ago, the President had not granted exemptions for big corporations. A year ago, Members of Congress had not gone to the President and asked for an exemption and got it. A year ago, we had not seen companies all over this country forcing people into 29 hours a week. A year ago we had not seen one big corporation after another dropping their health insurance coverage, such as UPS telling 15,000 employees: Your spousal coverage is being dropped because of ObamaCare. Your husbands and wives have just lost their coverage. So I would submit that the circumstances have changed.

Mr. KAINE. The last thing I would ask the Senator is—the three Senators who are now in the Chamber are each from different States. We all ran in 2012. I do not know about the presiding officer's situation. I was in that hypothetical, as you understand, running against a candidate who promised to repeal ObamaCare. I promised to work on reform efforts but to reject any effort to repeal or defund ObamaCare. The voters of Virginia chose the candidate who was not for repeal of ObamaCare. I do not know if it was the same situation in Connecticut or not. I suspect it probably was. We each represent one State.

There was also a national election in 2012, between a candidate, a President, who said that the Affordable Care Act was the law of the land and I am willing to work on it and improve it, but I will fight against efforts to repeal it or defund it, and a candidate who pledged to repeal the Affordable Care Act.

An election result in a Presidential election is listening to America, I believe. I am a believer in this system. I am a believer in democracy and the power of Presidential elections and mandates. I think the result in that election between the candidate who promised to maintain the Affordable Care Act and work to improve it and the candidate who promised to repeal the Affordable Care Act was not particularly close. I think it was a 53 to 47 percent election among the large size of a national electorate, rejecting the repeal of the Affordable Care Act position.

Is that something that this body should at least consider or take into account as we wrestle with this question?

Mr. CRUZ. I appreciate the question from the Senator from Virginia as well. Look, there is no doubt President Obama was reelected. I wish he had not been. I obviously did not support his election, but the majority of the American people voted for him to be reelected. That is to his credit.

I would point out that I do not agree with one of the premises of the question proposed by the Senator from Virginia, which is namely that the national election was fought over ObamaCare. I think the national election—No. 1, President Obama is a spectacularly talented candidate, a far more talented candidate than the Republican candidate. I think Mitt Romney is a good and decent man, but not the political candidate that Barack Obama is.

But, No. 2, once we got to the general election, much to my great dismay, Republicans did not make the election about ObamaCare. In fact, if you contrast the elections in 2010 and 2012, in 2010 Republicans ran all over the country on let's stop ObamaCare. The result was a tidal wave election for Republicans in the House of Representatives and in the Senate. It resulted in new personnel in both places. It resulted in Republicans taking over the House of Representatives. It resulted in a significant number of new Republicans in this body.

In 2012, Republicans did not focus. Indeed, the general election did not make nearly as much of an issue about ObamaCare and how it was failing the American people as it should have. As a consequence, I think an awful lot of people stayed home. I will commend the Obama campaign. They did a fabulous job of mobilizing their supporters. They also did a very good job of focusing on a lot of issues other than ObamaCare. Indeed, I would suggest to the Senator from Virginia, that if the premise of his question were correct, then President Obama would have campaigned on: I passed ObamaCare. Vote for me and let's preserve ObamaCare. We would have seen TV ads saturating that this is the signature achievement. It was very interesting. That was not the campaign President Obama ran. There was almost a bipartisan agreement not to mention ObamaCare; unfortunately, Republicans did far too little of it. But it is not like the President ran a lot focusing on it either.

Mr. KAINE. I have a comment and a final question. I am not skilled at how campaigns are run, but I would challenge the Senator's assertion. I think virtually everyone in the country who voted in the Presidential election in 2012 knew that one candidate, the President, would fight to maintain the Affordable Care Act, and another pledged to repeal it.

How much they did it in ads and on TV I cannot count. I actually saw a lot of ads about the very subject in the battleground State of Virginia. But I think the voters knew exactly the position of the two candidates on this issue. While it was not the only issue in the campaign, it was an important one. They had that before them as they made the decision.

The last question I will ask is a little bit of a rhetorical one but it is a sincere one. I very much hope that regardless of the outcome of this debate over the next few days—and I strongly want the outcome of this debate to be that government continues and that we continue to provide the services that we need to provide, and that we save the debate about health care reform for another day. But I very much hope that the Senator introduces legislation about health care reform ideas and that the legislation not be wrapped up with the question of whether government should shut down or not but that it be standalone legislation, that it not be wrapped up with a question of whether we should default on our debts or not, but that it should be standalone legislation.

I have a feeling that there are many Democrats and Republicans that would love to work on reform ideas. In this body and in the

House we have a somewhat limited bandwidth. We are trying to deal with a lot of different issues. Health care is a hugely important one.

Its connection to the economy is equally important, and I think there are a lot of Members here who would love to have a debate about reform.

But for the last 3-plus years the only debate has been about the repealing or defunding instead of about reform. That makes it a fairly simple vote for many of us. It makes it a simple vote for many of us who feel as though the will of this body has been expressed, that the Supreme Court has rendered an opinion about the Affordable Care Act, that the American public rendered an opinion about two positions in a Presidential election in 2012.

A defunding repeal strategy, which has been now done four dozen times by the House, is actually a pretty simple thing to move aside based on the foregoing, but if we set aside those efforts and try to take up the kinds of concrete reform ideas the Senator talked about earlier, I actually think there might be a number of things that we could all do together to improve the situation, but we don't need to do it while we are talking about the shutdown of the government or defaulting on America's bills for the first time in our history.

Thank you. I yield the floor, and I yield back.

Mr. CRUZ. I appreciate the question from the Senator from Virginia. Let me say I appreciate the good faith and seriousness with which he approaches this issue and the other issues before this body. One notable thing: Of the three Senators who are on the floor right now, all of us are freshmen. One of the things I appreciate about this freshman class, as all of us came to Washington before we were sworn in as Senators, we had a weeklong orientation process. We went and had dinners with our spouses, and we got to know each other as human beings. That is something that doesn't happen very often in Washington anymore. It used to happen in a bygone era, but it doesn't happen much anymore.

One of the interesting consequences that not many people have commented about—but it is something I find quite significant—is in the freshman class there were far more Democrats than Republicans, but to the best of my knowledge, no freshman has spoken ill of another freshman. I am not aware of it if it has happened. I think part of the reason for that was spending that time together, getting to know each other as people.

The Senator from Virginia and I disagree on a number of issues. Yet I hope and believe that we each understand that the other is operating in good faith based on principles he believes are correct. That is a foundation for actually solving problems and moving forward in this country.

One of the unfortunate consequences as you see both sides of this Chamber pommel each other is that many of us don't even know each other. One of the interesting dynamics, from my perspective, is that many of the senior Democrats frequently choose to say some fairly strident things directed at me. Many of them I don't really know. I haven't had the opportunity to get to know them, and I have had conversations with freshman Democrats asking the senior Republicans: Do you know them? The answer I have been told is, not really. We sit on committees, but most of us are on four or five committees. We are running from one hearing to another. You often run into a hearing, you ask a few questions, you run out, and you are off to the next meeting. You are meeting with your constituents, you are doing this and doing that. You don't have an opportunity to get to know each other. I am hopeful that the good will we have seen among the freshmen can spill over more broadly.

I wish to say also, on the point the Senator from Virginia made about reasonable and productive amendments to improve the system, look, it is very difficult to have the sorts of reforms I have talked about with ObamaCare in place because ObamaCare has so dominated the health care market. It has made government the chief mover and operator. You can't have positive free market reforms with ObamaCare there. The approach I am advocating doesn't work as long as ObamaCare makes the government the chief mover and operator. That is much the same in situations and nations that have adopted single-payer socialized health.

I would note that the Senator from Virginia expressed an interest in positive reforms to address some of the most egregious aspects of health care. I would encourage the Senator from Virginia to direct those comments to the majority leader of this body because the majority leader of this body has decided on this vote, that we will have one amendment and one amendment only, as far as I understand. That amendment will be funding ObamaCare in its entirety. The majority leader has decided we are not going to have amendments on the sorts of things the Senator from Virginia suggested, ways to improve the system.

If, for example, the majority leader does not want an amendment, apparently, on addressing the medical devices tax—a large majority of Senators in this body voted during the Budget proceeding against the medical devices tax because we understand it is killing jobs, destroying innovation, and it is one of the most punitive, destructive aspects of this bill. Yet the majority leader, as I understand it, said we are not going to have a vote on that. Why? Because that would actually affirmatively help fix things, and so we are not going to do that. I am putting words into the why, but that is the only reason I can think of.

Another example is Senator VITTER's amendment to repeal the congressional exemption. I understand many Members of Congress don't want to be in the exchanges, don't want to lose their subsidy, don't want to have the same rules apply to them that apply to millions of Americans. I understand that personally, but I think it is utterly indefensible for Members of Congress to be treated better than the American people. I think we ought to have a vote on the Vitter amendment.

I have stated before that I think it ought to be expanded so that every Member of Congress, all the congressional staff, the President, the political appointees, and every Federal employee should be subject to ObamaCare. They shouldn't be exempted. There shouldn't be a gilded class in Washington that operates on different rules than those of the American people. That would be a positive reform indeed. Indeed, I would suggest it would be a populist reform. Yet the majority leader has said: No, we can't vote on that. I am going to assume part of the reason is because having a debate on that, on the merits—the position that Congress should have a privileged position is indefensible.

Another example: The House of Representatives has voted to delay the individual mandate. They have said: Listen, if you are going to delay the employer's mandate for big businesses, why treat big businesses better than individuals and hard-working American families? Let's delay them both. If you are going to delay one, delay them both.

That passed the majority of the House—and, indeed, a considerable number of Democrats. I don't have the number in front of me, but a considerable number of Democrats in the House voted for that. The majority leader of the Senate has said: No, we are not going to vote on that.

Yet another instance: We have all been astonished and dismayed by the abuse that has occurred in the IRS that has been made public and has been admitted to. Quite a number of Members of this body would like to see the IRS removed from enforcing ObamaCare.

That is a position a large majority of Americans support. The majority leader of this body, as I understand it, has said: No, we can't vote on that. We are not going to have that positive reform. We are not going to have a vote. We are only going to vote to fund it all.

There are a great many amendments we could make that would make this situation better. It is only because the majority leader has decided to shut down the Senate to not make this process worse, but we are not having those amendments.

I thank the Senator from Virginia. I would urge him to make those arguments to the leader of his party and this institution so that we can have full and open debate and vote on these amendments because this isn't working. It is fundamentally not working. We need to respond to the American people. We need to listen to the American people, and we need to fix it.

At this point I wish to return to reading some more tweets. As the night goes on, I hope to read even more tweets. I would encourage anyone who would like to see—the folks in the gallery who just waved, I am not sure if they have their electronics. If you do tweet, it may end up here and I may have the chance to read it, the "MakeDCListen."

Make D.C. listen because "We the People" are on to you and will not stand for tyranny. Hoorah.

I like that.

Defund ObamaCare because if I can't get a job now, what hope will I have later. Make D.C. listen.

Make D.C. listen because it makes entry-level jobs disappear for young Americans.

Make D.C. listen because I want to keep my own doctor. Defund ObamaCare because we don't want government-run health care. Make D.C. listen.

ObamaCare is a job killer. We can't afford it. Make D.C. listen.

Make D.C. listen. If it is bad for Congress, they have no right to force it on their constituents. Vote to defund it.

I want my 40 hours. Make D.C. listen.

Start listening to the people instead of who is lining your pockets. We are the ones who vote. Make D.C. listen.

Here is a tweet from Greg Abbott, my former boss, the attorney general of Texas, who is running for Governor of Texas, and a very good man.

ObamaCare is destructive to our economy, to jobs, to liberty, and to health care access. Make D.C. listen.

Thanks, boss. I appreciate it, and I agree.

Make D.C. listen by committing to always cast your vote for those who do listen and act accordingly.

Make D.C. listen because government is too large already.

ObamaCare violates our rights. We cannot, as America, allow this "solution" to continue. Make D.C. listen.

Small business owners. If ObamaCare is implemented, I will be forced to drop my group insurance for my employees. Make D.C. listen.

When can the citizens expect our way. If everyone else is · getting them, shouldn't we make D.C. listen?

That is a great point. Why is it that President Obama treats giant corporations and Members of Congress better than hard-working Americans? I think it is indefensible. Yet this body right now, unless we act differently, is going to allow that status quo to continue.

The same Senators should live by the same rules as the American people and should not be controversial. It should be obvious. Make D.C. listen.

That is exactly right.

Congress has exempted itself and staffers from the monstrous law for an obvious reason. Don't we deserve the same? Make D.C. listen.

Make D.C. listen. Make Americans finally see what is in the bill, and we hate it.

Thank you for standing up to the status quo in D.C.

Senate phone lines are jammed. Start using facts, social media. Go to . . .

And it lists a private Web site for a list of Twitter accounts.

Make D.C. listen.

I think that point, by the way, is really quite potent, that as effective as the phones are—I think the phones are very effective—there is e-mail, Facebook, Twitter. There are an awful lot of ways for the American people to speak up and make DC listen.

Today the Cleveland Clinic saved my dad's life. The U.S. Senate saved their jobs. Make D.C. listen.

That is powerful.

How can any American support a law that punishes success. That is unAmerican. Defund ObamaCare now. Make D.C. listen.

Defund ObamaCare because it is a tax that was never read until it was passed. "We the People" demand representation. Make D.C. listen.

Defund ObamaCare because it will ruin our generation and will destroy America and the American Dream. Make D.C. listen.

ObamaCare is destructive to our country. Defund ObamaCare. Stand up for our freedom. Make D.C. listen.

If ObamaCare is so great, why is everyone not going to have it? Make D.C. listen.

The Congress, the President, and Federal workers have forgotten they work for us and should have to obey the same laws and rules we do. Make D.C. listen.

Make D.C. listen. My children cannot get full-time jobs because of ObamaCare. Can't wait to see how much my premiums will go up during open enrollment. Defund ObamaCare because it is not good enough for Congress. Make D.C. listen.

The American people are screaming to STOP OBAMACARE. Make DC listen. Leave us alone.

At this point I want to talk about the topic of rate shock. We all remember some 3½ years ago when President Obama told the American people that by the end of his first term the average American family's health insurance premiums would drop by $2,500. The end of his first term, as we know, was last year, and that hasn't happened. That has not been the effect.

What has happened instead? According to a Kaiser Family Foundation report in 2012, the average cost of premiums for family coverage has risen by more than $3,000 since 2008. Now, $3,000 compared to $2,500 is a $5,500 swing. That is a big swing. That is a big impact for any hard-working American family.

But you know who is impacted the most? Those who are struggling the most. Single moms, working one or two jobs trying to feed their kids, trying to put food on the table. You know, $5,500 a year is a real difference. The consistent pattern is that the people who are the biggest losers under ObamaCare are the most vulnerable among us—they are young people, African Americans, Hispanics, single moms. They are the ones not able to get jobs, they are the ones being laid off from their jobs, they are the ones being forcibly put into part-time work at 29 hours a week, they are the ones facing sky-rocketing health insurance premiums, and they are the ones losing their health insurance.

The actuarial firm of Oliver Wyman estimates premiums in the individual market will increase an average of 40 percent. The Society of Actuaries estimates an average premium increase of 32 percent in the individual markets.

The Obama administration unilaterally delayed a provision of the law that limits out-of-pocket payments—e.g., deductibles, copayments—to $6,350 per individual or $12,700 per family.

According to Avik Roy, a senior fellow at the Manhattan Institute and writer for Forbes.com:

> If you compare the cheapest plan on health care.gov to the cheapest "bronze plan" on the new Covered California insurance exchange, premiums for healthy 25 year olds will increase by 147 percent, a median of $183 on the exchange versus $74 today; and premiums for healthy 40 year olds will increase by 149 percent, a median of $234 on the exchange versus $94 today. And because California bars insurers from charging different rates based on gender—and so do Colorado, Maine, Massachusetts, Minnesota, Montana, New Hampshire, New Jersey, New York, Oregon and Washington—the war on young people's premiums will fare just as poorly for women in California and many other States. Despite ObamaCare subsidies, many Americans will still be paying higher premiums in 2014 as a result of ObamaCare.

Even with the government subsidy they are going to be paying higher premiums.

For example, Americans earning as little as $25,000 will still pay more, even including subsidies.

The Ohio Department of Insurance—we talked about this earlier, how every 4 years both parties focus rather intensely on Ohio. When it is a Presidential year, when it is a swing State, suddenly Ohio is the center of the universe. We get to 2013, a nonpresidential year, and Ohio seems to command an awful lot less attention in this body. But what is happening in Ohio? Well, the Ohio Department of Insurance announced ObamaCare will increase individual market health premiums by 88 percent. That is not a mild increase. That is not a percent or two. Eighty-eight percent is a big deal for a family struggling to pay their bills.

In California, ObamaCare is estimated to have increased individual health insurance premiums by anywhere from 64 percent to 146 percent.

In Florida, Florida's insurance commissioner Kevin McCarty told the *Palm Beach Post* that insurance rates will rise by 5 to 20 percent in the small group market and by 30 to 40 percent in the individual market.

If the men and women in America can easily afford to pay an extra 30, 40 percent or, in the case of California an extra 146 percent on health insurance, then we don't have anything to be worried about. But when I travel home that is not what the men and women of America tell me. That is not what Texans say. Texans say they are working hard to make ends meet; that their life has gotten harder because of ObamaCare.

A constituent in Vidalia, TX, wrote on September 19, 2013:

I decided to do some research on ObamaCare insurance for me and my husband since neither of us have any insurance. I used the calculator to calculate how much "affordable insurance" would cost us. I had really hoped this might be our chance to get insurance. To my SHOCK it would cost us $16,026, and this was for the silver plan, which only pays 70 percent. My husband is disabled and receives Social Security benefits, but they say he cannot get Medicaid for 2 years after he was approved. He has another year before he qualifies. He is 62 and I am 56, and we have been without insurance since he lost his job 4 years ago. There is no possible way to pay $16,026 from our take-home pay, plus have to pay an additional 30 percent cost on any health costs we may incur. This is not affordable health care. The crime of it all is that if my husband and I do not enroll we will be fined. This is crazy. Please stop this madness.

I will pass on some more words from Texans. Today we received welcome news of support from several of our friends in the Texas legislature who are backing our effort to fund the government and to defund ObamaCare. The Texas Conservative Coalition—67 members of the Texas legislature—released a letter which I would like to read. It begins:

Dear Senators Cornyn and Cruz and Texas Members of the House of Representatives: Representing the State of Texas, with its 26 million people, we write at this most urgent hour for you to do all you can to defund ObamaCare and fund the Federal Government.

We have done all that we can to help stop ObamaCare from harming Texans. No. 1, we refused to create the ObamaCare health exchanges and No. 2 we have refused to expand the Medicaid Program under the false pretense of taking Federal money now while burdening taxpayers with millions of dollars in new costs later.

But some of the most pernicious parts of ObamaCare can only be stopped at the Federal level. Only you can stop the Federal Government from enforcing the individual mandates. Only you can stop the government from creating a new budget-busting entitlement that will drive up the cost of insurance around the country. Only you can stop Federal bureaucrats from drafting and imposing thousands of pages of redtape. And only you can stop the Federal Government from destroying the quality of our health care system.

Therefore, we applaud the action of the United States House of Representatives on Friday, September 20, 2013, to pass a bill that defunds ObamaCare and funds the Federal Government. Next, it is up to Senators Cornyn and Cruz to hold the line and make sure Democratic Senate majority leader HARRY REID does not use procedural tricks to strip the defunding language from the House bill.

I would note—and this is not in the letter, this is me speaking—this is exactly the debate we are in the middle of right now. The vote on Friday or Saturday on cloture is going to be the critical vote in this battle in the Senate. If Republicans stand together, we can prevent HARRY REID from shutting off debate, we can prevent HARRY REID from funding ObamaCare using 51 Democratic votes on a straight party-line vote. But that is only if Republicans stand together. If Republicans, instead, choose to vote for HARRY REID, choose to vote for giving the Democrats the ability to fund ObamaCare, then that too will be our responsibility. And it will be incumbent upon each of us to explain to our constituents why we voted to allow Harry Reid and the Democrats to fund ObamaCare despite the fact it is destroying jobs and hurting millions of Americans.

Returning to the letter:

We know Republican Senators will need continued support from the Republican-led House to prevent Democrats from funding ObamaCare. Together, we can prevail. Remember the spirit of so many Texans who have fought much worse odds in the past. Stay strong, stay resolute, and do not give in.

I am thankful my home State of Texas has such principled conservatives among its elected officials to have fought hard to resist ObamaCare, and I am very grateful for their support and their encouragement. Their leadership is the reason Texas has one of the strongest economies in the Nation and is one of the fastest growing

States in the Nation. Texas is proof that conservative principles put in practice actually work and provide opportunity for the most vulnerable among us.

There is a reason why so many people from all across this country are moving to Texas, and it is because Texas is where the jobs are. If you look across this country, ObamaCare is killing jobs all over this Nation.

I want to look now at the impact to my home State of Texas. ObamaCare will devastate jobs, growth, and the economy. It hasn't even been fully implemented and yet it is already hurting Americans, even those in conservative States that have worked hard to resist the influence of ObamaCare.

According to the Advisory Board's Daily Briefing, 15 Governors are opposing Medicaid expansion. I applaud those conservative leaders—Governor Haley in South Carolina, Governor Walker in Michigan, Governor Jindal in Louisiana, Governor Bentley in Alabama, Governor Brownback in Kansas, and many others— but particularly Governor Perry in my home State of Texas. Texas leaders in the House and Senate elected statewide have stood united to resist the influence of ObamaCare in our State. But the tragedy is, even with their efforts, Texans still aren't exempt from its negative impact.

Governor Perry in March of 2012 said:

ObamaCare will cost the State of Texas at least $27 billion over the next 10 years.

Senator Jane Nelson, Texas Senator and chair of the Senate House of Health and Human Services, said in September 2012:

ObamaCare is the wrong approach to our health care challenges. It does more harm than good. It will hurt our economy, eliminate jobs, balloon the State budget, and perhaps most importantly stretch to the limit our already overburdened health care system.

Senator Nelson also observed:

Texas is a large, geographically diverse border State with challenges that are unique from other States. The one-size-fits-all approach of ObamaCare is wrong for Texas. If given the opportunity, we can design an efficient system that better meets the needs of our citizens.

In March of 2012 Senator Nelson observed:

ObamaCare creates more problems than it solves, ballooning the deficit, overwhelming our health system, and burdening employers at a time when they are just struggling to survive.

In March of 2010 Senator Nelson observed:

In Texas, I am deeply concerned about the devastating impacts Federal health care reforms will have on our State budget. The Health and Human Services Commission estimates it will cost up to $24 billion over a 10-year period. Considering our projected budget shortfalls for the upcoming legislative session will be somewhere between $9 billion and $16 billion, it is clear that our Health and Human Services budget—which accounts for a third of the total spending already—will continue to consume precious resources that would otherwise be available for our schools, our highways, and other important services. I am concerned that the Federal Government's plan will jeopardize our efforts on the State level. One size does not fit all, especially in Texas. Our State government spreads more health care dollars across more terrain than any other State. We have challenges along the border in our remote rural areas and in our inner cities that are unique to our State and our costs will be disproportionately high.

One could perhaps listen to those who say: Those are conservative Republicans. We expect conservative Republicans to oppose

ObamaCare. But how about others? How about those who are not conservative Republicans? On April 24, 2013, the United Union of Roofers published a press release opposing ObamaCare because it jeopardizes their existing health plans. Their press release read: Roofers union seeks repeal-reform of Affordable Care Act. Cites loss of benefits to members, harm to industry and multiemployer health plans.

Washington, DC. The United Union of Roofers, Waterproofers, and Allied Workers International President Kinsey M. Robinson issued the following statement on April 16, 2013, calling for a repeal or complete reform of the President's Affordable Care Act.

This is not the union calling for a slight adjustment. This is the union calling for repeal: Repeal the law outright.

Our union and its members have supported President Obama and his administration for both of his terms in office.

So these are President Obama's supporters. These are the labor unions.

But regrettably, our concerns over certain provisions in the ACA have not been addressed, or in some instances totally ignored. In the rush to achieve its passage, many of the act's provisions were not fully conceived, resulting in unintended consequences that are inconsistent with the promise that those who were satisfied with their employer-sponsored coverage could keep it. These provisions jeopardize our multi-employer health plans and have the potential to cause a loss of work for our members, create an unfair bidding advantage for those contractors who do not provide health coverage to their workers, and in the worst case may cause our members and their families to lose the benefits they currently enjoy as participants in multi-employer health benefits.

For decades, our multi-employer health and welfare plans have provided the necessary medical coverage for our members and their families to protect them in times of illness and medical needs. This collaboration between labor and management has been a model of success that should be emulated rather than ignored. I refuse to remain silent or idly watch as the ACA destroys those protections.

Let me read that sentence again, because that is coming from the leader of a labor union that has supported President Obama in two elections:

I refuse to remain silent or idly watch as the ACA destroys those protections. I therefore call for repeal or complete reform of the Affordable Care Act to protect our employers, our industry, and our most important asset, our members and their families.

Let me ask right now. Do Members of the Senate have concern for hard-working union members? Do Members of the Senate have concern for the families of hard-working union members who are saying in writing, We supported the President, but this law isn't working?

If Members of the Senate were listening to the people, this letter would get our attention. If Members of the Senate were listening to the people, Democratic Senators and Republican Senators would stand up and say, This thing isn't working.

The IRS employees union doesn't want to be subject to ObamaCare. The union representing IRS workers, tasked with enforcing ObamaCare, vocally opposes participating in the law's exchanges. IRS union leaders provided their members with a form letter expressing concern with legislation to "push Federal employees out of the Federal Employee Health Benefits Program and into the insurance exchanges established under the Affordable Care Act."

Now I want to focus on exactly what happened here. The IRS employees' union sent letters to their members, form letters, drafted to you and me, drafted to Members of this Senate, where the IRS employees union asked the IRS employees: Write a letter to your Senators, write a letter to your congressmen saying, Exempt us from

ObamaCare. Apparently, the IRS employees union believes Congress will listen to them.

How about the American people? These are the men and women in charge of enforcing ObamaCare. These are the men and women the statute gives the responsibility to go to every hard-working American and say, We are going to force you to participate in ObamaCare. They don't want to be in it. I would suggest that is not an accident. They know exactly what they don't want to be a part of, and the fact that they have sent those letters ought to be a warning call that sounds from the high heavens.

And yet another example—and this is an example I have made multiple references to tonight—is a letter from the Teamsters. I would note that neither Leader REID nor Leader PELOSI on the House side are on the floor. Neither are listening or participating in this debate.

> Dear Leader Reid and Leader Pelosi. When you and the President sought our support for the Affordable Care Act, you pledged that if we liked the health plans we have now, we could keep them. Sadly, that promise is under threat. Right now, unless you and the Obama administration enact an equitable fix, the ACA will shatter not only our hard-earned health benefits but destroy the foundation of the 40-hour workweek that is the backbone of the American middle class.
>
> Like millions of other Americans, our members are the frontline workers in the American economy. We have been strong supporters of the notion that all Americans should have access to quality, affordable health care. We have also been strong supporters of you.

This is directed to majority leader HARRY REID and minority leader NANCY PELOSI.

> In campaign after campaign we have put boots on the ground, gone door to door to get out the vote, run phone banks, and raised money to secure this vision. Now this vision has come back to haunt us.

Let me read that again. This is the president of the Teamsters describing the political efforts that members of the Teamsters all over this country have done to elect Democrats to the Senate and the House. In his words, he said, because of ObamaCare and their vision of supporting Democrats politically, "Now this vision has come back to haunt us." If that doesn't get the attention of the men and women in this body, I don't know what does.

The letter continues:

Since the ACA was enacted we have been bringing our deep concerns to the administration seeking reasonable regulatory interpretations of the statute and to help prevent the destruction of nonprofit health plans. As you both know firsthand, our persuasive arguments have been disregarded and met with a stone wall by the White House and the pertinent agencies.

The average American does not have the political sway that a major labor union like the Teamsters has. The average American especially does not have the political sway that a major labor union has with this President—a Democratic President—with a Democratic majority in the Senate. And yet the head of the Teamsters says that:

. . . their persuasive arguments have been disregarded and they have been met with a stone wall by the White House and the pertinent agencies.

If a powerful labor union with friends in high office in Washington is met with a stone wall, what is the average American met with? Do you think the reception is more welcoming to the average American? Perhaps the average American doesn't even get to see that stone wall to be rejected, doesn't even have the forum to raise those arguments to have them disregard and rejected.

The letter continues:

This is especially stinging, because other stakeholders have repeatedly received successful interpretations for their respective grievances. Most disconcerting of course is last week's huge accommodation for the employer community, extending the statutorily mandated December 31, 2013 deadline for the employer-mandated penalties. Time is running out. Congress wrote this law. We voted for you. We have a problem. You need to fix it. The unintended consequences of the ACA are severe. Perverse incentives are already creating nightmare scenarios.

"Nightmare." That is the word the Teamsters used. "Nightmare." Some Democratic Senators object to the use of the word "train wreck." Perhaps "nightmare" would be better. That comes from the Teamsters in writing, describing what ObamaCare is doing.

Nightmare is fitting. It is past midnight. Why are we here? Because the American people are experiencing the nightmare that is ObamaCare and we need to help them wake up from this very bad dream.

The Teamsters letter continues:

First, the law creates an incentive for employers to keep employees' work hours below 30 hours a week. Numerous employers have begun to cut workers' hours to avoid this obligation, and many of them are doing so openly. The impact is twofold. Fewer hours means less pay while also losing our current health benefits.

How does that sound? The majority leader told the American people on television that ObamaCare is terrific. Fewer hours meaning less pay and losing your current health benefits, that doesn't sound terrific to me. That doesn't sound terrific to the millions of Teamsters, the millions of union workers, the millions of hard-working Americans who are experiencing the negative consequences of ObamaCare.

The letter continues:

Second, millions of Americans are covered by nonprofit health insurance plans like the one in which most of our members participate. These nonprofit plans are governed jointly by unions and companies under the Taft-Hartley Act. Our health plans have been built over decades by working men and women. Under the ACA, as interpreted by this administration, our employees will be treated differently and not eligible for subsidies afforded other citizens. As such, many employees will be relegated to second-class status and shut out of the help offered to buy for-profit insurance plans. Finally, even though nonprofit plans like ours won't receive the same subsidies as for-profit plans, they will be taxed to pay for those subsidies. Taken together, these restrictions will make nonprofit plans like ours unsustainable and will undermine the health care market as viable alternatives to the big health insurance companies.

On behalf of the millions of working men and women we represent—

I would note, he didn't say on behalf of the hundreds or on behalf of the thousands. He said:

On behalf of the millions of working men and women we represent and the families they support, we can no longer stand silent in the face of elements of the Affordable Care Act that will destroy the very health and well-being of our members, along with millions of other hard-working Americans.

I want to remember that phrase, "We can no longer stand silent." I am going to return to it in a moment.

We believe that there are commonsense corrections that can be made within the existing statute that will allow our members to continue to keep their current health benefits and plans, just as you and the President pledged. Unless changes are made, however, that promise is hollow. We continue to stand behind real health care reform, but the law as it stands will hurt millions of Americans, including the members of our respective unions. We are looking to you to make sure these changes are made.

James P. Hoffa, General President, International Brotherhood of Teamsters.

I don't have to remind anyone that the Teamsters and Mr. Hoffa are not loyal Republicans. They are not even disloyal Republicans. They have been active foot soldiers in the army to elect President Obama and to elect Democrats to this body.

This letter describes ObamaCare as a nightmare. This letter describes how it is hurting millions of Americans, including the members of their respective unions. And interestingly enough, this letter uses the same phrase, "We can no longer stand silent," that the roofers union used. "We won't stand silent, either."

Why is it that both of these unions used that same phrase? Everyone in this body understands politics, understands sticking with your team, dancing with the team that brought you. No union is eager to criticize President Obama. They have too much invested in this administration. And there is a lot of pressure—a lot of pressure—on the labor unions. I can't imagine what the repercussions were to Mr. Hoffa and to the Teamsters after this letter was sent. I am quite certain it did not produce joy and celebration in the political classes of Washington.

I think it is quite striking, though, that both the roofers union and the Teamsters said we can no longer stand silent, because the pressure is enormous.

Let me tell you about another group that is right now standing silent that I hope can no longer stand silent and that consists of elected Democrats in this body. Elected Democrats in this body— these union men and women knocked on doors, worked to elect many Members of this body. If their union leaders cannot stand silent, I hope the politicians who pledged to fight for them won't stand silent either.

What a remarkable thing it would be to see a Democrat to have the courage of James Hoffa, to see a Democratic Senator stand and have the courage to say: You know, look, I supported ObamaCare. That is what Mr. Hoffa said. I supported it at first because I believed the promise that was made. I thought this thing might work, but we have seen it has not. It is a nightmare. It is hurting hard-working American families. Any Democrat who did so would be certain to receive serious repercussions from the party. Political parties do not like it when you rock the boat. I can promise you Senator LEE and I have more than a passing awareness of that in our respective party. But at the end of the day, if you are responding to the American people, if you are listening to the American people, you are doing their job. I hope in the course of this week that of the 54 Democrats in this body, we will see one, two, three—I hope we see a dozen who have the courage Mr. Hoffa showed, have the courage to speak out about the train wreck, about the nightmare that is ObamaCare, that is hurting Americans, that is killing jobs, that is pushing people into part-time work, that is driving up health care premiums and is causing more and more people to lose their health insurance. That is the courage we need.

But you know what. It will not come from business as usual in Washington. It will not come from wanting to be popular in the conference lunches. It will only come from elected officials making the decision, the radical decision to get back to the job we are supposed to do in listening to the people. Make DC listen. That is what we should be doing.

Mr. LEE. Will the Senator yield for a question?

Mr. CRUZ. I am happy to yield for a question without yielding the floor.

Mr. LEE. As I listened to the Senator's remarks, I am reminded of many events throughout our Nation's history. It is a storied history involving a lot of comebacks. There were a lot of instances in which the American people were up against a brick wall of sorts, in which a small group of Americans, often not just a minority but sometimes a minority within a minority, faced a substantial obstacle.

The founding of our Republic, at the moment of our independence, involved a battle against what was then the world's greatest superpower. Even within our own continent we did not have unanimous support. Even among our own people, at times it was a minority within an a minority who believed that the cause of independence was worthwhile, that it was worthy of the great effort that declaring independence and fighting a war for it would inevitably require.

Yet we persevered, we rallied together as a people, believing fundamentally that our cause was just. And it worked. We followed that formula many times when it has mattered and we have not backed away from fights when those fights were necessary. This may be one of those moments where even though those who are willing to fight against this law, those who are willing to take this effort are not in the majority, are in the minority—in this case in a sense we are a minority within the minority—it is still worth fighting.

I commend my colleague, the junior Senator from Texas, for his dedication, his commitment, his leadership on this issue. Senator CRUZ has never shrunk from this. He has been willing to fight hard for it. He has been willing to speak his mind even at moments when it was difficult, even at moments when many were suggesting it could not be done or should not be done. It reminds me of other examples we have seen over the years, of Senators who were willing to speak at great length.

I see our pages who are here tonight, pages who serve us well and who are willing to stay late at night, working hard. I am reminded that 27 years ago I was a page much like these who are serving us here today. I remember a young Senator then in his first term. His name was HARRY REID. I remember watching him speak at great length for 10, 12—I don't know, maybe 13 hours at a time. I am not certain what the issue was at the time, but I know it was important to him. I know it was an issue on which he was somewhat outnumbered. I know that I saw his colleagues approaching him. Some of them were quite critical of the effort in which he was engaged. Yet he stood by his message, he did not shrink from it, because he had an inner commitment to the people he represented and I respected that about him. I could tell he had that kind of tenacity.

I watched, as I was a Republican page at the time—I watched my Democratic page colleagues as they brought him a lot of water, hoping perhaps that eventually he would drink enough water that he would decide it was no longer in his best interests to continue speaking on the floor. Yet somehow he managed to stay speaking for, I don't know, 10, 12, 13, 14 hours at a time, and I have a great deal of respect for what he did at that moment. I hope there is some aspect of Senator REID that is able to sympathize with what Senator CRUZ is going through, that is able to respect the great level of commitment it takes to stand here, hour after hour, and engage in this discussion, a discussion that is important for the American people to have.

We all continue to hear from our constituents about some of the things ObamaCare might do, some of the things ObamaCare might do to the people rather than for them. I received this one from James in Utah. James writes:

> Sir, as a retired U.S. Marine Corps gunny, I would like to express my view and ask that you vote to defund ObamaCare. I am part of the security team here at—

And I have deleted the name of his employer.

> —and our new contract has a massive increase in the cost for health coverage. I fought for the people of this country. Now I ask the same from you. Please help us.
> Gunnery Sergeant Charlie Jones, U.S. Marine Corps, retired.

From Utah.

Then I hear comments such as this from constituent after constituent, from people who will write in from throughout my State and from throughout the country. Steven from Minnesota writes:

> Dear Senator LEE. Please do all you can to stop the implementation of ObamaCare. My work insurance went up 8.1 percent in January in anticipation of ObamaCare. I make about $40,000 a year. We do not have any extra money after bills. I would like to see health care available to everyone. We've gone without health care insurance at times but I believe that ObamaCare is

not the solution and will result in poorer quality health care overall, and hurt our economy.

Thank you for considering a Minnesota resident's concerns.

Steven, I am happy to consider your concerns and I am happy to share those with my constituents. This next one comes from Kevin from Massachusetts.

Dear Senator. I strongly urge you to approve and vote yes on the House resolution bill passed by the House and is now before the Senate that fully funds the Government and protects the full credit of the United States but defunds the Affordable Care Act as provided for in the bill and continuing resolution sponsored by Congressman GRAVES. It is unfair to exempt everyone with political connections from ObamaCare and not to exempt the rest of us. You must understand that ObamaCare is undermining American workers and selling out hard for union benefits. It is not fair for businesses to reduce workers' hours to survive. It is time to defund the Affordable Care Act until such time when it can be repealed and things can be straightened out and workers protected.

I urge you please to delay funding for ObamaCare now.

That is Kevin, from Massachusetts.

When we look at these examples and we read other similar examples like them from people writing from throughout my State of Utah, people writing from throughout the country, we see a consistent pattern. Americans are justifiably, understandably fearful of losing their jobs, of having their wages cut, of having their hours cut, in some instances losing access to health care—sometimes through a health plan upon which they and their families have relied on for many years. This is a difficult situation for them because health care is an especially unusually personal thing.

Access to health care is something people do not necessarily want to entrust entirely to their government. Yet that seems to be the direction in which ObamaCare inevitably takes us. It puts more and more of our health care into the control of the Federal Government and, as has been suggested on the floor tonight, as some of my colleagues, some of my Democratic colleagues from within the Senate have acknowledged, this is but a step in the direction of what they hope will be a single-payer, government-funded, government-run health care system, funded, operated, and administered entirely from Washington, DC.

There are some things government can do in the sense that there are some things that government is rather uniquely empowered to do. Providing, for example, for our national defense, that is something we do from Washington. That is a power that is entrusted to us by article I, section 8, of the Constitution with roughly one-third of the provisions of article I, section 8, being dedicated in one way or another to our national defense. That is something Washington can do. It is something Washington must do and that Washington is rather uniquely empowered to do under our constitutional system.

Health care is of course important, undeniably important. In many respects it is as important as national defense. The fact that it is important doesn't necessarily make it a responsibility of the Federal Government nor does it necessarily qualify the Federal Government as a practical matter, setting aside the constitutional question. It doesn't necessarily qualify the Federal Government as an effective health care provider. Many people fear the day when our Federal Government becomes much more empowered over the very personal decisions of our lives, particularly those affecting our access to health care.

Many people are also suspect of the new taxes imposed by this law, the new permutations this law will introduce into the lives of the American people. We have discussed several times today the manner in which this law was enacted, the manner in which it was introduced as a bill, brought to the floor of the House of Representatives after then-Speaker of the House NANCY PELOSI informed her Members that they needed to pass their bill and then they could find out what is in it.

One of the things we have not discussed as much is the fact that even after that was passed, without Members of Congress having ade-

226 STAND WITH TED

quate opportunity to review this legislation—even after that happened, setting aside the 20,000 pages of regulations that have been added to this corpus of Federal law up until this point, we have had two significant revisions of the law, revisions that were brought about not legislatively but by the judicial branch of government, revisions the judicial branch of government had no authority to impose.

I would like to talk about both of those. When the Affordable Care Act was challenged as to its constitutionality, there were two primary constitutional challenges brought to the attention of the Federal court system that ultimately made their way to the Supreme Court of the United States. One of those challenges involved a constitutional attack on Congress's authority to enact the individual mandate. The provision compelled individuals to buy health insurance—and not just any kind of health insurance but the kind of health insurance the Federal Government in its infinite wisdom deemed appropriate, necessary, essential, and indispensable to every American everywhere.

The argument presented in those constitutional challenges culminating at the Supreme Court of the United States was that Congress had acted pursuant to its authority under the commerce clause, article I, section 8, clause 3 of the Constitution, which empowers Congress to regulate commerce among the several States, Indian tribes, and foreign nations. The argument said that Congress does have the power to regulate interstate commerce, and the Supreme Court has interpreted that power rather broadly since 1937.

Yet, even under that extraordinarily broad interpretation of the commerce clause, the argument was that Congress doesn't have the power to regulate an activity. The failure to purchase health insurance is not an interstate commercial transaction. In fact, it is not a transaction at all. It is a failure to act.

The Supreme Court of the United States accepted that argument and concluded that even under the extraordinarily broad deferential standard of review used by the Supreme Court since 1937, this could not pass muster as a valid, legitimate exercise of Congress's commerce clause authority. The Supreme Court Justices rejected that argument by a vote of 5 to 4. Oddly, however, the Supreme

Court went on to conclude that the individual mandate was nevertheless constitutional—not under the commerce power but under Congress's power to tax. In essence, what they had was five Justices of the Supreme Court—led by the Chief Justice of the United States, the Honorable John Roberts—who, as I see it, effectively rewrote the individual mandate provision as a tax. They saved it only by recasting it as a tax or as a valid exercise of Congress's power to impose taxes.

There were a couple of problems with that interpretation. First and foremost, Congress could have imposed a tax as an enforcement mechanism to bring about compliance with the individual mandate provision. Yet it decidedly did not. It used language that—under at least a century's worth of jurisprudence—was clearly and unequivocally a penalty and not a tax. There is a long line of cases that help courts decide whether something is a penalty or tax. Under a century or more of jurisprudence, this was a penalty and not a tax.

It is also important to note that the House of Representatives initially considered language that would have attempted to enforce compliance with the individual mandate provision by means of a tax and using language that under a century's worth of jurisprudence would have been regarded as a tax. Yet, interestingly enough and not surprisingly, that language was rejected. That proposal did not carry the day. That proposal could not carry the day. Why? Well, most Americans understandably are reluctant to raise taxes on middle-class Americans. It was soundly rejected. It could not carry enough votes even in the Congress that was in place during the first 2 years of President Obama's administration. It could not carry the day in a Congress that was overwhelmingly Democratic in both the House of Representatives and in the Senate.

The Constitution requires that revenue bills originate in the House of Representatives. If this was a new tax, it would have to originate in the House. In a very significant sense, one could argue that the bill that ultimately became the Affordable Care Act, ObamaCare, did originate in the House. It came over here to the Senate and had its provisions stripped out and replaced by Senate language, but many people still consider that a House bill.

The problem here has a lot to do with the fact that the tax language did not originate in the House or in the Senate. Instead, it originated across the street with five lawyers wearing black robes whom we call Justices. Those five lawyers wearing black robes whom we call Justices are no more empowered than the Queen of England to impose a tax on the American people. Yet they imposed a tax on the American people. This is not OK. This is not acceptable. This was a lawless act. This is something we should be ashamed of as Americans. It was a sad, shameful moment when the Supreme Court of the United States took upon itself the mantle of a superlegislative body, which it is not.

Unable to bring about a massive tax increase on the middle class, Congress adopted what it could. What it did adopt the Supreme Court found to be unconstitutional on its own terms as it was written. The Supreme Court—apparently unwilling to do its job and all too eager to do the job of the legislative branch rather than acknowledging the unconstitutionality of that provision—simply resurrected it by rewriting it as something that it is not, was not, and never could be.

Interestingly, this was not the only insult to the Constitution in connection with that case. In the same dispute in which the Supreme Court rewrote ObamaCare in order to save it, in the same case in which the Supreme Court of the United States rewrote the individual mandate provision as a tax when in fact it was a penalty, they did something else: A separate and even larger majority—a 7-to-2 majority—concluded that another aspect of the Affordable Care Act as written could not withstand constitutional muster.

The Medicaid expansion provisions left the States with no option, no alternative, and no choice other than to accept a significantly expanded Medicaid Program, which is a program that is administered by the States. It is partially funded by the Federal Government but ultimately administered by the States.

The Supreme Court of the United States, citing longstanding precedence, said: This is not OK. Congress doesn't have the power to commandeer the State's legislative and administrative machinery for the purpose of implementing a Federal policy. Congress may not do that.

It is not within our power. Yet a large majority of the Supreme Court concluded that is exactly what Congress did in the Affordable Care Act. So faced with yet another constitutional problem, the Supreme Court adopted another rewrite that the Supreme Court of the United States was not constitutionally empowered to bring about. What the Supreme Court did in that circumstance was to just read in or write in an opt-out for the States so as to make it constitutional.

Some have tried to defend this by saying: Well, that is what courts do. When courts find that something is unconstitutional, they have to look a second time to see whether they can read into it a different interpretation that might be fairly plausible—a fairly plausible interpretation that could allow them to save it. But in this case there was nothing there. There was nothing that could allow them to do this.

The Court's job at that moment was to figure out whether the unconstitutional provision could be severed from the rest of the statute, whether it could be excised, sort of like a cancerous tumor, allowing the healthy tissue to remain with the cancerous tissue gone forever. There are rules and standards the Supreme Court is supposed to follow when engaging in this exercise, and whenever it does this, it follows decades-old severability jurisprudence. Well, that standard, I believe, if followed, would have inevitably culminated in the Supreme Court of the United States finding that the Medicaid expansion provisions could not be severed from the rest of the statute—the other provisions in the Affordable Care Act. I suspect that may well be why the Supreme Court did not engage in severability analysis. Instead, it rewrote the law.

So the Supreme Court of the United States rewrote ObamaCare not just once but twice in order to save it. This is not OK. This is not constitutional. This is not America.

The next response the defenders of this law usually bring up is, well, it is, after all, the Supreme Court's job to decide what is constitutional and what is not constitutional. So if they say it is constitutional, then it must be constitutional, and who is anyone else to second guess their judgment as to constitutionality?

OK. Well, I understand that argument. That argument is fine, perhaps, as far as it goes. You can't read too much into that statement. It is not fair to say that the Supreme Court is the sole expositor of constitutional meaning. It is true, of course, that within our Federal system the Supreme Court has the last word in deciding questions of Federal statutory and constitutional interpretation for the purpose of deciding discrete cases and controversies properly before the Court's jurisdiction. However, that does not excuse the rest of us from independently exercising our own judgment, nor is it the case that every constitutional infraction and every constitutional indiscretion is necessarily within the competence of the Federal courts to resolve.

In fact, there are countless circumstances in which, either because the courts might lack jurisdiction or because no plaintiff can be brought forward with article III standing necessary to challenge the Federal action in question or because the courts have recognized that there is a nonjusticiable political question at stake—for whatever reason, courts might not be competent to address a particular issue. In other circumstances, a case for whatever reason simply is not brought. In many circumstances the courts don't have occasion to address a constitutional infraction.

Regardless, we are never excused. We, as Senators of the United States, having taken an oath under article VI of the Constitution to uphold the Constitution of the United States, are never excused from our responsibility to look out for, protect, and defend the Constitution of the United States. When we see an unconstitutional action, we need to call it out as such, and we need to do whatever we can to stop the Constitution from being violated.

The Constitution was violated, the Constitution was distorted, and the Constitution was manipulated. It was defiled not once but twice by the Supreme Court of the United States when the Court rewrote the Affordable Care Act twice in this decision that was rendered at the end of June 2012.

This is one of many reasons why I think it is important for us to have this debate and discussion about whether we fully fund the implementation and enforcement of this law—a law that was never read by those who enacted it, a law that has become less popular rather than more popular subsequent to its enactment, a law that has now spawned some 20,000 pages and counting of new regulatory text.

This same law was rewritten not just once but twice by a supreme court of the United States that openly flouted the Constitution of the United States. They thumbed their noses at their own constitutional responsibilities. We are now being asked whether we should continue funding the implementation and enforcement of that act, and I think not.

In addition to the unconstitutional rewriting by the Supreme Court of the United States, we now have several instances in which the President of the United States himself has attempted to rewrite the Patient Protection and Affordable Care Act. The President of the United States has said that although enforcement of the employer mandate provision is set to begin on January 1, 2014, the President's administration will not implement and enforce that provision effective January 1, 2014. Although the President lacks any constitutional or statutory authority to make this decision, although the President has neither sought nor obtained a legislative modification from the legislative branch of government—Congress—the President is treating the law as if it contained that modification already.

There was another modification that took place with respect to the implementation of the out-of-pocket spending limits, the spending caps. This, too, was done without any legislative or any constitutional authority. There is another modification the President made with respect to proof of eligibility for subsidies on the exchange network set up by the Affordable Care Act. All three of these modifications were made by the President without any statutory authority, and they were, therefore, extra constitutional modifications.

As I understand it, a few weeks ago somebody asked the President of the United States why this was appropriate. Somebody challenged the President of the United States with regard to his authority on these modifications. His response was something similar to this: Under ordinary circumstances, under more ideal circumstances, perhaps I might have gone to Congress to get Congress to modify

232 STAND WITH TED

the statutory provisions in question, but these are not ordinary or ideal circumstances.

I am not sure exactly what he meant, but it sounds to me as though what he was saying was, I am in a tough spot so I have to do what I can do, what I can get away with, because I have a Congress that is now less cooperative, less inclined to cooperate with me, less inclined to do what I as President of the United States want Congress to do, than the Congress that was in place in 2010 when the Patient Protection and Affordable Care Act was enacted into law.

That is interesting. It is interesting on a number of levels because, No. 1, one of the reasons Congress is now less inclined to be coopera- tive with the President, one of the reasons the Congress is no longer as inclined to do the President's bidding is, interestingly enough, because of the Patient Protection and Affordable Care Act, because of the widespread public outcry that came from across this country as a direct result of the enactment of this statute.

It is not at all unusual to have a divided Congress. It is not at all unusual for one or both Houses of Congress to be under the control of a party other than the President's own political party. Yet it has never been the case and can never be the case if there is somehow an exception to the Constitution, if there is somehow an exception to article I's provision that all legislative powers granted by the Constitu- tion shall be vested in a Congress consisting of a Senate and of a House of Representatives.

The fact that the President finds political dissent within the Congress irritating does not make him a king. The fact that Con- gress will not always do the President's bidding does not vest him with the powers of a despot. When someone holding the office of President of the United States purports to wield legislative power, when the President of the United States purports to make law by the stroke of the executive pen, we have exited the territorial con- fines of constitutional government.

These are some of the reasons we have focused this debate back on ObamaCare. People are frequently bringing up the argument: This is law. This is settled law. Because it is settled law, you must fund it. First of all, I am aware of no constitutional command that says that simply because a law has been adopted, Congress must fund any and every provision authorized under that law. In fact, quite to the contrary. Because Congress holds the power of the purse, Congress may—Congress must—continue to have the authority to decide which programs to fund and which programs not to fund. Were it otherwise, we would have a straining set of circumstances in which one Congress could bind another Congress simply by passing a piece of legislation and not by a constitutional amendment.

That is not the case. It never has been the case. It never could be, should be or will be the case under our constitutional system today.

What we see is the fact that this is not simply a partisan political debate. Many are casting it as that. Many are pointing to the fact that we have some Republicans agreeing with some Democrats, but for the most part we see widespread disagreement between Republicans and Democrats. But that dramatically oversimplifies the matter. This is no longer simply a dispute between Republicans and Democrats. In many respects, this represents a dispute between the political ruling establishment in Washington, DC, on the one hand and the American people on the other hand.

One of the things we are often told we have to face is that we have to choose to keep everything funded or we have to choose to fund nothing. It is a frequent source of frustration to many who serve in this body. It certainly has been a frequent source of frustration to me and to the 3 million people I represent in the State of Utah. It is odd that we find ourselves in a position to vote on a continuing resolution that funds everything in government or nothing in government. It is a frustrating exercise we have to go through. Because of the fact that we have chosen to appropriate this way year after year, we basically have one opportunity to decide what we are going to fund in government and what we are not going to fund in government. I wish what we could do is, at a minimum, a bare minimum—it should be a lot more than this—but at a bare minimum, to have two different debates, two different discussions, both starting with the presupposition that we fund nothing but culminating in funding or not funding something; one that would deal with funding for ObamaCare and another one that would deal with funding for everything else in government. It would be nice if ObamaCare funding had to stand or fall on its own merits. If we were starting from zero when it came to providing ObamaCare funding and we had to justify it, we had to make the case for it, and we had to say, let's prove to the American people why we ought to be funding the enforcement of this law—this law that will make health care less affordable rather than more and this law that is being implemented in a fundamentally unfair manner, I think that would prove a very different debate and discussion. But very often the way things work in Washington, the way continuing resolutions work, is we are faced with a set of circumstances that don't accurately reflect the way we make decisions in any other aspect of our lives.

I sometimes am inclined to analogize this kind of continuing resolution spending default. This is a vast oversimplification, but suppose someone lived in a very remote area. Suppose the closest town to where they lived was at least 100 miles away, but there was one market, one grocery store just 1 mile from their home. It was the only grocery store within at least 150 miles, let's just say. One day the person's spouse calls them on their way home from work and says: Stop at the store. We need bread, milk, and eggs. The person goes to the grocery store and finds the bread, puts it in the cart, finds the milk and eggs, puts them in the cart, and goes to the checkout counter. The cashier checks out those things and then the cashier says: Wait a second. You can't just buy these things. You cannot just buy bread, milk, and eggs.

You say: Why on Earth can I not buy just these three items? This is all I need.

This is a different kind of grocery store. This is a grocery store patterned after the U.S. Congress. In order to buy bread, milk, and eggs, we are also going to require you to buy a bucket of nails, a half ton of iron ore, and you can use our wheelbarrow to take it out to your car, a book about cowboy poetry, and a Barry Manilow album.

You say: I don't want any of those things. And the cashier says: That is fine. Then you don't get your bread, your milk, and your eggs.

At that point, the shopper, not wanting to come home to a very disappointed spouse, is likely to say: Fine, even though I don't want the nails or the iron ore or the cowboy poetry book, and I definitely don't want the Barry Manilow album, I am going to buy those things because I can't buy the things I need unless I also buy those things.

That is how we spend in the Congress. Whether we like it or not—and most of us don't like it—that is what we are stuck with. So that is one of the reasons we are having this debate now, one of the reasons I think it is appropriate for us to have this debate in connection with this. It is unfortunate in many respects that we tie something so fundamental to who we are as a country, something so essential to our ongoing existence as a nation as national defense. It seems absurd that we should tie that to funding for ObamaCare. Yet that is where we find ourselves because of the fact that we have been operating under a continuous string of back-to-back continuing resolutions for the last 4 or 5 years.

It is time for us to start breaking away from those false and ultimately ridiculous choices. It is time for us to demand more as a people from our Congress. It is time for us as a people to start to demand independent debate and discussion, debate and discussion that far more closely reflects the will of the American people and their ongoing needs.

If the Senate must choose between standing with the longstanding interests, the entrenched interests of the political governing class in Washington on the one hand or, on the other hand, standing with the American people, I hope—I expect—that we will stand with the American people. If we ask any Member how constituents are feeling about the Affordable Care Act, how constituents are feeling about ObamaCare and its coming implementation and enforcement, the response we will get is that, at best, constituents are mixed. In many cases, they are apprehensive, they are uncertain. But overwhelmingly, we will find a lot of opposition from people who are seeing those all around them facing job losses, wage cuts, cuts to their hours, and cuts to their health care benefits.

How long are we going to have to continue to hear these things before we act? Are we as a Congress willing to just look at these things and say: Yes, well, bad things happen. Let's just allow them to happen. Are we willing to do that? Those who are Democrats, are they willing to do that saying, yes, I know this law is not perfect, but it is a speed dump that we have to cross over on our way to a single-payer system run by the health care system? As Republicans, are we willing to endure that, saying, yes, it is a train wreck, but the good news is it might inure to our political benefit if it gets in? I hope we are not willing to do that. I hope we have not descended to such a shameful, cynical low that we would be willing to allow those political interests to trump the needs of the American people who are calling out, crying out for help and for relief.

Ultimately, as we think about our responsibilities as Senators, as we think about our responsibilities as citizens, I hope we will reflect from time to time on the fact that we have all taken an oath to uphold this document, this 226-year-old document, a document that I believe was written by the hands of wise men raised up by their Creator for that very purpose, to help foster and promote what will become—what has become—the greatest civilization the world has ever known.

To the extent that we respect and honor this document, to the extent that we follow it, to the extent that we defend it, we uphold it at every turn, to the extent that we consider it not just a responsibility of the judiciary but also of the political branches of government, including our own branch, we have prospered as a country. And to the extent that we will return to those practices, we will benefit directly as a result.

So I have to ask Senator CRUZ, as a constitutional lawyer, as one of our Nation's preeminent appellate litigators, as one who has argued many times before the U.S. Supreme Court, and as one who clerked for the late Chief Justice William Rehnquist and now as a U.S. Senator, how does the Senator see this role, the role of what some describe as coordinate branch construction of the Constitution? What role does it play in this body? What role does the Constitution play in the Senate? Does it have a place or is that something that is supposed to be left to the nine men and women wearing black robes across the street who are lawyers and hold a different constitutional office than we do?

(Mr. SCHATZ assumed the Chair.)

Mr. CRUZ. Well, I thank my friend the junior Senator from Utah for his very fine, learned question. It is truly a privilege to serve in this body alongside a constitutional scholar, alongside a Senator who takes fidelity to the Constitution so seriously, so appropriately seriously.

Senator LEE's question is exactly right: How seriously do the men and woman in this body take the Constitution? How seriously do we take the obligation? Each of us swears to uphold the Constitution. Yet it is easy, particularly in an era in which the Supreme Court is deemed to be the primary arbiter of constitutionality, for Members of Congress, members of the executive branch, to say: That is their problem. We pass the laws; the Court figures out if they are constitutional.

I would very much agree with Senator LEE's proposition that doing so is an abdication of our responsibility, that every one of us has an obligation to not support any law that is contrary to the Constitution and to oppose any law that is.

I would note that among the House Members who joined us was Congressman JUSTIN AMASH. He came to the floor of the Senate to join us to support this effort. I note Congressman AMASH has the unique distinction of joining you and me and Senator PAUL in the description of being—I believe the term was "wacko birds," which, I for one— I am not sure to which particular avian species that refers, but whichever one it is, if it reflects a fidelity to the Constitution, a fidelity to liberty, and a willingness to fight to defend the principles this country was founded on, then I—and I believe I can speak for you and RAND and Congressman AMASH—and I think quite a few others of us are very, very proud "wacko birds."

We are talking about an important topic. We are talking about a topic that impacts millions of Americans. But at the same time, we cannot lose our sense of humor, and we cannot lose our sense of hope and optimism.

I will note that my staff has been with me here all night, tirelessly fighting because they believe in America. We believe in America. We believe there can be something better. You look at the explosion of government, the explosion of spending, the explosion of debt, the explosion of taxes, the explosion of regulation, the stagnation of economic growth, and it is easy to throw up your hands and say: Can we ever get back to that United States of America we once were?

But there are signs, glimmers of hope. Look right now at one of the
most popular television shows in the United States—"Duck Dynasty."
This is a show about a God-fearing family of successful entrepreneurs
who love guns, who love to hunt, and who believe in the American
dream. It is something that, according to Congress, almost should not
exist, yet a lot of wisdom. Millions of Americans tune in to "Duck
Dynasty." So I want to point out just a few words of wisdom from
"Duck Dynasty" that are probably good for all of us to hear.

Willie observed: You put 5 rednecks on a mower, it's gonna be epic.

Phil said: In a subdivision, you call 911. At home, I AM 911!

Si said: Some people say I'm a dreamer, others say, "If you fall
asleep at work again we're going to let you go."

Jase said: Redneck rule number one, most things can be fixed with
duct tape and extension cords.

(That is actually very true.)

Phil said: I think our problem is a spiritual one.

Phil also said: When you get older and you start dating, I want you
to be able to say one thing, "I can bait a hook."

(One day maybe Caroline and Catherine will be able to say that.)

Phil also said, very simply: Happy, happy, happy.

I say this to the junior Senator from Utah, when we defund
ObamaCare, we are all going to be happy, happy, happy.

Miss Kay said: Our marriage is living proof that love & family can
get you through everything.

Si said: I live by my own rules (reviewed, revised, and approved
by my wife) . . . but still my own.

Jep said: Faith, family, and facial hair.

Let me point out to the junior Senator from Utah that if we continue doing this long enough, we may have facial hair on the floor of
Senate. That is all right.

Willie said: Are you kidding me? I'm straight up hunger games
with a bow.

Si said: Ford F150, Chevy Silverado, Dodge Ram, Toyota Tundra. As a married man, these are the only pickup lines I am allowed to use.

Jase said: Where I come from, your truck is an exact reflection on your personality.

Si said: I make up people all the time to get out of stuff.

Si also said: A redneck walkin' into Bass Pro Shops gets more excited than a 12 year old girl going to a Justin Beaver concert.

Let me point out that that is Justin Beaver, B-e-a-v-e-r.

Si also said: Your beard is so hairy, even Dora can't explore it.

Si also said: Your beard's so stupid it takes 2 hours to watch 60 minutes!

And finally Si said: I am the MacGyver of cooking. You bring me a piece of bread, cabbage, coconut, mustard greens, pigs feet, pine cones . . . and a woodpecker, I'll make you a good chicken pot pie.

Let me suggest that kind of homespun wisdom is what this country was built on. It is who we are. Look, there are some things to chuckle on, but there is an awful lot of common sense.

On the same theme, I want to point to one of my favorite songs. It is a song that came out following the tragic attacks on this country of 9/11, but it speaks more broadly to who we are as Americans, that we can overcome any challenge, any obstacle, including, I think, the obstacle of ObamaCare—admittedly, a very, very different challenge than that which occurred on 9/11, but ultimately the American spirit and faith and freedom that underlie it will help us overcome every challenge. That is Toby Keith's song "Courtesy of the Red, White, and Blue."

Toby Keith observed—and, Mr. President, I am going to make a promise to you. I am not going to endeavor to sing because even if it might not violate the Senate rules, it would violate rules of musical harmony, human decency, and possibly even the Geneva Conventions. So I will not subject you to my musical rendition, but I will at least share the words from "Courtesy of the Red, White, and Blue."

[At this point, Senator Cruz recites the lyrics to "Courtesy Of The Red, White, And Blue (The Angry American)" by Toby Keith. The lyrics can be found on the various Internet sites.]

If you want to talk about the American spirit, it is hard to listen to that song and not think about who we are as a people, not think about the threats.

Let me give you an example of a different threat, a different threat to our liberty that every bit as much we have to rise up against. I want to read for you a statement of September 12, 2012, that Hobby Lobby put out on ObamaCare and religious freedom. Religious freedom is foundational to who we are. So let's read what David Green, the CEO and founder of Hobby Lobby Stores, Inc., stated.

When my family and I started our company 40 years ago, we were working out of a garage on a $600 bank loan, assembling miniature picture frames. Our first retail store wasn't much bigger than most people's living rooms, but we had faith that we would succeed if we lived and worked according to God's work. From there, Hobby Lobby has become one of the nation's largest arts and crafts retailers, with more than 500 locations in 41 states. Our children grew up into fine business leaders, and today we run Hobby Lobby together, as a family.

We're Christians, and we run our business on Christian principles. I've always said that the first two goals of our business are 1) to run our business in harmony with God's laws, and 2) to focus on people more than money. And that's what we've tried to do. We close early so our employees can see their families at night. We keep our stores closed on Sundays, one of the week's biggest shopping days, so that our workers and their families can enjoy a day of rest. We believe that it is by God's grace that Hobby Lobby has endured, and he has blessed us and our employees. We've not only added jobs in a weak economy, we've also raised wages for the past four years in a row. Our full-time employees start at 80% above minimum wage.

But now, our government threatens to change all of that. A new government health care mandate says that our family business must provide what I believe are abortion-causing drugs as part of our health insurance. Being Christians, we don't pay for drugs that might cause abortions. Which means that we don't cover emergency contraception, the morning-after pill or the week-after pill.

We believe that doing so might end a life after the moment of conception, something that is contrary to our most important beliefs. It goes against the biblical principles on which we have run this company since day one. If we refuse to comply, we could face $1.3 million per day in government fines.

Our government threatens to fine job creators in a bad economy. Our government threatens to fine a company that has raised wages four years running. Our government threatens to fine a family for running its business according to its beliefs. It's not right.

I know people will say we ought to follow the rules, that it's the same for everybody. But that's not true. The government has exempted thousands of companies from its mandates, for reasons of convenience or cost. But it won't exempt them for reasons of religious belief.

So, Hobby Lobby—and my family—are forced to make a choice. With great reluctance, we filed a lawsuit today, represented by the Becket Fund for Religious Liberty, asking a federal court to stop this mandate before it hurts our business. We don't like to go running into court, but we no longer have a choice. We believe people are more important than the bottom line and that honoring God is more important than turning a profit.

My family has lived the American dream. We want to continue growing our company and providing great jobs for thousands of employees, but the government is going to make that much more difficult. The government is forcing us to choose between following our faith and following the law. I say that's a choice no American—and no American business—should have to make.

Now, you might ask, what does that letter from Hobby Lobby have to do with Toby Keith's terrific song? I am going to suggest they have an awful lot to do with each other. Our Nation was founded by men and women fleeing religious persecution from across the globe, fleeing governments that sought to impose their rules to restrict the religious liberty of men and women.

Our Founding Fathers, the people who formed the United States of America, fled those countries and came here. Why? To establish a country where everyone could worship God with all of your heart, mind and soul, according to the dictates of your conscience. The men and women watching this at home—not all of you may share the religious convictions of the CEO of Hobby Lobby. You may or may not be Christians. If you are Christians, you may or may not share his faith and his interpretation of what his faith requires.

But if you look at the history of our country, the Federal Government is telling that CEO—the Federal Government is telling Catholic hospitals and Catholic charities that they must violate their religious beliefs. Why? Because government knows best. You know, there is a reason why the Bill of Rights begins with the First Amendment and why the First Amendment begins with protecting religious liberty, protecting the religious liberty of all of us, because it is foundational. The Founding Fathers who formed our country understood that if you did not have the freedom to seek out God, then every other freedom could be stripped away. Yet this administration has demonstrated a hostility to religious faith that is staggering, indeed.

In recent months, we saw an Air Force chaplain in Alaska face punishment and repercussions for posting a blog post in which he stated, "there are no atheists in foxholes."

Now, mind you, this was a chaplain. His job is to minister to the spiritual life of the men and women of the Air Force. Yet that statement was deemed inhospitable to atheists and inconsistent with the military and this administration. Now, the irony, of course, is that particular statement was said previously by a general named Dwight D. Eisenhower, who as we all know was President of the United States.

Indeed, President Dwight D. Eisenhower had more than a passing familiarity with the military. That statement comes from a speech

President Eisenhower gave to the American Legion—I believe it was in 1954—in which he was describing a story of four immortal chaplains. That story is a story young people do not learn any more. It is a story a lot of people do not know. President Eisenhower told it.

I had the opportunity recently to speak at the American Legion's national convention. I had the opportunity to share it. There were a number of particularly older veterans, World War II veterans, who knew the story of the four immortal chaplains. That is the story of the USS *Dorchester* that was hit by a U-boat torpedo and was sinking. There were four chaplains aboard that ship.

I believe two were Protestant, one was Catholic, and one was Jewish. They were handing out life vests. They realized they did not have enough life vests for the men and women on that ship. Each of those four chaplains removed his life vest and gave it to another passenger. Those other passengers were saved and those four chaplains stood together on the deck of the ship singing and praying as the ship went down.

The point of the story is, when the chaplains put their life vests on other passengers, gave their life vests, gave their lives for other passengers, they did not ask each passenger: Are you a Christian? Are you a Jew? Is your religious faith the same as mine? Because, as President Eisenhower explained, there are no atheists in foxholes, and they were there sacrificing for their fellow man.

You know religious liberty is foundational to who we are. One of the most pernicious aspects of ObamaCare is that it disregards religious liberty, when you have the Federal Government getting so intimately involved in health care. It has necessitated the Federal Government trampling on good faith religious beliefs.

Look, nobody has questioned the good faith religious beliefs of the owners of Hobby Lobby. Even if you do not share their views, what about your religious beliefs? If the government can order them to violate their religious beliefs, what is to stop them from ordering you to violate yours?

That is wrong. That is inconsistent with who we are as Americans. That is one of the many reasons Americans are fed up with what is happening under ObamaCare.

You know, earlier I was reading some of the stories from individual constituents. I would like to return to that. A constituent in Humble, TX, wrote on September 10, 2013:

I am one of many Americans adversely affected by Mr. Obama's health care. I just received a letter stating that as the Affordable Care Act draws fuller to close implementation, I will no longer have access to the group medical PPO plan, the group dental plan, or the group vision plan effective January 1, 2014. I am 62, in good health, but need health insurance. I do not know what my options will be if I can even afford a government-run plan.

That is not me speaking. That is reading a letter from one individual who is 62 years old who had insurance but is losing that insurance because of ObamaCare. Not working. It is simply not working.

Another constituent from Fort Worth, TX, wrote on September 9, 2013:

My husband was with IBM for over 30 years. We considered the health insurance was part of our salary. Two weeks ago, I found out that they are canceling the insurance for retirees and their spouses because of ObamaCare. They say they will give me a lump sum of money to buy another plan. But I assume once that money is gone, I will be responsible for the payments. Thank you for all you're doing to stop ObamaCare. By the way, my primary physician just closed his practice because of ObamaCare. He said he didn't think he could give the kind of care to his patients that they deserve.

There are two things there that are very striking. No. 1 is the situation of this woman so many Americans across this country are experiencing. They had a health plan they liked. They had health insurance they liked. We remember 3½ years ago when the President promised the American people: If you like your health insurance you can keep it. We now know that statement was flatly, objectively 100 percent false. We now know that it is not the case, if you like your health insurance you can keep it, because ObamaCare is causing people all over the country, like this woman in Ft. Worth, TX, to lose her health insurance.

They are understandably not happy about it. They are hurting. They are suffering. But, secondly, I think it is very interesting, the point about her primary physician. We are also seeing doctors leaving the practice of medicine, advising young students: Don't go to med school because ObamaCare is destroying the practice of medicine. If the goal is to expand access to health care, driving good physicians out of the practice of medicine is completely antithetical to that goal.

Another constituent, a retired couple from Bayou Vista, TX, wrote on the September 9, 2013:

> My wife and I are retired living on a fixed income. We worked hard our whole lives protecting our credit and saved enough money to buy a modest home in Bayou Vista, TX. If the insurance premiums being published in the local newspaper materialize, we will no longer be able to afford to live in our home. We could not sell it either. The facts, if left unchanged, will destroy many coastal communities and result in our personal financial ruin. We would have no choice but to walk from our mortgage. We would lose all of the investment we have made in this house. Our credit would be ruined.

These are the words of a retired couple living on a fixed income who managed to save up to buy a home for their retirement for their golden years. ObamaCare is threatening to turn their retirement into a nightmare. I remind you that the word "nightmare" is not mine. That word "nightmare" is the word of James Hoffa, the president of the Teamsters.

That nightmare is very real for that couple. It is real for so many Americans. Yet it is a nightmare. It is now late at night. I am going to venture to say most Members of the Senate are home in bed asleep while America lives the nightmare. If we were listening to the people, we would not be home asleep. If we were listening to the people, we would be experiencing that nightmare, we would be waking up—much like my little girls do sometimes when they have a scary dream—but we would be responding like any parent does when your child has a nightmare. You come in and try to make the nightmare go away.

America is experiencing that nightmare and it is even worse. Because here, the Senate caused that nightmare. We passed the law that is the nightmare for the American people, and Senators on both sides of the aisle have been telling the American people they are too busy, there are too many other priorities on their list to even talk about the nightmare that is ObamaCare.

That is wrong. That is fundamentally wrong. We need to make DC listen.

Mr. LEE. Would the Senator yield for a question?

Mr. CRUZ. I am happy to yield for a question without yielding the floor.

Mr. LEE. I wish to ask the Senator from Texas his reaction to a couple of stories that I think relate well to what the Senator from Texas is saying to us about the fact that Congress has adopted a law that has brought about a series of nightmares for the American people, only these are real. This is not some dream we are going to wake up from and discover that this is a figment of our subconscious mind that is causing us torment. It is real.

Sometimes we react as a lawmaking body to situations in such a way that we don't necessarily improve upon the status quo. We identify a problem, and we try to act. Sometimes the results aren't necessarily what we intend them to be. Sometimes the results can be quite the opposite of what was intended at the outset. I think this may well have been the case with the Patient Protection and Affordable Care Act which at the end of the day neither protects patients nor makes health care more affordable.

It reminds me a little bit of a story, something I experienced a few years ago when I was working at the Supreme Court. I shared an office with three other law clerks at the time.

We discovered something very interesting about our office space. During the summer months, when we started our clerkships, our office was almost unbearably cold, something that was unusual for me because I like an office or a home to be relatively cool, but this was unusually cold. It was so cold we were tempted to wear gloves in the middle of the summer indoors because our office was so cold. It was so cold that sometimes we would open our windows to our office, even though it was hot outside, and it would let in this hot, humid air. Sometimes we were tempted to build fires in the fireplace in our small office in the middle of the summer, because it was so cold in the office that our hands would get numb and we could barely write. That is a significant portion of a law clerk's job is to write, write a lot of material.

We would walk over to the thermostat thinking that might solve the problem. It was too cold, so we turned the thermostat up thinking that would make it a little bit warmer and, therefore, more tolerable in our office. First we would move it up a little. It didn't do any good. Then we would move it up a lot and it still didn't do any good. It was still freezing cold in our office in the middle of the summer in Washington.

When it came to be wintertime, we had a similar problem but at the opposite end of the thermometer. In the wintertime we found that our office was intolerably hot. It was hot all the time. It was so hot that we were sweating. It is hardly appropriate, when working as a law clerk at the Supreme Court of the United States, to wear shorts to work, especially in January, so we didn't do that. Because it was so hot we frequently found ourselves tempted to open the windows again, letting in very cold air from the outside. Because we were so hot we had to do something to balance out the temperature. Again, we went to the thermostat to no avail. It was intolerably hot so we, of course, turned the thermostat down, first a little, and it didn't do any good, and then a lot, and it still didn't do any good.

After a while we called the maintenance people of the building. In fact, we called several of the maintenance people in the building. It was an old building, finished in 1935. It was undergoing renovation at the time. The renovation went on for many years. We ultimately got to the top maintenance and management supervisor in the Supreme Court. He ended up spending a fair amount of time trying to find out what was wrong with our heating and air conditioning system, trying to figure out why on Earth it was so intolerably cold in our office in the summer and why it was so intolerably hot in the wintertime.

His conclusion was relatively simple, and it was not what we expected. He came to us and he said, OK, I have dismantled your entire system and I found the problem. Your thermostat was installed backward. When you turned the thermostat up, trying to make it warmer, it had the opposite effect. It was only making it colder. When you turned the thermostat down, trying to make it cooler, it was only making it hotter in your office, hence your problem.

As he said this, I looked out the window across the street at the Capitol, and I thought I wonder if there is something Congress can learn from this. Sometimes Congress, out of an abundant, legitimate, well-intentioned desire to achieve good in society will do something. Sometimes that something is the only thing Congress knows how to do at the moment. Why? Because Congress legislates. It is what we do.

As I have said before, sometimes when you are holding a hammer, everything starts to look like a nail. Sometimes when Congress acts, even with the best of intentions, it gets it wrong. The risk of this is especially high when Congress acts in 2,700-page increments that no one has read prior to passing those increments into law. I believe that is what happened here.

But the proper response to a broken thermostat, or a thermostat that is installed backward, is not to continue using the same thermostat. The solution has to be to fix the thermostat, to replace it. We have got a broken thermostat with this law and it needs to be replaced entirely.

I am also reminded of another story, a story that is somewhat related that helps us understand some similar points.

One night when I was a teenager, I think I was about 14 years old, I was out with my family. I grew up in a large family, seven children, but in Utah that is sort of a medium-sized family, but that is a discussion for a different day. We were out somewhere with the family. I think we had gone out for dinner, and we were headed home. As we were almost to our home, one of my younger sisters suggested to my dad that we go out for ice cream as a family. We were almost home, and recognizing that we were almost home, I all of a sudden realized I didn't want to go out for ice cream because I had homework. I asked my dad to keep driving home, drop me off at the house. The rest of the family could continue on and go and get ice cream together. That way I could stay home, get my homework done, and I wouldn't have to be up too late.

It all worked well. I had all my siblings in the car. That is a lot of kids in the car, but my dad pulled up in front of our house to let me out. I was in the back seat of the car. I opened the car door, and I put one foot out of the car, starting to get out. I wish to tell you something a little bit about my father—my late father, may he rest in peace; he died 17 years ago. He was a very good man, a wise man, a smart man. He was one of my greatest heroes in this life. He had many talents, but he was also very absentminded. Sometimes he wasn't paying attention, and this was one of those moments.

As I stepped one foot out of our Oldsmobile, my dad started to drive off with half of my body still in the car. Somehow the Oldsmobile ended up on top of my foot turned around backwards. That is a little bit hard to describe. The Oldsmobile, with a whole bunch of kids in it, weighs a lot. All of a sudden the Oldsmobile was on top of my foot as it was turned around backwards. I was trying to explain to my dad we had a problem, but all that came out were grunts and groans. I couldn't quite find the words to tell him that we had a problem, because I was in so much pain.

He realized at that point I was still in the car, but it still didn't occur to him that the car was on top of my foot. Finally I mustered the presence of mind to get out one word, one word that I knew I could pronounce, one word that would send the message unequivocally to my father: Get the Oldsmobile off of my foot. But I couldn't utter that many words, so I spit out one word. The word was "reverse." Dad, reverse. Well, he got that message. He put the car in reverse, and he got the Oldsmobile off my foot.

But for my ability to utter that one word in a relatively short period of time that seemed like an eternity under the circumstances, my foot may well have been broken, my siblings probably would have found that mildly amusing under the circumstances, and I probably wouldn't have gotten my homework done that night. As it turned out, I was able to avoid that and it was because I was able to utter that one word, reverse.

Sometimes when you are doing something that hurts someone, you have to reverse. You have to turn off that which has been turned on which has been harming people. This law, turned on 3½ years ago, is harming people. It is going to do a lot more if it remains in the on position. We need to put this car into reverse. We need, at a minimum, to halt the operation of this law.

The best way, I believe the only way at this point, to achieve that, short of repeal, is by defunding. Say: Look, at a minimum, let's halt the spending on further implementation and enforcement of this law while we get certain things sorted out as a country, while we figure out what else we can do.

The objections to this are many. Some say this can't ever happen. You don't have the political will to do that, and you don't have the political muscle to do that. It can't happen. We know one thing for certain. It is never going to happen if we don't try.

We also know a number of other can't-win battles have been fought and ultimately won. A few months ago, Americans were being told we are going to have significant gun control legislation, significant legislation that could eat away in a meaningful way through your privacy and your right to own a gun in this country. We are going to have some form of gun registration system. We were told this is happening, just accept it, just deal with it, there is nothing you can do about it. A few people in Congress disagreed with that conclusion. A few people in Congress resisted, and we stopped it.

Only a few weeks ago it was regarded as an indisputable truth that we were going to get involved in some kind of military strife in Syria. A swelling group of lawmakers from both Houses in both political parties started expressing reservations with that idea. Before long people stopped saying resisting that effort was impossible. After a while, they stopped saying it was improbable, and after a while movement to resist getting the United States involved in military action in Syria became absolutely unstoppable.

In one way or another, I believe the effort to stop ObamaCare might bear some resemblance to this. It might operate under a somewhat different time-frame. Initially, people said the effort to stop this law was one that was impossible.

I think we are reaching the point at which it is being described by many as improbable. In time, as more and more Americans join this cause, as more and more Americans reach out to their Senators and their Congressmen, this effort will become absolutely unstoppable.

Because the American people love freedom, the American people were born to live free. The sons and daughters of America have freedom as their birthright, and they don't take particularly well to micromanagement from a large, distant, national government—one that is slow to respond to the needs of the people, one that often approaches the people with something that does not exactly resemble deep sympathy or compassion, because this is not what large national governments are all about.

A large national government can do certain things well. It can do certain things no one else can do well. But it can't be all things to all people, least of all physician and general caretaker to all. When we try to do all things, we often cause far more problems than we resolve.

So in this circumstance, we have to remember the lesson we learned from the thermostat, the lesson I learned while working at the Supreme Court; that sometimes if you have a broken thermostat, what you do might actually be having the opposite effect of what you are trying to do. What you are trying to do might actually make matters worse if your thermostat's broken, if it is installed backward.

We also have to remember that sometimes when you get into a position where you are causing harm or you could cause more harm unless you change direction, that you sometimes just have to reverse. This, I believe, is one of those times.

To reframe all of this, we are here at nearly 2 in the morning on an otherwise perfectly good Tuesday night. I guess now it is Wednesday morning. We are here because we feel strongly about how best to proceed with a funding mechanism passed by the House of Representatives. The House of Representatives last week responded to a call from the

American people—a call to do something very important, a call to keep the Federal Government funded and operating but to do so while defunding ObamaCare. Once that was passed by the House, once that started making its way over to the Senate, we in the Senate were faced with several alternatives.

I believe there are two very good alternatives to addressing that. One is to vote on the House-passed continuing resolution that funds government but defunds ObamaCare on an up-or-down basis, either pass it or don't pass it, but pass it or don't pass it in as-is condition based on how it was passed by the House.

That is one good option. Another option would be to subject that same House-passed continuing resolution that funds government but defunds ObamaCare to an open amendment process, a process by which Senators, both Republicans and Democrats, may propose alterations to that continuing resolution as they deem fit. This would require us to debate, discuss, and vote on a number of amendments.

Either of these alternatives would be equally acceptable. I can see arguments for either one of them. But what is not acceptable is for the Senate majority leader to do as he is expected to do by many, which is to say we will have one amendment and one amendment only to the House-passed continuing resolution and that amendment will be one to gut the continuing resolution of a provision that was the "without which not" measure of the entire bill to gut the defunding language.

At the same time, the majority leader is expected widely to fill the tree, meaning to say no other amendments will be allowed. This is it. There is no more. If he is going to do that, he is not going to have my help doing it, and because he is not going to have my help doing it, that means I must vote no on cloture on the bill.

In other words, HARRY REID is expected to ask his Members, and is expected to be followed by the 53 other Members in his caucus, for a total of 54 Democrats who will vote yes when it comes to cloture on this bill, who will vote yes knowing full well HARRY REID and the 53 Democrats who follow him, for a combined total of 54, will vote on cloture on this bill. This doesn't mean they are in support of the

House-passed resolution as adopted by the House, funding government but defunding ObamaCare. Quite to the contrary, this means they are in favor of gutting it, of severing, of cutting out its most important single provision.

If HARRY REID and the 53 Democrats who follow him want to do that, that is their prerogative. As a Republican who was elected to combat ObamaCare, to try to stop it, I will not be voting for cloture on the bill for that very reason. That could change, of course, if HARRY REID decides to bring up this continuing resolution for a vote as is, on its own merits, as it was written or, alternatively, if HARRY REID decides to bring up the House-passed continuing resolution under an open amendment process, allowing Senators to propose, debate, discuss and, ultimately, vote on amendments.

But what is not acceptable is for him to allow one and only one amendment, one gutting the continuing resolution of its most important provision. With him doing that, the Democrats can oppose this if they want. I will not be joining them, and I don't believe they need Republican help if that is what they want to do. If they do want Republicans to vote with them, I will not be among them. My job is not to make it easier for them to gut the House-passed resolution.

I stand with the House of Representatives. I stand behind Speaker BOEHNER and the Republicans who assisted him in getting this passed. I want to get this passed. I would like to pass it as is. If we can't pass it as is, on a single as-is vote, I want to see us with an open amendment process. The Senate majority leader is proposing neither.

So I ask Senator CRUZ: How does the Senator see this, how could one possibly see a "yes" vote on cloture on the bill, under the circumstances I have described, as a vote in favor of the House-passed continuing resolution that funds government while defunding ObamaCare?

Mr. CRUZ. It is a very good question the Senator from Utah poses, and I would note there is only one way; that is, if you are trying to confuse and deceive your constituents. There is no intellectually honest way to do it.

If you ask any rational person: If the Republicans vote along with HARRY REID and 53 Senate Democrats to allow HARRY REID and 53

Senate Democrats to fund ObamaCare, have they stood for defunding ObamaCare? Of course not. It is not a difficult question. It is not complicated.

Those who want to confuse their constituents want complication. Those who have, at least initially, stated they intend to vote to allow HARRY REID and the Democrats to fund ObamaCare are at the same time—often within hours of those statements—telling their constituents: I am leading the fight to defund ObamaCare, you can't have it both ways. You cannot have it both ways. You are either willing to stand for your principles and not just on an empty show.

There was an exchange earlier with the Senator from Illinois where he was saying he wasn't surprised by the House vote. He was certain of those votes because they had voted 40-some-odd times to defund ObamaCare. But there was a big difference in this Friday vote, a big difference in why the commentators in DC, the pundits, and all of the learned gray beards said this one wouldn't happen. The other 40-some-odd times were symbolic votes. They never had a chance to pass it into law.

It is not difficult to get Republicans to vote in symbolic votes against ObamaCare. Indeed, in this body I have introduced two amendments this year that at the time, when there were 45 Republicans in this body, all 45 Republicans voted against it. We are going to have another vote. If Majority Leader REID is successful in shutting off debate on funding ObamaCare, then all 46 Republicans will have to vote against it, and they will tell people: Hey, I voted against him, when it didn't matter. They will leave out the "when it didn't matter" part. They will leave out that I voted to allow HARRY REID to do that, but then once the matter was decided, I cast a vote against it to confuse my constituents.

We wonder why Americans are cynical about politics. They are cynical about politics because too many leaders in this body, too many Democrats and too many Republicans are not listening to the American people.

Let me read statements from a number of think tank leaders across the country.

Matthew J. Brouillette from the Commonwealth Foundation in Pennsylvania.

Giving more citizens health insurance is not the same as giving them health care. The tragic outcome is that ObamaCare will harm the very Pennsylvanians it purports to help.

Francis X. De Luca from the Civitas Institute of North Carolina. ObamaCare is about neither health nor care. It is about forcing Americans to buy a service they may neither need nor want. In the end, it will reduce the availability of health services for citizens while making those available more costly.

That sounds like a great option: Fewer choices than the ones you have and more expensive. No wonder James Hoffa, head of the Teamsters, calls ObamaCare a nightmare. No wonder so many Americans are suffering and asking for Congress to listen to their pleas to give them the same exemption President Obama has already given huge corporations and Members of Congress.

Connor Boyack from the Libertas Institute in Utah:
The Affordable Care Act is unfair, invasive and an illegitimate burden on taxpayers. In attempting to remedy certain health care problems, it follows the historical pattern of government intervention and creates even more of them.

Ellen Weaver from the Palmetto Policy Forum in South Carolina. South Carolinians are already starting to feel the front end of the shockwave as several local employers cut work schedules to part time. And we are left to imagine the ultimate decimation on the budgets of Palmetto State families as personal rates skyrocket and people are forced off their current insurance that we were promised we would be able to keep. In fact, just last week, Palmetto Policy Forum's president received a letter telling her she would be losing her private policy. And this is just the beginning of the promised "trainwreck."

Sally Pipes from the Pacific Research Institute in California.
Unless ObamaCare is repealed and replaced, America will be on
the "road to serfdom" and there will be no off-ramp. We will be
headed for a single-payer, Medicare for all system such as exists
in Canada. Americans will face long waiting lists for care,
rationed care, and a lack of access to the latest treatments and
procedures. Where will the best doctors and we as patients go to
get first-rate care?

Interestingly enough, the majority leader of the Senate, HARRY
REID, agrees with Ms. Pipes. Both Sally Pipes and Majority Leader REID
say the end result of ObamaCare is—and indeed is designed to be—
single-payer, government socialized health care. The only difference
is that Majority Leader REID thinks that is a good idea and Sally Pipes
and the American people think that is a terrible idea. Because we don't
want our care rationed, we don't want government bureaucrats
deciding who gets health care when, we don't want waiting periods,
and we don't want low-quality health care, which is what happens at
the end of this road if we continue down it.

Justin Owen, the Beacon Center of Tennessee.
ObamaCare presents the most dangerous threat to Tennesseans'
jobs and health security than anything coming out of
Washington. And that says a lot these days.

Paul Gessing of the Rio Grande Foundation, New Mexico.
ObamaCare locks in the worst aspects of American health care.
Rather than restoring the patient-doctor relationship, it puts
the IRS and the Federal Government alongside insurance companies between patients and their doctors.

Matt Mayer, Opportunity, OH.
ObamaCare is distorting insurance markets, forcing Ohioans to
make changes they do not want to make and expanding one of
the least effective and most costly government programs in
U.S. history.

Mike Stenhouse from the Rhode Island Center for Freedom and Prosperity.

In Rhode Island, not only will up to 75 percent of those currently uninsured remain uninsured after ObamaCare is implemented, but our State has still not determined how to pay for its wasteful exchange after the Federal subsidies end.

Scott Moody from the Maine Heritage Policy Center observed: The Maine Heritage Policy Center has profiled several Maine businesses employing hundreds of Mainers that simply can't afford to absorb the increased costs under ObamaCare. In fact, in one case the higher ObamaCare costs will consume anywhere from 54 percent to 134 percent of the company's profits.

This burden could ultimately put this company out of business, which would not only mean no health insurance for their employees, but it would also mean no jobs either.

Doesn't that describe the nightmare James Hoffa of the Teamsters was talking about—employees losing their jobs, employees being forced into part-time work and losing their health insurance all at the same time? No wonder the unions are speaking out or remaining silent no longer.

How long will it be until we see Democratic Senators who have the courage of James Hoffa to remain silent no longer and to speak out for the men and women of America who are losing their jobs, who are being forced into part-time work and are losing their health insurance? How long will it be before all 46 Republicans do more than give speeches against ObamaCare and actually stand and fight this fight, stop saying we can't win it and actually stand up and start to win it?

Paul Mero from the Sutherland Institute in Utah: The ACA is a hallucinogen for its recipients and defenders in the search for prudent ways to address the medical needs of our uninsured. A true Utah solution will rely on our people, not the federal government.

Mike Thompson from the Thomas Jefferson Institute in Virginia: It looks as if those on the low end of the income scale will be harmed as part time employees will see their hours cut and full time employees moved to part time. Small businesses, the engine of job creation, are seeing their health care costs rising forcing them to employ fewer people than they would otherwise.

Wayne Hoffman of the Idaho Freedom Foundation: Obamacare is destroying the quality of health care in Idaho. The onslaught of new regulations and the fear of what might come next from Washington is not only raising costs, it has prompted countless Idaho doctors to give up medicine or join large hospital or group medical practices. As a result, the close knit doctor-patient relationships that have endured in many of our communities have vanished entirely.

Do you like your doctor? Do you like continuing to see your doctor? With ObamaCare, that relationship is in jeopardy. Why do you think so many Americans are unhappy with this law?

Janie White of the Wyoming Policy Institute: ObamaCare is closing businesses in the small populated state of Wyoming. Full-time is going to part-time and in a state where small business is prevalent, it's hurting an entire state; not just one industry.

Dave Trabert of the Kansas Policy Institute: Scholars at Kansas Policy Institute estimate that Medicaid is expected to consume 31% of Kansas' General Fund Budget by 2023 under Obamacare and its proposed Medicaid expansion. The "woodwork effect" of Obamacare alone is expected to cause over $4 billion in tax increases or spending reductions for other government services in just the first ten years of Obamacare.

Gary Palmer of the Alabama Policy Institute:
Because of the Budget Control Act, which the Republicans
passed in 2011, spending reductions for the next fiscal year
are already set in place by law and will require approximately
$1.3 trillion in discretionary cuts over the next eight years.
These cuts can either be done through another round of
sequestration in which the Obama Administration will
determine what is cut, or it will be done proactively by
defunding ObamaCare which, according to the latest
Congressional Budget Office (CBO) estimate, will cost $1.85
trillion over the next 11 years. Keep in mind that in 2010 the
CBO estimated that Obamacare would only cost $898 billion
for the first 10 years. With the U.S. already facing a $16 tril-
lion debt and continuing to run a trillion dollar annual
deficit, and with all the uncertainty surrounding what
Obamacare will actually cost, defunding Obamacare would
be an act of fiscal responsibility as intended by the passage of
the Budget Control Act.

Carl Graham from the Montana Policy Institute:
Obamacare has already resulted in the consolidation and cen-
tralization of the health care industry in Montana, removing
choices and competition, especially in the state's rural areas.

Andy Matthews of the Nevada Policy Research Institute:
At a time when Nevada is already suffering under the highest
unemployment rate in the nation, the so-called Affordable
Care Act now threatens to do even more damage to the Silver
State's jobs picture. Every day I hear from frustrated business
owners who would like nothing more than to hire new
employees but can't because of the many barriers to hiring that
this law has created.

Trent England of the Freedom Foundation in Washington State:
Washington State's Freedom Foundation reports some small
businesses are already being told their health insurance rates

will double, punishing some of the state's hardest working people, hurting job creation, and stifling economic growth.

Robert Alt from the Buckeye Institute for Public Policy Solutions in Ohio:

So far, Obamacare has been a game of drawing straws: a good deal for the IRS and others who have the ability to secure exemptions for themselves: Congress, a motley group of companies with connections, some unions, and friends of the Obama administration; and the short straws being won by average Americans, medical professionals, small businesses, the overwhelming majority of seniors who are happy with their current plans, and our children and grandchildren. The results of this rigged game are an invasion of privacy, increase in healthcare and insurance costs, loss of freedom, distortion of the free market, and a host of changes Americans never hoped for.

Jim Stergios of the Pioneer Institute in Massachusetts:

The ACA will slow the future of innovation in Massachusetts, especially in the medical device field, which faces hundreds of millions of dollars in new taxes. In addition, the so-called "cadillac-tax" that will burden many Massachusetts Chevy drivers: Over half of the citizens of the state by 2018, including union members, and hundreds of thousands of the middle-class.

Kim Crockett from the Center for the American Experiment in Minnesota:

Minnesota has one of the finest health care systems in the world. It is unfortunate that Gov. Mark Dayton has whole-heartedly embraced the incursion of federal authority in our state. The ACA is anything but affordable and threatens the delivery of quality care to all but the most financially secure Minnesotans. The gross misallocation of local, state and federal resources could instead have been used to improve health care.

Instead we are bureaucratizing it. We continue to advocate for portable, patient-owned defined contribution plan as an alternative to one-size-fits-all health care.

Jim Vokal of the Platt Institute of Nebraska:
At the expense of middle class, every day Nebraskans, Obamacare's implementation will cause undue hardship on the families and the younger generation all across the state. Governmental intervention rather than personal choice is not the Nebraska way.

Ashley Landess from the South Carolina Policy Council:
SC business owners are forced to close their doors and sell off family businesses, not only b/c they can't afford the mandate but because they can't even predict the cost—and neither can anyone else.

Brett Healy from the John K. MacIver Institute for Public Policy of Wisconsin:
Before Obamacare, Wisconsin had one of the better health insurance markets in the country that covered the vast majority of our citizens. Now, under Obamacare, Wisconsinites will see insurance premiums increase on average 51% and in many parts of the Badger State, we will have only one company to choose from and no consumer choice. In Wisconsin, the Affordable Care Act is proving to be not affordable at all and the uncertainty surrounding its implementation is weighing on our employers and holding back our economic recovery. Wisconsinites deserve better.

J. Robert McClure, III, from the James Madison Institute in Florida:
In Florida, where tourism and seasonal hiring are a way of life, small businesses and large ones are confused and frustrated as to how to move forward. Arbitrary delays and enforcement by the federal government of this invasive and unwieldy law have

created a climate of paralysis in Florida when it comes to job creation and planning. In a state of roughly 19 million people, where the economic climate is poised in every way to take off, no organization be it in business, education, healthcare or government knows how to proceed. The Affordable Care Act has only created stagnation and insecurity in Florida—with a hefty price tag to come, paid for on the backs of every taxpayer in the state.

State representative Geanie Morrison from the Texas Conservative Coalition:
The so-called Affordable Care Act is not even fully implemented, and is already costing jobs, leading to costly increases in insurance premiums, and promising billions of dollars in new taxes. Texans should not have to shoulder the cost of Obamacare, which is why we implore our Texas delegation to defund this unpopular, unworkable, and unaffordable law.

And Finally, Jim Waters of the Bluegrass Institute of Kentucky:
Obamacare will devastate Kentucky's already-struggling economy. We already have entire areas where expectant mothers in rural areas must drive two hours to see an ob/gyn. But there will be nowhere that any Kentucky family or small-business owner can go to hide from the increased costs and destruction of our personal liberties resulting from this policy of redistribution.

That list of quotes spans the country. It wasn't just one region. It wasn't just Republican States. It wasn't just Democratic States. Those are quotes from think tanks in North Carolina, Utah, South Carolina, California, Tennessee, New Mexico, Ohio, Rhode Island, Maine, Utah, Virginia, Idaho, Wyoming, Kansas, Alabama, Montana, Washington State, Massachusetts, Minnesota, Nebraska, South Carolina, Wisconsin, Florida, and in the State of Kentucky.

Let me ask everyone watching: Have the Senators from each of those States come out and said they will defund ObamaCare? Have the Democratic Senators from each of those States said: I have listened to my constituents, I have listened to the people who are losing their jobs, who are being pushed into part-time work, who are seeing health insurance premiums skyrocket or losing their health insurance. Have the Democratic Senators representing those States said that?

And have the Republicans representing those States said, we will stand together, and Republicans will be united against cloture on this bill because we are not going to vote to allow HARRY REID and the Democrats to fund ObamaCare, to gut the House Republican bill? And if they haven't, it is a reasonable question to ask why. Why aren't elected officials listening to the people? We need to together make D.C. listen.

Mr. LEE. Will the Senator yield for a question?

Mr. CRUZ. I am happy to yield for a question without yielding the floor.

Mr. LEE. I have two sons and a daughter. My two sons are twins. They are teenagers. They are good boys. They are both 4.0 students, and I couldn't be more pleased with them. They work hard.

I had an experience with them about 1½ years ago that comes to mind. I was driving down the street with them in my car one day. We were listening to the radio, as I often do with them. We were listening to a popular song familiar to all three of us, a song we had heard on many, many occasions.

On this particular occasion I started noticing the lyrics more than I had on previous occasions in the past. All of a sudden, for whatever reason, I noticed that these were not good lyrics. These were not wholesome lyrics. These were not lyrics that any God-fearing father of teenaged boys would necessarily want his sons listening to. All of a sudden I pointed out to my twin sons, turning down the radio, These were terrible lyrics, and I asked them: Have you ever really listened to the words of this song? Do we like the message that is in this song?

My son John didn't miss a beat. Without hesitating, without batting an eye, John looked right at me and said, Dad, it is not bad if you don't think about it. I immediately thought it was funny that was his response. This was teenage reasoning at its very best. It is not just teenage reasoning. It is the way a lot of us think about things by saying certain things aren't bad if you don't think about them.

In many respects, that is reflective of what we face in our country today. A $17 trillion debt growing at a rate approaching $1 trillion a year isn't bad if you don't think about it. Having a 2,700-page health care law with 20,000 pages of implementing legislation isn't bad if you don't think about it; having between $1.75 trillion and $2 trillion a year in existing Federal regulatory compliance costs is not bad, if you don't think about it; having the world's highest corporate tax rate, at least the highest corporate tax rate in the developed world, isn't bad if you don't think about it. A lot of these problems we face are not bad, but only if you don't think about them.

The problem is in the Senate it is our job to think about these problems. It is our job to think about the fact that we have on the books a law called the Patient Protection and Affordable Care Act that will make a lot of things worse for a lot of people, a law that will have an effect not consistent with the lofty sounding title of that law, an effect that will actually result, in many instances, in health care that is both unfair and less affordable.

We have to think about what our responsibilities are. We have to think every single day about how this is going to affect the American people. We have to be willing to say we are not going to allow certain things to persist, things that would harm the American people, and that means we have to listen to the American people when they cry out for help.

They have cried out for help in recent weeks as they have asked Congress again and again to defund ObamaCare, as they have asked Congress to keep government funded. They don't want a shutdown. We don't want a shutdown. I know I don't want a shutdown. I don't think Senator CRUZ wants a shutdown. In fact, I don't think I know any Member of Congress of either House or either political party representing any of our country's 50 States who wants a shutdown.

What we want is to keep government funded. What the American people want is for us to fund government while defunding

ObamaCare. That is precisely what the House of Representatives has done. I salute the House of Representatives. The House of Representatives, the Republican leadership, has been thinking about it. They have been thinking about this law and the many problems it threatens to create for our Nation's 300 million-plus people.

We have to think about the fact that every time we make a law we are expanding the reach of this government. We have to think about the fact that we became an independent nation, a nation that flies its own flag rather than the Union Jack, a nation that pays tribute to the sovereignty of the people rather than to the supposed sovereignty of a monarch. A couple of centuries ago this was not just an act of rejection of the idea of having a monarch, this was not just a rejection of the Union Jack, this was not just a statement to the effect that we did not want to sing "God Save the King" or "God Save the Queen." We became our own Republic at least in part because we were subject then to a large distant national government, a large distant national government that was so far from the people that it was sometimes slow to respond to the needs of the people, and that national government based not in Washington, DC, because Washington, DC, did not exist then. What is now Washington DC was then part of the colony of Maryland.

Our national capital, based in London, taxed the people too much. It regulated the people too aggressively, too oppressively. When the people called out for help, that government was slow to respond to their needs—in part because it was so far from them, so distant from them. It was not just distant from them in terms of measurement, in terms of geography, but also distant from them in that its interests were somewhat detached from those of the American people.

Ultimately we became our own country. Ultimately we declared our independence, we fought for it, we won our independence. Instinctively, reflexively, quite understandably we established a national government because we knew we would need one. We knew that each of these Thirteen Colonies could not exist independently as a freestanding Republic. We knew we would need a national government to provide for those basic things that a national government generally must provide.

We knew that national governments, at least our national government in this circumstance, would need to be in charge of a few basic things such as national defense. Yet we feared what national governments could do because we know that when governments become big there is a greater risk toward tyranny—even if it is a type of tyranny that exists only by degrees. We knew that the risk of this kind of tyranny—some might call it soft or incremental tyranny—exists even in republics, even when democratic forces are at play. We knew this type of risk of soft tyranny, as some would describe it, is greatest within national governments.

The bigger the nation, the more powerful the government and the fewer the restrictions on that government, the greater the risk that the rights of the people will be undermined; the greater the risk the people of that great nation will become subjects rather than sovereigns—which of course they should always be.

So for that very purpose we put in place a very limited-purpose national government, originally under the Articles of Confederation. We put together a weak national government. It was so weak in fact it was ineffective. It was not able to do the things our basic national government needed to do. Congress, under the Articles of Confederation, had some powers but they proved to be not enough. It had no power of raising revenue independently of the States. It had no power of regulating commerce or trade between the States and with foreign countries. So after a period of just a few years under the Articles of Confederation, our Founding Fathers came together in that hot, fateful summer of 1787 in Philadelphia and they put together a compromise document. They said we need a national government that is at once strong enough to be able to do what a National Government must be able to do in order to protect us so we can be a nation. Yet we also need those powers to be sufficiently limited that the risk of tyranny, even incremental tyranny or tyranny by degrees, will be kept to a minimum.

So our Founding Fathers wisely came up with a list, a list of powers that we knew the national government would need powers that we knew needed to be exercised at the national level. Those powers, the vast majority of which are found in one part of the Constitution—

often overlooked but perhaps the single most important portion of the Constitution, at least for our purposes here—the part of the Constitution we have to look to more frequently here, article I, section 8.

Article I, section 8, has 18 clauses and goes through the basic powers of Congress. Congress, of course, has the power to tax and the power to spend within the powers authorized by the Constitution. Congress has the power to regulate trade—referred to in the Constitution as commerce—among the States, with foreign nations and among the Indian tribes. Congress has the power to coin money and regulate the value thereof; develop the uniform set of laws governing naturalization or what we would today call immigration; the power to provide for our national defense; to declare war; the power to come up with a system of laws dealing with bankruptcy; to establish a uniform system of weights and measures; to establish postal roads. There are a few other powers, but this is the basic gist of them.

Then there is my favorite power, the power to grant Letters of Marque and Reprisal, a power that we too often fail to recognize, a power I wish we would get to debate and discuss longer and more frequently in the Senate. A Letter of Marque and Reprisal was effectively a hall pass issued by the U.S. Congress in the name of the U.S. Government that entitles the bearer of that hall pass to be a pirate on the high seas. Regardless of how long I might serve in the Senate, I hope one day to be granted a Letter of Marque and Reprisal so I can become a pirate as I longed to be as a child. You are all invited to join me when I get that Letter of Marque and Reprisal.

The point is the powers of Congress are limited. These are powers that James Madison cited in defending the Constitution against people who questioned him, against those who feared this Constitution might give rise to a general purpose national government, one empowered with so many powers that it could become a tyrant. He tried to set at ease the concerns of the people in Federalist 45 when he said:

> The powers that would be granted to the newly established federal government upon ratification of the Constitution are few and defined while those reserved to the States are numerous and indefinite.

He was right and he was persuasive. Upon the advice of James Madison and others, the States ratified the Constitution. They did so with that very understanding, that this body, the legislative body created by the Constitution, the U.S. Congress, consisting of a Senate and a House of Representatives, would possess legislative powers that were not so broad as to encompass all the day-to-day interactions of human beings. We would not possess what people refer to as general police powers. We do not have the power to make whatever law we think is a good idea. A good idea is not nearly enough. We have to find something in the Constitution that puts us in charge of legislating within that area to promote that good idea. We have to find something in the Constitution that gives us the power to do it.

During the first 100, maybe 150 years of our Republic as it operated under the Constitution, we followed pretty closely this document, what some describe as the enumerated powers doctrine. Sure, there were arguments from time to time over this or that legislative proposal. There were arguments that arose, for example, over whether we should have a national bank.

You had debates among and between the political branches of government, meaning Congress and the Presidency, that often centered on the principles of the Constitution. It was very common to have constitutional concerns brought up on the floor of this body or on the floor of the House of Representatives as a basis for halting serious consideration of a legislative proposal on grounds that it simply was not within Congress's power to enact.

It was not necessarily considered acceptable to say let's let another branch of government think about it. Let's let the Supreme Court iron it out. Let's let the Supreme Court decide whether it is constitutional. Within the political branches of government, frequently proposals were stopped on grounds that they were unconstitutional.

Fast forward 130, 140, 150 years, and things started to change. The Supreme Court, early in the administration of President Franklin D. Roosevelt, pushed back on a lot of FDR's more aggressive attempts to expand the reach, the size, the scope, the cost of the Federal Government. It resisted those and said: Look, regardless of what the policy merits might be of this Federal program or that one, we still have a limited purpose as the Federal Government and not an all-purpose national government. That limited purpose—the national government—has to find something in the Constitution each time it legislates. If it fails to do that, then no matter how good of an idea it is, it can't fly.

By the end of F.D.R.'s Presidency, the Court changed course. There are a number of reasons for this, but the prevailing theory is that the Supreme Court got scared. It got scared as a result of F.D.R.'s Court-packing plan.

In 1935, the Supreme Court moved into its new building across the street, the shining marble palace we see just outside the door to the Senate. The Justices liked their new white marble palace. They enjoyed it. They didn't want F.D.R., or any other President, raining on their parade by packing the Court and fundamentally altering the nature of the Court's composition. So for that reason, many theorized, the Court changed its position. The Court stopped resisting F.D.R.'s attempts at expanding the Federal Government's power.

People trace the change in jurisprudence to a number of different moments. I think one of the pivotal moments occurred in 1937 when the Supreme Court of the United States decided a case called the NLRB v. Jones & Laughlin Steel Company. In that case, the Supreme Court adopted an early version of what has become its modern common clause jurisprudence. The Supreme Court started concluding that where there is an activity that is commercial or economic in nature, Congress may regulate that activity so long as there is a substantial connection between that activity and interstate commerce. It was in that case that the Supreme Court, for the first time, smiled upon Federal regulation of what were previous to that time considered local activities, such as labor, manufacturing, agriculture, and mining.

That is not to say those things should not be regulated by any government anywhere. It is not to say the Supreme Court—prior to NLRB v. Jones & Laughlin Steel—ever suggested otherwise, but it is to suggest that prior to that case regulation of local activities, such as labor, manufacturing, agriculture, and mining were considered more appropriate for State and local governments and not for our national government. Within the next 5 years, the Supreme Court solidified its position on the commerce clause, and in many respects it allowed its power to reach a high watermark in the 1942 case of Wickard v. Filburn.

Let's talk about that case for just a minute because I think it bears on what we are talking about. That case involved a farmer by the name of Roscoe Filburn. He got in trouble with the law. You might be asking yourselves: What did farmer Roscoe Filburn do? What did he do to get in trouble with the Feds? Was he a bank robber? No, he didn't rob a bank. Was he a drug dealer? No, he didn't do that. Was he a murderer or a kidnapper? No. You want to know what Roscoe Filburn did? He committed a grave offense against the United States. He grew too much wheat. Yes, scary but true. Roscoe Filburn grew more wheat than Congress, in its infinite wisdom, saw fit for any American to grow in any 1 single year.

By then Congress decided it needed to regulate every aspect of human existence, if possible. It even had the wisdom and foresight necessary to direct the entire economy right down to how much wheat a particular farmer could legally grow. Roscoe Filburn was fined many thousands of dollars for growing too much wheat. That was a lot of money in those days.

Fortunately, Mr. Filburn had a good lawyer. Mr. Filburn was determined not to allow his life to be micromanaged by Federal officials in Washington, DC. Mr. Filburn challenged the enforcement of this law against him with a theory. He said: Look, the statute I have been accused of violating was enacted pursuant to the commerce clause of the U.S. Constitution, article I, section 8, clause 3. The commerce clause applies to interstate commerce or commerce for trade occurring between the States and not intrastate commerce—commerce within a State. Commerce which is within a particular State is not subject to Congress's authority and the commerce clause.

Roscoe Filburn argued—through his lawyer—that the wheat he grew in excess of the national wheat production limit never entered interstate commerce because it never entered commerce at all. Roscoe Filburn used that wheat entirely on his farm. He used some of it to feed his animals, some of it to feed his own family, and he reserved the balance of that grain to use as seed for the following season.

So on that basis, he said: Look, you can get after me for any reason you want. You can get after me, if you want, for violating this wheat production limit, but the fact is this law can have no application here because this wheat never entered interstate commerce or any other form of commerce. It never left my farm.

Interestingly enough, the Supreme Court of the United States saw it differently. The Supreme Court of the United States found that even that wheat that never left Roscoe Filburn's farm was subject to the long arm of Congress and the long arm of the Federal Government. It was subject to that same Federal power that James Madison once described as few and defined. All of a sudden the supposedly few and defined powers were broad enough somehow to extend to Roscoe Filburn's pernicious wheat.

The Supreme Court said, in essence, that this wheat, because it was grown and used on Roscoe Filburn's farm in excess of the grain production limit imposed by Federal law, it was grain that Roscoe Filburn would have otherwise purchased but did not have to purchase on the open market, a market that was distinctively interstate.

Because he grew it and used it on the farm and did not buy it somewhere else, thus by growing too much wheat, Roscoe Filburn shamefully distorted and undermined the interstate market and wheat. He undermined it in the sense that it drove the price in a different direction than Congress, in its infinite judgment, saw fit to direct the economy. So the Supreme Court of the United States upheld the fine that was assessed against Roscoe Filburn. The reasoning of the Supreme Court employed in Wickard v. Filburn is a fascinating study in legal and verbal gymnastics. It is a fascinating study in the idea that everything affects everything else. They basically said that the wheat Roscoe Filburn grew on his farm affects the interstate wheat market in much the same way that butterflies flapping their wings in Brazil can affect weather patterns in North America.

We are somehow asked to have faith that this does, in fact, happen. I am told that climatologists can prove there is an impact by the butterflies in South America on weather patterns in North America. I don't know how, but you have to make a lot of inferences before you get there. But as many inferences as has to be made with the butterflies, I think there are even more inferences that have to be drawn with respect to Roscoe Filburn's wheat.

I remember studying this case in my high school history class. I remember arguing with my history teacher about this. I remember my history teacher eventually telling me: Get over it, Mr. LEE. The Federal Government is big and powerful, and that is just the way things are. Yet I think we have a certain responsibility to look back through our history and to question from time to time the judgments of the Supreme Court of the United States, especially when those judgments enable the Congress to extend its power far beyond what Madison described as few and defined powers.

In a sense, what we have done ever since Wickard v. Filburn is we continued to expand Federal authority beyond that. We have never fully retreated from that high watermark. What we have seen is a perpetually expanding national government, one that is capable of imposing an estimated $2 trillion in Federal regulatory compliance costs alone, a Federal Government that imposes a couple of more trillion dollars in taxes a year from the American people, and manages to spend between $3.5 and $4 trillion every single year. That is a very big government.

Since Wickard v. Filburn, there are only two instances in which the Supreme Court of the United States has invalidated an act of Congress as being beyond the scope of Congress's power under the commerce clause. Sometimes I almost add a third, but then I remember the Supreme Court stopped short on that third.

The first two involved a case called the United States v. Lopez, which is a case from 1995 where the Supreme Court invalidated the Gun-Free School Zones Act prohibiting the bare possession of a handgun within a school zone. The Supreme Court concluded that the bare possession of a gun was not commercial activity at all. It was not interstate commercial activity. It was not interstate commerce, and they couldn't get to the point where they could conclude that this was a valid subject of Congress's commerce clause authority.

The second case was decided in 2000. It was a case called the United States v. Morrison in which the Supreme Court invalidated provisions of the Violence Against Women Act, including that those provisions attempted to regulate acts of violence, however reprehensible, were themselves neither interstate or commercial.

Then, of course, in 2012 the Supreme Court sort of invalidated the penalty provisions attached to the individual mandate in the Patient Protection and Affordable Care Act. I say they sort of invalidated that provision because the Supreme Court of the United States concluded that provision, though enacted pursuant to the commerce clause, could not be defended as a valid exercise of Congress's power under the commerce clause. To that extent, they concluded it was unconstitutional.

But then the Supreme Court went on somehow to conclude that this was a valid exercise of Congress's power to impose taxes even though Congress had attempted unsuccessfully to pass this as a tax, even though new taxes have to be introduced in the House of Representatives and passed into law by both Houses of Congress and signed into law by the President, even though the Supreme Court of the United States has no authority to levy taxes, impose taxes or create taxes.

The Supreme Court of the United States created out of whole cloth a new tax which it imposed on the American people. They imposed a middle-class tax hike, which the Court has no power to impose. It has no power to levy taxes. Yet the Court did it anyway.

When I tell that story, I get asked all the time: How then did the Court do it? If the Court has no power to do it, how did it do it? It just did. It just declared it to be so and the rest of us were expected to accept that and get over it and move on, just as I was told by my high school history teacher to accept, get over, and move on from Wickard v. Filburn because the Federal Government is big and powerful and we can live with it. Well, we all just have to live with it but only as long as the American people put up with it, only as long as the American people are willing to accept it.

The American people have never been enthusiastic about ObamaCare—not from the beginning. Their satisfaction with this law has not improved over time, and it has not been enhanced. The American people don't deserve to have to live under a law that imposes a massive middle-class tax hike on the American people, one that was not imposed by the people's elected representatives in Congress but instead was imposed by five of nine lawyers who wear black robes and sit in big fancy chairs in the building just across the street from us.

The American people deserve to live under a system where the laws are written by men and women of their own choosing, who serve in increments of 2 years in the case of Members of the House of Representatives and in increments of 6 years in the case of U.S. Senators.

Supreme Court Justices, of course, are smart men and women—every one of them. They are very intelligent, well-trained individuals. I am convinced that each and every one of them loves this country and wants to serve it well. Yet the members of the Supreme Court of the United States are not elected. They are not subject to election at regular intervals, and that is one of the many reasons we don't trust them with the power to write law. It is one of the many reasons we don't trust them with the power to impose taxes. They are there to decide cases and controversies based on the law and the facts before them.

In the case of the Patient Protection and Affordable Care Act, they rewrote the law not just once but twice—once by transforming what was enacted as a penalty into a tax in order to save that law from an otherwise certain doom, a doom necessitated by important constitutional limitations; the second time when the Court concluded by an even wider margin—7 to 2—that Congress had violated the Constitution by imposing on the States a mandate to expand their Medicaid Programs without giving them any reasonable alternative, any available alternative. The Supreme Court, again by a 5-to-4 margin, after 7 to 2—after the Justices, by a margin of 7 to 2, had found that this was unconstitutional, five of them—by a margin of 5 to 4—saved the provisions simply by rewriting the law, by inserting into the law an exception in the law that the law did not provide.

I believe it may have been Shakespeare who originally penned the words "he will cheat without scruple who can without fear." I have also heard it attributed to Benjamin Franklin. I am not sure which of them was the originator of that quote, but I have heard it attributed to both. Regardless, there has to be a legal corollary to that. When Supreme Court Justices are able to make law, when Supreme Court Justices are able to impose taxes and no one calls them out on it, that is when the people have to live with that. That is when they get away with it. That is when they are allowed to cheat the American people out of their right to have their laws made by men and women of their own choosing, to have their taxes increased, if at all, only by men and women of their own choosing. This was wrong. This was a dastardly, cowardly act, one we can't simply ignore.

One of the things I found so offensive, so appalling, so disturbing, so distressing was the fact that in the wake of this decision, so many people—many of them from my own political party—praised Chief Justice Roberts for his participation in this dastardly, inexcusable act of rewriting the Affordable Care Act not just once but twice in order to save it. They praised him. Some of them said that this showed he was willing to cross the aisle at the Supreme Court. Well, that is a problem. There is no aisle in the Supreme Court of the United States. They sit along a bench. At the center of the bench is the Chief Justice. There isn't an aisle. In fact, particularly once they have been appointed by the President and confirmed by the Senate, Supreme Court Justices operate in a world in which partisan political affiliation has no meaning. This wasn't reaching across the aisle.

Some suggested that this was somehow a statesman-like act by the Chief Justice, an act that revealed that he was willing to sort of balance various interests, an act that some Republicans even were convinced was carefully and wisely engineered to procure a Republican partisan victory in the 2012 election cycle. That is absolutely nonsense, first of all. As a political matter, we saw that it turned out not to work at all. I don't necessarily think there is any validity to the theory that that is what the Chief Justice was trying to bring about. If it was, that would amount to an utter betrayal of his judicial oath. It would also reveal him to be a really bad political tactician, but that is not the Chief Justice's job. It is not the job of any justice or any jurist. The job of any jurist is to decide each case before the court based on the law and the facts of the particular case.

Some have suggested that this was designed to protect the enumerated powers doctrine or at least the idea that there is some limit to Congress's power under the commerce clause. I believe that is utter nonsense. This didn't do that. In fact, I think it blew a hole a mile wide in the enumerated powers doctrine because what this suggested is that, OK, the Supreme Court is going to pay at least lipservice to the idea that the power of Congress is, in fact, limited. But if Congress colors outside the lines, if Congress doesn't utter the magic words, if Congress really does something quite wrong in drafting such that its power can no longer be appropriately assigned, its power can no longer be appropriately justified under the commerce clause, then all of a sudden the Supreme Court of the United States will find some other basis in the Constitution upon which to rest this authority.

This is really disturbing because if the Supreme Court can do that and if the Supreme Court can do that even to raise taxes, then Congress can pass all kinds of laws in theory purporting to be simply exercises of its regulatory power under the commerce clause and then rely on the Supreme Court of the United States to say: Yes, OK, this may not be a valid exercise of Congress's power under the commerce clause, but we will rewrite it as a tax. We will rewrite it as a tax and thereby uphold it, thereby stand behind it.

So we get back to the question—a question I get asked all the time by people around my State, by people across the country when they hear about this decision. They ask: How can the Supreme Court of the United States do this? How can the Supreme Court of the United States get away with it?

Well, they can do it because they wear the black robes. They can do it because they have the printing press that prints out those decisions with the fancy wording of the Supreme Court behind it. They can do it because the people still regard the decisions, the rulings of the Supreme Court of the United States as legitimate.

I do have to point out another aspect of this ruling. In the same ruling in which the Supreme Court of the United States concluded that the Patient Protection and Affordable Care Act's individual mandate provision was a valid exercise of the taxing power, the Supreme Court of the United States also said—with, by the way, the concurrence of Chief Justice Roberts, who was the author of the majority opinion upholding it as a valid exercise of the taxing power—that same opinion authored by the same Chief Justice concluded that this same provision was not a tax for purposes of a law called the Anti-Injunction Act. Had the Supreme Court of the United States not reached that conclusion, had it reached the same conclusion under the Anti-Injunction Act that it reached under the constitutional aspect of the challenge, and had the Court concluded that this was, in fact, a tax and not a penalty, as it did under the constitutional analysis, then the Supreme Court of the United States would have been without jurisdiction to hear the case because the Anti-Injunction Act said: If it is a tax, you can't review the statute being challenged until after it has been enforced, which meant that no legal, no judicial challenge could have been properly brought, could have been countenanced by an article III court of the United States until, at the earliest, sometime in 2014, after enforcement of the individual mandate began.

So it was very odd that the Court, led by the same Chief Justice, concluded at once that this was a tax for purposes of constitutional analysis but that it was not a tax for purposes of the Anti-Injunction Act. Here again, how does the Court get away with that? It gets away with it because we recognize the validity, the legitimacy of the decision.

But the more people learn about this, the more they read about it, the more they become upset. I have yet to explain this to a constituent who isn't deeply disturbed by it. I have yet to explain this to anyone who can really defend it on its own merits.

So we see that this was a law that was put in place quite improperly. It was a law that was put in place not by an elected legislative body but instead by a judiciary that, at least for purposes of this case, transformed itself into a judicial oligarchy of sorts, a judicial legislative body—one of the many reasons we need to defund the implementation of this law. It was unconstitutional as written in two respects and would have been invalidated but for the Supreme Court of the United States rewriting it not just once but twice.

We have to ask ourselves these questions from time to time: Where do we go with this? What do we do with it? That is where we get back to where we are now, where the House of Representatives boldly stood behind the American people and decided to keep funding the government, funding the operations of government while defunding ObamaCare. That bill, that continuing resolution is now moving over here. That continuing resolution is now before us.

Sometimes we have to ask ourselves these questions of what is it that we are funding, why is it that we are funding it, and why is it that we should continue to stand behind a law that is causing so much harm to the American people—a law that was improperly brought into being in the first place, a law that was improperly upheld and sustained, ultimately rewritten by the Court, improperly, unconstitutionally rewritten by the President of the United States.

So I wish to ask Senator CRUZ, does the Senator know how long the Hundred Years War lasted?

Mr. CRUZ. Well, I thank my friend from Utah for his remarkable discourse on constitutional law.

As for the latest question he asked, one might think the Hundred Years War lasted 100 years, but think again.

It was 116 years.

Things are not always as they seem.

(Ms. BALDWIN assumed the Chair.)

Mr. LEE. Can the Senator tell me, where do Chinese gooseberries come from?

Mr. CRUZ. I yield for this question. Most would say China. But think again. Chinese gooseberries actually come from New Zealand.

The way things are labeled are not always, in fact, what they are.

Mr. LEE. If the Senator will yield for another question.

Mr. CRUZ. I will yield for a question without yielding the floor.

Mr. LEE. Commercial airplanes, as far as I know, all airplanes in the United States, have within them something called a black box—a black box that records the events of the cockpit. It also records critical operating data from the airplane so that in the event of an accident, the data and the voice recordings can be reviewed to try to figure out what happened.

Does the Senator know what color the black box is?

Mr. CRUZ. I say to Senator LEE, I do. A lot of people would say it must be black. If we were dealing with ordinary English language, it would be black. But perhaps airplane manufacturers think like Congress because the black box on an airplane is orange.

Mr. LEE. There is something called a Panama hat. Can the Senator tell me what part of the world the Panama hat comes from?

Mr. CRUZ. I will yield for that question and note it could possibly be Panama. You might think if you call it a Panama hat it would make sense that it would be Panama. But, no, think again. Ecuador. Ecuador makes Panama hats. I do not know that anyone makes Ecuador hats.

Mr. LEE. The device known as a camel's hair brush, does the Senator know what it is made of?

Mr. CRUZ. I yield for that question. Curiously enough, I do. You might think a camel's hair brush must be made of camel's hair. There are lots of camels. They have hair. Surely you can make a brush. Well, maybe you can. I do not know if you can. But a camel's hair brush is made of squirrel fur. It makes you wonder. The squirrels apparently have a very bad marketing department if they give their fur that gets credited to the camels.

Mr. LEE. What color is a purple finch?

Mr. CRUZ. Again, I will yield for the purpose of that question to note a purple finch—listen, similar to most husbands, I have a color palate of about six colors. I remember once my wife asked me, with regard to a tile—we were redoing our bathroom. It was a white tile. She was long distance. She said: What shade of white? I will note that was a question I was utterly incapable of responding to. I was not aware there were shades of white, and my vocabulary does not cover such things. I finally dropped it in a FedEx envelope and simply sent it to her. I was like: It is a white tile. I know nothing beyond that.

But yet your question: What color is a purple finch? I would tend to think it would be purple, but I would think wrong if that were the case because a purple finch is crimson red.

Mr. LEE. There is a chain of islands off the coast of Spain, a chain of islands known as the Canary Islands. Can the Senator tell me after what animal were these islands named?

Mr. CRUZ. I will yield for the purpose of that question as well. Indeed, I can tell you that. Now, you would think, if you call a chain of islands the Canary Islands, it must be a bird, maybe a bird in a coal mine but some sort of bird. Think again. The Canary Islands are named after a dog. I would note, the Canary Islands are a chain of islands I have some real connection to because my grandfather, my father's father, was born in the Canary Islands. Indeed, he moved to Cuba when he was 1, was raised in Cuba. My father was born in Cuba, was raised in Cuba.

The lesson from all of these is striking. Labels do not always mean what they say. Some might wonder, what does this chain of insightful questions from my friend, the junior Senator from Utah—how does it relate to the issue of ObamaCare?

If we look at Senator Lee's tremendous discourse of the Constitution—and I would note, by the way, there is not another Senator in the Senate who could give that constitutional lecture that my friend Senator Lee did, sharing with this body. I wish all 100 of us had been here to hear that because a lot of Senators—all Senators would be well served by learning or relearning those basic constitutional principles.

Mr. LEE. But the question is, Would any of them be willing to listen to it or interested in it or would most of them consider it a form of torture?

Mr. CRUZ. I yield for the purpose of that question as well—and they might well.

One of the striking things—and although under the rules of the Senate I am not allowed to ask Senator Lee a question, I can pose a rhetorical question to the body, and should Senator Lee have thoughts on that rhetorical question, he can choose to ask me a question that might contain his thoughts on that rhetorical question posed to the body.

So given that sort of convoluted reasoning, which may explain why we are in the Senate with the odd and precarious procedures that govern this body, I am going to ask this rhetorical question to the body, which is, Senator LEE explained that the Supreme Court of the United States upheld ObamaCare, after concluding it exceeded the commerce clause authority of Congress, by concluding that it was a tax. By calling it a tax, it was able to force it into a different line of jurisprudence and uphold it under the taxing clause, the taxing power of Congress.

I would ask rhetorically of this body, was it an accident that the ObamaCare statute did not call the individual mandate a tax? Maybe it was a scribe's error. Maybe it was they meant to call it a tax, they thought it was a tax, and a clerk writing just wrote the wrong word. So instead of "tax," the word "penalty." Surely that is not consequential. It must purely have been an accident. As a related component of that, was it an accident that the President of the United States went on national television and told the people of America, while this was under consideration, this is not a tax.

He affirmatively said this is not a tax.

Mind you, the argument that the U.S. Department of Justice made, the Obama administration made to the Supreme Court was this is a tax, although the statute did not say it. The argument the Supreme Court ultimately found persuasive was: This is a tax, although the statute said it was a penalty and not a tax.

The question I would rhetorically pose is: Was it an accident or is there perhaps another reason why elected politicians would not call something a tax?

Mr. LEE. Will the Senator yield for question?

Mr. CRUZ. I will be happy to yield for the purpose of a question.

Mr. LEE. Hearing the Senator from Texas, I started humming the theme to "Jeopardy," while stating lots of these things in the form of a question. It does occur to me it is absolutely certain there was a reason why this was not called a tax when it was presented to the Congress. The reason is tax hikes are unpopular. Tax hikes are especially unpopular when they are directed at the American middle class. Tax hikes are especially unpopular when they are directed at the American middle class, when they are presented by a President who ran specifically on a campaign of not raising taxes on the American middle class, which, of course, nearly all candidates for President will promise and in this case did promise.

So, no, it is not by any means an accident that this happened—the fact that language, consistent with 100 years' worth of jurisprudence, language that was used in this law, created a penalty. There is a very clear distinction between a penalty under Federal law and a tax under Federal law. A tax under Federal law is something that is an obligation, a generalized obligation to fund government; whereas, a penalty is something that involves both a requirement under Federal law and a provision exacting a payment as something that occurs in response to non-compliance with that requirement. So no, this was not an accident at all.

So I would ask Senator CRUZ whether this aspect of the Affordable Care Act—and also the fact that ObamaCare is called the Patient Protection and Affordable Care Act—doesn't it strike the Senator that this, in so many ways, is a misnomer in much the same way that the Hundred Years' War did not last 100 years, Chinese gooseberries come not from China but from New Zealand, that the black box is orange, that Panama hats come from Ecuador, that camel hair brushes are made of squirrel fur—by the way, I do not ever want to try one of those; it does not sound pleasant—that the purple finch is actually red and that the Canary Islands are named after a dog? So, too, the Patient Protection and Affordable Care Act is a name that does not accurately describe the finished product because this is a law that will make health care less affordable rather than more, and it is a law that subjects patients to a lot of harm rather than protecting them.

Does that mean we should think again about ObamaCare in the same way that we need to think again in the answers to some of these questions?

Mr. CRUZ. I think the good Senator from Utah is exactly correct. Indeed, as he quite rightly explained, it was not an accident that Congress deliberately did not call the individual mandate in ObamaCare a tax, nor was it an accident that the President of the United States explicitly said it is not a tax, because the effort was to represent to the American people that it was something quite different.

Indeed, again, asking a question rhetorically to the body—I know Senator LEE is aware; I know many other Senators are aware—of a lot of cases in the Supreme Court, the commandeering line of cases that provides that one of the things this body cannot do, Congress cannot do, is commandeer a State legislature, commandeer a State law-making apparatus or a State executive agency to implement, to carry out Federal law and Federal policy.

Indeed, the Supreme Court has explained the reasoning behind the commandeering line of cases; that fundamental to our democratic system, fundamental to our constitutional system is the notion of accountability, the notion that the voters should be able to determine who is it that put this policy in place.

If Congress could commandeer and force State legislatures to carry out Federal policies, it might be that voters would get mad at the State legislators, and they would be mad at the wrong people because if the decisions were coming from Congress and yet it was the State legislators being commandeered into acting, that would frustrate the principles of accountability that underlie our constitutional structure.

So the Supreme Court has explained that to make the democratic system work, the voters need to be able to understand who has made a decision, what that decision is, and if they do not like it, they need to be able to, as they say colloquially, throw the bums out.

The Affordable Care Act in Congress, declining to call it a tax. I might ask, did the Supreme Court's rewriting the statute to call it a tax for Congress, to call it a tax for the President—despite the fact that both had said it was not—did that contravene the accountability principles that underlie the Supreme Court's commandeering doctrine that underlie the constitutional principles of, frankly, a republican form of government, where we may know who our elected officials are and what their actions are, and that they may be held accountable for those actions so that a democratic republic can function?

Mr. LEE. Will the Senator from Texas yield?

Mr. CRUZ. I will yield for the purpose of a question without yielding the floor.

Mr. LEE. It occurs to me, as I think of this question that I am about to ask the Senator, that, inevitably, one constitutional violation facilitates another. It cannot be that you violate one aspect of the Constitution, in this circumstance, especially, where you are tinkering with the lawmaking power in ways that impact both federalism—the relative power of States and localities, on the one hand, vis-a-vis the Federal Government on the other hand—and also when you manipulate the power to legislate, the power to impose taxes.

Anytime you distort the operation of the legislative power, anytime you allow the judicial branch to commandeer the legislative machinery from Congress, you are also distorting the accountability you describe. In other words, you have in the Patient Protection and Affordable Care Act a massive intrusion by the Federal Government into the sovereign authority that is retained by the States and by the people.

The bigger the legislative package, the bigger the intrusion, and the greater the potential threat to federalism. The more removed that legislative package is from the people's elected representatives in the House and in the Senate, the greater the potential distortion that is at play in the constitutional system.

What we have at the end of the day is a new tax. Nobody knows who to blame. When the people are upset that they are going to be paying this tax, who do they blame? They go to their Members of Congress. You ask any Member of Congress who is still here who was here when this was enacted, any Member of Congress who voted for the Patient Protection and Affordable Care Act, and I can pretty well guarantee you they are going to say: Oh, no, I did not vote for a middle-class tax hike. I did not vote to impose a new tax on middle-class Americans. No. No. I voted for this, but I did not vote for that because this imposed a penalty and not a tax.

I know that because even in the wake of the Supreme Court's ruling in 2012, people who supported this legislation in the House and in the Senate and in the White House continued to insist: No, this is not a tax, this is a penalty. This notwithstanding the fact that the Supreme Court of the United States concluded it could not be upheld as a penalty, that it can be upheld only as an exercise of Congress's authority to tax, an authority which Congress decidedly did not exercise. So the accountability is thrown off severely.

This is what prompted me to introduce a piece of legislation, S. 560. S. 560, which stands in rather stark contrast to the Patient Protection and Affordable Care Act with its 2,700 pages and 20,000 pages of implementing regulations—S. 560, 1 page.

Here is what it says, to paraphrase: Section 1501 of the Patient Protection and Affordable Care Act, the individual mandates provision, is hereby amended as follows: Nothing in this provision shall be interpreted as a tax or as a valid exercise of Congress's power to tax pursuant to article I, Section 8, clause 1, or the 16th Amendment.

You see, the part of S. 560 is that it gives those who voted for ObamaCare, those in Congress who still defend ObamaCare, something other than a tax on the middle class, an opportunity to register that belief, to register that belief by a vote, a vote that would say yes, I do not believe this is a tax, and it should not be considered as a tax by the courts, and it should not be upheld by the courts as a tax. It should not be construed under any circumstance as a tax, because we do not regard it as that.

The interesting thing, of course, is that that is naturally the way people who are the law's biggest defenders would like to vote in some respects, because they want to tell the American public, and they are still telling the American public: It is not a tax, it is a penalty. But if, in fact, they actually put their vote in that direction, if they put their money where their mouth is and they pass that into law, guess what happens to the Supreme Court's ruling. What would happen to the Supreme Court's ruling in that circumstance, if we were to pass S. 560 into law? Let's assume that somehow magically it passed the House and the Senate and President Obama signed it. Perhaps it united both parties behind this concept that this is not a tax. What then would become of the Supreme Court's ruling upholding the Patient Protection and Affordable Care Act on that basis?

Mr. CRUZ. It is an excellent question from Senator LEE. The answer is quite simple. If Congress acted to make clear that nothing in the Affordable Care Act created a tax, that would remove the entire basis for the Supreme Court's upholding ObamaCare. Indeed, it would be a relatively simple matter in subsequent litigation for the Court to conclude under the matter it has already concluded that the other bases for upholding the act are not present.

When have you elected officials who go to the people, and go to the people as Senator LEE still quite rightly noted and still say it is not a tax, you would think they would happily vote for it, except there is a vested interest. I would note there is a difference between calling this a tax when Congress said and says it is not, and the examples we went through of the Hundred Years War and the purple finch, and that those are relatively innocuous misnomers, where there is something designed to be actively deceptive.

Indeed, another one you could add to that litany we went through is you might think if an act were titled "An act to amend the Internal Revenue Code of 1986, to modify the first-time homebuyer's credit in the case of members of the Armed Forces," you might think that is the title of an act that would concern something about the first-time homebuyer's credit, perhaps even members of the Armed Forces. Depending on the content of it, it might even be an act that Senator LEE and I together would support.

Yet think again. That act is ObamaCare. This is the 2,000-plus pages of ObamaCare, a little bit worse for wear. Right on the cover of it on page 1: December 24, 2009, ordered to be printed and passed. Resolved, that the bill from the House of Representatives, titled H.R. 3590, entitled, an Act to amend the Internal Revenue Code of 1986, to modify the first-time home-buyer's credit in the case of members of the Armed Services and certain other Federal employees, and for other purposes, do pass the following.

Then what was this amendment that was done? Strike out all after the enacting clause and insert. Everything for the first-time homebuyer's credit, everything about the Armed Forces, that all got erased. The title stayed there but it all got erased. Suddenly, ObamaCare was born.

That was a creature, that was a fact that came out of the procedural games that had to be played to force ObamaCare into law on a straight party-line vote. But I would note that this body has not forgotten how to play those games. Indeed, I would ask again rhetorically to the body, is the game the Democratic majority of Congress played in passing ObamaCare, saying it was not a tax, when in fact it was a tax, when it was not a tax, any different than what right now some members of the Republican conference are doing when they say they will vote for cloture in order to give HARRY REID and the Senate Democrats the ability to fully fund ObamaCare, and that they will do so because they want to defund ObamaCare? Is that fundamentally any different, presenting one story to tell the voters and a different story in terms of what will happen in this body? When it comes to accountability, I wonder if we are seeing much the same games played out again, games that undermine the integrity of this institution, games that undermine the confidence the American people have that our elected representatives listen to us.

Mr. LEE. Will the Senator yield for a question?

Mr. CRUZ. I am happy to yield for the purpose of a question without yielding the floor.

Mr. LEE. It certainly is important that we call something by an appropriate name. It was important back then that the Congress properly name what it was doing. It was appropriate back then for the Congress to say: We are enforcing the individual mandate through a penalty and not through a tax. In fact, it was so important that but for Congress's decision to make this a penalty and not a tax, it would never have passed in the first place.

What you call something and what you make of it can mean all the difference between passage and failure of a particular legislative proposal. When you dress something up in different language, something might appear to be more palatable than it actually is. Certainly, it could be argued that if there are people among us—if there are Republicans among us who are saying that if you support the House-passed continuing resolution, then you must vote for cloture on the bill, cloture on the House-passed resolution, that would not be accurate, in my opinion. I would respectfully but strongly disagree with someone who would make that claim. I certainly do not believe it is accurate to say that if you support the

House-passed continuing resolution, the one that keeps government funding but defunds ObamaCare at the same time, I think it would be inaccurate to say you must vote yes on cloture on the bill in this circumstance.

It is not to say that in every circumstance you would have to vote no. In fact, it seems counterintuitive when you first approach it, say why would you vote no on cloture on a bill that you liked. There is one circumstance where I can see where you would want to do that. It is a circumstance in which the continuing resolution you want to support moves over from the House of Representatives, and there are three alternatives the Senate could consider, but the Senate chooses only the third, three doors the majority leader could choose to open. He chooses only the third.

The first door is one in which he says: Okay, we are going to vote on this. We are going to vote on it up or down on its merits as is. We are going to vote on it as it was passed by the House of Representatives.

Behind door two is another option. We are going to allow amendments. We are going to allow individual Members, Democrats and Republicans, to submit amendments as they deem fit. We will debate and discuss those amendments. We will consider them. We will vote on them. Some of them may pass, some of them may not pass. But we will get to amendments. Door one is okay. Door two is okay. They are both appropriate. I would be okay with either one. I would vote yes on cloture on the bill if we were going to go through either of those first two doors.

But door three is the one the majority leader appears likely to open. And behind door three is a very different alternative, one where the majority leader says: I do not want to vote on it as is. But I also do not want to allow an open amendment process. In fact, I am going to allow one and only one amendment. That amendment will gut the continuing resolution passed by the House of the single most important provision relative to its ability to pass the House, the provision defunding ObamaCare.

Door 3 is unacceptable. Door 3 is unacceptable because it allows the majority leader to gut the House-passed continuing resolution funding government but defunding ObamaCare.

I find door 3 unacceptable. Because I find door 3 unacceptable, I am not going to help the majority leader get there. If he wants to get there with the help of himself, his own vote, and the 53 Democrats who follow him in his conference, that is fine. Let them do that. If he wants to try to convince some Republicans to join him in that effort to make it easier for him to gut the House-passed continuing resolution, to strip out the language defunding ObamaCare, then that is the prerogative of anyone who may go along with him. I choose not to do that because I was elected to fight this law, not to facilitate its implementation.

I don't want to facilitate its implementation. I therefore don't want to facilitate the demise of what I regard as the single most important provision of the House-passed continuing resolution. I will therefore vote against cloture on the bill.

I ask Senator CRUZ, how does he view the upcoming cloture vote? I am speaking here not on cloture on the motion to proceed but on the cloture on the bill, on the House-passed bill, the continuing resolution.

Mr. CRUZ. I thank my friend from Utah for that question.

On the motion to proceed, on the decision of whether to take up the bill, I think there is widespread agreement that we should take up this bill as there is no more important bill we could be debating now than this. Indeed, in my view, there should not only be 3 Senators in this Chamber, there should be 100. The urgency facing this country from ObamaCare is such that we have nothing better to do. When James Hoffa, the president of the Teamsters, says that ObamaCare is a nightmare, frankly, Senators shouldn't be asleep while the Nation is undergoing a nightmare.

The vote that matters is the vote on cloture on the bill. It will occur on either Friday or Saturday of this week. On that vote, 60 Senators, vote yes for cloture. That is a vote to shut off debate, a vote to say we will not debate anymore. What it does is it opens the door, it sets the stage. It allows the majority leader HARRY REID to fully fund ObamaCare with just 51 Democratic votes. That means for the Republican side of the aisle that any Republican who votes along with HARRY REID—and you quite rightly know that Leader REID and presumably all of the Democrats will vote for cloture on a bill with which most, if not all of them disagree. They get the joke. There is no mystery to this when the majority leader has announced: I am going to shut off all other amendments and I am going to add one amendment to totally gut the bill and to transform it, to do to this bill what they did to this bill.

Can you imagine if we were debating cloture? This is actually a very good analogy. Imagine if this bill were coming over, the bill that was turning into ObamaCare, and we had the same procedural arrangement—cloture vote first at 60 votes and then all amendments to be approved at 51 votes. Imagine if Republicans said: I support an act to amend the Internal Revenue Code to modify the first-time home buyer credit in the case of members of the Armed Forces. That is a good idea, so I am voting yes for cloture.

That is the bill I supported. It is the bill that came over, and it is the bill that I have right now.

Imagine if that were the scenario, and imagine that majority leader HARRY REID had announced: Once we get cloture, I am going to offer an amendment to strip every word of that bill you say you support, strip it all out and to replace it with 2,000 pages of ObamaCare.

I would suggest that any Republican who stood up and said: I am voting for cloture to give HARRY REID the ability to strip out the bill that I support—which he said he is going to do—and to replace it with a bill that I say I oppose and not just oppose slightly, that I say I oppose passionately, I would suggest that would be beyond irrational. Indeed, it would be so irrational to do that, and I would suggest no Member of the Senate is capable of such irrationality. This means, if they are saying that, it is for a deliberate purpose. It is because they affirmatively desire that outcome and yet they wish to be able to tell their constituents something different. It is fundamentally the same dynamic that leads to the cynicism about Washington that "our elected leaders don't listen to us."

I wish to note on a different front that serving in an elected office is a tremendous privilege. It is a humbling experience. You get to meet people from all over the State, sometimes from all over the country. You get to meet incredible people. You get to meet people who have done remarkable things.

One of the people I have been privileged to meet is my colleague and friend Senator MIKE LEE. We have learned tonight a number of extraordinary things about him, a number of things that border on the superhuman.

No. 1, we have learned that Senator MIKE LEE would be willing to purchase a ton of rocks and a Barry Manilow record simply to bring his wife milk and eggs. That is extraordinary matrimonial fidelity.

No. 2, we have learned that Senator MIKE LEE as a boy could be run over with a Buick filled with seven people and not have his foot injured. That, too, is extraordinary and superhuman.

No. 3, we have been privileged with a tour de force constitutional lecture with no notes, with no materials in front of him that, frankly, was reminiscent to me of a former boss of mine.

Senator LEE is the son of a legend in law. His late father, Rex Lee, was the Solicitor General of the United States. I did not have the opportunity to meet his late father but have known him by reputation for much of my life because he was revered as one of the finest Supreme Court advocates who ever lived. I think MIKE was all but weaned on the Constitution as a young lad.

The discourse Senator LEE just presented to this Nation reminded me of my boss, former Chief Justice William Rehnquist, who, like Senator LEE, had a deep love for the Constitution and, like Senator LEE, had an encyclopedic knowledge of the Constitution and could weave the battles we have had to rein in government power to protect individual liberty into a tapestry of narrative that explained what it is we are fighting for.

I will say that as we stand here now at 3:35 in the morning, I feel privileged. I feel fortunate to be standing side by side with my friend.

I will say this: If ever I am threatened by a Buick with seven people in it, I want to put MIKE LEE between me and the Buick.

Mr. LEE. Will the Senator yield for a question?

Mr. CRUZ. I yield to the gentleman without yielding the floor.

Mr. LEE. First, by way of clarification, it was not a Buick but an Oldsmobile.

Those were not rocks I was purchasing in my hypothetical; it was instead a half ton of iron ore. I am not sure it is critical to the merits of the story, but I did think that deserved some clarification. I am not certain that I would, in fact, do that. I wish to be very clear. I did engage in a transaction like that.

It does remind me of how we are often asked to vote here. We tie together program after program. Things are funded not on their own merits but on the merits of other programs. When you tie every single piece of government spending together, then all of a sudden it becomes a must-pass piece of legislation. Everybody sinks or swims together, and it becomes a practice of collusive spending in which Congress funds things not because each program deserves to be funded but because nobody wants to have his ox gored, and that does become a problem.

I appreciate the Senator's comments about my late father. He has been dead for the last 17 years. We miss him. We have missed him every day since then.

The Journal of the American Bar Association once referred to him as "Huck Finn in a morning suit," referring to the ceremonial dress worn by the U.S. Solicitor General. They regard him as sort of the Huckleberry Finn character. It was not typical that a boy from the Rocky Mountains, as he used to describe himself, ends up in that position, but he loved that position and loved it very much.

It is worth noting that I have met the father of the junior Senator from Texas. He is an inspiring speaker. He is a true patriot. Even though he was not born or raised in this country, the Senator's father has a great love of the United States of America that is unparalleled, certainly unexceeded by almost anyone I have ever met. He is one who certainly can understand the angst the American people feel about laws like ObamaCare. He is someone who I think can understand that in many respects the very best kinds of jobs program the Senate could enact, as my friend Jared Stone from Danville, CA, recently told me, would be legislation defunding ObamaCare. As my friend Jared Stone pointed out to me, ObamaCare presents a sort of double whammy for the American people. At once, it imposes a massive new tax on the middle class and at the same time kills job opportunities for the middle class. Most people who work in real jobs or want to have a good job understand this. That is why the overwhelming majority of Americans want the Senate to defund ObamaCare.

This is a principle that I think the father of the junior Senator from Texas understands very well. The father of the junior Senator from Texas came here as a young man, initially working at a restaurant waiting tables, as I recall. This was a young man who had escaped tyranny in various forms, originally the form of tyranny Cuba saw under Castro's predecessor, Fulgencio Batista.

The Senator's father had quite an experience coming to this country. I was wondering if the junior Senator from Texas would be willing to share a little bit more about his father's story, the story of Rafael Cruz, how he came to this country, and how the Senator's father might look upon ObamaCare based upon his rather unique experience coming to this country.

Mr. CRUZ. I thank my friend from Utah for his very kind comments regarding my father, and I will say that he and I—I will paraphrase Sir Isaac Newton, who said: If I have seen a little bit further, it is by standing on the shoulders of giants. I will say one thing. Senator LEE and I are both fortunate. We are blessed to be the sons of fathers whom we admire immensely and who, I think for both of us, played a big part in trying to raise us to be principled, to fight for liberty, and to fight for the Constitution.

When you think about the journeys to freedom that constitute who we are as American people, all of us have a story. It doesn't matter—in any group you go to, you could get 1,000 people in an audience, and each person could come up to the microphone and tell their family story of someone who risked everything to be here.

My dad as a kid was born in Cuba. We mentioned earlier that his father had come from the Canary Islands when he was 1. As a young man—my dad was 14 when he began to get involved in the Cuban Revolution. At the time, Batista was the dictator. Batista was cruel, corrupt, closely aligned with the Mafia, and he was oppressive.

The revolution occurred—dad was a 14-year-old boy, and I am looking at the pages who are sitting here now who are older than 14, and I would suggest, if you could imagine at the age of 14 finding yourself in a war, finding yourself fighting a war, hoping to liberate the country, being asked to fight against the army, and being asked to fight for freedom. The revolution was being fought on behalf of Fidel Castro, and indeed my father was one of many freedom fighters who fought on behalf of Castro. My father didn't know Castro. He was a kid. He was not a high ranking person in the revolution. I can tell you, my dad and the kids who were fighting, none of them knew at the time Fidel Castro was a communist. As my father describes it today, he says: Look, we were all 14- and 15-year-old boys. We were too dumb to know about that. We were just fighting for freedom. We just wanted to get out from under the boot of Batista.

For 4 years my father fought with the revolution. When he turned 17, my dad went out and partied. He was enjoying himself. He was a 17-year-old young revolutionary. He was in a white suit. You know, Senator LEE, Latinos love white suits. He was in a white suit and he was partying it up in Havana and he disappeared.

For several days my grandfather went looking for him. My grandfather—my grandparents knew their son was involved in the revolution. He hadn't hid that from his parents. And they also knew if your son is involved in the revolution and he disappears, it is a bad, bad thing. Well, after searching for him for several days—searching the jails, searching around—they found my dad. He was in a jail. He had been imprisoned, and he had been tortured.

I will confess to this day I don't know a lot about what happened. Different people have different experiences. My father doesn't talk much about it. To the best of my knowledge, other than our colleague Senator JOHN McCAIN, whom all of us respect immensely for his tremendous service and sacrifice to this Nation, I am not aware of any of our colleagues in this body who have experienced anything like imprisonment and torture—and what my father experienced was a tiny fraction of what JOHN McCAIN went through in the years he was in that Vietnam prison. But my dad, when I was growing up, never would really tell me what happened there.

But I remember one night when I was a kid—I think I was in high school, maybe junior high or high school, I don't remember—my dad and I had gone to see the movie Rambo. My dad and I both liked movies. He had taken me to see Rambo, and it was a fun movie to see as a kid. It happened that night—my parents owned a small business, and my dad had one of his clients over for dinner—that during the course of dinner, my father was talking to his client, and he was feeling a little gregarious, and he started talking. He said: You know, my son Ted and I went to see Rambo this evening. And you might remember there is a pretty nasty scene where Rambo is strapped to a bed frame and being subjected to electric shock. Not a very pleasant scene in the movie. My dad was saying: You know, the Cubans weren't nearly so fancy when it came to torture. We watched the movie Rambo. They didn't have any fancy bed frames and electric shock or anything. The Cubans were much more simple in their torture. Basically, they would just come in every hour and beat the living daylights out of you. They would just beat you, and beat you, and beat you. Then they would leave, come back in an hour and do it again.

I can tell you my grandmother said when my dad came out of that jail cell in Cuba the white suit he was wearing, you couldn't see a spot of white on it, that every inch of that suit was covered with mud and blood from where he had been beaten. And my father's teeth, she said, were dangling from his mouth in shards. Today, my father is a pastor in Dallas, and his front teeth are not his own because when he was a kid they were kicked out of his mouth in a Cuban jail.

He got out of that jail and at that point my grandfather told him, he said: Look, Rafael, they know who you are now. In fact, the Batista police were following my dad hoping he would lead them to others in the revolution. The only reason he got out is they thought: Well, maybe if we let him go he will be dumb enough to go to some other people in the revolution and we can track them down too. So my grandfather said: Listen, they know who you are. At this point they are just going to hunt you down and kill you. You can't stay here.

So my father applied to three U.S. universities. He applied to the University of Miami, he applied to LSU, and he applied to the University of Texas. It was pure happenstance that the first one to let him in was the University of Texas. Had it been otherwise, had it been the University of Miami, I might today be a constituent of our friend MARCO RUBIO. But it so happened it was the University of Texas, and that led to my father getting on a plane in 1957 when he was 18.

I want again to talk to the pages who are here. Some of you may be 18 or near it. I want you to imagine at the age of 18 getting on a plane and flying away from your family, thousands of miles away to another country—to a country where you don't know anybody, you don't have any family, and you don't speak the language. Imagine walking off the plane.

My father had the suit on his back. He couldn't take anything with him. He couldn't take a suitcase or anything. He was wearing a suit. The one possession he had was a slide rule that was in his pocket. I see looks of somewhat confusion on the faces of the pages. I note anytime I talk to young people they have utterly no idea what a slide rule is. That was the one possession he had that he had taken from Cuba. And my grandmother, before he left, sewed $100 into the inside of his underwear. She wanted him to have at least a little money when he landed.

So in 1957 he shows up in Austin, and his first priority was to get a place to live. So he went and found a place to live. And then he had to get a job. And the job he got was washing dishes. Why washing dishes? Because you didn't have to speak English. He couldn't speak English. He made 50 cents an hour. He didn't have to talk to anyone. He could take a dish, stick it under hot water, scrub it, and move on to the next one. That he could do.

My dad worked 7 days a week washing dishes and then as a cook to pay his way through the University of Texas. And times were tight. I can't imagine. I didn't have to go through that. I don't believe Senator LEE had to go through the experience of going to school full time and working full time. My dad worked 7 days a week while he was going to school full time as a student. It wasn't that he wanted to. He didn't have any other alternatives. There wasn't anyone else providing for him.

I remember a couple of stories my father told me of his time in college. With the indulgence of the Chair, I will share those stories because they are stories, I think, of the American experience; they are shared experience.

The great thing about working in a restaurant is they let you eat while you work. So during the 8 hours, he would eat those 8 hours. The other 16 hours he wouldn't eat. It was even better when he got promoted to being a cook, because as a cook you really got a chance to eat. For example, one of the things the restaurant served was fried shrimp. My dad had a policy that anyone who ordered a dozen shrimp, he would cook 13 and eat one. During the course of the day a lot of people would order fried shrimp, and he would just eat one steadily throughout the day. My dad used to try to drink 6 or 7 glasses of milk during the day. He figured there was no percentage in water, and he needed the nutrients. Because when he left, he was going another 16 hours without eating until he came back to work the next day. He didn't have money for food.

There was one little exception. There was a coffee shop he found in town. He went in one day, and he splurged. It was one of the few times he actually spent money, and he spent money for a cup of coffee. Another gentleman in the coffee shop came in and ordered some toast. My dad saw the waitress take out of a bag a fresh loaf of bread, take both of the heels and throw them away, and then take two other slices of bread, put them in the toaster and toast them. My father said: What are you doing? You are throwing away perfectly good food. And she said: well, we can't serve the heels.

When you are desperate and you are hungry, you have incentive to do all sorts of things, and so my father said: Listen, do me a favor. Save them for me. Just save them for me. You can't serve them, I will eat them. He used to go into that coffee shop, and that waitress very kindly would save the heels when she opened a new loaf. When he would come in she would have five, six, or seven heels. She would toast them and give him butter, and he would order one cup of coffee and have five or six heels of toast and drink his coffee.

Another similar story. There were a lot of immigrants at the University of Texas who didn't have two nickels between them, and he went over to some friends who I think were brothers and they invited him over for dinner. He was sitting down for dinner with a big pot of black beans. Cubans love black beans. When he was reaching in to get black beans, they said: Watch out for the nail. Watch out for the nail? What on Earth are you talking about? These two brothers explained: Look, we don't have money for food. So what little money we have, we have enough to have beans each night, and we have enough to purchase a little tiny paper-thin steak. The brothers said: Initially, we started to cut the steak in half so we would each eat it. To be honest, we both left hungry and we weren't happy with that. So we decided instead of doing that, we would take a nail, drop it in the beans, and we would fish for the nail. Whoever got the nail with their beans got the whole steak and the other brother didn't get any steak at all.

They said: Rafael, since you are our guest—and he was kind of waiting for them to say we are going to give you the steak, but they were not quite that generous. But they said: Since you are our guest, we will give you half of the steak and we are going to fish for the nail for the other half.

One other story. In his freshman or sophomore year, I'm not sure which, my dad and a couple of other Cubans who were students there decided they wanted to have a Christmas dinner. The Cuban tradition of Christmas is to roast a whole pig.

Indeed, if I may digress, when I was dating my wife Heidi—Heidi is the love of my life, she is my best friend. She was raised in California. She and her whole family are vegetarians. I remember Heidi brought me back to meet her parents for Christmas, and we were sitting there having Christmas dinner. I would note that a vegetarian Christmas dinner is just like any other Christmas dinner except the entree never comes. Everything else is wonderful, but you keep waiting for them to bring out the entree and it is not there.

My now in-laws, who are wonderful tremendous people, who were missionaries and just wonderful people, they were trying to get to know this strange young man their daughter had brought home. And they said: Ted, tell us, how does your family celebrate Christmas? I said: Well, we are Cuban, and the Cuban tradition is that on Christmas Eve we roast a whole pig.

I must tell you the look of abject horror. If you can imagine a table full of California vegetarians, when I said we roast a whole pig. I don't think if I had said we consumed live kittens it would have more horrified them than that so viscerally carnivorous tale.

But my dad and a couple of his Cuban buddies decided they wanted to have a Christmas dinner, and to actually celebrate. So they drove to a farm just outside of Austin. They found some farmers in central Texas and said: Listen, is there any chance we could somehow buy a little piglet from you? Can we do something so we could get it and roast it? We would like to have it at Christmas Eve dinner. These farmers decided they wanted to have fun with my dad and these kids, so they said: Tell you what. We will take this little piglet and let him loose in a corral filled with mud. If you can catch it, you can have him for free. My dad and his friends chased that piglet for close to an hour, running around in the mud. They finally caught the piglet, the farmers gave it to them, they took it home, and they roasted it for Christmas Eve.

The epilogue to the story about my in-laws is that when Heidi and I became engaged, her mother called her and said: Sweetheart, are you prepared to catch the pig? Thankfully Heidi reassured her she was quite confident in our marriage that there would be no pig catching that she would indeed be carrying out, and that has indeed proven true.

All of us have stories about our families. My father has been my inspiration ever since I was a kid because I think it is a great blessing, a tremendous blessing to be the child of someone who has fled oppression, to be the child of someone who came here seeking freedom. It makes you realize that what we have in the United States of America is precious, it is wonderful, it is unique, and we cannot possibly risk giving it up.

At the same time, I am amazed at how commonplace my father's story is. Every American has a story just like that. Sometimes it is us, sometimes it is our parents, sometimes it is our great-great-grandparents. But I have yet to encounter someone who doesn't have a story like that in their background, often closer than one might think. I think the most shared characteristic among all of us as Americans is we are the children of those who risked everything for freedom.

Sometimes people ask, what differentiates Americans from, say, Europeans, Americans from other countries? I think more than anything it is in our DNA to value liberty and opportunity above all else.

When ObamaCare was being passed 3½ years ago, I think the proponents believed—in fact, they stated—that once it is in place Americans would come to love it and would give up their liberty, would give up their freedom in exchange for bread and circuses. Yet 3½ years later we see ObamaCare is less popular now than it was then. That is true all over the country. That is true in every region. That is true among Republicans, among Democrats, among Independents, and among Libertarians.

There are several reasons for that. One is simple facts. Forget party ideology affiliations. The simple fact is this isn't working. If you look at it on its face, it is a train wreck, as the Democratic Senator who was the lead author of ObamaCare has described. On its face it is a nightmare, as James Hoffa, the president of the Teamsters, has described it.

ObamaCare in practice is killing jobs all over this country. It is causing small businesses to stay small, not to grow, not to create jobs. It is causing Americans all over this country to forcibly reduce to 29 hours a week. Do you know who is being reduced the most? It ain't the rich. It ain't, as the President likes to put it, the millionaires and billionaires. The millionaires and billionaires are doing great. They are richer today than when President Obama was elected.

I think the biggest lie in politics is the lie that Republicans are the party of the rich. I think it is a complete and total falsehood. The rich do great with big government. Business does great with big government. Why? Because big business gets into bed with big government.

What have we seen with ObamaCare? The rich and powerful get special exemptions. Big businesses? The President exempts them. Members of Congress? The President exempts us. It is the little guy who doesn't have an army of lobbyists, doesn't have special interests, the little guy is the one left out.

So who are the people losing their jobs? Who are the people forcibly having reduced hours? Who are the people facing skyrocketing health insurance premiums? Who are the people having their insurance dropped? It is people such as the disabled retirees whose letters I was reading earlier today. It is people like my father.

If ObamaCare was the law in 1957, when my father was washing dishes, I think it is a virtual certainty that he would have found his hours forcibly reduced to 29 hours a week—if he had been lucky enough to get a job in the first place. He might not have been hired at all. That is happening to people all over the country. The people who are losing under ObamaCare are people like my dad, teenaged kids who don't speak English, who are recent immigrants, who are Hispanic, who are African Americans, single moms.

I have a good friend who is now a justice on the Texas Supreme Court whose mom was a single mom and waited tables. He computed the distance she walked as a waitress to bring him up. I don't remember the exact measurements, but it was some remarkable number of times walking from the Earth to the Moon and back that she walked so her kids could have a better life. That single mom who was waiting tables, her son is now a justice in the Texas Supreme Court. That is the story of America. But if ObamaCare had been in place, that single mom waiting tables is working 29 hours a week. Try feeding a family on 29 hours a week. You can't do it. It cannot be done.

So what happens instead? People get their hours forcibly reduced. They either can't earn enough to feed their family so they leave the workforce altogether and they go on welfare. Not that they want to. They want to be working. But if Congress has passed a law so that the only job they can get is 29 hours a week, that is not enough to feed their family. Right now one in seven Americans is on food stamps. What a travesty. It is not a travesty from the perspective of the budget; it is not a travesty from the perspective of the taxpayers. It is a travesty from the perspective of those people on food stamps who would rather be working, who would rather have the dignity of work to provide for their family and to climb the economic ladder.

My dad started washing dishes, but he didn't stay there. After washing dishes he got a job as a cook. After a cook he got a job as a teaching assistant. After a teaching assistant he got hired at IBM as a computer programmer. Then he started his own business. If he doesn't get hired washing dishes, he doesn't get the next job as a cook, he doesn't get the next job as a teaching assistant, he doesn't get the next job at IBM, he doesn't get the next job starting his own business.

If you look at those single moms who are waiting tables and suddenly get their hours reduced to 29 hours a week, if she ends up giving up, going on food stamps, going on welfare, saying I can't earn enough in the market to provide for my family, not only does that have devastating effects on her and on her kids, but it also means she won't have a chance to move up the ladder. She won't have a chance to get that next job. Maybe if she was waiting tables, she would get promoted to being assistant manager and then manager. Maybe she would have another opportunity moving up the ladder. But if she doesn't get on that first rung, we know to an absolute certainty you won't go to the second or third rung. What a travesty.

This is a country of unlimited opportunity, and ObamaCare is cutting off that opportunity. It is shutting down that opportunity. Those are who are hurt the most under ObamaCare.

There are many reasons why ObamaCare is problematic. It is problematic because it is the biggest job killer in America. It is a train wreck because it is forcing more and more people to be driven into part-time work 29 hours a week.

The second thing the single mom can do—suppose she doesn't give up. Suppose she says, Darn it, I want to work to provide for my kids. I am not going to give up. I am not going to go on welfare and stop working in the workplace. The other option is to go find another job. So then she has two jobs at 29 hours a week. Her kids now see less of their mom. And, by the way, neither one gives her health care. So the Affordable Care Act and all the great benefits of that haven't helped her at all. Instead of being at one job where she could work and focus on that one job and potentially climb the ladder to different opportunities, she is working two part-time jobs. Part-time jobs are much harder to advance in your career with. She is also dealing with commuting. She has got to get from one job to the other. For a single mom whose time is at a premium, who would like to be at her kids' soccer game if ever she could work the schedule to do that, if she has to drive from one place to the other back and forth, there are a lot of soccer games that single mom is never getting to, not to mention the headaches of having two different jobs and two different bosses. If you have boss No. 1 who says, I want you to work Tuesday morning, and boss No. 2 says, I want you to work Tuesday morning at my place, how do you balance those? Both of them say, I don't care about your other job. I need you here. What a nightmare.

ObamaCare is a train wreck. It is a nightmare because it is killing jobs, because it is driving up health insurance, because it is causing more and more people to lose their health insurance. But it is also fundamentally wrong for a broader reason: because it infringes on our liberty.

The Federal Government is telling every American: You must purchase health insurance. The individual mandate, we are going to make you purchase health insurance. If not, the IRS is going to come and find you.

The Federal Government is telling Catholic charities and Catholic hospitals, Christian companies like Hobby Lobby: You must pay for health insurance procedures that violate your religious dictates. They may not violate everyone's religious dictates. There may be a lot of people in this country who have no religious qualms about that whatsoever, and that is fine. Each of us is entitled—indeed, encouraged—to seek out God Almighty with all of our heart, mind, and soul as best we can, and we will follow different paths. But I guarantee you, if the Federal Government can tell Catholic charities and Catholic hospitals: You must violate your religious beliefs or we are going to fine you out of business; if the Federal Government can tell that to Hobby Lobby, a Christian company, they can tell that to you too. Whatever your religious beliefs happen to be, if the Federal Government can say: Violate your religious faith or we are coming after you, that is a dangerous Rubicon we have crossed.

We are a nation that was founded on liberty. Always defend liberty. You can't go wrong with that as a mantra.

In the interest of that, I would like to share a few excerpts of one of my favorite books, *Atlas Shrugged* by Ayn Rand. Let me encourage any of you who have not read *Atlas Shrugged* to go tomorrow and buy *Atlas Shrugged* and read it. What is interesting is in the last 3 years sales of *Atlas Shrugged* have exploded, because we are living in the days of Ayn Rand. [In following pages, Senator Cruz read from Ayn Rand's *Atlas Shrugged*, Some quotes have been abridged. The full quotes can be found in the *Congressional Record*.]

I will share a few excerpts that are all fundamentally about liberty and the liberty that ObamaCare infringes.

Productiveness is your acceptance of morality, your recognition of the fact that you choose to live—that productive work is the process by which man's consciousness controls his existence, a constant process of acquiring knowledge and shaping matter to fit one's purpose of translating an idea into physical form, of remaking the earth and the image of one's values— . . . that to cheat your way into a job bigger than your mind can handle is to become a fear-corroded ape—

There is a phrase you don't hear often in modern parlance.

—on borrowed motions and borrowed time, and to settle down into a job that requires less than your mind's full . . . decay—

My, is that happening across this country as a result of ObamaCare, people being forced to settle down into jobs that require less than our mind's full capacity.

—that your work is the process of achieving your values, and to lose your ambition for values is to lose your ambition to live—that your body is a machine, but your mind is its driver, and you must drive as far as your mind will take you, with

achievement as the goal of your road— . . . that your work is
the purpose of your life . . . that any value you might find outside your work . . . must be travelers going on their own power
in the same direction. . . ."

A few other excerpts.

What is morality, she asked. Judgment to distinguish right and
wrong, vision to see the truth, and courage to act upon it; dedication to that which is good, integrity to stand by the good at
any price.

Boy, that is counsel the Senate should listen to. That is counsel I
would encourage for every Democratic Senator who feels the urge
of party loyalty, to stand by their party, to stand by ObamaCare
because it is the natural thing to do. Yet we saw union leaders, we
saw the roofers union, we saw James Hoffa of the Teamsters say they
cannot remain silent any longer. Why? Because of the suffering
ObamaCare is visiting on so many working men and women. It is a
nightmare, according to James Hoffa of the Teamsters. I encourage
my friends on the Democratic side of the aisle, as difficult as it is to
cross one's party leaders—I say with perhaps a little familiarity with
the consequences of so doing that it is survivable and that ultimately
it is liberating; that the Democratic Senators of this body maintain
their fidelity, their loyalty not to the party apparatus, not to the
party bosses, but to the men and women who sent them here, to the
men and women like the union members of the Teamsters who are
pleading with Members of Congress: Hear our suffering. ObamaCare
is a nightmare.

With that prism in mind, let me reread Ayn Rand's excerpt:

What is morality, she asked. Judgment to distinguish right and
wrong, vision to see the truth, and courage to act upon it;
dedication to that which is good, integrity to stand by the
good at any price.

You know, at any price? Look, at the end of the day, a Member of the Senate bucks his or her party leadership, and to be honest, the prices are all pretty piddly. What a coddled world we live in that we think that if someone says a cross word to you at a cocktail party or, God forbid, even worse, leaks a scurrilous lie to some reporter, that truly is a grievous insult. Goodness gracious, compared to what the people have gone through, compared to the suffering my dad went through being tortured in a Cuban prison, that is all mild. To be honest, compared to the single moms who are just wanting to provide for their kids, give them a good home, give them a good example, help them get a good future, the retribution any political party can impose on us for daring to buck the leadership is so mild and inconsequential, it is not even worth mentioning.

Let me encourage every Democratic Senator to try to meet that definition of morality:

> Judgment to distinguish right and wrong, vision to see the truth, and courage to act upon it; dedication to that which is good, integrity to stand by the good at any price.

Let me encourage my Republican colleagues, there may be some Republicans who are inclined to vote for cloture on this bill, to give majority leader HARRY REID and the Democrats the ability to fund ObamaCare on a straight party-line vote, as some of my colleagues have publicly said they are so inclined. It is my sincere hope that between now and the vote on Friday or Saturday, their better angels prevail.

Listen, any Democrat who crosses the aisle to vote with us will face swift retribution, but at the end of the day we have a higher obligation. We have an obligation to the constituents who sent us here.

Any Republican—I know there are some Republicans who are saying: I am going to support cloture. I am going to support giving HARRY REID the ability to fund ObamaCare. Why? Because my leadership is telling me to, and I am a good soldier. I will salute and march into battle in whatever direction leadership instructs.

I will confess that Republicans are sometimes even more susceptible to such commands to being orderly. Let me commend to every Republican, ask yourself that same test that Ayn Rand laid out.

What is morality, she asked. Judgment to distinguish right and wrong, vision to see the truth, and courage to act upon it; dedication to that which is good, integrity to stand by the good at any price.

I can tell you this: If any one of the 46 Republicans in this body asks not what does our party leadership want us to do but asks the more important question of, what do our constituents want us to do, I tell you this: If I get any gathering of Texans, Texans are not conflicted. If I ask a gathering of Texans—and by the way, it doesn't matter what part of Texas—east Texas, west Texas, the panhandle, down in the valley.

I was in a gathering down in the valley a few weeks ago. The Rio Grande Valley in Texas is the poorest part of the State.

My friend Senator LEE knows the valley well because he was a missionary down in the valley. In fact, he has darned good Spanish as a result of living in the valley in Texas. In fact, I think that gives Texas a reason to claim him unofficially as a third Senator. He may not acquiesce to that, but we will claim him anyway.

I was at a gathering in the valley a few weeks ago, 200, 300 people. I would guess a significant percentage if not a majority of the people in that room were probably Democrats. A majority of them were Mexican Americans.

You know, I try to make a policy of giving the same remarks standing for the same principles regardless of whether I am talking with a group I think will necessarily agree with me or will not.

The bulk of the remarks I gave to that group before taking Q and A from the group for some time were focused on defunding ObamaCare, and it was really striking that in that group, which was largely if not predominantly Hispanic Democrats in the valley in Texas, when it came to defunding ObamaCare, to stopping the train wreck that is ObamaCare, the result was rousing sustained applause and cheers. Why? Because if you get out of the partisan prison that is Washington, it is not complicated.

There is a reason why labor unions want out. There is a reason the Teamsters, who describe that they have been knocking on doors as loyal foot soldiers for the Democratic Party, are saying: This is a nightmare. Repeal ObamaCare. Repeal it because it is a nightmare.

There is a reason why Members of Congress, why Majority Leader REID and Democratic Senators who support ObamaCare so much for the American people said: Good golly, get us out from under it. We certainly do not want to be subject to the same rules the American people are.

There is a reason why the IRS employees' union is saying: Even though we are enforcing ObamaCare, please get us out from under it.

Under the objective facts, this is not working.

I urge every Republican who is here, before you make a decision how to vote on cloture on this bill on Friday or Saturday—and I think certainly in the time I have been in the Senate this is the most consequential vote I will cast and I believe any Member of this body will cast during the time I have been here—I ask every Republican to ask not simply what this party leadership wants you to do but what is the right thing to do for your constituents. If you gather 100 of your constituents together in a room and you ask them: How should I vote on this motion—let me frame it a little more explicitly because, you know, politicians are sometimes crafty characters. Some politicians say: I could get 100 of my citizens, and I could frame in some abstract procedural way how I would vote on the cloture to take up the bill to do the whatchamacallit and it would really be supporting the House bill. What do you think? We can talk fast enough that we can confuse some people in the room for a few minutes.

But let me suggest to any Republican Senator, gather at random 100 of your constituents—I am going to suggest even broader: not 100 Republicans, 100 constituents—and pose the following question to them: Should I as your Republican Senator vote to allow HARRY REID and the Democrats to fully fund ObamaCare with no changes, no improvements to address the train wreck that is ObamaCare on a purely party-line partisan vote of only Democrats? I will wager all the money in my bank account that every one of the—by the way, you could pick the bluest State for which a Republican Senator represents that State—I will wager that in that State, if you grab 100 of your constituents, it would not be a 50–50 proposition. I don't even think it would be a 60–40 proposition. Your constituents overwhelmingly would say: No, don't vote to give HARRY REID the ability to fund ObamaCare without fixing this train wreck, without stopping this nightmare.

All that it takes for us to do the right thing is to listen to the people. It is not complicated. It is not rocket science. Listen to the people.

Ayn Rand in *Atlas Shrugged* also held:

> The nation which once held the creed that greatness is achieved by production is now told that it is achieved by squalor.

She also observed:

> Fight for the value of your person. Fight for the virtue of your pride. Fight for the essence of that which is man: for his sovereign rational mind. . . .
>
> God has created men and women to be free creatures. It is not benefiting anyone to strip them of their liberty, to make them dependent on government.

I cannot tell you how many times I have said: Thank the good Lord that when my dad was a teenage immigrant in Texas 55 years ago, how grateful I am that some well-meaning liberal did not come and put his arm around him and say: Let me take care of you. Let me give you a government check. Let me make you dependent on the government. Don't bother washing those dishes. Don't bother working. I am going to take care of your every need. And by the way, don't bother learning English. I respect your culture so much that I am going to lock you out of the business and professional classes in this country. I am going to make sure that if you do work, you are almost surely going to be consigned to menial labor because you cannot communicate with the significant majority of Americans.

What a destructive thing to do to someone. If someone had done that to my father and he had listened, I am hard-pressed to think of anything that would have been more destructive.

At the end of the day these points are not partisan or ideological; they are common sense. They are who we are as Americans. Ask any abuelo or abuela: What do you want for your grandkids? Do you want your grandkids dependent on government? Do you want your grandkids receiving government support or do you want them working? Do you want them working in a job, working hard? Do you want them climbing the economic ladder to success? Do you want them in a career where they can have a better life than you had and their parents had? Do you want them working in a job? I don't know of a grandmother in this country who would find that a difficult choice. That is a choice that is basic common sense. It is fundamentally destructive to the human spirit not to be able to work and stand on your own feet.

After standing here for 14 hours, I can say that when you are standing on your own feet, sometimes there is pain and sometimes some fatigue that is involved. But you know what. There is far more pain involved in rolling over, far more pain in hiding in the shadows, far more pain in not standing for principle, not standing for the good, not standing for integrity. That is what it means to be an American. We do the hard things.

To all the Republicans who say fighting this fight is going to be very hard, I sure hope they didn't run for the Senate because they wanted something easy to do. I sure hope they didn't run for the Senate because they wanted to avoid hard challenges. To the Democrats who say, I couldn't buck the party leadership, gosh, it would make the White House mad, make the party leadership mad, and make our leadership in the Senate mad, we have to be united, Team, team, team. We are not a team. We represent the people. You know the team that each of us is on? It is the American team. It is a team where we have an obligation to the men and women who sent us here. Let me be clear: We have an obligation to all the men and women who sent us here. I have an obligation not just to Republicans in the State of Texas and not just to those who voted for me in the State of Texas, although there were quite a few voters in the State of Texas who voted for President Obama and voted for me.

If you listen to Washington conventional wisdom, they would suggest that is impossible. I was pleased to get a number of Texans who did that. Even those who voted against me and disagree with everything I am doing, I still have an obligation to represent them and to try to use my best judgment and try to listen to them and fight for them.

I am convinced that every one of the 26 million Texans in my State will be better. They will have a better future, a better life, and an environment where economic growth comes back and small businesses are thriving and creating jobs and not shrinking. They will have opportunities so they are not forced into part-time work but will have fulltime opportunities so more people who are like my dad—teenaged kids who can't speak English—can get that first job washing dishes. That first job helps them to get the second job, the third job, and the fourth job.

I believe in the American dream with all of my heart and might. The American dream is being jeopardized by ObamaCare, and that is a travesty that should outrage and horrify everyone in the Senate. For everyone on the Republican side who said this is hard, we might be blamed; there might be some political blame; let's let it all collapse—I have heard Republicans say, especially the pundits, Gosh, to get on TV—I will tell you that one of the best ways to get on TV is to just advise and then run away from any battle that matters. They put you on TV a lot if that is your advice.

What they say is, if Republicans stand and fight this fight, the President and Harry Reid might force a shutdown and Republicans might get blamed and, gosh, that could hurt us politically. Beyond that you might hear—and this is the very clever Republicans—ObamaCare is such a train wreck and a nightmare that we just need to sit quietly. James Hoffa said he couldn't sit silent anymore, but Republicans say to sit silently and let ObamaCare collapse on its own weight.

Never mind that Harry Reid said when it collapses on its own weight, it will lead us to single-payer socialized health care. Why? Because it will destroy the private health insurance. Never mind that.

We have been told that if we do nothing, it will collapse on its own weight and everyone will blame the Democrats.

Let me make it very clear: Who cares? Listen, if everyone will blame the Democrats, then consider me the person trying to actively save the Democrats from that blame. I would gladly celebrate any Democrat brave enough to stand and say: Listen, I used to think ObamaCare was a good idea. I supported it, and I am persuaded by the facts and by my constituents. This thing isn't working. People are hurting.

When President Obama reversed course and listened to bipartisan calls to submit his decision to launch a unilateral military attack on Syria to the will of Congress, I happily and loudly praised President Obama for submitting to the constitutional authority of this party. When he went even further and listened to the calls from the American people not to put us in the middle of that sectarian war, I again happily and enthusiastically praised President Obama for being willing to change his mind and turn back because he listened to the voice of the American people. That was the right thing to do.

For everyone who thinks this is hard, I would like to turn to some of my favorite remarks from a Republican President who I suspect many on the Democratic side of the aisle admire as well because he was one of the most progressive Republicans, although he was not shy in any way, shape or form.

Indeed, Teddy Roosevelt was once giving a speech, and he was shot during the speech. He finished the speech before seeking medical attention. There was an old episode on "Saturday Night Live"—the pages have probably never seen this—that was "Quien es mas Macho," which means who is more macho. You know what. Teddy Roosevelt quien es mas macho. If you get shot while giving a speech and stand there and finish the speech, you win. Even Sean Connery is looking at him and going, wow, that guy is tough.

I will read the words Teddy Roosevelt delivered at the Sorbonne in Paris on April 23, 1910. These are words for everyone who thinks this fight is too hard or that we shouldn't take a risk or we shouldn't risk political blame. These are words that every one of us should listen to:

It is not the critic who counts; not the man who points out how the strong man stumbles, or where the doer of deeds could have done them better. The credit belongs to the man—

Or the woman—

who is actually in the arena, whose face is marred by dust and sweat and blood; who strives valiantly; who errs, who comes short again and again, because there is no effort without error and shortcoming; but who does actually strive to do the deeds; who knows great enthusiasms, the great devotions; who spends himself in a worthy cause; who at the best knows in the end the triumph of high achievement, and who at the worst, if he fails, at least fails while daring greatly, so that his place shall never be with those cold and timid souls who neither know victory nor defeat.

Yes, you can avoid risk. You can avoid doing the hard thing. You can avoid doing the things where you might get politically blamed. You can stay silent and hope that the other party gets blamed because there will be political benefits for that. But I am going to suggest to you that is not doing our job. That is not what we were elected to do.

We were elected to stand and fight to do the hard things for the men and women of this country because it is an extraordinary and breathtaking privilege to serve in this body. I cannot tell you how it brings me virtually to tears to think about the opportunity I have to stand here at a time when our Nation is threatened as I have never seen before. You know what. The tears that I talked about, and am now experiencing a little bit, are a very small reflection of the very real tears I have seen from men and women all across Texas.

Men and women have looked me in the eyes and said: I am scared for my country, my kids, and my grandkids. We are losing America. We are losing the wonderful free enterprise system. We are losing the prosperity. We are losing growth.

Will my kids and grandkids have a better life than I did? I don't think so. I cannot tell you how many Texans have said that. You know what. When you say that, that is not something you say like reporting the weather: It is sunny today and 78 degrees. That is heartbreaking. As Americans, it is fundamental in who we are. We believe in a better tomorrow. We believe morning can come to America, and we believe our kids and grandkids will live with a better challenge.

If we continue down this road, we will be mired in what I call the great stagnation. Over the last 4 years, our economy has grown on average at 0.9 percent a year. If we continue down this road, we will allow young people to be what economists are starting to dub "the lost generation." I am sorry to tell young people that is what economists are calling them right now. This generation is coming of age at a time when there is no economic growth and no real prospect for that to change.

What it means as a practical matter is that young people are not getting that first job or they are getting jobs—and as Ayn Rand observed—that are far less than their mind, their capacity, and their talent is capable of. What that means is they don't get their next job or their next job, so they don't develop to their full potential, and that stays with young people for decades to come.

This body needs to listen to the American people. We need to make DC listen.

Mr. LEE. Will the Senator yield for a question?

Mr. CRUZ. I am happy to yield for a question without yielding the floor.

Mr. LEE. My question relates to the nature of our government and the nature of our system which is a system of laws. One of the reasons America has been attractive to so many people over the last few centuries and one of the reasons people have wanted to move here from all over the world is that this has always been a land of opportunity. It has been a place where you can be born into one station in life and die in a much better station. We worry that land of opportunity might cease to be. We worry about the fact that people are being trapped at the bottom rungs of the economic ladder and finding it increasingly difficult to move up along that ladder.

One of the reasons this is the case is because the distinction between what is properly within the domain of government and what is properly within the domain of people is sometimes blurred. In other instances, that which is properly within the domain of the Federal Government and properly within the domain of the State and local governments in this country is blurred.

On other occasions, it is because what is properly within the domain of the legislative branch is usurped by the executive branch or the judicial branch or a combination of the two. The more our legal system becomes deteriorated, the less faithful it becomes to the blueprint that was created for our government some 226 years ago, and the more we struggle in this country.

I quoted James Madison earlier. I referred to something he said in Federalist No. 62. I have the actual text of the language, which I largely paraphrased earlier, and I wish to expand on it a little more and explain some of what he was saying.

He writes:

It will be of little avail to the people that the laws are made by men of their own choice, if the laws be so voluminous that they cannot be read, or so incoherent that they cannot be understood; if they be repealed or revised before they are promulgated, or undergo such incessant changes that no man, who knows what the law is today, can guess what it will be to-morrow. Law is defined to be a rule of action; but how can that be a rule, which is little known, and less fixed? Another effect of public instability is the unreasonable advantage it gives to the sagacious, the enterprising, and the moneyed few over the industrious and uninformed mass of the people. Every new regulation concerning commerce or revenue, or in any way affecting the value of the different species of property, presents a new harvest to those who watch the change and can trace its consequences; a harvest, reared not by themselves, but by the toils and cares of the great body of their fellow-citizens. This is a state of things in which it may be said with some truth that laws are made for the few, not for the many.

In another point of view, great injury results from an unstable government. The want of confidence in the public councils damps every useful undertaking, the success and profit of which may depend on a continuance of existing arrangements. What prudent merchant will hazard his fortunes in any new branch of commerce when he knows not but that his plans may be rendered unlawful before they can be executed? What farmer or manufacturer will lay himself out for the encouragement given to any particular cultivation or establishment when he can have no assurance that his preparatory labors and advances will not render him a victim to an inconstant government? In a word, no great improvement or laudable enterprise can go forward which requires the auspices of a steady system of national policy.

But the most deplorable effect of all is that diminution of attachment and reverence which steals into the hearts of the people, towards a political system which betrays so many marks of infirmity, and disappoints so many of their flattering hopes. No government any more than an individual, will long be respected without being truly respectable; nor be truly respectable, without possessing a certain portion of order and stability.

We see in this an age-old warning, a warning about what happens when governments do certain things which tend toward voluminous legislation, excessive regulation, and deliberate manipulation by those who have access to the power lovers of government, whereby they may commandeer the economic machinery of an entire civilization—commandeer it to their advantage, and thereby secure a position at the top end of the economic spectrum of that society. When people do this, they very frequently use really long, really complex laws. They necessarily rely on extensive regulation, the kind of regulation that can be found in a 2,700-page law passed by Members of Congress who have not read it, who pass it after being told they have to pass it in order to find out what is in it, who do so only to discover later that this 2,700-page piece of legislation has become 20,000 pages of regulation.

As we stand this evening, or this morning, or whatever we call this time of day as we move forward together on this path toward standing with the American people, I invite my colleagues to join me on a journey back to a place and time not unlike our own. It was a turbulent time of deep division within our young Republic. George Washington recorded the events of March 4, 1797—his last day as President of the United States. Washington wrote:

> It was with a heavy heart that I left my room today thinking not so much of myself as of our country . . .

Walking out onto Chestnut Street in Philadelphia, Washington continued:

> I was plain George Washington now, neither general nor President. Suddenly I realized I was not alone. People were following me, at first only a few, then a swelling crowd.
>
> For a long moment, I stood face to face with them—the young cobbler, the carpenter, the storekeeper, the laborer. All of them stood facing me. They said not a word. I realized that providence was showing me a vision of America, of what it will become. I could feel assured that, come what may, whether it be political bickering . . . or any other evil in government, . . . our country rests in good hands, in the hands of its people . . .

A similar crowd we might say gathers every time people converge at a townhall meeting. It is not necessarily a crowd consisting of carpenters, storekeepers, laborers, and cobblers. It might well consist of a crowd including schoolteachers, Web designers, business consultants, mothers and fathers and friends.

Every time I hold townhall meetings, as I look around the crowd and I see groups of people represented from those groups I described, I think about the fact that today, as in Washington's time, the hands of our great Nation rest in good hands. It rests in the hands of its people.

So hand in hand and acting on the instincts of our better angels and connected in the principle of civil society and in the principles that allow our country to be great, we know that we the people and not we the government will form a more perfect union and help ensure that the vision of George Washington becomes the destiny of the Nation.

Our discussions tonight have been about keeping the country in the hands of the people and making sure the government serves the people and not the other way around, making sure the people are in charge of their own government; that whenever the things that government does become destructive of the ability of the people to achieve happiness and secure their own lives and their liberty and their pursuit of happiness, it is important that the people restore to themselves the power which is rightfully theirs.

Throughout the history of the world, in many civilizations, people have called that idea radical. They have called it crazy. They have called it insane. Here we call it a very American ideal.

Here, tonight, we have been talking a lot about this law. We have been talking a lot about our ability to defund this law which we believe has become destructive of the people. We have been told by some of our colleagues—some from within our own party—that this effort is futile, that we shouldn't fight it because, as we are told over and over, we don't have the votes. Those things can change and they do change when the people speak to their elected representatives and they ask their elected representatives to do that which they were sent to our Nation's capital to do.

There is a man named William Morris, a man whose political philosophy I don't share in many respects, but a man who occasionally said things that were profound and reflect broader truths.

William Morris once wrote:

One man with an idea in his head is in danger of being considered a madman; two men with the same idea in common may be foolish, but can hardly be mad; ten men sharing an idea begin to act, a hundred draw attention as fanatics, a thousand and society begins to tremble; a hundred thousand . . . and the cause has victories tangible and real; and why only a hundred thousand? Why not a hundred million and more . . . ? You and I who agree together, it is we who have to answer that question.

So when we find ourselves with an idea in our head, when we find ourselves listening to people, people who might begin with a chorus of one calling out for Congress to do something to protect the American people, we might be inclined to dismiss that one idea coming from that one person as the product of madness. When two people join together, when 10, when 100, 1,000, 10,000, and so forth—with each order of magnitude, we find that the idea acquires more potency, the idea acquires more lasting power, the idea moves more and more people.

The idea to defund ObamaCare is not new. It has been discussed since 2010, since shortly after the law's enactment, since about the time when many people were predicting that the Republican Party might gain control of at least one House of Congress. That is when it began in earnest.

We hoped, we expected, that once the Republican majority took hold, once Republicans took control of the House of Representatives in January 2011, in the wake of the 2010 election cycle, that the defunding of ObamaCare would be imminent. In fact, H.R. 1, the continuing resolution, as I recall, was filed at the beginning of the last Congress and originally was written to defund ObamaCare. I am not quite sure why that didn't move forward, but many expected it would happen. It didn't happen. We have continued to pass continuing resolution after continuing resolution since January of 2011 to keep the government funded and we have done so without defunding ObamaCare. There have been reasons for that. There were many who expected the Supreme Court would invalidate ObamaCare, thus obviating the need for Congress to go through the process of defunding it and later repealing it. That didn't happen.

There were those who expected that a Republican would be elected to President of the United States in the 2012 election cycle, thereby making it possible for ObamaCare to be repealed or perhaps at least stalled out with the assistance of the President and with the assistance of an Executive order suspending many of its major provisions. That, of course, didn't happen. We are now at the point when we are being asked to fund the operations of government potentially for the last time between now and the time when the law's major operative provisions will take effect.

This will not be the end of the debate, assuming this effort either does or doesn't succeed. I have no doubt this debate will continue for some time. If we do not succeed in defunding ObamaCare at this point, it doesn't mean the cause is lost forever. It may nonetheless mean it becomes far more difficult to stop this law.

Once a law such as this takes effect, it is frequently suggested it will be much harder to stop, much harder to defund, and much harder to repeal down the road. So before we take this step, I think it is appropriate that we consider very seriously defunding this law's implementation and enforcement, especially in light of taking into account the potentially devastating impact this law will have, could have, and is already having on our Nation's workers, the impact it is having with regard to wages, to employment opportunities, to access to health care, and to the cost of health care. We have to take that very seriously, as the House of Representatives has done in passing this continuing resolution.

As we take that up, we have to remember the fate of this Nation lies in good hands. It lies in the hands of the American people—the people who were represented well by the House of Representatives when it passed the continuing resolution funding the operations of government, while defunding ObamaCare.

I ask Senator Cruz the question: What can we do as citizens, what can we do as Senators, to make sure the hands of our government will, indeed, remain in good hands, in the hands of its people, rather than in the hands of a perpetual oligarchy, albeit an elected oligarchy, a bipartisan political establishment that might limit the freedom of the American people?

(Mr. DONNELLY assumed the Chair.)

Mr. CRUZ. I thank my friend from Utah for that very fine question. The answer as to what we can do is to do what we must, as Americans, what we always have, which is to take the responsibility on ourselves, on our shoulders, to step forward, to engage.

Edmund Burke famously said: The only thing necessary for evil to prevail is for good men to do nothing.

One of the tremendous aspects of the American character is Americans have never been willing to sit back and do nothing.

People all over this country are disillusioned. They are disillusioned because Washington does not listen to us. They are disillusioned because Democratic Senators do not listen to the people and Republican Senators do not listen to the people. I understand that disillusionment. I feel the same way. Everywhere I go in Texas that sentiment is expressed. I do not think there is a State in the Union where they do not feel that sense.

But there are moments—moments in time when we can change that. You think back to earlier this year, to another filibuster that occurred on this Senate floor with our friend Senator RAND PAUL, when he was standing up to the administration's drone policy.

Senator PAUL began that filibuster, if I remember correctly, at 11:45 a.m. When he started, virtually every Senator in this Chamber viewed what he was doing as an odd crusade. They did not support it. They did not even understand it. What matters if the Federal Government can use a drone to target a U.S. citizen, to kill a U.S. citizen on U.S. soil? What matters that, thought most Senators.

Senator PAUL began a brave crusade. I would note, during that filibuster, I was honored to stand side by side with my good friend Senator LEE as we were the first two Senators to stand in support of that and to battle the length of those 13 hours in defense of the Constitution.

During the course of that filibuster, we saw what happens when the American people get engaged. Because the American people got engaged at an incredible level, and it forced a change. For 3 consecutive weeks, President Obama had refused to do what he did that very next day, which was admit in writing that the Constitution limits his authority to target U.S. citizens.

Indeed, earlier that day before the filibuster began, it so happened that Attorney General Eric Holder was testifying before the Senate Judiciary Committee. Senator LEE and I were both there as part of that testimony. I remember an exchange with the Attorney General where three times I asked the Attorney General if, in his view, the Constitution allowed the U.S. Government to kill a U.S. citizen on U.S. soil if that individual did not pose an imminent threat, and three times he responded: I do not think it would be appropriate to do so.

The first time he gave that response, I responded to the Attorney General. I said: Mr. Attorney General,.you seem to have misunderstood my question. I was not asking about propriety. After all, he was not there testifying as an etiquette columnist for the local newspaper. I said: You are the Attorney General of the United States. You are the chief law enforcement officer for the United States of America. Does the Department of Justice have a position on whether the Constitution allows the U.S. Government to use a drone to target and kill a U.S. citizen on U.S. soil if that individual does not pose an imminent threat? Again, the response was: I do not think it would be appropriate.

After the third time, I almost felt as if the response was: I do not understand this Constitution to which you are referring. Finally, he conceded in that back and forth: Well, when I say "appropriate," I mean "constitutional," which I find a curious notion that somehow "appropriate" and "constitutional" are coterminous.

You want to talk about what the American people can do? We saw during that, had not that filibuster and the American people mobilized, President Obama would have never admitted in writing what he admitted that next day, which was the Constitution limits his authority. And that matters.

We saw another example with the gun debate. Following the tragic shooting in Newtown, CT—which every one of us was horrified at—the President, sadly, did not come out and say: Let us go after violent criminals.

And listen, I think we should come down on violent criminals like a ton of bricks. Instead, the President, unfortunately, took it as an opportunity to go after the Second Amendment rights of law-abiding citizens, instead of targeting violent criminals, those who would prey on the innocent.

The conventional wisdom in Washington was the momentum behind those efforts was unstoppable. Indeed, all the talking heads, the same talking heads who during RAND's filibuster said this is foolish, this is a fool's errand, this cannot work—the American people rose up and spoke and that was proven wrong.

During the gun debate, those same talking heads—it is interesting, in the world of punditry there are no consequences for being proven wrong. You just keep going back to making those same gosh darn predictions. And you know what. If you keep making the same prediction often enough, eventually it is going to prove right.

In the gun debate all those same talking heads said: You cannot stop it. This is unstoppable. What happened again? The American people got involved by the thousands, by the tens of thousands, calling their Senators, emailing their Senators, speaking out at townhalls, saying: Defend the Second Amendment right to keep and bear arms. We want the constitutional rights of law-abiding citizens to be protected.

I remember on the floor of this Senate, when it came for a vote, every single proposal of the President that would have undermined the Second Amendment was voted down. That astonished observers. They said it was impossible. It was impossible until the American people engaged.

As we discussed not too long ago with Syria, the President advocated, said he was going to engage in a unilateral military strike within days. It was imminent. It was happening. There was bipartisan support from the leadership of both Houses of Congress. All those same pundits—Mr. President, if you are noticing a pattern here, there is a pattern here. These same pundits over and over again said: Whatever President Obama says, that is inevitable. It cannot be stopped. There is nothing we can do about it. There is nothing to see here. Move on.

At first the President, quite rightly, listened to bipartisan calls to submit that decision to the constitutional authority of Congress. I was quick to praise him for doing so. And, second, even more difficult, the President showed the wisdom, the prudence to listen to the voice of the American people when the American people spoke out overwhelmingly and said: We do not want to be involved in a sectarian civil war in Syria when we do not have a dog in the fight, when the rebels are in some significant way allied with Al Qaeda, Al-Nusra, radical terrorists, when there is no national security interest in getting us in the middle of this. It was overwhelming, and the entire ship of state turned on a dime. What was inevitable stopped. And it stopped because of the American people.

So the question my friend Senator LEE asked—what can the American people do? Do the same thing. But let me tell you now, you have to do it 10 times louder. You have to do it in even greater volume. Because I am sorry to say, Members of this body are dug in at a level they were not dug in on drones, at a level they were not dug in on guns, at a level they were not dug in on Syria.

The Democrats in this body, I am sorry to say, have not yet shown the willingness to speak out like James Hoffa of the Teamsters has, have not yet shown the willingness to speak out for their constituents and say: ObamaCare is failing and it is not working.

The Republicans in this body—there are quite a few of them who are angry we are having this fight. They believe it is not worthy of the time of this institution. They find themselves offended that the American people would expect us not just to have a symbolic show vote on a ObamaCare but actually to do something. Goodness gracious, this is Congress. We do not do something. Let's have another symbolic vote, and then we can put out a press release.

About an hour ago, a member of my staff showed me that this discussion—even though virtually every Senator has gone home and gone to sleep—that this discussion, this debate is not just trending No. 1 in the United States, but in one way, shape, or form is trending No. 1, No. 2, No. 3, and No. 4. I have never seen anything like that.

No. 2, I will confess, is Duck Dynasty, but I am going to claim Duck Dynasty as part of it since not too long ago I took the opportunity to read some words of wisdom from Duck Dynasty and I suspect that is not entirely disconnected.

I have to admit, I have seen things trend No. 1. I have never seen them trend Nos. 1, 2, 3, and 4 all at the same time.

Given the Senate Chamber has been largely empty for most of the night, it is self-evident that kind of involvement from the American people is not a factor of personalities. It is not a factor of myself or MIKE or anyone else. And by the way, everyone who wants to distract from the subject of this debate will try to make it about personalities. If they can get the Washington press corps to write stories about personal flights, about back and forth, about civil war—my goodness, how many times have we seen the words "civil war" in the last week in the press? I am wondering if reporters have it now on a macro: "Alt" "C" and it types "civil war." Who cares? You know what. If you get out of Washington, DC, I do not know anyone who cares. What Americans care about is they want jobs back. They want economic growth back. They want to get back to work. They want their health care not to be taken away because of ObamaCare. Every effort to talk about anything else is all a deliberate effort to distract from the issue that matters.

The reason this is trending Nos. 1, 2, 3, and 4 is because, for a moment, at least, some in this body are listening to the American people. I hope and believe and think that a great many Americans want to believe that more of us will do so, that more of us on the Republican side of the aisle and more of us on the Democratic side of the aisle will forget party, forget the battle, and actually listen to the people and fight to fix these problems.

The question Senator LEE asked is: What can the American people do? I will say, nothing gets the attention of elected representatives more than hearing from their constituents in jaw-dropper numbers, in phone calls and emails and tweets and Facebook posts.

Some Members of this body express annoyance that why would their constituents have the temerity to dictate to us—the solons of Washington—what to do. The answer is simple. Because our constituents are our boss. We work for them. They have every right to dictate to us.

I will note, on a lighter note, my friend Congressman LOUIE
GOHMERT, who has been here all night, handed me something that
was quite nice. It is from the *Daily News*. It ran on Friday, November 4,
1949. It is entitled "Ode to the Welfare State." It reads:

> Mr. Truman's St. Paul, Minn., pie-for-everybody speech last
> night reminded us that, at the tail-end of the recent session of
> Congress, Representative Clarence J. Brown (R-Ohio)
> jammed into the Congressional Record the following poem,
> describing its author only as "a prominent Democrat of the
> State of Georgia":
>> It is titled "Democratic Dialogue."
>> Father must I go to work?
>> No, my lucky son.
>> We're living now on Easy Street
>> On dough from Washington.
>> We've left it up to Uncle Sam,
>> So don't get exercised.
>> Nobody has to give a damn—
>> We've all been subsidized.
>> But if Sam treats us all so well
>> And feeds us milk and honey,
>> Please daddy, tell me what the heck
>> He's going to use for money.
>> Don't worry bub, there's not a hitch
>> In this here noble plan—
>> He simply soaks the filthy rich
>> And helps the common man.
>> But father, won't there come a time
>> When they run out of cash
>> And we have left them not a dime
>> When things will go to smash?
>> My faith in you is shrinking son,
>> You nosy little brat.
>> You do too damn much thinking son,
>> To be a Democrat.

That is from the *Daily News*, Friday, November 4, 1949, apparently inserted into the CONGRESSIONAL RECORD by a Member of Congress. [Representative Clarence J. Brown (R-Ohio)].

Let's take it a different direction. We talked about liberty, liberty that is at stake here. I want to talk about that same principle. On one level, on the real, on the personal, on the hardworking American families, they are facing a loss of jobs. They are facing small businesses that are not growing. They are facing skyrocketing health insurance premiums. They are facing losing their health insurance.

But on another level, we are facing an assault on liberty. Before, we went through some of Ayn Rand's *Atlas Shrugged*. Now, I want to go further back to 1850, to read some excerpts from a classic that I would recommend to everyone to read, Frederic Bastiat's, *The Law*. *The Law* is a primer in free enterprise.

> Though expansion of government programs may be tempting, the designers often have selfish aims, and the program almost always thwarts the liberty and prosperity of the people.

He warns of the dangers of programs and the way in which government programs deprive the people of their rights. So Bastiat observes:

> Life is a gift from God, which includes all others. This gift is life—physical, intellectual, and moral life.
>
> But life cannot maintain itself alone. The Creator of life has entrusted us with the responsibility of preserving, developing and perfecting it. In order that we may accomplish this, he has provided us with a collection of marvelous faculties. And He has put us in the midst of a variety of natural resources. By the application of our faculties to these natural resources, we convert them into products, and use them. This process is necessary in order that life may run its appointed course.
>
> Life, faculties, production—in other words, individuality, liberty, property—this is man. And in spite of the cunning and artful political leaders, these three gifts from God precede all human legislation, and are superior to it. Life, liberty, and property do not exist because men have made laws. On the

contrary, it was the fact that life, liberty, and property existed beforehand that caused men to make laws in the first place.

Each of us has a natural right—from God—to defend his person, his liberty, and his property. These are the three basic requirements of life, and the preservation of any one of them is completely dependent on the preservation of the other two. For what are our faculties but the extension of our individuality? And what is property but an extension of our faculties? If every person has the right to defend even by force—his person, his liberty, and his property, then it follows that a group of men have the right to organize and support a common force to protect these rights constantly.

Thus the principle of collective rights—its reason for existing, its lawfulness—is based on individual right. And the common force that protects this collective right cannot logically have any other purpose or any other mission than that for which it acts as a substitute. Thus, since an individual cannot lawfully use force against the person, liberty, or property of another individual, then the common force—for the same reason—cannot lawfully be used to destroy the person, liberty, or property of individuals or groups.

Property and plunder. Man can live and satisfy his wants only by ceaseless labor; by the ceaseless application of his faculties to natural resources. This process is the origin of property.

But it is also true that a man may live and satisfy his wants by seizing and consuming the products of the labor of others. This process is the origin of plunder.

Now, since man is naturally inclined to avoid pain—and since labor is pain in itself—it follows that men will resort to plunder whenever plunder is easier than work. History shows this quite clearly. And under these conditions, neither religion nor morality can stop it.

When, then, does plunder stop? It stops when it becomes more painful and more dangerous than labor.

It is evident, then, that the proper purpose of law is to use the power of its collective force to stop this fatal tendency to plunder instead of to work. All the measures of the law should protect property and punish plunder.

But, generally, the law is made by one man or one class of men. And since law cannot operate without the sanction and support of a dominating force, this force must be entrusted to those who make the laws.

That would be us.

This fact, combined with the fatal tendency that exists in the heart of man to satisfy his wants with the least effort possible, explains the almost universal perversion of the law. Thus it is easy to understand how law, instead of checking injustice, becomes the invincible weapon of injustice. It is easy to understand why the law is used by the legislator to destroy in varying degrees among the rest of the people, their personal independence by slavery, their liberty by oppression, and their property by plunder. This is done for the benefit of the person who makes the law, and in proportion to the power that he holds.

I would note throughout the course of this debate, the central theme I have been focusing on is the disconnect between Washington and the people and the practice right now of Democrats and Republicans not to listen to the people. Let me read again that sentence from Bastiat written in 1850—not written in response to the Senate in 2013—in 1850. He says:

This is done for the benefit of the person who makes the law, and in proportion to the power he holds.

It seems almost as though Bastiat were writing about Congress right now, about the Obama administration granting exemptions from ObamaCare to the friends, to those with political influence, the giant corporations, and to Members of Congress. Why do Members of Congress get an exemption from ObamaCare that hard-working American families do not?

Bastiat tells us this 160 years ago. This is done for the benefit of the person who makes the law and in proportion to the power he holds. Bastiat goes on to talk about the victims of lawful plunder.

> Men naturally rebel against the injustice of which they are victims. Thus, when plunder is organized by law for the profit of those who make the law, all the plundered classes try somehow to enter—by peaceful or revolutionary means—into the making of laws. According to their degree of enlightenment, these plundered classes may propose one of two entirely different purposes when they attempt to attain political power: Either they may wish to stop lawful plunder, or they may wish to share in it.

Now, let me note at this point, this goes directly to the question Senator LEE asked a little bit earlier this morning: What can the American people do? The plundered class, the hardworking American families that are finding their jobs going away, that are finding economic growth stripped away, they are finding themselves forcibly put into part-time work. They are seeing their health insurance premiums skyrocket or are seeing their health insurance jeopardized or taken away. They can come together and force our elected officials in both parties to listen to the people—make DC listen. That is what Bastiat is talking about there.

> Woe to the nation when this latter purpose prevails among the mass victims of lawful plunder when they, in turn, seize the power to make laws! Until that happens, the few practice lawful plunder upon the many, a common practice where the right to participate in the making of law is limited to a few persons. But then, participation in the making of law becomes universal. And then, men seek to balance their conflicting interests by universal plunder. Instead of

rooting out the injustices found in society, they make these injustices general.

As soon as the plundered classes gain political power, they establish a system of reprisals against the other classes. They do not abolish legal plunder. (This objective would demand more enlightenment than they possess.) Instead, they emulate their evil predecessors by participating in this legal plunder, even though it is against their own interest.

It is as if it were necessary, before a reign of justice appears, for everyone to suffer a cruel retribution—some for their evilness, and some for their lack of understanding.

It is almost as if that sentence was written about ObamaCare. I would suggest when you read that sentence and then you pick up and read the letter from James Hoffa of the Teamsters saying: We knocked on doors. We supported President Obama. We block walked. We phone called. We supported your agenda. Now we have discovered that this law, which is your signature achievement that you fought for, is a nightmare that is hurting millions of Americans and their families. That is what James Hoffa said. Or, as Bastiat said:

It is as if it were necessary, before a reign of justice appears, for everyone to suffer a cruel retribution—some for their evilness, and some for their lack of understanding.

Bastiat continued.

Enforced Fraternity Destroys Liberty.

Mr. De Lamartine once wrote to me thusly: Your doctrine is only the half of my program. You have stopped at liberty; I go on to fraternity.

I answered him: The second half of your program will destroy the first. In fact, it is impossible for me to separate the word fraternity from the word voluntary. I cannot possibly understand how fraternity can be legally enforced without liberty being legally destroyed, and thus justice being legally trampled underfoot.

Legal plunder has two roots: One of them, as I have said before, is in human greed; the other is in false philanthropy.

At this point, I think that I should explain exactly what I mean by the word plunder. Plunder violates ownership. I do not, as is often done, use the word in any vague, uncertain, approximate, or metaphorical sense. I use it in its scientific acceptance—as expressing the idea opposite to that of property [wages, land, money, or whatever.] When a portion of wealth is transferred from the person who owns it—without his consent and without compensation, and whether by force or by fraud—to anyone who does not own it, then I say that property is violated; that an act of plunder is committed.

I say that this act is exactly what the law is supposed to suppress, always and everywhere. When the law itself commits this act that it is so supposed to suppress, I say that plunder is still committed, and I add that from the point of view of society and welfare, this aggression against rights is even worse. In the case of legal plunder, however, the person who receives the benefits is not responsible for the act of plundering. The responsibility for this legal plunder rests with the law, the legislator, and society itself. Therein lies the political danger.

The Law and Charity. You say: There are persons who have no money, and you turn to the law. But the law is not a breast that fills itself with milk. Nor are the lacteal veins of the law supplied with milk from a source outside the society. Nothing can enter the public treasury for the benefit of one citizen or one class unless another citizen or other classes have been forced to send it in.

If every person draws from the treasury the amount that he has put in it, it is true that the law plunders nobody. But this procedure does nothing for the persons who have no money. It does not promote equality of income. The law can

333 CLARION CALL 333

be an instrument of equalization only as it takes from some persons and gives to other persons. When the law does this, it is an instrument of plunder.

I would note the adage that any legislator who proposes to rob Peter to pay Paul can always count on the support of Paul.

Going back to Bastiat:

With this in mind, examine the protective tariffs, subsidies, guaranteed profits, guaranteed jobs, relief and welfare schemes, public education, progressive taxation, free credit, and public works. You will find that they are always based on legal plunder, organized injustice.

Legislators Desire to Mold Mankind.

Now let us examine Raynal on this subject of mankind being molded by the legislator. The legislator must first consider the climate, the air, and the soil. The resources at his disposal determine his duties. He must first consider his locality. A population living on maritime shores must have laws designed for navigation. . . . If it is an inland settlement, the legislator must make his plans according to the nature and the fertility of the soil.

Frederic Bastiat—1915—explained principles of liberty that continue across the ages, principles of liberty that we owe it to every man and woman in America to protect his or her life, liberty, and property. ObamaCare does violence to the natural rights of every American; it does violence to their opportunity.

Do you know the cruelest joke of all? ObamaCare has been justified: Let's help the least among us. That is a noble goal. We should all care about helping the least among us. The cruelest irony is that the people who are being hurt the most by ObamaCare are the least among us.

The rich, as the President frequently inveighs, millionaires and billionaires, are not hurt by ObamaCare. They are doing just fine. In fact, they are doing better. The richest segment of this country is doing better today than they were when President Obama was elected.

Who is getting hurt? Who is losing their jobs? Who is not finding jobs? Who is getting their hours forcibly reduced to 29 hours a week? Who is losing their health insurance?

I have read one letter after another from people across Texas and across this country, and not one of these letters said: I am independently wealthy, cruising on my yacht in the Caribbean, and yet ObamaCare has crimped my style. That is not what is happening. These are letters I read from the retired couple in Bayou Vista who had saved their whole life to buy their home, and now they are at risk of losing their home because of ObamaCare. Let me read from another constituent in Houston, TX, my hometown, who on July 11, 2013, wrote:

> My wife and I are currently both working jobs where there is no provided health care coverage. My wife is a self-employed physician and I am in sales. We have never gone without health coverage our entire lives.
>
> My father was in the military, so I had health care until I graduated college. My wife had coverage through her parents until she graduated. We never wanted to go without coverage, so anytime our coverage had a break we went ahead and bought catastrophic short-term coverage, even knowing we would have coverage soon.
>
> While my wife was in medical school, I had employer coverage, and I bought an individual policy for her because it was much less costly than group coverage. When my employment status changed and neither of us had employer coverage, I bought individual policies for both of us. We would not risk going without health insurance.
>
> Because we were both young and healthy at the time, the policies were very affordable, about $130 a month. Purchasing coverage was a no brainer.
>
> While in her residency, we got family coverage through her work. When she finished her residency in 2012, neither of

us had employer coverage, so it came time for another policy. We looked around at all the options for a family of four, two 30-year-old adults, a 2-year-old boy and a newborn girl. We found a HTIP plan for $400 a month with a $10,000 deductible.

We also had scrimped and saved so that in the event we had a catastrophe we would have a deductible coverage. After that our plan paid for 100 percent. This is the best coverage I had ever purchased. I had become an educated consumer in health care, shopping around for the best deals on medications, and informing doctors of our situation so they coded it properly. When we needed care we opted for urgent care and physicians' offices instead of emergency rooms.

Many of my young healthy friends now have these plans, either individually purchased or through their employers. As of January 1, most of these plans will go away for us, as most of my friends are around 30 years old. These plans are actually decreasing the cost of health care as they inspire us to be educated consumers. Unlike what the President said, I don't get to "keep my plan."

I never thought that not purchasing insurance would be an option for my family. I have done a fair amount of research using the IRS info, current and estimated prices, even my own insurance company's estimates. It looks like for the cheapest, bronze plan, the estimated cost will be about $1,600 per month, which is $20,000 per year. We don't qualify for subsidies.

If I choose not to comply, I would pay a fine which, for us, amounts to about $2,000 and save the $18,000 balance in a bank account. Our fine will max out at about $5,000, so I will still have $15,000 per year. I will now begin paying cash for my health care and negotiate with doctors and hospitals myself.

As I get older I will consider big insurance when it looks like the cost-benefit ratio is better. No one in my family has ever gone without coverage because health care is the No. 1 priority on our list. It still is, but this individual mandate has caused us to consider going without insurance for the first time. I would gladly keep my fine if I could keep my current insurance, but that is not an option either.

Here is one of my friends' stories. He is a high school teacher and his wife is a stay-at-home mom with two kids. His district pays for all of his coverage and none of his spouse's. This year they opted to purchase an individual plan for her because it was more affordable, $150 a month versus $500. Beginning January 1, she will be forced into the exchange, where her estimated cost will be about $400.

They currently cannot afford this, and they don't qualify for a subsidy because her employer offers coverage for her, even though her income would qualify her for a 50 percent subsidy. They will choose not to have insurance coverage on them.

Many of the young, healthy people I have talked to told me they plan to go without insurance—people who currently purchase individual plans—because the coverage would be too expensive and the fine for most of them is much less than the coverage.

As was told to the American people, if you like your health coverage, you can keep it. We now know that promise was simply, objectively, 100 percent false. For Americans all over this country, the facts are otherwise.

It is incumbent on us, representing our constituents, to look to the reality of these facts.

Look to the young people. I don't think you could design a plan designed to harm young people more than ObamaCare. It is more than a crying irony that some 70 percent of young people voted for the President. I recognize that young people didn't necessarily understand the consequences of ObamaCare and how it is impacting their future. It is one of the things on which I hope this debate will focus.

If you are a young person coming out of school, have some student loans, and let's say you are hoping for a job and for a future, if you can't get that first job or if you are forced into part-time work, you are not going to gain the skills you need to get that second job, the third job, the fourth job, or to build a career, to get married, and to provide for your family.

We read earlier from the *Wall Street Journal* describing how economists now talk about young people as the "lost generation." One of the striking consequences of this is that young people are putting off marriage and putting off kids. We know that has societal consequences. That has societal consequences that are altogether detrimental. And they are doing it not for matters of individual choice, they are doing it because the economy is so terrible for young people that they have no options. They have no options to provide for a spouse, to provide for kids, so they rationally choose not to begin those families until they have a job sufficient to provide for their families.

This thing isn't working. Every one of us owes it to our constituents to listen, to listen to the young people who are suffering, to listen to the single moms, to listen to the seniors, to listen to those with disabilities, to listen to the African Americans, to listen to the Hispanics who aren't getting jobs, are getting forcibly put in part-time work, facing skyrocketing health insurance premiums, and who are losing their health insurance.

We can vote party loyalty. That is easy to do. It is the way Washington often works. We can vote and say: Congress is exempted. We have special rules that apply to us, so it is not our problem.

Yes, it hurts hard-working Americans. If there is one thing Washington knows how to do, it is ignore the plight of hard-working Americans. Or we can show a level of coverage that has been rare in this town and step up and say we will risk retribution from our own parties. We will stand up and speak the truth. We will stand up and champion our constituents. Elected officials need to listen to the people. Together, we must make D.C. listen.

Mr. LEE. Will the Seantor yield for a question?

Mr. CRUZ. I yield for a question without yielding the floor.

Mr. LEE. As the Senator was mentioning, the fact that it is time for people to stand for their own rights and it is time for the people's elected representatives in Washington to stand for them reminds me of the fact that sometimes people do take this challenge, and sometimes they don't. Sometimes people will square their shoulders heading into a challenge, and other times people will simply engage in shoulder-shrugging and ignore problems all together.

A few years ago I was traveling through southern Utah with my family, and we went to a restaurant. It was sort of a fast food restaurant that had a salad bar. For some strange reason, instead of ordering a cheeseburger, I ordered a salad. I don't know why, but I got the salad bar. I went through the salad bar with my plate, and I was putting all of these horribly healthy foods on my plate—lettuce, vegetables. Then I saw at the end of the salad bar something that I didn't expect, a little bonus. There was a little tub of chocolate pudding, and I thought, this is fantastic. I can feel like I am eating a healthy meal because I am eating a salad, but I get chocolate pudding in with salad, so I put a bunch of that on my salad plate.

I sat down a few minutes later, and, of course, rather than eating the salad, I went right for the pudding. There was only one problem: The pudding was disgusting. It was spoiled rotten. It tasted as if it had been left out overnight unrefrigerated for 3 nights in a row, which is not a good thing.

I immediately thought, I have to find somebody who works here. I have to tell someone that the pudding is bad so that they don't have to deal with any other customers eating rotten pudding. I found the nearest employee of the restaurant. I said to her in a sort of hushed tone of voice: Hey, the pudding is bad. You need to do something about it. You need to replace it. It is rancid. It is spoiled rotten. Please do something about it.

She looked at me with a sort of blank stare. She couldn't have been older than maybe 17 years old, and she just said: I am not on salad. Then she walked away. My response to that was, I am not suggesting that you are on salad.

I all of a sudden wondered whether I had stumbled across some rift among the employees of this particular fast food establishment. Maybe she didn't like the implication that she was one of the salad bar attendants. Maybe that was a bad thing. I don't know. All I know is that it was kind of strange because she worked for the same employer who ran the salad bar. I would have thought she would have cared about that. Instead, she said: I am not on salad, shrugged her shoulders, and walked away.

I wonder if that is sometimes what we have too much of here in Washington: I am not on salad. I am not on ObamaCare. I am not on excessive regulation. I am not on dealing with a law that is going to result in a lot of Americans losing their jobs, having their hours cut, their wages cut, or losing access to their health care benefits.

Well, our problems are acute. Our problems are, in fact, chronic. We have to do more than shrug our shoulders. What we need right now is more shoulder-squaring than shoulder-shrugging. We have to have people who will follow the admonition of Ronald Reagan, who declared more than 30 years ago that it is morning in America again. As it is now morning in Washington again, it is an appropriate time of day for us to bring this up. To paraphrase the words of Ronald Reagan, as spoken in his speech at the Republican National Convention in July 1980, and to apply those same words today, let me just say as follows:

> Our problems are both acute and chronic, yet all we hear from those in positions of leadership are the same tired proposals for more government tinkering, more meddling and more control, all of which led us to this state in the first place. Can anyone look at the record of this administration and say: Well done? Can anyone compare the state of our economy when this administration took office with where we are today and say: Keep up the good work? Can anyone look at our reduced stand in the world today and say: Let's have more of this?
>
> We must have the clarity of vision to see the difference between what is essential and what is merely desirable, and then the courage to use this insight to bring our government back under control and make it acceptable to the people. It has long been said that freedom is the condition in which the government fears the people and tyranny is the condition in which the people fear the government.

Throughout the duration of our history as a republic, we have enjoyed liberty, we have enjoyed freedom, and we have had a notable absence of tyranny. Sure, there have been excesses from time to time. We have kept those under control because the government has always been in good hands—in the hands of its people. When the people weigh in from time to time and decide they have had too much of something, it ends up having a benefit for everyone. Everyone benefits when the people speak and are heard. Everyone benefits when the people's elected representatives are willing to square their shoulders and stand up to a challenge rather than shrug their shoulders and walk away saying, as it were, I am not on salad.

Today, we are all on ObamaCare. We are all on it in the sense we can't walk away from it. We are all on it in the sense that we have no choice but to confront the many challenges facing our people. There is not widespread agreement as to what we can or should or must or might do.

In the absence of consensus, and understanding the widespread disruption to our economy this will create once it is fully implemented, some have suggested that a good compromise position might be to delay its impact. And the best way to fully delay it is to defund it—defund it for at least 1 year. The President himself has acknowledged the law is not ready to be implemented as written. The American people are reluctant to confront the many economic challenges this law presents. It is, therefore, appropriate that we do this, and it is appropriate the House of Representatives passed a continuing resolution to keep government funded while defunding ObamaCare.

It is for that position we have been speaking, and it is for that position that we continue to insist that as we approach the cloture vote this week, that I and Senator CRUZ and a few others will be voting no on cloture on the bill because we support the House-passed continuing resolution—H.J. Res. 59. We support that, and because we support it, we cannot support a process that would enable Senator REID, the Senate majority leader, to strip out, to gut the most important provision within that resolution—the ObamaCare defunding legislation—by a simple majority vote without allowing any other votes on any other amendments, without allowing for an open amendment process, without ever allowing Members of this body to have an up-or-down vote on the legislation as a whole, as it was enacted, as is.

That is what we are fighting for. Is this difficult? Yes, absolutely it is. Do we have consensus within our own political party? Of course we don't. That is one of the reasons we are standing here today, to persuade our colleagues and to persuade more of the American people to join in with us. No one Senator can do this alone. Not one of us, certainly by means of our persuasive abilities, will be able to do this. But with the American people, we can do a lot of things.

It wasn't very long ago, it wasn't even 2 weeks ago when people were still saying it would not be possible to pass a continuing resolution such as H.J. Res. 59—one that keeps government funded while defunding ObamaCare. Yet when the people weighed in strongly in support of this measure, it became possible. I hope and I expect the same can be true in the Senate.

So I would ask Senator CRUZ: What is the best way the American people, in confronting this challenge and others similar to it, but in particular this challenge confronting ObamaCare, can square their shoulders and avoid the kind of shoulder shrugging that has resulted in so much expansion of government almost as if by default?

Mr. CRUZ. I thank my friend from Utah for that very fine question, and I wish to thank the American people for doing exactly what Senator LEE just asked—for over 1.6 million Americans signing a national petition to defund ObamaCare.

You want to know why the House of Representatives voted overwhelmingly on Friday to defund ObamaCare? The answer is simple: Because the American people rose and demanded it. At the end of the day, the House of Representatives is the people's House. I salute the House conservatives who fought and fought hard to get this done. I salute the House leadership. I salute Speaker BOEHNER for listening to the people.

It is not surprising the House of Representatives would do that first. For one thing, the House is designed to be the people's House. In our constitutional structure, the House has a different role than the Senate. The House of Representatives is up for election every 2 years like clockwork. In the House, you run, you get elected, you may get a little bit of a breather, enjoy Thanksgiving and Christmas with your family, and then you promptly turn around and start getting ready for the next election 2 years hence. Given that, the House is, by its nature, more responsive to the people because the risks are higher in the House to not being so. The House has shown over and over, when the elected representatives stop listening to the American people, the American people are very good, to use an old phrase, at throwing the bums out.

The Senate, on the other hand, is similar to a battleship. It turns slowly. Part of that is by constitutional design. Part of that was the wisdom of the Framers. In any given 2-year cycle only one-third of this body is up for election. It is one of the things that is interesting. If you look at those Republicans who have publicly said they intend to vote for cloture, they intend to vote to give HARRY REID the power to fund ObamaCare with 51 Democratic votes, they intend to give HARRY REID the power to gut the Republican continuing resolution, most of those Republicans who have said that are not up for election in 2014.

It is amazing how it can focus the mind if you have to actually stand before the citizens. I suppose some of the Republicans who are up in 2016 and 2018 might think: There will be time. There will be time. The voters will forget. The only way to move the battleship of the Senate is for the American people to make it politically more risky to do the wrong thing than it is to do the right thing.

When we were reading Bastiat's *The Law*, he talked about how do you prevent plunder. You make it more risky to engage in plunder than in hard work. The same is true of politics. You make it more risky not to listen to the voices of the people. How do you do that? The only way that has ever worked is a tidal wave of outpouring. It is what we saw with drones, it is what we saw with guns, and it is what we saw with Syria. But here it has to be bigger. It has to be bigger than any of those three. Why? Because the resistance is more settled in. The Democratic side of the aisle, the party loyalty is deeply entrenched.

I hope by the end of this week we see some brave Democrats who show the courage James Hoffa of the Teamsters showed. We haven't yet. I hope that changes. I hope by the end of this week we see a lot more Republicans, even Republicans who are not up in 2014 but who may have some chance by the next election cycle the voters will have forgotten. I am not convinced of that, but it is easy for politicians to convince themselves of that. I hope we see Republicans saying: Listen, this is a conscience vote. This is a vote to do the right thing.

I have to say that in my time in the Senate this is the first time I have seen Republican leadership actively whipping the Republican conference to support HARRY REID and give him the power to enact his agenda. I have never seen that before. I am quite confident it is not what Texans expect of me. I am quite confident, when each Republican goes back to his or her home State, it is not what their constituents expect of them.

I am also quite confident, if and when we return home and stand in front of our constituents and are asked: Senator, why did you vote yes on cloture to give HARRY REID the power to fund ObamaCare, to gut the House continuing resolution, I am quite confident if the answer was: Our party leadership asked me to do that; I am expected to be a good soldier, to salute and to march into battle—you know what, none of us were elected by party leadership. That is true on the Democratic and Republican side.

Listen, if we see Democratic Senators showing courage on this issue to break, I have no doubt the Democratic leadership will be very unhappy with them. I don't want to sugarcoat what the reaction would be. On the Republican side, none of us were elected by our party leadership. We have a different boss. Our boss is the American people. Our boss consists of the constituents who elected us. I am going to submit, if you strip away all the procedural mumbo jumbo, all the smoke and mirrors, our constituents would be horrified to know the games we play, to know this is all set up to be a giant kabuki dance—theater—where a lot of Republicans vote to give HARRY REID the authority to gut the House continuing resolution to fund ObamaCare and they go home and tell their constituents: Hey, I was voting in support of the House. Boy, with support like that, it is akin to saying you are supporting someone by handing a gun to someone who will shoot you.

We don't have to speculate. It is not hypothetical that maybe, kind of, sort of, possibly if you vote for cloture ObamaCare will be funded and the House of Representatives' continuing resolution will be gutted. We know that because HARRY REID has announced it. So any Republican who casts a vote for cloture is saying: Yes, I want HARRY REID to have the power to do that, and then I will vote against it once it no longer matters, once it is a free symbolic vote. I don't think those kind of games are consistent with the obligation we owe to our constituents.

I made reference to the IRS employees union asking to be exempted from ObamaCare, and the union sent a letter where they asked their members please send. I want to read that letter. This is prepared, presumably, by the union bosses at the IRS employees union.

> Dear Leader REID and Leader PELOSI:

Interestingly enough, this letter is directed to the Democratic leaders.

> When you and the President sought our support, you pledged that if we liked the health plans we have now, we could keep them. Sadly, that promise is under threat.

By the way, who is saying this? The IRS employees union, the people in charge of enforcing ObamaCare on us, the American people.

> Right now, unless you under the Obama administration enact an equitable fix, the ACA will shatter not only our hard-earned health benefits, but destroy the foundation of the 40-hour workweek that is the backbone of the American middle class.

I think this letter I am reading may not be the IRS employees union; it may be, in fact, the Teamsters letter. I am going to set that aside and see if we can get the actual IRS union. It is a great letter.

I may read it again in the course of this discussion. But I don't think that is the IRS letter since it is signed by James Hoffa. I am pretty confident that was not the IRS employees union.

Instead, let me read another note from a constituent. But don't trust me; don't trust any politician on what is happening on ObamaCare; trust the people.

A constituent from Spring, TX, wrote on April 12, 2013:

> My late husband worked for the same company for over 40 years. Because of ObamaCare, this year that company decided it would no longer offer supplemental insurance to Medicare. The program I was forced into has increased my monthly premium by almost $100. Not only that, but the prescription plan has increased the drug plan—a generic one at that— by 30 percent.

Ridiculous. This body—Democrats and Republicans—needs to listen to the people. Together, we must make DC listen.

Mr. RUBIO. Would the Senator from Texas yield for a question without yielding the floor?

Mr. CRUZ. I am happy to yield to my friend from Florida for a question without yielding the floor.

Mr. RUBIO. My first question is, What did the Senator do last night?

Mr. CRUZ. I thank my friend from Florida for that question. I had a delightful night. I had a chance to read Bastiat, Rand, and read some tweets. There are few things more enjoyable than reading tweets. And I hope that the Senator and I and Senator LEE and many other Senators who participated in this—I hope we have had some positive impact on moving this debate forward and making clear to the American people both the train wreck, the nightmare that is ObamaCare, in the words of James Hoffa, the president of the Teamsters, but also that right now too many members of this body are not listening to the American people, and the only remedy for that is this week the American people demanding that we make DC listen.

Mr. RUBIO. Would the Senator from Texas yield for a followup question without yielding the floor?

Mr. CRUZ. I am happy to yield for another question without yielding the floor.

Mr. RUBIO. First an observation. It is interesting how much times have changed around here. If a decade ago you were to tell someone you were tweeting on the Senate floor, that would not be a positive thing. People would think that meant something else.

The world has changed a lot, and I think the Senator highlighted earlier in some of the speeches given here what a positive development that has been. It wasn't so long ago that in order to be able to do something in politics, to make a difference, to mobilize people to take action, you needed the benefits of the formal organizations that existed. You needed groups or the establishment—or whatever term people want to use—to get things done. But one thing that has really completely changed American politics is that anybody can become a political activist now. Because of access to social media, because of access to Facebook and Twitter and Vine and Instagram and all these other programs, anyone can now take action and speak out. Anyone can now connect with like-minded people halfway across the country or halfway around the world and begin a cause.

In many respects, that is what I think you see happening in this country now. There is a lot of talk about how Washington has changed, how there are things happening now that didn't used to happen before. I am convinced that one of the reasons is because people now have access to things that are happening in real time and they have the ability to speak out on these things in real time.

It used to be that you had to turn on the TV at 6:00 in the evening or 6:30 to watch the evening national news. Not anymore. News is reported on a minute-by-minute basis. Even as I speak now, there is someone out there covering it, there are people out there saying something about it. By and large, it has been a positive development because it has empowered individual Americans from all walks of life not just to be aware of what is happening in this Capitol but to engage in it, to speak out, and to be heard. At the end of the day, this Republic depends on that—on an informed citizenry who is also able to speak out on the issues of the day and communicate with the people who work for them.

Let me tell you what I hear from the people I work for in the State of Florida. I hear tremendous concern about the future. We focus a lot around here on specific issues, and we should. The national debt is a crisis. Our Tax Code is broken. Our regulations are out of control. We are talking about ObamaCare right now, which has been hugely detrimental to the American economy and to the aspirations of individual Americans. But overriding all of this is the central concern that I find increasingly on the minds of people. Let me describe it.

I know that as a country we are divided on a lot of issues. Look at the polls. Look at the elections. I know the country is divided on a lot of important issues. That is why this body and Congress are struggling to find consensus on many of the major issues we confront.

But let me tell you what I believe is still the unifying principle that holds our Nation and our people together. That unifying principle is the belief that anyone who is willing to work hard and sacrifice should be able to get ahead, the idea that if you are willing to work as hard as you can and make sacrifices, you should be rewarded for that with a better life.

By the way, when we talk about a better life, it is not a guarantee that you will ever be a millionaire or a billionaire, but it generally means the ability to find a job that is fulfilling, helps you feel like you are making a difference in the world, a job that allows you to do something you love for a living, and a job that pays you enough money to do things like buy a house, provide a stable environment for your family, and save so your kids can go to college and so that you can retire with dignity and security.

As a people, we are unified in the belief that it is unfair that people who are willing to work hard and sacrifice, as the vast majority of Americans are—it is unfair when people who are willing to do that cannot get ahead, when those people are held back. We have been told our whole lives that if you work hard, if you sacrifice, if you go to school and graduate, if you do all these things, you will get ahead, that this is that kind of country.

But now people are starting to wonder if that is still true. Across this country increasingly people are starting to wonder, that which we know as the American dream, is that still alive? They want to believe it still is. They believe in America, but they are starting to wonder if that formula I have outlined—hard work and sacrifice lead to a better life—if that formula still works. Why are they wondering that? It is not hard to understand. They are working hard. They are working harder than they ever have. Look at median incomes in America. Look at the people who feel as if their lives have stagnated. They are working hard. They are sacrificing. Not only are they not getting ahead, sometimes they feel as if they are falling behind.

Put yourself in the place of someone who is 56, 57, 58 years old and worked their whole life at some company or industry. Suddenly, they are laid off and they can't find anyone to hire them. They were getting ready for retirement. Now they don't know when that is ever going to happen.

Put yourself in the place of a student. You graduated high school. While your friends were out playing around, you were studying so you could get good grades and get into a good school. You did that. You went to college. While your friends were out partying, you studied. You graduated with a 3.5, 4.0. You went to grad school and graduated from there as well. You did everything that was asked of you. Then you graduated, and you couldn't find a job in your career field. And here is what is worse: You owe $30,000 or more in student loans.

By the way, that is an issue I know. I know Senator LEE has confronted that as well. I had $100,000 in student loans when I graduated. I grant you, it was a wise investment in my education, but it was an anchor around my neck for many, many years. My parents were never able to save enough money to provide for our education, so I had to do a combination of grants, work study, and student loans. When I came to the Senate, I still had those loans. There were months when my loan payments were higher than our mortgage.

So you look at these things and you understand what people around the country are facing.

Think about the small businesses. You used to work for someone. You were an employee, and then one day you decided: I can do this job better than my boss can, so I am going to quit this job and I am going to risk it. I am going to take every penny I have access to, I am going to max out my credit card, I am going to take out my life savings, and I am going to open a small business because I believe in my idea. And I will guarantee that for most people who did that, those first years were tough. This idea that you open a business and tomorrow you are on Facebook is usually not the case. Usually you struggle those first few years. Oftentimes, people fail in business two or three times before they finally succeed.

Interestingly enough, as part of this process one of the most rewarding things I have been able to do is travel the country and meet and interact with very successful people in business and in life. It is amazing how many people you meet who—when you ask them how they got started and how they achieved, they usually focus on all the times they failed before they achieved. They take pride in the struggle because it means that they earned it, that they earned what they have. They take pride in that.

But put yourself in the position of someone who went through all that, someone who started this business by taking out a second mortgage on their home and literally came upon one Friday when they didn't know how they were going to make payroll or stay open but somehow they persevered and made it through, and now that business is open and functioning and yet it is struggling. And they are wondering—after all these years of hard work and sacrifice, they feel as though they are slipping backward instead of moving ahead.

There is a growing sentiment in this country about these things. Let me tell you why that is so dangerous. What I just described to you is what we have come to know as the American Dream. There is this idea among the minds of some that the American dream is a material thing, that the American dream is about how much money can you make so you can own more things. That may be an element of it for some people, but the American dream is largely about being able to earn for yourself a better life.

You can only understand the American dream by viewing it from a global perspective. For those of us who were born and raised in this country, who have lived here our whole life, who don't know anything else, sometimes it is easy to take what I am about to tell you for granted. In most countries around the world, for almost all of human history and even today, it doesn't really matter how hard you are willing to work and how much you are willing to sacrifice. If you don't come from the right family, if you are not well connected, you don't get into the right schools and then you don't get into the right jobs.

Put yourself in that position for a moment. Imagine now that you have big hopes, big dreams, and big talent, and your hope is to do something with it. By the way, it doesn't have to mean making a lot of money. Maybe you want to serve in philanthropy. Maybe you want to make a difference setting up a foundation. Maybe you are an artist or a musician. Whatever it may be, imagine now being trapped with all that talent and unable to put it into use. You would say that is unfair, and I would tell you that was the human condition up until 200 years ago everywhere in the world, and it is still the human condition in many parts of the globe today. The American dream is that here that is not true. Here, we believe that is wrong. Here, we believe that is unfair. Here, we believe all Americans— Democrats, Republicans, Liberals, Conservatives, everyone—we all believe it is unfair and it is wrong that someone should be prevented from achieving a better life because of where they come from, whom they come from, or where they started out in life. We believe that is unfair. We believe that is wrong. That is the American dream. That is us—the notion that you should be able to achieve whatever you were meant to be, to be able to fully utilize your talents in whatever way you find meaningful, the ability to have a career instead of a job, all these sorts of things.

That is what we are on the verge of losing, in the minds of many Americans, and that is supremely dangerous to the country. Why? Because I personally do not believe there can be an America as we know it without the American dream. Without the American dream, America is just another big powerful country, but it is no longer an exceptional one. That is what is at stake in all these debates we are conducting in this body.

What are the impediments? What is creating these problems we are facing? There may be more, but I have identified three that I hope we will focus on more.

The first, by the way, is societal breakdown. It is real. This idea that somehow you can separate the social well-being of your people from their moral well-being is absurd. The social well-being from the economic well-being—the idea that you can separate those is absurd. If you are born into a broken family, the statistics tell us that the chances that you are going to struggle significantly increase. The destruction of the family structure in America, the decline of it, is a leading contributor to poverty and educational underperformance.

The question for policymakers here in Washington is what can we do about that? Can we pass laws that will make people better parents? Can we pass government programs that will make families better? The answer is usually not. But I can tell you what we can start doing. We can start recognizing this is a real factor. This is not about moralizing. This is not about imposing our religious views or values on anyone. This is a free country. You have the right to believe in anything you want or believe in nothing at all. But you better believe this: It doesn't matter how many diplomas you have on the wall. If you don't have the values of hard work and sacrifice and respect and perseverance and self-discipline, if you don't have those values you are going to struggle to succeed, and no one is born with those values; no one. Those values have to be taught and they have to be reinforced.

One of the things that made America exceptional, one of the things that allowed the American dream to happen is that in this country we had strong families and strong institutions in our society that helped those families instill those values in children. Today there are millions of children growing up in this country who are not being taught these values because of societal breakdown. We refuse to confront it at our own peril. We better recognize it and start acting on it as a nation because I am telling you, children who are born into broken families, living in substandard housing, in dangerous neighborhoods, with no access to health care and with difficulty accessing good schools, these kids have five strikes against them. They are going to struggle to make it unless someone addresses that, and we are losing an entire generation of talent because of it. We better address it in a way that is good for the country and also good for those families.

The second issue, I would tell you, that is contributing to this is we have a significant skills gap in America. What that means is 21st century jobs require more skills than jobs ever have. Here is a graphic example. Go to the grocery store. I was there Saturday. There used to be 12 checkout lines. That meant 12 cashiers, right? Twelve cashier jobs. Now there are eight checkout lines and the other four are these machines where you run the card over the scan. That means those four or five cashier jobs are gone, right? Yes, but those jobs have been replaced by the jobs of the people who installed those machines, the jobs of the people who built those machines, the jobs of the people who maintain those machines. A graphic example of the 21st century. The job has been replaced by a new job, but the new job—to be a cashier you have to be trained on the site. My mom was a cashier. But to build, fix, and maintain those machines you have to have a higher level of skills you have to learn in school somewhere. Too many people don't have those skills. We have to fix that. For the life of me I don't understand why we stigmatize career education in America. There are kids who don't want to go to Harvard or Yale. They don't want to go for a 6-year degree or a 7-year degree program. They want to fix airplane engines. They want to be electricians and plumbers. Those are good-paying jobs. We need those people. We should be teaching kids to do that while they are still in high school so they can graduate with a diploma in this hand and a certificate that makes them job ready in the other. We should do that.

Beyond that, our students today, many of them are nontraditional students. They are not just 18- or 19-year-olds who just graduated from high school. There, for example, a single mom is working as a receptionist at a dental clinic somewhere and she is the first one to get laid off every time things go wrong. How can she improve her life? By becoming an ultrasound tech or becoming any of these other paraprofessions you find in medicine. But to do that she has to be able go to school. How is she going to do that if she has to work full time and raise her kids? We have to answer that. Whether it is online programs or flexibility in study or programs that give you credit for life experience and work experience, we have to answer that.

We have to also address workers who in the middle of their lives have lost their job, a job that is never coming back. They need to be retrained. By the way, the traditional college route will still be the ticket for upward mobility for millions of Americans but better figure out how to pay for it because right now you have kids graduating with $30,000 and $40,000 around their neck and that is going to prevent them from starting a family, buying a house, and moving ahead. We had better figure out why it is that every time more aid is made available to these students it gets gobbled up by these tuition increases. We better address that problem and we better address the skills gap.

Here is the third, and it goes right to the heart of what Senator CRUZ from Texas is dealing with here. The free enterprise system is the single great eradicator of poverty in all of human history. Free enterprise, American-style free enterprise, has eradicated more poverty than all the government programs in the world combined. You want to wage a real war on poverty? Encourage free enterprise. Why? Because free enterprise is an economic system that rewards people for hard work, sacrifice, and merit. Free enterprise does not ask what did your parents do for a living? Who do you know? Where do you summer? Who do you hang out with over the summer? What clubs do you belong to? Free enterprise doesn't ask that. Free enterprise wants to know what is your idea? Is there a market for it? Are you willing to work hard and sacrifice and persevere? If you are, there is no guarantee, but if you are, you have a real opportunity to make it. You want to know proof that that works? I have 200-some-odd years of American history to show you. It works.

In fact, it works so well that other countries are trying to copy it in their own version. Why are there millions of people in China today that just a generation ago lived in deep poverty and now are consumers in the middle class? Why? Is it because they headed even more in the direction of communism or because they opened their economy to free enterprise principles? The same is true in Brazil, Mexico, India, all over the world. What are the countries that are finding increased prosperity and growth in the middle class doing? They are inching toward free enterprise, not away from it.

Does that mean there is no role for government? No, of course there is a role for government. There is an important role for government. It provides for our national security. It is hard to grow your economy when you are under attack. It provides for internal security. You know, it is hard for people to invest in an economy if they don't know there is a court system that is going to enforce property rights, if they believe crimes will go unpunished.

We believe in a safety net. Free enterprise doesn't work without a real safety net—not as a way of life. You cannot live your whole life on welfare and food stamps and disability unless you are truly disabled. That is what the real safety net is there for. It is there to help people who cannot help themselves and it is there to help people who have fallen to stand back up and try again. We believe in a safety net—not as a way of life but as a backstop to make people feel the confidence that they can invest in the future.

What else should government be doing? As I have talked about—national security, infrastructure, the roads and bridges we build in this country. It is not a jobs program but it does create the backbone for the economy to function. The problem is the most important thing government should do in all of our policymaking decisions is we must ask ourselves, before you do anything—you pass a law, you create a new program—ask yourself: Will this foster the free enterprise system or will it undermine it?

To answer that question, you have to first recognize how the free enterprise system works. What creates prosperity and opportunity? Here is what creates it. When someone invents something new, a new product, idea, or service, when someone starts a new business or when someone grows an existing business, that is what creates opportunity and middle-class prosperity in the free enterprise system, that is what makes upward mobility possible, that is what allows people to climb out of where they started in life and improve it and leave their kids even better off—when people innovate, when they invest by starting a new business or expanding an existing one.

As policymakers, every time we make a decision around here, if you want to help the middle class, the people who are trying to make it, make America the best place in the world to innovate, to start a new business or to expand an existing business.

Do you want to know what is wrong in America today with our economy? Look no farther than a series of government policies—by the way, pursued by both political parties, although my opinion is I have not seen anything like the last 6 years—but a series of policies that have undermined the free enterprise system, policies that make it harder, not easier, to start a business, to expand an existing business, and to innovate.

Chief among them right now before us is what the Senator from Texas has been talking about all night—ObamaCare. That is why we are passionate about this. If you watch the news a little bit, you would think this is all because it is President Obama's idea and the Republicans are against it because it is his idea and that is what is happening here. That is absurd. I certainly have an ideological objection to the expansion of government. But my passionate objection, at least why I am on the floor here today and why Senator CRUZ is on the floor all night, it is not because of ideology or theory, it is the reality that this law is going to hurt real people. It is going to hurt real people. I have met those people. I have talked to those people. If you have been to a Walgreen's lately you know those people, too.

Why? Because Walgreen's has announced that because of ObamaCare it has to get rid of its insurance program that its employees are generally happy with. That is why they are still working there, right? Now they get thrown into the great unknown.

Here is the problem with that. Imagine if you are chronically ill or imagine if you have children and you have this preexisting relationship with a doctor. They know your history. You can call them when you need them. They are responsive. That is why you are going there all these years. Now you get thrown on this new insurance program and the doctor is not on the plan anymore. In fact, what we are hearing from these new exchanges that are being set up is one of the ways we are going to lower costs is limit our networks: less doctors, less hospitals. That is how we are going to save some money and make these things affordable. That is what we are going to put people into? So all of a sudden these doctors you have been going to these years, you cannot go to them anymore? That is wrong. That is hurting real people.

How about this for an example. Imagine now these small businesses I have met. I know the Senator talked about this, Senator CRUZ. I met a restaurant owner—we had a small business meeting here a couple of months ago—from Louisiana. He testified. He has great ideas. He has calculated that there is a market for him to open a new restaurant. He owns a chain. He wants to open one more. He is not going to because of ObamaCare, because the costs create uncertainty about the future for him, because he is worried about triggering mandates he cannot calculate for.

You may say he is a business owner, he already has X number of restaurants, why does he need anymore? Some people would actually say that. It is not him we are going to worry about. He would be the first to tell you I am going to be OK. Who is not going to be OK? If you open that new restaurant, he was going to hire 20 or 30 new people. There are 20 or 30 people in Louisiana right now who could have had a job, a job that could have helped them to provide for their family, a job that could have helped them to pay for their school. Those jobs are not going to be created. That is just one example. There are multiple examples.

How about this one? How about if you are a part-time worker now. The backbone of our economy can never be part-time work, but there is always a place for part-time work. I worked part time before. I think the Senator has talked about when he had to work part time before. Others have. There is a place for that in our economy. Primarily it helps young people and retirees. For young people, it helps them to work their way through school. Imagine, now, if you want to work your way through school because you don't want to owe $50,000 in student loans and you are in central

Florida and you work for Sea World and right now maybe you are working 32 hours a week part time and using the rest of the time to go to school. But here comes ObamaCare so now Sea World has announced instead of 32 hours we are going to move you to 28 hours. That is real money. That is real money. That is hurting real people.

Here is one that doesn't get a lot of attention. Medicare Advantage is a great choice program. It is not perfect. There are ways to improve it, but it is a program on Medicare that basically allows patients on Medicare to sign up in a managed care system that manages their care but for that, it adds additional benefits to their package. My mom is a Medicare Advantage patient. I can tell you the outcomes are generally better than for people who are in the fee-for-service system and the services they offer are valuable.

In my mom's case she needs transportation to and from doctors' visits. That is one of the services the Medicare Advantage Program provides. ObamaCare takes money out of Advantage. You would think they are taking money out of Medicare Advantage to shore up the finances of Medicare because it is going bankrupt. No, they are taking the money out to fund ObamaCare.

So what is going to happen practically is that at some point here over the next few months, beneficiaries on Medicare Advantage are going to get letters in the mail and those are going to inform them of services they were once receiving and are no longer receiving.

With all the uncertainty created by ObamaCare, is it making America the easiest place, or an easier place, to start a business? No. Does ObamaCare make it easier to grow an existing business? Absolutely not. Does ObamaCare encourage innovation in the marketplace? Of course not. On the contrary, it undermines innovation in medicine. It undermines advances in medical technology that have added years and quality to the lives of millions of people.

This thing is a complete disaster, and now we are being asked to take the taxpayer dollars and pour more money into this broken thing? Of course we are passionate about being against that. So I go out across the State of Florida, and everywhere I go I have people who voted for the President telling me this thing is hurting them.

This is not a partisan issue. There are Democrats who are hurt by this. There are supporters of the President being hurt by this.

Earlier this evening—I lost track of when it was—Senator CRUZ read letters from the Teamsters Union and from other unions across the country. We received news that the union representing IRS workers who are in charge of enforcing this law through the fines or the tax—or whatever they decided to call it—want to be exempted from it. They don't want it to apply to them.

By the way, all these exemptions that people are begging for—whether it is Members of Congress or IRS employees or unions—is shining a light on this reality. Big government always benefits the people who have access to power. That is true everywhere in the world. Why? I will tell you why. Big government always writes a lot of regulations, rules, and has a lot complexity.

So if you are a multibillion-dollar corporation, a powerful labor union or a billionaire, you can come and hire the best lawyers in America and they will help you figure out the loopholes in those laws. Let me tell you what else you can do: You can hire the best lobbyists in Washington to help you get those loopholes written in.

You may not be shocked to know this, but in politics, sometimes businesses use government regulations and laws to give them an edge over their competitors and to keep other people from coming into their industry and competing against them. It happens because in big government that is possible. Big government always helps the people who have access to power because they are only ones who can afford to navigate it. So if you are a major corporation or major labor union, you can either deal with the impacts of ObamaCare or you can work to get an exemption or a waiver or what have you from it.

Who can't? I will tell you who can't. The person trying to start a business out of the spare bedroom of their home. By the way, I met someone like this. They weren't at a Starbucks, they were at a Dunkin' Donuts. They were using the free wi-fi, and that was their business. They were in the corner of the Dunkin' Donuts, and that is where they started their software business. Do you think they can comply with the complicated rules and regulations? They can't.

ObamaCare will force people either to go underground in their operations or not do it at all. It is not a question of why ObamaCare will fail, it is an example of why big government fails, and it is not fair. It is not fair for people in this country who are willing to work hard and are willing to sacrifice. It is not fair that we are making it harder on them through government policies being pursued.

By the way, ObamaCare is not the only one. We have a broken Tax Code. If I asked you: Please design for me a Tax Code that discourages people from investing money and growing their businesses, you would give me the U.S. Tax Code today. We have to fix that.

Our regulations are completely out of control. There is no cost-benefit analysis at all. These people write regulations here in Washington, and no one ever asks the question: How many jobs will this destroy? How many jobs will not be created because of this? No one asks those questions. They measure the theory behind what it might do, such as the environmental benefit and the societal benefit, but no one ever does the cost-benefit analysis. There is no employment impact statement attached to these laws. Think about the absurdity of that.

Here we are with a huge number of people dropping out of their search for jobs, a huge amount of underemployment, a vast majority of the new jobs being created are part-time jobs, and we are passing regulations that make it harder for people to create jobs and opportunities. It is crazy. The regulations are out of control.

We are going to deal with the debt. In about 6 or 7 days the debt limit debate is going to come up. They want to raise it again. The President said: I am not negotiating on this. Let's just raise it again. Never mind the fact that he stood on the floor of this Senate less than 10 years ago and said that raising the debt limit back then was a failure of leadership.

Now things have changed because a $17 trillion debt is no longer pressing in his mind, and that is problematic. Why? Is the debt just an accounting problem? That is how they talk about it on the news. They talk about the debt as just an accounting problem. They say: They just spend more money than they take in, but if they only raised more taxes on richer people, they would pay off the whole thing. That is not true, guys.

If we took every penny away from people who made over $1 million this year, it doesn't even make a dent in this. Any politician who says: All we have to do is raise taxes and the debt is under control is lying to you—period.

The sooner we confront the debt, the better off we will be as a people. The debt is growing because we have important government programs that are structured in a way that is not sustainable. They spend a lot more money than they take in, and it only gets worse from here.

Medicare, Medicaid, and Social Security are important programs. My mom is on two of them. I would never do anything to hurt her benefits or people like her and that is why I am so passionate about reforming them. Those programs are going bankrupt, and we are going to have to deal with it. We cannot continue to spend $1 trillion more than we take in and not deal with it. The problem is the longer we wait to deal with it, the harder it is going to be to deal with it.

It is no different than medical conditions, right? Think about this for a second: Is there any disease or medical condition that you know of that is easier to treat the later you catch it? Is there? Is there any medical condition that is easier to fix the longer you wait to deal with it? Of course not. What are doctors always talking to us about? Early detection.

It is the same with the debt. The longer we wait to address this issue, the harder and more disruptive it is going to be to solve it, and that is what is driving our debt. People want to focus on other things such as foreign aid. They say: Cut foreign aid. That is less than 1 percent of our budget. That is not what is driving our debt. It is not even defense spending.

Are there ways to save money in defense contracting, of course there is, but that is not the driver of the debt. The driver of our debt are these unsustainable programs that if we want to save them, we must fix them. The debt is not an accounting problem. Why? First of all, it is a moral problem.

Never in the history of this country has a generation of Americans said to their kids: Guys, we are going to run up your tab and you figure out how to pay for it later. We have never had that happen in the history of the United States, but that is what they are doing. It is wrong. But it is more than that. This is not just about what taxes will be 50 years from now on our kids, this is about the jobs that are being destroyed right now.

Let's go back to the simple equation of how jobs are created. Jobs are created when someone invents something or when someone starts a new business or expands an existing business. People look at this debt and say they are going to have to deal with that debt one day through a debt crisis. They are going to have to raise taxes, make disruptive changes in the government in the future. They are not encouraged about investing in the future now because they are fearful about the uncertainty provided by the debt. They are fearful.

So there are jobs right now that are not being created. Right now there are jobs in America that do not exist and were not created. They were going to be created but were not created because of the national debt.

We are going to have a debate in a few days about it. The attitude from a lot of people around here is: Of course, we have to raise the debt limit, and we should not do anything about it. I stood on the floor of the Senate—my chair was back there in 2011—and I said: When are we finally going to deal with this thing? Well, 2½ years later and we are still not dealing with this thing.

This complaisance and lack of emergency about these issues is puzzling. You know what my fear is? My fear is that we fast forward 50 years into the future and historians are going to write that the country was falling apart, they were destroying the free enterprise system, the American dream was crumbling, and these guys stood by and did nothing.

That is what I feel is happening right now. It feels like the horror movies where you scream at the screen: Don't go in that room. Don't do it. But they do it anyway. In some ways, everything we are facing with the debt and ObamaCare is similar to a horror movie.

We know how it ends if we stay on this path. We know what happens in the horror movie if they open the door. The bad guy is on the other side.

It is the same thing with the issues we are facing. We know what happens if we continue on the path we are on now—we decline as a nation. The sad part is that doesn't have to happen.

There is no reason the 21st century cannot also be an American century. There is no this reason the next generation of Americans cannot be the most prosperous people who ever lived, but it requires us to act. It requires us to reform our Tax Code, not as a way of raising taxes but as a way of creating new taxpayers through economic growth. It requires us to deal with regulations.

By the way—and I think the Senator from Texas would agree with this—ObamaCare, as much as anything else, is a massive authorization to write a bunch of rules. It is not just a law, it is a bunch of regulations that are hurting job creation, discouraging investment, and discouraging people from starting a new business or expanding an existing business. We have to fix that, and we have to deal with the debt.

All of these issues have to be dealt with. None of them get easier to fix as time goes on. They all get harder and more disruptive.

I don't know how the Senator from Texas did this for 18 hours. I am already tired.

I guess I will just speak personally. The one issue that makes me so passionate about all of this in its sum total—I often wonder what would my life would have been like if America had never existed. What if in 1956 there wasn't a place my parents could go to where people like them had a chance for a better life? I doubt very seriously whether I would be standing on the floor of the Cuban Senate. There isn't one now.

I can't imagine what my life would be like if America never existed. If God had not given my parents the opportunity to come to the one place on Earth where people like them—born into poverty and little formal education—actually had a chance to build a better life.

I think about the millions of people out there trying to do what my parents and Senator CRUZ's parents did—what so many of our parents did, by the way. The great thing about this country is when you tell your story, everybody has one just like it. We are all the descendants of go-getters.

Every single one of us is the descendant of someone who overcame extraordinary obstacles to claim their stake on the American dream. They overcame discrimination or poverty. In many cases they overcame this evil institution of slavery. This is who we are as a people. We are all the descendants of go-getters.

I think about how that has changed the world. There is literally no corner of this planet that you cannot go to where you will not find people who feel frustrated and trapped. I cannot tell you how many times I meet people from abroad who disagree with all sorts of things that America does. Yet they have a begrudging admiration for it. You know what that admiration is rooted in? That someone just like them who came from where they come from, is doing extraordinary things. They are doing things they never could have dreamt of in the Nation of their own birth.

I think we should all ask ourselves: What would the world look like if America was not exceptional? What if America was another rich country in the world with a big military and some power, but it wasn't special? What would the world be like? The answer is: The world would be more dangerous, less free, and less prosperous. So when we debate the future of our economy—and in many ways we are debating the future of the world.

If America declines, I want you to ask yourself this: Who replaces us? The United Nations replaces us? Really? Who replaces us? China? China doesn't even care about the rights of their own people. Why would they care about the rights of people anywhere else? Who replaces us? Russia? Who replaces us on the world stage?

If America declines, who will inspire people around the world to seek not just freedom but economic opportunity? Who will stand as proof that it is a lie to tell people they can't achieve? Who will stand as an example that that is not true if America declines?

The one thing that will lead quickest to America's decline is not simply the debt or taxes or these unconstitutional violations we see on a daily basis. The quickest way to decline is to undermine the

American dream and lose our identity as the one place on Earth where anyone from anywhere can accomplish anything. That is the fast track to decline. That is why we are so passionate about ObamaCare. It is a direct threat to the American dream.

The irony of it is that ObamaCare was sold as a way to help the people who are trying to make it. How was it sold to people? Here is how it was sold to people: If you are working class, if you are poor and you can't afford health insurance, the government is going to provide you with health insurance. Tell me the truth. That is what a lot of people perceived this to be. If they don't have insurance now, this is going to allow them to now have insurance—maybe for free, if not at a very low cost. By the way, anyone who already had insurance, this wasn't going to hurt them at all. That is how it was sold. That is how it was sold to people: This is going to be cheap, easy-to-get insurance for people who are struggling.

I understand why someone who is struggling to make it would look at it as something that is appealing. Guess what. That is not what it is. People who have existing health insurance right now, many of them are going to lose it. When they told us we could keep what we had, they were not telling us the truth. People who were told this is going to provide them access to cheap, quality health insurance, guess what. I can't tell people what they are going to get because it doesn't exist yet. But theoretically, on October 1, people are going to have a chance to sign up for one of these exchanges and here is what I predict we will find: less choices, a higher price than we anticipated, perhaps higher than we can afford, and less choices in hospitals and doctors included in those exchanges. This is a disaster all the way around. By the way, while these exchanges are being set up, people may ultimately be getting a notice from their employer that they are going to reduce their hours or maybe even their job. So that is why this is a fight worth having.

It is interesting to see it—Senator CRUZ has not had a chance to see it because he has been here—but it is interesting how the news covers all of this. Political reporters—and they have a job to do—always cover this through the political angle: Who is going to win? Who is going to lose? If this is a college football game, who is the winner and who is the loser on the scoreboard and all of that kind of thing? They love to talk this up, and there is a place for that. People aren't shocked to know there are politics around here.

This issue is so much deeper than that, though. It really is. There is not a lot of attention being paid to that. I think we should, because it is having an impact on real people in a real and powerful way. All of this attention being paid, if we watch the news among the political classes, the process: When are they going to vote? Who is going to win the vote? Who is going to vote which way?

That is fine, guys. I understand that is part of this process and we all enjoy watching it from time to time, right? What they are missing is the why. Why is someone willing to stay up all night—two people, basically, willing to stay up all night to speak about this? Why are people willing to fight on this issue? Why are so many Americans against it? The why. No one is asking the why. The answer is because it is undermining the opportunity for upward mobility. That is why. We are not fighting here against the President; we are fighting for people—for people who voted for us and people who will never vote for us; for people who voted for Mitt Romney and for people who voted for Barack Obama—for real people; people who may never agree with us on any other issue, but they are going to be heard about ObamaCare. People who, as we speak here, are about to wake up, get their kids ready to go to school, put in 8 to 10 hours at work, come back home, try to make dinner while they make sure their kids are doing homework, put them to bed. By the time all that ends, they are exhausted, and they have to get up and do it all over the next day and the next day and again the next week. The last thing these people need is another disruption in their life. The last thing these people need is to go to work tomorrow and be informed: I am sorry, but we are cutting 4 hours out of your work week. I am sorry, but we are changing your insurance plan, so that doctor you have been taking your asthmatic child to or that doctor you have been going to for your pregnancy, you are not going to be able to see them anymore because this new insurance plan does not include them. That is the last thing people need, and that is what they are going to get. That is wrong and it is unfair.

I will close with this, and I alluded to it earlier. I hope we will do everything we can to keep America special, to keep it the shining city on the hill, as Reagan called it, because as I outlined earlier, I think the future of the world depends on it, the kind of world our children will inherit depends on it.

I think it is important to remind us that America has faced difficult circumstances before. In fact, every generation of America has faced some challenge to what makes us exceptional and special— every single one. They were different, but they were challenges. This country had a Civil War that deeply divided it. This country lived through a Great Depression. This country lived through two very painful world wars. This country had to confront its history of segregation and discrimination and overcome that. It had a very controversial conflict in Vietnam that divided Americans against each other.

In the midst of all that, it had to wage a Cold War against the expanse of communism. We forget, but there were many commentators in the late 1970s and early 1980s who would ask Reagan, Why don't you accept the fact—not just Reagan, but anybody—we have to accept the fact that Soviet expansion is here to stay. That was a real threat. Again, it is easy to forget that, but that was the way the world was just 25 years ago.

Every generation of America has had to face challenges and confront them, and every generation has. Not only have they solved their problems, every generation has left the next better off—every single one. Now it is our turn.

We have a very important choice to make, and it is a pretty dramatic one. We will either be the first generation of Americans to leave our children worse off or our children will be the most prosperous Americans who have ever lived. It is one or the other. There is no middle ground, in my mind, on that. When we debate the future of this health care law and ObamaCare, we are debating that question.

I am reminded of the story of the Star-Spangled Banner and how it was written. I was reading it this morning. During the attack on the fort, it was hard to imagine that after that bombardment the United States could survive. After that bombardment the notion was there is no way they are going to make it through the night. But that next morning when the Star-Spangled Banner—when that flag was hoisted, when it was raised, it was a signal to the British and the world that this idea of freedom and liberty had survived. It is interesting how time and again that idea has been tested, both in external and internal conflict. My colleagues may not realize this, but when the Senate is in session, the flag is up. So, usually, when I am walking in early in the morning to the Capitol, there is no flag up at 5 in the morning because there is nobody here. I didn't have my TV on this morning, but I looked over at the Capitol and I said, My goodness, the flag is still up; these guys are still talking. I am glad they are, because what is at stake is the future of our country, economically'in ways just as dramatic as those challenges we faced at the inception of the Republic. This debate is not just about whether a program named after the President will stay in law; this debate is about a program that undermines the American dream, about the one thing that makes us special and different from the rest of the world, and if there is anything worth fighting for, I would think that is. If there is anything worth fighting for, I would think the American dream is worth fighting for. I think remaining exceptional is worth fighting for.

I think after its history of poverty eradication, the free enterprise system is worth fighting for. I think as someone who has directly benefited from the free enterprise system, I personally have an obligation to fight for it. I hope we will all fight for it not just on this issue but in the debate to come next week. This is what this is all about.

I will close by asking the Senator from Texas, as I highlight all of these challenges we face, is this issue, at the end of the day, about us fighting on behalf of everyday people who have no voice in this process, who can't afford to hire a lobbyist to get them a waiver, who can't afford to hire an accounting firm or a lawyer to handle all of this complexity? At the end of the day the rich companies in America are going to figure this out. They may not like it, but they can deal with it. They shouldn't have to, but they can. The people we are fighting for are the ones who cannot afford to navigate this.

I ask the Senator from Texas: Isn't this what this is all about?

Mr. CRUZ. Mr. President, I thank the Senator from Florida for his inspired comments and for his question. He is absolutely right. This fight is about whether hard-working Americans get the same exemptions and the same benefit President Obama has given big corporations and Members of Congress.

I wish to respond to the inspirational remarks of Senator RUBIO by making five comments, the last two of which I think may well be likened to Senator RUBIO who will be inspired to ask a question in response to it.

The first point is a very brief one, which is to simply thank the Senator from Florida for telling that story about the flag. I will confess as we stand here a few minutes before 7 a.m., I am a little bit tired. Senator LEE is probably a little bit tired. I will tell my colleagues, the image of the dust clearing, the smoke clearing, seeing the Star-Spangled Banner waving under the rockets' red glare, that vision is inspiring and I appreciate it. It was very kind of the Senator to tell that story and it is very meaningful, so I thank him.

Secondly, Senator RUBIO talked about how the political reporters have been focusing predominantly on the game, on the political process. He is right, I haven't seen any of the news coverage; we have been here on the Senate floor so I don't know what the coverage is. But what he reports doesn't surprise me because that is the nature of political reporting in Washington. So I am going to make a request directly to those reporters who are covering this proceeding—those reporters who are reporting this proceeding—to endeavor to have at least half of what they say be focused on the actual substance of this debate, on the fact that ObamaCare is a train wreck that is killing jobs, that is forcing more and more Americans to part-time work, that is driving up their health insurance premiums, that is causing more and more Americans who are struggling to lose their health insurance. My real request would make all of the coverage to be on that, but I know that is too much to ask. But I am going to suggest if all of the coverage or most of the coverage is on the political process, on this personality or that personality, or who is up or who is down, or how this impacts the 2042 Presidential election, I am going to suggest two things. No. 1, that is not doing the job you have stepped forward to serve and do. All of us have a job. Those of us in this body elected to serve have a job to listen to the people and to fight for the men and women of America, but those of you who serve in the media have a job to report to the men and women of America what is happening, and not just on the political game.

Secondly, I want to say, if you just report on the personalities and political gains, you are taking sides on this issue. Why is that? Because those who want to keep ObamaCare funded, those who want, on Friday or Saturday when cloture comes up for a vote, for Members of this body to vote for cloture, to give HARRY REID the ability to defund ObamaCare with 51 partisan Democrat votes, they want all the coverage to be about the personality, about the politics—about anything, anything, anything other than the substance. So if you choose to cover just the personalities and the politics, you are doing exactly what some partisans in this body would like, and that is, I am going to suggest, not responsible reporting. I know each one wants to be a responsible steward of informing the public, and it would strike me that the debate we have had here impacts people's lives in a way that nobody gives a flip about the politicians involved.

A third observation about Senator RUBIO's question, when he compared ObamaCare to a horror film, I enjoyed that comparison. In fact, in my mind, I heard the music from "The Shining"—not "The Shining," from "Psycho" in the shower scene. And it occurred to me that perhaps one of the great philosophical conundrums with which we must all wrestle is whether ObamaCare is more like Jason or Freddy. That, indeed, is a difficult question. You can put forth a powerful argument for Jason because ObamaCare is the biggest job killer in this country and when Jason put on his hockey mask and swung that machete, there was carnage like nothing else. On the other hand, we could make a powerful argument for Freddy, because as James Hoffa, the president of the Teamsters said, ObamaCare is a nightmare. It is a nightmare for the men and women of America.

While the Senate slept, the men and women of America didn't get a respite from the nightmare that is causing them to lose their jobs, never getting hired, causing them to be forced to be reduced to 29 hours a week, driving up their health insurance premiums, and jeopardizing their health care.

The only way they get a respite from that nightmare, the only way we stop—there was a movie "Freddy Vs. Jason." I forget. They fought each other. I forget even what happened in that movie. But the only way we stop Jason and/or Freddy is if the American people rise up in such overwhelming numbers that the Members of this Senate listen to the people and we step forward and avert this train wreck, we step forward and avert this nightmare.

Those are three observations I wanted to make at the outset. Then I want to make two more. I would note, Mr. President, as you know well, the rules of the Senate are curious at times. While I am speaking, I am not allowed to pose a question to another. I am allowed to answer questions, but not to pose a question to another Senator. But there is no prohibition in my asking a rhetorical question to the body, which may, in turn, prompt Senator RUBIO to ask a question of his own and to comment perhaps on the rhetorical question I might raise.

The rhetorical question I would raise to the body—and I have two I want to ask—but I want to start the body thinking about Senator RUBIO's family story. And listen, I am inspired by Senator RUBIO's story every time I hear it. I am inspired. Part of it is because his family, like mine—we share many things in common. His parents, like my father, fled Cuba. His father was a bartender. My dad washed dishes. His mother, I believe, cleaned hotel rooms, if I remember correctly. My mother was a sales clerk at Foley's Department Store.

The question I would ask the Chamber is: What would have happened if when Senator RUBIO's parents came from Cuba, when they arrived here, if ObamaCare had been the law of the land? What would have happened to his father and mother as they sought that job as a bartender, cleaning hotel rooms, if we had an economy with stagnant growth, where jobs were not available, and they were not able to get hired? What would have happened if they had been lucky enough to get that job and their hours had been reduced forcibly to 29 hours a week against their wishes? What would have happened if they had faced the economic calamity for working men and women—for those struggling—that is ObamaCare? I wonder—

I have thought many times about what would have happened to my parents. I know it would have been catastrophic in our family. But I wonder how it would have impacted the Rubio family if ObamaCare had been the law when Senator RUBIO's parents came to this country seeking the American dream. Would it have benefited them or would it have harmed them?

(Mr. MANCHIN assumed the Chair.)

Mr. RUBIO. Will the Senator from Texas yield for a question without losing the floor?

Mr. CRUZ. I am happy to yield for a question without yielding the floor.

Mr. RUBIO. I heard the rhetorical question the Senator posed to the body, and it involved a direct question about how my family would have confronted those challenges, so let me back up and talk about that for a second because while it is my family—and I always refer to it—the reason why I got in politics and my view of the issues of the day are all framed through my upbringing, as all of ours are. You cannot escape where you come from or what you were raised around. It influences the way you view the world and the way you view issues, and the experience my family had has influenced me.

I earlier talked about the student loans I once had. I paid them off last year, by the way, with the proceeds of a book, which is available now in paperback, if anyone is curious. But anyway, all joking aside, when I wrote that book, it required me to go back and learn a lot more detail about my parents. Because like anybody else, when you grow up you listen to your parents talk and you kind of repeat it to other people, but when you are growing up and you are in a hurry, you do not always have time to sit down and listen to the details. This actually forced me to go back and learn details about their lives.

What ended up happening is I ended up meeting and discovering two people whom I never knew. I knew something about them. I had grown up with them. But I knew my parents in their forties and fifties. I did not know them in their twenties and thirties. Sometimes when you are young, you forget your parents used to be young too.

Sometimes you forget that when they were your age, they had their own dreams and their own hopes and their own aspirations. And they certainly did.

It reminds me, as I learned about these stories, I learned that when they came to this country, it was not an instant success. The immigrant experience rarely is. You do not just get here and a week later you are running a very successful company or whatever. It does not work that way. My parents struggled. They were very discouraged those first few years. My dad bounced from temporary job to temporary job. My mom was hurt in an accident making aluminum chairs at a factory. She cut her hand.

They struggled. Those first years were tough. But they persevered, and what ended up happening was my father found a job as a bar assistant, basically, on Miami Beach. Then eventually, through hard work, he was promoted to bartender, and then one of the top bartenders at the hotel. It was not going to make him rich, but it made him stable.

By 1966, 10 years after they had arrived, they felt so confident in the future they bought a home. Five years after that, they were so confident that even though they were both over 40 years of age, they had me and then my sister a year and a half after that.

The Senator asked the question rhetorically to the Chamber—and I am going to answer it—what would it have been like if a program such as this would have been in place? But it is not just a program such as this. It is not just ObamaCare. It is all the other things the government is doing. To answer that question, I have to focus on why they had opportunities to begin with.

Why was my dad able to raise our family working as a bartender at a hotel on Miami Beach, and then in Las Vegas, and then back in Miami? Because someone who had access to money risked that money to open that hotel. That was not a government-run hotel. That hotel existed because people who had access to money—I do not know if they borrowed it; I do not if it was their own; I am not sure of the history behind it—but someone with access to money said: Instead of leaving it in the bank or investing it in another country, I am going to risk this money and open and operate this hotel. The result is the jobs my parents had existed.

But that is how you open a business. How does it continue? How does that business survive? It survived because Americans—after they were done paying their taxes and all their other bills—had enough money left over in their pocket to get on an airplane and fly to Miami Beach or to Las Vegas and stay three or four nights at the hotel where my parents worked.

The answer to the Senator's question is, the reason why my parents were able to own a home and provide us a stable environment in which we grew up was because free enterprise works. Free enterprise works. It encouraged someone with access to money to open those hotels, and it left enough money and prosperity in people's pockets after they paid their bills and their taxes so they could take a vacation and go to hotels where my parents worked. Without people in those hotels, there is no job for our parents. They were able to achieve for us what they did because of free enterprise.

To answer the Senator's question about the impact of ObamaCare, anything that would undermine free enterprise would have undermined those hopes and those dreams. And ObamaCare is undermining it.

I cannot say for certain what would have happened. But here is a possibility. ObamaCare could have encouraged the hotel they worked at to move employees from 40 hours to 28 hours, hire two bartenders part time instead of one. That would not have been good. ObamaCare could have led them to hire two cashiers at the Crown Hotel in Miami Beach instead of one—two part-timers like my mom. That would not have been good. Even beyond that, because ObamaCare is cutting people's hours all over the country, because ObamaCare is keeping people from getting hired all over the country, because ObamaCare is costing people their jobs all over the country, I suspect the number of visitors to that hotel would have been diminished.

When you lose your job, when you get moved from full time to part time, the next move you make is not to get on an airplane and go on vacation. The next move you make is to scramble to make up the difference. That is called personal discretionary spending, and people do not do that when they are uncertain about tomorrow.

ObamaCare would have made many Americans uncertain about tomorrow. It is going to make many Americans uncertain about tomorrow. The bottom line is, it would have directly and indirectly harmed my parents' aspirations for themselves and our family.

Here is what is troublesome. There are millions of people in this country today trying to do what my parents did. If you want to find them, walk out of this building and walk three blocks to the nearest hotel and you will meet them there. They clean the hotel rooms. They serve food at the restaurants. They cater the banquets, as did my dad or the gentleman or the lady standing behind that little portable bar serving drinks at the next function at which we speak. They are right down the street.

They are in the halls of this building. You will meet them. They have a little vest on. You will see them with a little cart, cleaning the bathrooms and the floors and providing an environment where we can work. These are people who are working hard to achieve a better life for themselves and oftentimes for their children. These are folks, many of whom have decided: I am going to sacrifice and work a job so my children can have a career.

I cannot tell you how many of the people who work in this building I have talked to, such as the company that caters our lunches or are in the cafeterias here. I cannot tell you how many of them have said to me the reason why they are working these jobs is because they hope one day their children can do something such as stand on the floor of this Senate.

I say to Senator CRUZ, that happens to be our story. That happens to be the American story too. We forget that some of the greatest heroes in the American story are not the people who have been on the cover of magazines. Some of the greatest heroes in the American story are not people who have had movies made about them. Some of the greatest heroes in the American story are not the famous people who are on CNBC being interviewed all the time about how successful they are. They are heroes too. But some of the greatest heroes in the American story are people you will never learn about, about whom books will never be written, whose stories will never be told. Some of the greatest heroes in the American story are people who have worked hard at jobs—back-breaking jobs, difficult jobs—so their children can have careers.

I want you to think about what that means. Think about reaching a point in your life when you realize, you know what, for me, this is about as far as I am going to be able to go—because of age, because of circumstances—but now the purpose of my life will become making sure all the doors that were closed for me are open for my children. Imagine that. Because that is what millions of people are living right now.

It is not that they are not talented, it is not that they are not smart, except they are 45 or 40 or 46, and time is running out on them. But what America is going to give them a chance to do is, it is going to give them a chance to open doors for their children that were closed for them.

They are not going to be able to leave their children trust funds. They are not going to be able to leave their children millions of dollars. They are not going to be able to leave their children a home even. But they are going to be able to allow their children to inherit their unfulfilled dreams and fulfill them.

There are millions of people in this country who are trying to do that right now. There are people who work in this Capitol who are trying to do that right now. There are people working within blocks of here who are trying to do that right now. ObamaCare is going to make it harder for them to do that. It is ironic because ObamaCare was sold as a plan to help people like that. Instead, because it undermines the free enterprise system, it is hurting them.

Many of those people who are being hurt may not have realized it yet. I think the job of leadership is to explain the consequences to people. But in the end, I feel as though we have an obligation to fight on their behalf. I feel as though we—especially those of us who are a generation removed from that experience—have a special obligation to fight for that.

The American story is not the story of people who have made it and then say: Now everyone is on their own. The American story is the story of people who have succeeded and want others to succeed as well. That, by the way, is one of the fundamental differences between the view of big government and the view of free enterprise. Big government believes that the economy cannot really grow, and so what we need government to do is divide it up among us. Right? The economy is a limited thing. There is only so much money to go around, so we need the government to step in and make sure the money is distributed fairly. That is what we are going to use taxes for. That is the view big government has.

What makes America different is we rejected that. We said that is not true. We believe in free enterprise, and free enterprise believes the economy can always continue to grow bigger.

That means if you are successful you can stay successful, and other people can become successful as well. What makes America special is that free enterprise believes you do not have to make any-body worse off in order to make someone better off. That is different from the rest of the world, and it works.

I remember growing up, especially when I lived in Las Vegas. There were not a lot of—back then, especially, there were not a lot of family friendly things to do on the weekends. One of the things we used to do—my parents liked to do this—they would drive us through the nice neighborhoods with the nice houses. I remember Liberace's house was in Las Vegas. It was one of the nice houses.

They would drive us through these neighborhoods and they would show us these houses. When we looked at these houses they would not say to us: Look at the people living in those houses, look at how much money they are making. That is unfair. Right? They are making all that money, and that is why we are struggling. The reason why we live in a small house is because people like them live in big houses.

They did not teach that to us. On the contrary. Do you know what they used to say to us. Look at what these people accomplished through hard work and sacrifice. That can be you if that is what you want. Look at what these people were able to do. That can be you.

That is the difference in some ways between us and the rest of the world. We have never been a place of class envy and class warfare. We have always pointed to these stories as an example of what you can do as well. We celebrate success in America. It inspires us because we know it is not a zero sum game. We know that you can be successful and I can be successful. We know that you can have a successful business and I can have a successful business.

We know that in order for me to be more prosperous I do not have to make anyone less prosperous. That is a big deal, because that is not the way the world has functioned for most of its history. For most of its history, governments did not view it that way and peoples did not view it that way. They always viewed that there had to be a winner and there had to be a loser. One of the things that made us really unique is that we never viewed it that way. In America we have viewed it as you can be a winner and I can be a winner. We can both benefit from each other, because that is how free enterprise works.

In free enterprise you need your customers to be well off. You need your customers to be doing well economically. You cannot afford to bankrupt people by raising your prices because then they cannot buy stuff from you. It is all interrelated. Last year during the campaign there was this big debate about job creators, whether or not you realize it. Every time you go shopping at a department store you are a job creator. Every time you order something on the Internet you are a job creator. Every time you spend money in our economy you are a job creator.

Some people open a business. But every American is a job creator because in the free enterprise, the better off you are the better off we are. And we can all be better off. That is not the direction we are headed. That is one of the things that they are trying to influence in this debate on ObamaCare. They are trying to argue that this is an effort to deny people something. Not true. This is an effort to protect people from something, especially people that are vulnerable to this. I repeat; I am telling you that I have talked to a lot of successful people, people that are making a lot of money or have made a lot of money. They do not like ObamaCare but they are going to be fine with it. They are going to deal with it. They can afford to deal with it. They do not like it. They are going to have to make decisions in business that they do not want to make. But they are going to figure out how to deal with this one way or the other.

At the end of the day, they are going to be fine with whatever we do. They are not going to be the ones who are going to be hurt by this. The ones who are going to be hurt by this are the people who are trying to make it, the people whose hours are going to be cut, whose jobs are going to be slashed, who are going to lose benefits that they are happy with.

Sadly, because they are so busy with their lives, working and raising their kids, they may not realize why all of this is happening until it is too late. So the question the Senator posed to the body was a very insightful one. It goes to the heart of what this debate is about: Who are we fighting for? What are we fighting about?

I fear that too many people that are covering this process think this is all about an effort to keep the President from accomplishing something that he feels strongly about. Not true. This is an effort to fight on behalf of people who are going to be hurt badly. This is an effort to fight on behalf of people who do not have the influence or the power to fight here for themselves. That is why we are here. This is an effort to fight on behalf of people who are trying to do what my parents did. This is an effort to fight on behalf of the people who are trying to start a business out of the spare bedroom of their home—probably in violation of the zoning code, but they are trying to do it.

This is an effort to fight on behalf of the people who are working every single day to achieve their full potential. This is an effort to fight on behalf of people who are working hard at jobs that are hard to get up for in the morning to go do. But they are going to go do it, because the purpose of their life is to give their kids the chance to do anything they want.

Do you how many people I know like that? You cannot walk 10 steps in my neighborhood without running into people like that. The whole purpose of their life, the singular focus of their life, is to make sure that their kids have a chance to do all the things they never got the chance to do. Do you know how many people there are like that around this country? They depend on the jobs that are being destroyed by ObamaCare. They depend on the opportunities that are not being created because of ObamaCare. That is wrong. I hope we will be successful with this effort.

Now, people are going to focus on how the vote is going to go down. This is not going end here, guys. We are not going to stop talking about this no matter how the vote here ends up. We are going to continue to do everything we can to keep this from hurting the American people because it undermines the essence of our Nation.

The reason why I am so passionate about this goes right to the heart of the question the Senator asked, because ObamaCare and big government in general make it harder, not easier for people that are trying to do what my parents did to achieve their dreams.

I think the question of Senator Cruz goes to the heart of what this debate is all about. I would yield back to the Senator to encourage him to continue to highlight the impact that this law is having on real people and their real lives, because I think it is going take some time to break through the narrative that this is all a big political fight, that this is between the President and his opponents.

Whether this law was called ObamaCare or not, we would have to oppose it, because it is hurting real people who are trying to achieve the American dream.

Mr. CRUZ. I thank the Senator from Florida for his answer on how the law would have impacted his family. I will say this: I have no doubt that at every gathering in every hotel where Senator Rubio speaks, there is not a bartender, there is not a waiter, there is not a dishwasher in the room who does not look over and think: I wonder if some day my daughter, my son, could be in the Senate.

What an extraordinary statement. Do you know what. If we were in almost any other country on earth you could not say that. In most countries on earth, if you are not born into a family of power and prestige and influence, you have no chance whatsoever of serving in a position of significant political leadership. Only in America. That is the opportunity this country is. I have no doubt of the inspiration it serves every day when Senator Rubio shares his story.

I have no doubt also that Senator Rubio is right that if ObamaCare had been the law when his parents came from Cuba, when they were immigrants, when they were looking for jobs, when they wanted to support their family and eventually their young family when they had kids, that if they had not been able to get those jobs or if they had had their hours forcibly reduced to 29 hours a week so they could not earn enough to provide for their children, to give them the food, to give them the education, to give them the housing that they needed, it could have had a dramatic impact.

If ObamaCare had been the law, it may very well have been the case that Senator MARCO RUBIO would not be in the Senate right now, because it may have been that his parents would have struggled so much to make ends meet that they would not have been able to provide for him as a young boy the way they did, to give him the opportunities they gave him. He might not be here and our country would be far the poorer.

I know for me and my family, if my dad had not had that opportunity to get a job washing dishes for 50 cents an hour, if my mom had not gotten the opportunity to get her first jobs, there is a very good possibility I would not have had the chance to represent Texas.

When you cut off opportunity for those who are struggling to climb the economic ladder, it impacts for decades. It does not just impact them, but their children and their children's children. That leads to a second rhetorical question that I want to ask the Chamber, but it would not surprise me if it prompts, in turn, a question from Senator RUBIO.

That is, Senator RUBIO and I both have the privilege of representing States in which there is a tremendous Hispanic community. We both come from the Hispanic community, were raised in the Hispanic community. We both have the great honor of representing a great many Hispanics, he in Florida, me in Texas.

Some of the discussion of the Hispanic community focuses on his parents, like my father, who were young immigrants struggling, who may not speak English and who are on the first or second rung of the economic ladder. That describes a great many in the Hispanic community but there are others who are not necessarily in that circumstance.

In the United States there are right now approximately 2.3 million Hispanic small business owners. The Hispanic community is tremendously entrepreneurial. There are roughly 50 million Hispanics in the United States. That means roughly 1 in 8 Hispanic households is a small business owner. So the question I would pose, rhetorically, to the Chamber, is, what is the impact of ObamaCare on the Hispanic community? What is the impact of the crippling impact on jobs, of the punitive taxes, of the 20,000 pages of regulations? What is the impact on those 2.3 million Hispanic small business owners? What is the impact on economic growth and achieving the American dream? What is the impact on the Hispanic community, because I am convinced there is no ideal that resonates more in the Hispanic community than the American dream, than the idea that any one of us, regardless of who our mother or father is, regardless of where we come from, any one of us through hard work and perseverance, through the content of our character can achieve the American dream.

The question I would pose: Has ObamaCare made it easier or harder to achieve the American dream? How has ObamaCare impacted the Hispanic community?

Mr. RUBIO. Would the Senator from Texas yield?

Mr. CRUZ. I would yield for a question without yielding the floor.

Mr. RUBIO. The Senator asked actually a great question. We talk about people who are trying to make it. We talk about the people who are working hard to sacrifice and to leave their children and families better off.

A disproportionate number of people who are trying to do that find themselves in minority communities. You asked about the Hispanic community. I live in a Hispanic neighborhood even now. I live just blocks away from the famed Calle Ocho, 8th Street, in Miami.

If you have never been, I encourage you to come. The President visited an establishment about 4 blocks from my house, I think back in 2010 when he was in town campaigning for one of the candidates. Literally, I mean literally, every business, one after another after another is a small family-owned or family-operated business.

Every single one. It is the bakery, next to the dry cleaner, next to the liquor store, next to the grocery store, next to the uniform shop that sells uniforms next to the gas station, next to the banquet hall. It goes on and on and on. I invite you to come down and see it. There is a Popeyes there, and you will find a McDonald's. But even those franchises, by the way, are owned by families.

Literally, every business on 8th Street, on Calle Ocho, just blocks away from my house, one after the other after the other, is a small business. So are all of my neighbors.

I have a neighbor who runs an electronic alarm company and another neighbor who runs a pool-cleaning business. I am just speaking about my neighborhood. That is the story of the country.

Listen, there are very successful people, Americans of Hispanic descent, who started out as a small business and now are a big business and have been very successful too of course. It is sort of like the rest of the population. It reflects the concerns of whatever challenges they are facing.

But an enormous percentage of Americans of Hispanic descent also happen to be people who are trying to accomplish the American dream. Perhaps the strongest burning desire you will find in minority communities in general—and in particular the one I know best, the Hispanic community—is that burning desire to give their kids the chance to do everything they couldn't. Maybe by the time you got here you were already into your late twenties or early thirties. Because you could succeed, there are many stories of people who have come here at that age and have accomplished extraordinary things. They started in small business, and before you knew it they were being publicly traded. That is a great part of the American story. We celebrate that.

But there are also countless people who worked jobs their whole life. That is what they end up doing. They worked those jobs so their kids could have the opportunity to get ahead. That is a very prevalent story in the Hispanic community.

Interestingly enough, the Hispanic community is very diverse on a lot of different things. Obviously, we have a strong Cuban-American presence in South Florida, but we also have a significant presence from South America. My wife's family is from Colombia. We have a very vibrant Venezuelan community, by the way, coming to the United States to escape Big Government gone horrible.

They just posted—if you read this yesterday—posted military officers at the toilet paper factory in Venezuela because they are not producing enough toilet paper. They think it is some sort of capitalist, imperialist plot to deny the people of Venezuela toilet paper. They have now stationed troops at the toilet paper factory.

This is a country where many of those who find themselves on the American left love going down and extolling the virtues of Chavez, about how great a country it was. They can't—well, let me not say on the Senate floor what they cannot do anymore—but they are struggling to provide toilet paper for their people.

That is how Big Government works. If you want to see another socialist paradise, go to Cuba. The infrastructure is struggling and people are trying to get out of that economy. There are no political freedoms in Cuba, but the economic freedoms are a disaster.

It is because Big Government does not work. Compare that to Chile, to Panama, to Colombia. Compare Colombia to Venezuela, two countries living next together.

A decade ago Colombia was caught in a deep struggle with drug lords and drug cartels. They still have problems with the guerrillas and the FARC, things such as that, but Colombia has turned things around. Why? Two things; one, real leadership at the political level; and, two, free enterprise. They embraced free enterprise.

We have a free-trade agreement with Colombia. There is prosperity in Colombia. Compare that with next-door Venezuela, an energy-rich country, a country that is rich with oil, a country that has natural resources and advantages that Colombia doesn't have, Venezuela. They can't even produce toilet paper because Big Government failed.

In fact, there has been a massive migration of experts in the oil industry leaving Venezuela and moving to Colombia. Compare to Mexico. Mexico still has some challenges, but Mexico has a vibrant middle class. There is a real middle class in Mexico, and it is growing. Look at the moves the new President is making. They are not going to open the oil industry there the way we would do it in the United States, but they are going to make changes to the oil industry because they want to grow and they want to create prosperity.

This holds great promise for our country. Stronger integration between Canada, the United States, and Mexico is very promising. We can cooperate on all sorts of things from energy to security issues.

I think that holds great promise. North American energy has the opportunity to displace energy coming from unstable parts of the world such as the Middle East.

But how is Mexico growing its economy? What is Mexico thinking in order to grow its economy and provide more prosperity for its people. They are thinking about embracing more free enterprise.

Look at the countries in Latin America that are succeeding: Peru, Chile, Panama, Mexico, Colombia. I hope I am not leaving anyone out. These are countries that are moving ahead.

They have struggles and challenges, and it is not a clear upward trajectory because there are challenges in the global economy, but they are moving ahead.

Look at the countries that are a disaster: Cuba, Venezuela, Bolivia, Ecuador, and Nicaragua. What is the difference? What is the starkest difference between these countries other than perhaps the individual lunacy of some of these individuals in this country. What is the difference?

The difference is the countries that are failing and embarrassing their people are the countries that are embracing Big Government and socialism. The countries that are providing middle-class opportunities and upward mobility are the countries that are embracing more and more free enterprise.

When you ask about the Americans of Hispanic descent, these are the countries they came from. They came here to get away from Big Government. Why is there a vibrant and growing Venezuelan community in Miami-Dade County where I live? Because Big Government is destroying Venezuela.

Why are there over 1 million Cuban exiles living in Miami, New Jersey, and concentrated in different parts of the country, including a sizable community in Houston, TX? Because they came here to flee, not just Big Government, but the oppression that comes from very Big Government, socialism and Marxism.

Why do people cross the border from Mexico and come into the United States in search of jobs and opportunities—because for a long time Mexico didn't embrace free enterprise policies. It is now increasingly—and what is happening in Mexico, a vibrant and growing middle class, a sense of upward mobility. Every country has challenges. They have challenges in Mexico, but they are trying to turn it around and they are doing some good things to try to do that because they are embracing free enterprise.

The unique thing about it, Senator CRUZ, is that Americans of Hispanic descent, particularly those here in the first generation or the second, have come here to get away from Big Government policies, because in countries that have Big Government, you are trapped. You are trapped. In countries that have Big Government, the people that come from powerful families and powerful enclaves, they are the people who keep winning.

In places where the government dominates the economy, as is disproportionately the case, and the countries that immigrants come here from, those are the places where the same people keep winning.

The biggest company 50 years ago is still the biggest company. The richest family in the country is still the richest family. The President is the grandson and the son, over and over.

That is what Big Government does. It traps people in the circumstances of their birth.

What happens if you are a talented, ambitious, and hard-working person living in a country like that, frustrated and trapped? You try to get to the only country in the world where people like you even have a chance, the United States.

We have millions of people living in this country of Hispanic descent that experience that, that know what it is like to live in a place where you are trapped in circumstances of their birth. The reason why they love America is because here they are not limited by that.

I have said oftentimes—and I think you would share this perception in the story of your father, Senator CRUZ—it is true that immigrants impact America. It is true they do. Immigrants impact America, they contribute to America, they change America.

But I promise you that America changes immigrants even more. You find that in the Hispanic community, the impact that America has on immigrants once it opens opportunities for them. Long before my parents became citizens, they were Americans in their heart. That is still true. You will still find that out there in the His-panic communities. You will still find people who understand how special this country is because of the opportunities it is giving them and their children. This is why I think they will and are starting to understand how damaging this law may be.

If you watch Spanish-language television, they are running these advertisements now, talking about sign up for ObamaCare, it is good for you. They are making it sound like this is going to be cheap and free insurance for people. When you are working hard 10, 12 hours a day and not making a lot of money, maybe your employer doesn't provide health insurance and along come these politicians telling you we are going to give you health insurance cheap and free. It is enticing, but it is not what is going to happen. When people realize that, not only are they going to be upset, they are going to be livid.

When they go to work one day and they tell them: Guess what. You are now a part-time worker, they are going to be livid. When they go to work because they are working part-time because of where they go to school and they lose hours, they are going to be livid.

When they go back to work one of these days, they may be work-ing at one of these places where they have health insurance, as over 70 percent of Americans do, and they are happy with it. All of a sudden they found out: You know that health insurance you have, that is not our health insurance anymore. You have to go on this Web site and shop for a new one.

If they go on the Web site today they can't shop for anything. It isn't set up yet. They are going to be livid.

When we talked about defending people who are trying to make it, people who are working hard to persevere and move ahead, I think that is the epitome of what you will find in the Hispanic community in this country. That is the typical story of people who are here. They are working hard to get ahead and they want their children to have a better life than them.

There is only one economic system in the world where that is possible and that is the American free enterprise system. ObamaCare directly undermines it. If for no other reason we should repeal

ObamaCare because it undermines the free enterprise system—the single greatest eradicator of poverty in human history, the free enterprise system. It is the only system in human history that allows people to emerge from poverty and into a stable middle class and beyond, the free enterprise system. It is the only economic system in human history that rewards hard work, sacrifice, and merit, the American free enterprise system. ObamaCare is undermining it.

As I yield back to the Senator, is it not the case that what we are doing is not to stand against ObamaCare. We are fighting against the only system in American history, American free enterprise, where upward mobility is possible for so many people.

Mr. CRUZ. I thank the Senator from Florida for his passion, for his heartfelt commitment to opportunity and understanding.

This is not about the rich and powerful. We are rich and powerful. The rich and powerful are just fine with ObamaCare. Indeed, the rich and powerful are better than just fine with ObamaCare. The rich and powerful get special exemptions. The rich and powerful get treated better because they are buddies with the current administration. Big business and giant corporations get exemptions from ObamaCare. Members of Congress get exemptions from ObamaCare.

Mark my words, if Congress doesn't act to defund ObamaCare to stop this train wreck before the end of the President's administration, unions are going to end up getting an exemption from ObamaCare. It is going to be everyone who is a political friend of the administration, has juice and has power, will get extensions.

The people who are left, you have nothing to worry about unless you don't happen to have several high-paid Washington, DC, lobbyists on your staff, unless you happen just to be a Hispanic entrepreneur, a single mom or a hard-working American trying to provide for his or her family, then maybe you will have something to worry about. But you are not going to get the exemption because what the Senate has been saying to you is exemptions for everybody else but not for hard-working American families.

I believe if it doesn't apply to everyone, it should apply to no one. The Senate shouldn't be picking and choosing winners and losers and who are the favored political class.

The Senator from Florida talked about Cuba. Some, particularly in Hollywood, like to lionize Cuba as this workers' paradise, but I would note Cuba has socialized medicine. Majority leader HARRY REID has stated his intention that he believes ObamaCare will lead, inevitably, to socialized medicine, to single-payer, government-provided health care. Some in Hollywood have lionized Cuba as this workers' paradise. Yet I am reminded of a comment President Reagan said in the midst of the Cold War.

The funny thing he said is if you go to the Berlin Wall and look at the Berlin Wall, the machine guns all point in one direction.

The same thing is true about Cuba. People talk about, the workers' paradise. The funny thing about Cuba, the rafts all go in one direction.

In the decade since Fidel Castro seized control and began brutally oppressing the people of Cuba, destroying that once great Nation I am not aware of a single instance since the day of that revolution of one person getting on a raft in Florida and heading over to Cuba—ever. I am not aware of it ever happening. So if socialized medicine is this oasis, if we are to believe the Michael Moores of the world in Hollywood, one would expect Floridians to be jumping on rafts. You know, that 90 miles, it crosses both ways. In fact, Floridians can probably get a better boat than they can in Cuba, but nobody goes that way. They flee to freedom. They flee to America.

What gives freedom such vibrancy—you want to talk about what matters to the Hispanic community, you want to talk about what matters to the African-American community, you want to talk about what matters to single moms? It is the opportunity to work. It is the opportunity to get a job. When we talk about what matters to young people, it is the opportunity to start a career and to move toward advancing to providing for your family, to having the dignity and respect of working toward your dreams, toward your passions, toward your desires. ObamaCare is stifling that, and that is a tragedy. It is a tragedy. And the only way it will stop is if this body begins to listen to the American people. Together, we must make D.C. listen.

Mr. ROBERTS. Mr. President, would the distinguished Senator from Texas yield for a question?

Mr. CRUZ. I am happy to yield for a question without yielding the floor.

Mr. ROBERTS. How is the Senator doing?

Mr. CRUZ. I thank the Senator from Kansas. And I will tell the Senator, I am doing fabulous. I am inspired and I am motivated by the American people.

Mr. ROBERTS. I saw a black car down there in the parking lot with a Texas license plate, and I figured that was the Senator's. Didn't see him in it. Everybody was wondering as they got up this morning, after listening to the Senator last night, whether he would still be standing, but here he is. I appreciate this.

I think the thing I appreciate the most—and the question will follow, Mr. President—is how the Senator has conducted himself because throughout the night he has had some folks at least making their point of view, which is obviously very different from his. Sometimes folks in this body get a little critical—arrows and slings—and although not necessary, those wounds heal. But in each and every case of a person who has brought a different point of view, the Senator has very deftly and very skillfully, acting like a Senator, respected their point of view. Not once did I see him do anything else.

I gave up about midnight, by the way, my wife about 11. She fell asleep. But I thank the Senator for that. I thank him for being truly senatorial and basically doing what Senators do; that is, respect everybody's point of view.

I especially liked the comment of BERNIE SANDERS, whom I also like. You wouldn't know it, but he does have quite a sense of humor. A different point of view but very honest about it. So I thank the Senator for that.

If the Senator wants breakfast, if he is about ready to sit down, I will be happy to buy him breakfast. But we will let that go.

The other thing I want to ask is how does the Senator feel coming here as a new Senator and knowing how the Senate used to operate and knowing that in the Senate I came to, every Senator, on an important issue, had the opportunity to offer an amendment. It could be germane or it could not be germane. But for the last 5 years that has not been the case. There have been a few exceptions when we have had what is called regular order. Folks back home don't know what regular order is, but it is the way the Senate used to operate. It is the difference between the Senate and the House. It is the reason I left the House and ran for the Senate, because I wanted to have that opportunity to be an individual Senator.

Last year I made a reference to the farm bill, which has somewhat something to do with what the Senator is talking about because it involves the ability of America to feed not only us but a very troubled and hungry world. Of course, food helps your health, obviously, but you show me a country that cannot feed itself and I will show you a country that is in chaos. So we do farm bills. They are much maligned. Right now not too many people even care about them, but they are terribly important. And farmers and ranchers now see no certainty out there because, like the health care law, at the end of this fiscal year the farm bill is going to expire, and they wonder what on Earth we are doing. We are in a perfect storm.

In the last farm bill—not this one, in the last farm bill—in talking to the majority leader—whom I affectionately call Smoking Joe because he is a fan of boxing and Joe Frazier—I said: We can do this in 2½ days. And the chairperson of the committee, Senator STABENOW, also obviously weighed in, but we did the farm bill in 2½ days. That was a record.

The first amendment on the farm bill was the amendment of the Senator from Kentucky dealing with Pakistan and saying no more aid to Pakistan until they freed that doctor who was very helpful to our intelligence community with regard to what happened with Osama bin Laden. What did that have to do with the farm bill? Nothing.

RAND PAUL came to me and said: Do you think we can get this amendment?

I said: Yes. We have an open rule.

There were 73 amendments considered—73; this last farm bill, only about 10, probably less than that. Senator THUNE had very key amendments, Senator JOHANNS had very key amendments, Senator GRASSLEY had key amendments, and I, the former chairman of the

House agriculture committee, the former ranking member, had some key amendments. All of the senior members on the agriculture committee, all of us who had contributed to that process were locked out—sorry, it is over, no amendments. What is that all about?

We have a one-person rules committee in this Senate. And if there is anything I am upset about, it is the lack of ability and the lack of opportunity for the Senator from Texas or Kentucky or Kansas or anybody else in this body to offer an amendment.

So here we are—what is it—5 days away from the law that says: Prescribed by law, these exchanges and everything that has anything to do with the unaffordable health care act is going to take place. And the Senator has demonstrated time and time again, with every allegory one can possibly come up with, how this is a train wreck.

Yesterday afternoon, when the Senator started—well, it was in the evening—I came to the floor and said: Look, isn't it worth the fight, isn't it worth the effort—and the Senator is making the effort, and I appreciate that so much—knowing this is the first, second, and third step—skip to my Lou, my darlin'—going right into socialized medicine? And who says that? Well, let's start with the President; then the Secretary of Health and Human Services, Kathleen Sebelius; then NANCY PELOSI in the House; and then the distinguished majority leader here saying: Yes, we want a single-payer system.

A single-payer system means national health care; it means socialized medicine; it means, as the Senator has pointed out during all of this rather unique and incredible time he has taken before the Senate, the government pays for it, which means we all pay for it and premiums go up and the insurance companies have a heck of a time and there will be exactly what the Senator has described in Cuba. I am hoping it won't be that bad, but at least he has pointed it out.

So my question to the Senator is, after all of that rambling rose, wouldn't it be nice, wouldn't it be in the best interests of this body, wouldn't it be in the best interests of Americans to open this Senate, go back to regular order, and at least have an opportunity to offer amendments?

Some of the folks who were somewhat critical of the Senator said: Well, what are you going to offer?

There are about five amendments I would like to offer. I don't know what the Senator thinks the key amendments are that he would like to offer as a positive answer as opposed to shutting down the Affordable Health Care Act with a lack of funding. We could only do that partially because a lot of it gets in with taxes, and that is the mandated funds we allegedly can't touch. But would the Senator please list about two or three amendments he would like to offer.

I think I would like to see the medical device tax repealed, but, again, that is one of those mandatory things we have to deal with in the Finance Committee, of which I am a member. But let's get on the positive side of this and say: OK, if the Senator had the opportunity to offer amendments and everybody else had an opportunity to offer amendments—and the Senator has spent a great deal of time here overnight. What was it—2:40 in the afternoon? That is what they keep flashing on the news. Quite frankly, I was listening to Ray Price singing "For the Good Times," and I flipped over to FOX News, and there you were again. I thought, my Lord, there he is, still standing and still talking.

So give me just about three amendments the Senator might offer. We shouldn't do more than three things because people forget about it after three.

There is one other thing I want to mention. I got a lot of derision and a lot of criticism when this bill was first passed. I serve on the HELP Committee—Health, Education, Labor and Pensions. We spent a great deal of time on this bill. I had three amendments to prevent rationing by the rationing board. Everybody says they are not rationing, but they are. So those decisions are not being made by the patient and doctor, they are being made by appointed bodies or we can use the term "bureaucrats." That is usually a pejorative term. At any rate, I was upset, and I said: We are riding hell for leather into a box canyon, and there are a lot of cactuses in the world. We don't have to sit on every one of them, but, by golly, we are. We are about to do that. And I had some other allegories we use in Dodge City, KS, and I had a few marine stories to tell, and then I got derided even on national news: Oh my gosh, here is this cowboy from Dodge City. I am not. I am an old newspaper person.

At any rate, I am in here saying we are going into a box canyon only to find out four or five other people now have referred to it as a box canyon. We are in it. Everybody understands what a box canyon is, and we have to ride out. So when we are riding out, what are we going to do, I would ask the Senator from Texas. Give me three amendments.

Mr. CRUZ. I thank the Senator from Kansas for his very fine question, and I will make a couple of general points about the Senator from Kansas first, and then I will answer his important question.

I want to say that Senator ROBERTS is an old lion in the Senate. He was here last night, he was here this morning supporting us, and that is a big deal. The Senator from Kansas is a respected leader of this body, a gray-beard, and, I would note, a very well-liked Senator.

One point I will make about Senator ROBERTS is that, in my humble opinion, I think he is one of the two funniest Senators in the Republican conference. I would say Senator ROBERTS and LINDSEY GRAHAM both have a fantastic sense of humor.

Mr. ROBERTS. Will the Senator yield on that point?

Mr. CRUZ. I will be happy to yield for a question but not yield the floor.

Mr. ROBERTS. Well, the question is, some people are funny and some people are humorous. I may be one of the most humorous, but Senator GRAHAM is truly funny.

Mr. CRUZ. I will note on that question that I can provide no response other than to say, as they say in mathematics, QED. That point is granted.

But I will note that for the Senator from Kansas, as a respected senior Senator, to come and support this effort and even more importantly for the Senator from Kansas to have the courage to disagree with party leadership and express a willingness to vote against cloture—because doing so would allow the majority leader of the Senate, HARRY REID, to fund ObamaCare on a straight party-line vote with no input from Republicans—takes courage.

I guarantee you, it is noticed that Senator ROBERTS is standing with us. It is noticed that Senator SESSIONS is standing with us. It is noticed that Senator ENZI is standing with us. It is one thing for the young

Turks, it is one thing for those who have been dubbed the "wacko birds" to be willing to stand and fight, but when we see senior elder statesmen of the Senate standing side by side, I would suggest we are starting to see what I hope will happen this week, which is seeing Republicans unify.

I would like to see all 46 Republicans vote together on cloture on Friday or Saturday, whenever that vote occurs. I would like to see all of us stand together and vote against cloture because we say we can't, in good conscience, with the commitments we have made to our constituents, vote to allow the majority leader to fund ObamaCare on a straight 51 partisan party-line vote. I would like to see that happen, and I would note that Senator ROBERTS' presence here at night and in the morning is beneficial to making that happen. I hope it causes other respected leaders in our party to give a second thought that perhaps the division in the Republican conference is not benefiting the Nation or benefiting the Republican Party. Perhaps it is not serving the interests of our constituents.

Before I answer the question directly, that point is an important point to make—that the Senator's support is significant.

I also wish to acknowledge Senator ROBERTS' very kind compliment about the way I have endeavored to conduct myself.

Senator MIKE LEE has always conducted himself with respect for the views of others, not speaking ill of any Member of this Senate—Republican or Democrat. That is certainly what I have endeavored to do, and it is meaningful.

Senator ROBERTS comments that it is his judgment we have had some modicum of success achieved. I would note that characterization is at least mildly at odds with what one might think if one simply read the New York Times. If one read the New York Times, one would expect that perhaps I am leaning over, biting my colleagues with bare fangs. So I appreciate the observation of the Senator from Kansas that, in his judgment, we have not conducted ourselves that way. The reason is simple: The New York Times wants to spill gallons of ink on personalities, on people, on politics, and on anything except the substance.

I would have been perfectly happy if not a single story coming out of this ever mentioned my name. If every story just focused on:

ObamaCare, is it working or not? Is it helping the American people or is it hurting? If every story simply said the Senate stayed in session all night because ObamaCare is a train wreck; because ObamaCare is a nightmare—in the words of James Hoffa, the president of the Teamsters; because the American people are losing their jobs or being forced into part-time work or are facing skyrocketing health insurance premiums or are losing their health insurance, that is why the Senate was here. So I would be thrilled if all of the coverage focused on the substance instead of the distraction that is the silliness that is the back and forth.

Senator ROBERTS posed a very important question, and it went to process. It went to how this proceeding is moving forward.

There used to be a time when this body was described as the world's greatest deliberative body. I don't think anyone familiar with the modern Senate would describe it as that, because this body doesn't work anymore. This body is no longer a deliberative body. This body is now an instrument of political power used to enforce the wishes of the Democratic majority, both on the minority but more importantly on the American people, disregarding the American people's views and the American people's concerns.

So what are we told? In the Senate of days of old there were two cardinal principles that were the essence of what it meant to be in the Senate: one, the right to speak; and, two, the right to amend. For a couple of centuries any Senator could offer any amendment on just about anything. That is what made this process work, open amendments.

Did that make a few people take votes they didn't necessarily want to? Yes. But if we are being honest with our constituents, that shouldn't trouble you. If you are telling your constituents what you believe and if you are voting your principles, there shouldn't be a vote you are afraid of. Votes are only problematic if you are trying to tell your constituents one thing and trying to do something else in Washington.

What is the process that is supposed to play out here on this continuing resolution and this continuing resolution to defund ObamaCare—to fund all the Federal Government and defund ObamaCare?

We are told that, first, there is going to be a vote on cloture on the bill to shut off debate. If 60 Senators vote to do so, if Republicans cross the aisle and join HARRY REID and Senate Democrats in shutting off debate, we are told we will get one amendment—apparently drafted by the majority leader HARRY REID—and that amendment will fund ObamaCare in its entirety and will gut the House bill, will deliberately do it. That is the stated intent. We are also told that other amendments will not be allowed.

In the course of this discussion we have discussed a number of other amendments, all of which I think would be terrific. One amendment the Senator from Kansas mentioned would be an amendment to repeal the medical device tax. I would note that is an amendment which we had a vote on in the budget process, and an overwhelming majority of Senators in this body voted for it. My recollection is nearly 80 Senators voted for it. Yet it didn't pass into law because of the peculiarities of the budget process. So that is an amendment presumably that, if it were allowed, would be adopted. I would suggest that is perhaps the reason why it won't be allowed: because it would be adopted.

Repealing the medical device tax would take one aspect of ObamaCare—the punitive, crippling tax that is hammering the medical device industry, that is driving medical device companies out of business or near out of business, that is hammering jobs and that is restraining innovation—that is restraining medical device innovation. We know with certainty that if there is not innovation, if there is not research and development, if there is not investment in medical devices, there will be new medical devices that aren't discovered. There will be people whose pain is not alleviated, whose suffering is not alleviated, perhaps whose lives are not saved. So that would be one of them.

Another amendment I think we ought to have a vote on would be Senator VITTER's amendment to revoke the exemption that President Obama, contrary to law, unilaterally put in place for Members of Congress and their staff. Senator VITTER's amendment would subject every Member of Congress, every staff member, and the political appointees of the Obama administration to the exchanges just as millions of Americans are going to be.

Indeed, I supported an amendment that some Republican Senators have talked about that would expand Senator VITTER's

amendment to all Federal employees because our friends the Democrats frequently tell the American people what a wonderful thing
ObamaCare is: Look at this tremendous benefit we are bringing the
American people. If it is so wonderful, then the majority leader and
the Democratic Senators and the congressional staff should be
eager to get it if it is such a tremendous improvement. If it is so
wonderful, President Obama—after all, his name is on the bill,
ObamaCare in the popular vernacular—should be eager to get—
his political appointees who are forcing it on us should be eager to
get it and the Federal employees should be eager to get it. We all
know they are not.

We all know this exemption came after a closed-door meeting in
the Capitol with the majority leader HARRY REID and the Democratic
Senators where, according to press reports, they asked: Please let us
out from under this, because it will be so devastating, we don't want
to lose our health care.

I understand that. Look, I would not be eager myself to be on the
exchanges. I am certainly not eager for my staff to be on the
exchanges. Many of them are very concerned about it. I may lose
very good staff over it. But I think there is a broader principle, which
is that different rules should not apply to Washington that apply to
the American people.

If we are willing to subject millions of Americans to the exchanges,
if we are willing to let people lose their health insurance, as is happening all over this country—take the UPS. UPS recently sent letters to
15,000 employees saying you are losing your spousal coverage. Your
husbands and wives who were covered are losing their coverage.

President Obama promised: If you like your plan, you can keep it.
That has proven categorically wrong.

A great many of those husbands and wives who had health
insurance may be forced onto these new exchanges with no
employer subsidy. That is a lousy place to be. It is exactly the lousy
place to be that Members, Senators, and congressional staff are
complaining, Don't put us in that briar patch. But if Congress is
going to put the American people in that briar patch, then you had
better believe we should be there with them. And if we don't like it,

the answer isn't exempt us, the answer is exempt the American people. If it is intolerable for us to endure, it should be intolerable for the American people.

Another amendment I think we ought to vote on is an amendment stripping the IRS of enforcement authority on ObamaCare. We have seen the political abuses the IRS is capable of. I don't know anyone who is eager to have the IRS have the world's largest database of our health care information.

(Mr. DURBIN assumed the Chair.)

Mr. ROBERTS. On that point, would the Senator yield for a question?

Mr. CRUZ. I am happy to yield for a question without yielding the floor.

Mr. ROBERTS. There are six Federal agencies in the meta database that are involved in it. When I kept inquiring, when the distinguished chairman of the Finance Committee, Senator BAUCUS, asked the representative from the Center for Medicaid and Medicare Services—CMS, referred to in the health provider community as "It's a Mess"—and said, Who is the navigator? This is before we understood that it was pretty much all community organizers. There are three basic organizations in Kansas, 1.5 million, and so they are out there knocking on doors.

The problem is we don't know what people are signing up for, or they don't know and I don't know, and we have made all sorts of inquiries.

Finally I got the 16 pages that you have to fill out to be eligible to sign up and the 61 pages that you had to fill out then to be a member of the exchange. That got a lot of news. So they reduced the number by simply reducing the font size from about 16-point or 12-point down to 8-point. They said, Just read more carefully. I got to page 3.

I would not put down the information they wanted to know. There have been stories about scammers who are looking at these regulations or these signup sheets—no matter how big they are— saying, Aha, if they have to give their Social Security number, I can call them and say it is the law and you are going to have a lot of fraud and abuse. Maybe the IRS can take a look at that.

One other thing about the IRS. The Finance Committee in a bipartisan effort—we haven't held many hearings, but we are getting closer and closer to what happened with the IRS denying people First Amendment rights. I would give a lot of credit to Senator HATCH and Senator BAUCUS working in a bipartisan effort.

Along about November there is going to be quite a story. There is a V, and we have Lois Lerner here, and it goes up here to the Justice Department and it goes wider. We are getting a lot of communications. We are not making a lot of hearings about it, not standing in front of the mirrors. So we will get there.

But the Senator makes an excellent point about the IRS. With all the problems they have had over this denial of First Amendment—not only to the tea party groups, conservative groups, but pro-Israel groups and a whole bunch of other groups, and they are still doing it.

Consequently, the Senator has made an excellent point. Why on Earth would we want the IRS to be in charge of your health care, not to mention five other agencies, in a huge database? That information should be between you and your doctor, and you should have to break down the doggone doors in the dead of night in order to get that kind of information, as opposed to giving it to the Federal Government with all those different agencies with all sorts of opportunity for fraud, abuse, and virtually everything else.

I am sorry to get wound up on that, but the Senator made an excellent point and I am trying to think of a question to make this legal.

Doesn't the Senator think this is a trail we don't want to go down?

Mr. CRUZ. I thank the Senator from Kansas for that excellent question. I would like to make two points in response, and I want to give an opportunity to the Senators from Kentucky and Oklahoma who are both waiting, I believe, to ask questions, so I want to move expeditiously, allowing them to do so. Before that, it is important to address the very good point the Senator from Kansas raised.

I would say as the first observation, there are at least three more amendments that ought to be voted on in connection with the continuing resolution. One the Senator from Kansas suggested is an amendment defunding these navigators, defunding this slush fund that is being used to basically fund liberal special interest groups in the

States, much like the stimulus, yet another plan that is used to write checks to groups that are little more than political action groups. That would be a vote we should have.

Another vote we should have is a vote to protect the privacy of our information. The IRS has created the largest database in history of our personal health care information, and there has been report after report that the protections and the privacy of cyber security are pitifully, woefully inadequate; that there are identity thieves, that there are unscrupulous characters getting ready to mine those databases.

The Senator from Kentucky, who shortly will ask a question, has been a leader on privacy. The idea of the Federal Government collecting personal information about all of our health care and then putting it in one place so, A, the Federal Government can have it; and, B, if it is poorly secured, anyone can break in and steal it. We ought to have an amendment to require real protections for our privacy before any of this goes online.

Yet another amendment we ought to have is—the President has unilaterally delayed the employer mandate. We ought to have a delay of the individual mandate. I note the House passed that and a substantial number of Democrats voted for it.

That went through 6 amendments and I am pretty sure we could come up with more. I note that earlier in the evening I had an exchange with Senator KAINE from the State of Virginia who asked a question. I forget the exact terms of it, but to paraphrase, he said: Can't we work together on improving ObamaCare, stopping it from being—he didn't say this, but this is me saying it—to stop it from being this train wreck, the nightmare, the disaster that it is? My answer was: Absolutely. We should fix it, we should have amendments, and I listed some of these we discussed now. The problem is, I suggested to the Senator from Virginia, you should address your concern to majority leader HARRY REID, because he is the one who is shutting down the process, saying the Senate is not going to operate with open amendment, we are not going to have an opportunity to improve it.

Let me make a final point. In terms of the political theater that is Washington, why does this matter right now? There are lost

Republicans who would like votes on everything I said, and there is some virtue to getting a vote. But to be honest, many Republicans are fighting to get that vote in some context where it is purely symbolic. They are real happy because every Republican can vote together and every Democrat can vote against it, and then it can become fodder for a campaign ad.

Let me suggest a far better approach is to have these amendments voted on in a context where they can be passed into law. The continuing resolution is that context. Everyone understands that at one stage or another. This is must-pass legislation. Everyone understands that we will fund the Federal Government. We have to fund the Federal Government. Nobody wants a government shutdown.

We may get one if HARRY REID and President Obama force one, but nobody wants it. So voting on it now in the context of this continuing resolution is different from a symbolic vote, a political vote, because it actually could fix these problems. It is not simply Washington symbolism. That is why I find it all the more striking that so many Senate Republicans are suggesting they may be willing to vote with majority leader HARRY REID and with the Senate Democrats to cut off debate, to allow one amendment drafted by the majority that would totally fund ObamaCare that would gut the House bill and shut off every other amendment.

If this were any other context, my colleagues on the Republican side would be up in arms. We would see the so-called old bulls of the Senate united in saying the process is being abused, and we would get 46 Republicans voting against cloture.

By the way, nobody, if there were any other context, would make the silly arguments that voting for cloture is really supporting the bill. The majority leader has indicated that once cloture is granted he is going to introduce an amendment to gut the bill and go the exact opposite way, allowing him to do so in a 51-vote partisan vote. That is not supporting the bill; it is undermining the bill.

The stakes of this fight right now are whether this body is willing to listen to the American people—whether Democrats are willing, whether Republicans are willing. I would say what has to happen to change how this body operates is that we must make DC listen.

Mr. INHOFE. Will the Senator yield for a procedural question?

Mr. CRUZ. I am happy to yield for a question without yielding the floor.

Mr. INHOFE. Last night at 10 o'clock I was privileged to be down here with the Senator and we went over a lot of things. Something happened this morning. I went home, I went to bed, I ate. I am back here now.

The Senator from Kentucky has been waiting 40 minutes. I am not going to use his time, but what I would like to do is this. Something happened after I left last night, after a statement I made having to do with Hillary health care. I want to share that with the Senator. But I do not want to do it now on his time. Hopefully, if you are going to be here at 9 o'clock I would like to get back in line and share what happened last night after I left here. Is that all right?

Mr. CRUZ. I thank the Senator from Oklahoma. I can tell him as I said at 2:30 in the afternoon yesterday that I intend to stand against ObamaCare as long as I am able to stand. At this point I feel confident that at 9 a.m., I will still be able to stand. There will come a point when that is no longer the case, but we have not yet reached that point.

Mr. INHOFE. I appreciate the Senator from Kentucky allowing me to come in front of him.

Mr. PAUL. Will the Senator from Texas yield for a question?

Mr. CRUZ. I am happy to yield for a question of the Senator from Kentucky without yielding the floor.

Mr. PAUL. There has been some discussion. The Senator from Kansas recently put this question forward, how we would fix ObamaCare if we were allowed to. I think there are two parts to that. The first part of the question is, will we be allowed to offer any amendments to try to make ObamaCare less bad, to try to fix ObamaCare? Will Republicans, which is virtually half of the country, be allowed to participate in this process at all?

ObamaCare was passed with entirely Democratic votes, not one Republican vote. It is a policy that has been very partisan. It is a policy that now even supporters of ObamaCare are saying: My goodness, this is going to really be a problem for the country. But the Senator is exactly right, we are getting ready to go through a process where there are going to be no amendments on fixing ObamaCare. There will not be one thing offered.

Former President Bill Clinton is saying there are problems with it, the Teamsters, Warren Buffett, the 15,000 people at UPS who lost their spousal insurance are saying there is a problem with this. Are we going to be allowed to offer amendments?

It appears as if there will not be any amendments. It appears there is nothing forthcoming that there will be a need to debate. This is important for the American people because this is being portrayed as the Republicans are obstructionists, that Republicans don't want to do this, Republicans don't want to do this.

It is exactly the opposite. The President wants 100 percent of ObamaCare as he wrote it, as the Democrats wrote it, with no Republican input. So when we go around the country and people say why can't you guys get along, figure out some way of making our health care system better, it is because we are getting 100 percent of ObamaCare as written by the President and it is his way or the highway.

What he is talking about is really, even though they say the opposite, he wants to shut the Government down. They salivate at shutting the government down. Over the last 3 months as the Senator brought this issue forward, who has been talking about shutting the government down? Has the Senator been talking about it? No. Have I been talking about it? No. We have been specifically saying we don't want to do that. Who talks about shutting the government down, nonstop, every day? The Democrats, the President, and their liberal friends in the media.

As I get to my question, what I want to ask is about how we would fix it. I think Senator ROBERTS is right. The other side says they don't have any answers, they are not willing to fix ObamaCare. The truth of the matter is we have been talking about this for years now but we have been drowned out by the ObamaCare I want everything all the time, everything I want I am going to get. There are many fixes for our health care.

I am a physician and practiced for 20 years. I saw it every day. The No. 1 complaint I got: Health insurance costs too much. So what did ObamaCare do for health insurance costs? It drove them up. It did absolutely nothing. Even they are admitting it. But you have to understand why health care costs went up. Health care costs went up because we are mandating what health insurance.

People say I would like to have my kids covered. Sure we can cover your kids, but it is not going to be free. It is going to have a cost. So everything the people say they want is not free. It elevates the price of your health insurance. When you elevate the price of health insurance, what happens? Poor people have more difficulty buying their health insurance.

What else did ObamaCare do that we did, that is exactly the opposite of what we should do. There is something called health savings accounts that originated about 10 or 15 years ago. They were expanded gradually and they were the best thing to happen to health care probably in the last 30 years. But what happened? We went the opposite way. ObamaCare is now narrowing the health savings account. Why are the health savings accounts important? Because you can save money tax-free, you can carry it over from year to year, and then you can buy higher deductibles. So contrary to what people think, it may be counter-intuitive to some people, the way to fix health insurance is to have higher deductibles, because what does that mean? Cheaper insurance. You want cheaper and cheaper insurance. As you have higher deductibles, you have cheaper insurance. When you have cheaper insurance, you have all this extra money that you can use to pay for day-to-day health care. When you do that, what happens? You drive the price of health care down. I know that is exactly right.

As you increase deductibles, as you get the consumer involved in health care, your prices go down. In my practice as an ophthalmologist, there are two things that insurance did not cover at all and the prices were reduced most dramatically in the two areas in which the health insurance did not cover anything. If you want to buy contact lenses, most of the time health insurance doesn't cover it. The price went down every year. Lasik surgery to get rid of the need for glasses, much more expensive but the price went down for 20 years because the consumer paid.

What would the consumer do—or the patient? The average patient calls 4 doctors before they have Lasik surgery, so the thing is they drive prices down. People say I don't want to pay more out of pocket, I want to pay less. That is a natural impulse to want to pay less. You may pay less at the door, but you are paying more for premiums. Or if you are not paying it and your employer is paying more for premiums, what ends up happening is there are fewer jobs.

I know the Senator from Texas is familiar with philosopher and parliamentarian and French writer Frederic Bastiat. Bastiat often talks about the seen and the unseen. It is the consequences that are visible to the naked eye before you get started, but then there are the things you didn't realize were going to happen, the unintended consequences. It is like saying let's have government build the hospitals. Let's have government hire the doctors. Let's have government build everything. We would see all these bright, shiny things and we would not see where the money came from, where the money was not spent, where the economic growth could have occurred. What we have to think about when we think about ObamaCare is we have to think about do you believe in freedom or coercion? ObamaCare is riddled with mandatory, mandatory this, mandatory that, I think there are several mandates.

When you hear the word mandate that is not freedom, that is your government telling you that you have to do something. It should be about mandatory versus voluntary. We should have bills that originate here that say you are free to do things. We have gone the opposite way. We are taking away freedom and we are adding mandates. At its core, ObamaCare is about freedom versus coercion and as you add in these levels of coercion, not only do you lose your freedom, they cost money so it becomes more expensive.

We took a health care system where 85 percent of the people had insurance and we made it more expensive for everybody. We made it more expensive by mandating what goes into the insurance. For example, for a 30-year old, or for a 32-year-old, it is illegal to buy a high deductible policy. You will not hear this. ObamaCare has made it illegal to buy a high deductible policy. You can get it under age 30 but not over 30. Why would you want that? Maybe you are a plumber in your own business and you want to have a $5,000 deductible so up can pay $1,000 a year in premiums or $2,000 a year in premiums. But how do you ever get there? You never get there unless you allow freedom. You need the freedom of the marketplace. Instead of limiting it, realize what you are getting. When you ask for ObamaCare you are getting ObamaCare, you are getting mandates, but you are getting limited choices. Freedom means choices. Mandates, coercion, means less choices.

The exchanges will be very few choices. I will be on the exchanges. I will have to go to the exchange in Kentucky and buy my insurance. I am not very happy about it. In fact I think if I have to do it I think Justice Roberts ought to have to do it. Justice Roberts loves ObamaCare so much I am for voting to have Justice Roberts trot on down to the ObamaCare registry, the ObamaCare index, and get his insurance like the rest of us.

We talked about some amendments to include people, I think everybody, all Federal employees. If ObamaCare is so good, everybody ought to get it. The thing is we would be so fed up that we would rebel in this country. That is what I think the Senator from Texas has started, hopefully a rebellion against coercion, rebellion against mandates, a rebellion against everything that says that big government wants to shove something down your throat, they say take it or we will put people in jail. People say we aren't going to put anybody in jail. The heck they won't. You will get fined first. If you don't pay your fines, you will go to jail. They are telling you that you have to take their health insurance as they conceived of it, with absolutely no Republican input. Not one Republican vote, and they are unwilling to have any amendments.

What is this fight about? This fight is about whether or not we are going to have a society or a Congress where we can debate over how to fix things. ObamaCare is a disaster. Even its own authors are now saying it is a train wreck waiting to happen. Even the President, who is in love with this ObamaCare, is saying it is going to be a problem. He is delaying the individual mandate. He is delaying the individual mandate.

But realize on another level what some of our complaints are. Some of our complaints are that by making it mandatory, and by him doing it after the fact, he is not obeying the law. This is pretty important.

We talk about the rule of law a lot of times around here, but what is important about the rule of law is that Congress passes legislation and the President can sign it and execute it. ObamaCare was passed with only Democratic votes. But here is the thing, he is now amending it after the fact.

We saw one of the union officials coming out with a gleeful smile on his face from the White House. Is he going to get a special deal that nobody else gets? Is the President going to come to your town or my town in middle America and meet with me and give people in my town an exemption? No. He has been giving exemptions to his friends. This is patently un-American, and it is unconstitutional. We will fight this through the court cases, but it will take a year or so before we can get to the Supreme Court.

Can the President amend legislation? Can he write legislation without the approval of Congress? That is what he is doing. His argument would be: I am trying to fix the problems the legislation created. Yes, the legislation was 2,000 pages and nobody read it, and then they created 20,000 pages of regulations.

We have no idea who to call in many of the States. If you do know who to call and there has been an exchange set up, there are limited choices. Where you might have had hundreds of choices, you will now have two or three choices. Where you once had freedom, you are going to have coercion. Where you once had the ability to buy cheaper insurance and pay your out-of-pocket expenses on a day-to-day basis yourself and buy cheaper insurance, it will no longer exist because the government now says they know what is best for you. They know what you should do. Your choices have gone out the window.

We talked about amendments. If we were allowed to have amendments and the ability to try to fix ObamaCare, I would try to bring the price down. The best way to bring the price down is not to tell people they have to have a deductible or an HSA, but it is to expand their ability to choose an HSA. An HSA is a health savings account.

Before ObamaCare, you could put $5,000 a year in your HSA, and now it has gone to $2,500 a year. If you have a child who is autistic or a child with spinal bifida or a child with a severe learning disability, you can spend $10,000 a year on their health care in trying to help them adapt to life.

Right now what is happening is they are limiting that ability. Health savings accounts should be unlimited. We should take them from $2,500, where the President has squashed them, and make them unlimited. If you get lucky and don't get sick, your health savings account should be able to go into your kid's education. Health savings accounts should not be for just the family but for every individual of the family. They should be enormous over time, and then you would buy cheaper insurance.

This is also the answer as to how you drive the price down. Here is something, as a physician, people would say to me: I went to the hospital and had heart surgery that cost $100,000. When I looked at my bill very closely, the mouthwash was $50, and I was infuriated. I would say: Did you call? Did you try to negotiate with the hospital? They would answer: No, my deductible is $50.

When you have a low deductible and you don't have to pay, you are not connected to the product. Unless you are connected to the product, prices don't come down. This is a fundamental aspect of capitalism. That is why when you go to Walmart or any retail store such as Hobby Lobby, the prices are bid down because there is competition and you ask about the price.

Think about it. If you went to Walmart and your copay was $10 every time you went to Walmart, would you ever look at any prices after you paid $10? You can see what would happen to the entire retail world if we had health insurance for buying goods. If you had a health insurance copay of $100 to buy a car, the price of cars would go through the roof because you wouldn't care about the price. This is about having some sense.

The people who gave you ObamaCare are not bad people. They have big hearts but not necessarily big brains. They want to help people, but they have not figured out that the unintended consequences of ObamaCare are that part-time workers will have less hours, and full-time workers, who are on the margin, as far as their hours go, with a business that is struggling will lose their jobs.

If I have 51 employees, I may go back to 49 employees if I am struggling. If I have 1,000 employees, and I provide health insurance for them but my competitor decides to dump them on the government exchange, maybe I have to do that too so I can compete because maybe I have to offer the lowest price. Maybe the end result of ObamaCare is the people it was intended to help are precisely who it is going to hurt.

I think we have to think this through. We have to think as a society whether we are for choice or against choice, whether we are for mandates or for volunteerism. I think it is very important that we look beyond the immediacy of what we are trying to do, and, as I said, I don't discount the motives of the people on the other side. I think they want to help people, but I think they are going to hurt the people they want to help.

As we look at this ObamaCare debate and this disaster, there is another question you might ask: If ObamaCare is such a great thing, you would think you could give it away—this is something that will be free. And they are having trouble giving it away. So what have they done? They are spending tens of millions of dollars to advertise to you that it is such a great thing. If you can't sell somebody something that is free, I think there is a problem. ObamaCare is free and they can't sell it. They have enlisted the President now to sell it. They are going to barnstorm all across America selling something that is free. They will have government agents on planes flying hither and yon, knocking on your door, saying: Please take this free health care. Please sign up for free health care. If you cannot sell free health care, there must be a problem with it.

We are spending tens of millions of dollars on TV, and millions more having people going door to door to convince people that it is a good idea. Ultimately we should try to help those who cannot help themselves, but in order to figure out how you want to help the 15 percent who don't have health insurance, we should have looked at the problem more carefully. Of the 15 percent who don't have health insurance, one-third of them are young and healthy and make more than $50,000 a year. So one-third of the problem had nothing to do with not being—well, it did have something to do with not being able to afford it. It had to do with the health insurance costing too much. So we should have tried to figure out how we lower health care costs, and if you are a young, healthy person, we should have expanded health savings accounts. There are ways we could fix this.

What I would ask the Senator from Texas is: Does he see a way forward? Does he see that we can get the other side to come forward and tell the American people that, yes, we made some mistakes? We made some mistakes, and even our friends are telling us we made these mistakes and we want to work with you. Because I think the problem, the perception out there is that we don't want to work with them, but it is completely the opposite of the truth. The truth of the matter is, as I see it, they won't work with us. They won't open the process and we can't have a debate. We are having a debate, but where is the other side? Why can't we influence legislation? Why can't we be part of trying to fix health care? I don't know if ObamaCare is fixable, but health care is fixable.

The main problem of health care is price. It costs too damn much. Can we fix that? Could they come to the Senate floor and say: We are going to have amendments, we are going to have an open amendment process, and we are going to try to fix ObamaCare?

Does the Senator see an opening where maybe the President would compromise and come and say: Yes, I am willing to work with you in order to fix health care in this country?

Mr. CRUZ. I thank the Senator from Kentucky for his very fine question. The answer is absolutely yes, I believe there is an opening to do that. I believe we can address the train wreck and the nightmare the American people are facing that is ObamaCare. We can address the very real harms that are being visited upon Americans as a result.

I want to note that the Senator from Kentucky has been a clarion voice for liberty. That is one of the many things I appreciate about my friend Senator RAND PAUL. I think my favorite phrase from his question is a phrase that occurred about midway through his question where he said something to the effect of: We need a rebellion against oppression. I like that phrase. That is a particularly excellent turn of a phrase. I will confess that it reminded me of a movie series that was in the theaters when the Senator from Kentucky and I were both kids—young adults—and that was the "Star Wars" franchise and the discussion of a rebellion against oppression. I think it captures a lot of what is going on here. We started this debate some 18 hours ago talking about the divide between the Washington establishment that is not listening to the American people, that is forcing its will on the American people, and the people of this country.

I will confess that phrase of rebellion against oppression conjured up to me the Rebel Alliance fighting against the Empire—the Empire being the Washington, DC, establishment. Indeed, immediately upon hearing that phrase, I wondered if at some point we would see a tall gentleman in a mechanical breathing apparatus come forward and say in a deep voice, "MIKE LEE, I am your father."

This is a fight to restore freedom for the people. This is a fight to get the Washington establishment—the Empire—to listen to the people. And just like in the "Star Wars" movies, the Empire will strike back. But at the end of the day, I think the Rebel Alliance—the people—will prevail.

The Senator from Kentucky asked: Can we actually make real progress in this? Yes, if the people do it. To be perfectly honest, the Senator from Kentucky can't get it done; I can't get it done; Senator MIKE LEE can't get it done. I don't think there is an elected official in this body who can get it done. Only the American people can speak with a loud enough volume that it forces, No. 1, all 46 Republicans to unite, as we should be uniting, against cloture and say: No, not a single Republican will vote to give HARRY REID and the Democrats the ability to force through a single amendment that guts the House continuing resolution, that funds ObamaCare, and has 51 partisan Democratic votes and shuts out all other amendments; and No. 2, if the people rise up in sufficient numbers.

I believe the Democrats have good faith. We will ultimately have no choice but to do the same thing—listen to the people. During this debate we have read and we have discussed the letters from the roofers union, the letter from the Teamsters. Each of them used the same phrase: They "could remain silent no more." Both of those letters began by saying they were Democrats who supported the President, who supported Democrats for the Senate, supported Democrats for the House, who had campaigned and worked for them, yet they "could remain silent no longer" because ObamaCare is hurting millions of Americans. In the words of James Hoffa, president of the Teamsters, it is a nightmare.

If they can remain silent no longer, then I say to the Senator from Kentucky, I do have faith that there will be Democratic Senators who will feel the same pang of conscience to remain silent no longer but to actually speak up for the American people. But it will only happen when Republicans are united. If Republicans are divided and throwing rocks at each other, we cannot expect Democrats to cross their leadership. The Republicans have to unite first in order to get Democrats to come together and listen to the people. You want to know what this whole fight is about? Together we must make DC listen.

Mr. PAUL. Mr. President, I have a followup question for the Senator from Texas.

Mr. CRUZ. I am happy to yield for a question, but I will not yield the floor.

Mr. PAUL. One of the questions that should not only be asked of the Senator but should be asked of the President: Why doesn't the President voluntarily take ObamaCare? It is his baby, and if he loves it so much, why doesn't the President take it? He could voluntarily go on the exchanges. I am sure they would welcome him down at the DC exchanges. In fact, I think that ought to be a question they ought to ask him at the press briefing today: Mr. President, are you willing to take ObamaCare? If you don't want it, why are we stuck with it?

So if the President can't take it, if Chief Justice Roberts doesn't want it—here is the thing. If we want to see a rebellion, we should ask Federal employees to take ObamaCare—that is what my amendment says—not just Congress. I am willing to take it. I don't want it. I absolutely don't want it, and I have been frank about it. I am not a hypocrite. I didn't vote for it, I think the whole thing is a mess, and I don't want it. But the thing is, if I have to take it, I think the President ought to get it. He ought to get a full dose of his own medicine.

I think Justice Roberts should get it. I think he contorted and twisted and found new meaning in the Constitution that isn't there. So if he wants it so much, if he thinks it is justified, if he is going to take that intellectual leap to justify ObamaCare, he ought to get it. There are millions of Federal employees. They don't want it. Guess who they vote for usually?

I think it is a partisan question. I think if we were to put it forward and say ObamaCare is such a wonderful program for everybody, let's give it to the Federal employees, my guess is we wouldn't get a single vote from the opposition party, but we will not even get a chance because they don't want to talk about it: ObamaCare is good. We want to shove it down the rest of America's throat, but we exempt ourselves.

I have a constitutional amendment. I frankly think Congress should never pass any law if they are exempted from it. I think there is an equal protection argument for how it would be unconstitutional for us to do so. Yet we have done it repeatedly.

But my question to the Senator from Texas is, What does he think? Does the Senator from Texas think maybe we should ask the President to come down today and sign up for ObamaCare? I think we should ask him that today, every day, and henceforth: Mr. President, if it is such a good idea, why don't you get it?

Mr. CRUZ. Mr. President, I thank the Senator from Kentucky and my answer is, yes, yes, a thousand times yes. Indeed, if the Washington press corps would focus on the substance of this debate, on the issues that matter to the American people, the reporters would ask the question at every news conference the President conducts and at every opportunity they have: Mr. President, are you willing to be subject to ObamaCare, to be put on the exchange that millions of Americans are being forced to do? They would ask the majority leader of the Senate, and indeed every Democratic Senator who met with the President and who, according to press reports, at whose behest Members of Congress were exempted.

If the press were doing the job of a watchdog press holding leaders accountable, actually speaking truth to power, they would ask every Democratic Senator not once, not twice but over and over and over: Are you willing to be put on the exchanges without an employer subsidy, just like millions of Americans who are losing their health insurance because of ObamaCare? If not, why?

As I have noted multiple times during the course of this debate, I very much support what Senator PAUL suggested about making every Federal employee subject to ObamaCare. Let me be clear. Doing that is a lousy thing to do to Federal employees. It is a lousy thing to do to Members of Congress. It is a lousy thing to do to congressional staff. None of them like it. As the Presiding Officer and I know well, it is hard to find an issue that causes more dismay, if not panic, among congressional staff than the idea that they might be thrown into the exchanges with no employer subsidies, as will millions of Americans; ironically enough, including, presumably, many of the staff who worked on drafting ObamaCare, and it is why the American people are so fed up with this. It is a manifestation good enough for thee but not for me.

Washington plays by separate rules. The rich and powerful, those who stroll through the corridors of power, they get exemptions, just not hard-working Americans. If you are at home and it happens to be the case that you have two or three high-paid Washington lobbyists on your payroll, you may be in good shape. You might get an exemption. But if you don't have the ability to walk into the West Wing, if you don't have the ability to pull the levers of power, then what President Obama, the majority leader, and the U.S. Senate are saying to you is you are out of luck. We answer to the friends of this administration but not to the American people. Listen, I think under no circumstances should Members of Congress be treated better than what we are doing under the law, forcing upon millions and millions of Americans.

I would note that during the course of this debate, I have been privileged to receive support from a great many Senators but two in particular I wish to mention right now: Senator Rubio and Senator Paul. I wish to mention them because on any measure of hipness or coolness, I will readily concede I can't hold a candle to them. Indeed, I remember in the debate over drones, Senator Rubio began quoting from rap lyrics, and I will confess to being clueless enough that I didn't even know what he was referencing. I was sure it was something far too hip for me to know. Although I will note I did read Toby Keith lyrics, but that is probably not quite the same genre, and I will note that Senator Paul has a following of, as he describes it, folks in Birkenstocks and beards and earrings, a different sort of cool that again I could not remotely hope to compete with. I am a lawyer from Texas.

But what I can try to do to keep up—because, after all, we all have a little bit of competitiveness in wanting to keep up—I would like to provide a little more detail about something I referenced earlier, which is the speech that Ashton Kutcher gave at the Teen Choice Awards. To be honest, referring to the Senator from Florida and the Senator from Kentucky as cool, as terrific human beings, as both of them are, it is almost oxymoronic, because I think I will take it as a given that there is no politician on the planet who would actually qualify as cool. Ashton Kutcher I don't know and I don't expect to ever meet. Yet at the Teen Choice Awards he gave a speech that I thought was remarkable. He was there to accept an award for playing Steve Jobs in the movie "Jobs," and he did much more than accept a trophy. He talked about the importance of hard work.

His speech was so remarkable that I took the opportunity and tweeted out because, frankly, Ashton Kutcher can reach young people in a way that I never can, that no Member of the Senate can, and I thought the message was important and it is important because of a principle that is imperiled by ObamaCare. Let me read from the relevant portions of Mr. Kutcher's speech. He said:

I believe that opportunity looks a lot like hard work. I have never had a job in my life that I was better than. I was always just lucky to have a job. Every job I had was a stepping stone to my next job, and I never quit my job until I had my next job. So opportunities look a lot like work.

He went on:

The sexiest thing in the entire world is being really smart and
being thoughtful, and being generous. Everything else is—

And he used a mild expletive for manure.

It's just "manure" that people try to sell to you to make you
feel like less. So don't buy it. Be smart, be thoughtful, and
be generous.

Then he ended his speech by saying:

Everything around us that we call life was made up by people
that are no smarter than you. You can build your own things.
You can build your own life that other people can live in. So
build a life. Don't live one, build one. Find your opportunities,
and always be sexy.

I salute that message. I think it is a message that I hope every young
person in America hears. But it is also a message that embodies what is
imperiled by ObamaCare.

What Mr. Kutcher talked about "I was always just lucky to have a
job. I never had a job in my life that I was better than," it makes me
think about my father. When he came from Cuba, his first job was
washing dishes making 50 cents an hour. He was lucky to have that
job. He certainly was not better than that job. If he hadn't had that
job—the next sentence Mr. Kutcher said: "And every job I had was a
stepping stone to my next job." As we have discussed during this
debate, if he hadn't had that first job, he wouldn't have gotten his
next job as a cook. If he hadn't had that job, he wouldn't have gotten
his next job as a teaching assistant. If he hadn't had that job, he
wouldn't have gotten his next job as a computer programmer at IBM.
If he hadn't had that job, he wouldn't have been able to start a small
business and work toward the American dream.

We want to talk about the tragedy of ObamaCare. It is the millions of young people, the millions of single moms, the millions of

Hispanics, of African Americans who are struggling, who want to achieve the American dream and who, because of ObamaCare, can't find a job. Because of ObamaCare small businesses are not hiring, they are not expanding. Small businesses create two-thirds of all new jobs.

That first job washing dishes, if ObamaCare were the law in 1957, I think there is a very good chance my father never would have gotten that job washing dishes. If he had gotten the job, if ObamaCare were the law, I think it is virtually certain his hours would have been forcibly reduced to 29 hours a week, and he couldn't have paid his way through college on 29 hours a week. So one of two things would have happened. He either would have had to drop out of college or he would have had to get a second job at 29 hours a week and juggle the balance between each of them.

That is what is so critical about this issue, is maintaining the opportunity for those struggling to achieve the American dream.

Secondly, I wish to share with my colleagues some more material. During the wee hours of the morning, we had the opportunity to consider some excerpts from Ayn Rand. I want to point to some more excerpts from Ayn Rand that I think are relevant to the battle before this body.

First, from *Atlas Shrugged*:

We are on strike, we, the men of the mind. . . . against self-immolation against the creed of unearned rewards and unrewarded duties . . . against the dogma that the pursuit of one's happiness is evil against the doctrine that life is guilt.

Another on the filibuster, on the effort of the American people to get Washington to listen to us, from *The Fountainhead*:

Integrity is the ability to stand by an ideal.

Also from *The Fountainhead*:

. . . no speech is ever considered, but only the speaker. It's so much easier to pass judgment on a man than on an idea.

That particular quote I think more than anything is addressed to our friends in the media. I wish to read it again:

> . . . no speech is ever considered, but only the speaker. It's so much easier to pass judgment on a man than on an idea.

I, like every Member in this body, am a flawed human being, a man of many imperfections. If a reporter wants to write on those imperfections, there is no shortage of material. But as long as they are writing on those, they are not talking about the ideas. As long as they are writing about the personality, they are not talking about the American people who are suffering. As long as they are writing about the personalities, and the back-and-forth, the game playing and the insults and all of the nonsense, they are not talking about the millions of Americans who are desperate for greater opportunity, desperate for a job, desperate for work to provide for their families, desperate to hold on to their health insurance. We read letter after letter after letter of real live people who are losing their health insurance.

Another quote:

> Fight for the value of your person. Fight for the virtue of your pride. Fight for the essence of that which is man: For his sovereign rational mind. Fight with the radiant certainty and absolute rectitude of knowing that yours is the Morality of Life and that yours is the battle for any achievement, any value, and grandeur, any goodness, any joy that has ever existed on this earth.

Another from *The Fountainhead*:

> Throughout the centuries there were men who took first steps down new roads armed with nothing but their own vision. Their goals differed, but they all had this in common: that the step was first, the road new, the vision unborrowed, and the response they received—hatred. The great creators—the thinkers, the artists, the scientists, the inventors—stood alone against the men of their time. Every great new thought was opposed. Every

great new invention was denounced. The first motor was considered foolish. The airplane was considered impossible. The power loom was considered vicious. Anesthesia was considered sinful. But the men of unborrowed vision went ahead. They fought, they suffered, and they paid. But they won.

Let me suggest that quote speaks directly to the millions of Americans who are speaking up right now, who are saying Washington says we can't stop ObamaCare. Washington says we have to accept this train wreck, this nightmare. There is nothing we can do. Yet the message, as Rand says, is that if the American people stand together, if they believe in their vision, together we can make DC listen.

Indeed, also from *Atlas Shrugged* in terms of the divide we see in this body, as Rand observed:

There are two sides to every issue: one side is right and the other is wrong, but the middle is always evil. . . .

(The Acting President pro tempore assumed the Chair.)

Mr. President, I would suggest that comment speaks volumes to this dispute. As we observed during the middle of the debate, there are some Members of the Democratic Conference—indeed, one we discussed: Senator SANDERS from Vermont—who openly embraces his ideas. Indeed, there was a time when he ran for public office not as a Democrat but as a Socialist.

Mr. SANDERS and I agree on very little when it comes to public policy. But I will say this, I respect his fidelity to his principles. I respect the honesty with which he embraces them. And as I observed earlier in this proceeding, I would far rather a Senate with 10 BERNIE SANDERS and 10 MIKE LEES to a Senate where the views, the actual commitments, are blurred by obfuscation.

When it comes to the Republican side of the aisle, there are some Senators who have been quite open in saying they do not think we can defund ObamaCare. I will respect any Republican Senator who says: I am convinced we cannot do this and, therefore, I am voting for cloture because we cannot do it, and so I am voting against it. I do not agree with that. I think that is a defeatist philosophy. But it is an honest philosophy.

I would suggest it is far different for a Republican to say: I am going to vote for cloture, I am going to vote for HARRY REID and 51 Democrats the ability to fund ObamaCare in its entirety with no amendments, no changes whatsoever, but at the same time I am going to go to my constituents and say: I fully, I enthusiastically support defunding ObamaCare. Indeed, I am leading the fight. That is not being honest with the American people.

If we are to listen to the people, part of listening to the people is being honest with the people. Part of listening to the people is embracing, quite candidly, the position we hold. If those Members of this conference want to disagree with this strategy and say we agree with HARRY REID, that ObamaCare should not be defunded on the continuing resolution, then let them say so openly, not cloaked in robes of procedural deception and obscurity. Let them say so openly to the American people. And let them make their case. That has the virtue of truth.

On ObamaCare, in *Atlas Shrugged* Ms. Rand wrote:

> There's no way to rule an innocent man. The only power any government has is the power to crack down on criminals. Well, when there aren't enough criminals, one . . . declares so many things to be a crime that it becomes impossible for me to live without breaking laws. . . .

That is a profound insight on the train wreck, on the nightmare that is ObamaCare.

One statement the Senator from Kentucky made that I would disagree with slightly—the Senator from Kentucky said President Obama is committed 100 percent to ObamaCare, to making no changes, no alterations, to defending it as is, not to improving it. Actually, I do not think that is accurate. I think what the President has done is far worse than that, actually, which is the President has opposed legislative changes to fix the tremendous failures in ObamaCare that are hurting the American people, but the President has over and over unilaterally—abusing executive power—disregarded the law.

When the President decided unilaterally that the employer mandate that was set to kick in on January 1 of next year would be delayed for a year for big businesses, there is no basis in law for him to do so. The statute says otherwise. But his decision was simply: L'etat c'est moi. I am the state; therefore, this is delayed.

Likewise, when the President made the decision that the eligibility verification for subsidies, written into the statute, would not be enforced, that is contrary to law. The President does not have the authority to disregard the statute. If he does not like it, he can come to Congress and ask for an amendment. But the statutes written in the law books are binding law, and he simply announced: No, they are not. I am not going to enforce it.

Of all the different unilateral changes, that may be the most consequential. It is one of the least discussed, but it is consequential because its effect is essentially to encourage liar loans. Whether you are eligible for subsidies or not, just say you are, and we are not going to check to find out.

Perhaps most egregious was the President's action exempting Members of Congress. The statute provides that Members of Congress shall be subject to ObamaCare, shall be put on the exchanges without employee subsidies, just like millions of Americans.

Mr. President, as you and I both know well, that had Members of Congress, that had congressional staff in a panic. So majority lead Harry Reid and Democratic Senators met with the President and, according to the public press accounts, asked for an exemption, said: Please exempt us—although the statute is clear. It was written that way, I would note, because of my friend, Senator Chuck Grassley, who added that amendment on the principle that if we are going to put a burden on the American people, we should feel it, we should have skin in the game.

According to the press reports, the President said he would take care of the problem. Shortly thereafter, his administration did so and said: We are going to disregard the law of the land. We are going to disregard the statute.

Let me say, when the President of the United States begins picking and choosing which laws to follow and which laws not to follow, when the President of the United States looks at this mess that is ObamaCare and begins pulling out the eraser and saying: I am going to erase this part of the statute, I am going to erase this part of the statute, and I am going to pick that it applies to these people, but I am going to pick that it does not apply to these people, that is the height of arbitrary enforcement. It is also contrary to his constitutional obligation. Article II of the Constitution obliges the President to take care that the laws be faithfully executed. To deliberately, willfully, and openly refuse to enforce the law is the antithesis of taking care that the laws be faithfully executed. Indeed, it is taking care to refuse to faithfully execute the laws of the United States.

That is the pattern we have seen. For any President to do so, Democrat or Republican—and I can tell you this: If there were a Republican President in office, and he were saying: I am going to disregard the laws of the United States, I can promise you I would be right here on the floor of the Senate decrying that Republican President, just as loudly as decrying President Obama for disregarding the law.

Look, I think ObamaCare is a disaster. I think it is a train wreck. I agree with James Hoffa, the president of the Teamsters: It is a nightmare. But I do not think the President can just say: I am going to refuse to apply it to everyone. You have not heard me call on President Obama granting a lawless exemption to everyone. He did not have authority to grant an exemption to big business. He did not have authority to grant an exemption to Members of Congress. He does not have authority to grant an exemption to the American people. Only Congress does.

That is why Congress needs to act. That is why this body, why Democrats in this body, why Republicans in this body, need to listen to the American people. Together we must make DC listen.

Mr. INHOFE. Will the Senator yield?

Mr. CRUZ. I am happy to yield to the Senator from Oklahoma for a question but not yield the floor.

Mr. INHOFE. I mentioned a few minutes ago, when I was here last night something was said, and I went back and I got some phone calls because people did not believe it. I say to my good friend Senator CRUZ, I think sometimes people like you who are living this issue 24 hours a day—literally 24 hours on this day—may assume people understand the significance of some things that they do not. Because I got these phone calls last night when I was talking about—and I quoted our leader here in the Senate, Senator HARRY REID. A couple days ago on the PBS program "Nevada Week in Review," Senate majority leader HARRY REID was asked whether his goal was to move ObamaCare to a single-payer system, and his answer was: "Yes, yes. Absolutely, yes."

I know I said this last night. But a lot of people did not realize that because there is—and if the Senator does not mind, I am going to take a few minutes here to kind of set the question up because I think it is important.

As the Acting President pro tempore will remember, since he was in the other body when I was elected many years ago to the House of Representatives—I recall at that time nobody thought the Republicans would ever be a majority of anything, the House or the Senate. I know that would have pleased the Acting President pro tempore. It is kind of interesting because we became very good friends, and yet we are philosophically apart from each other.

But I observed four things, and I did not think about this until this morning and how this subject fits into this. At the time Republicans were totally insignificant in the House of Representatives, so I spent my time sitting on the floor, and I listened and I observed some things, and I actually wrote a paper about this. I am going from memory now, but I recall in this paper I said there are, in my opinion, four flawed premises on which Democrats' policies are based, and I listed those four flawed premises. They were: The cold war is over. We no longer need a strong military. Punishment is not a deterrent to crime. Deficit spending is not bad public policy. And then the fourth one: that government can run our lives better than people can. Well, I kind of went through that.

I remember so well that one time there was an amendment on the floor—and I know those who were there at the time will recall this—that we were going to take some of these closed bases, because of the cost of incarceration for prisoners, and we were going to take those and take the fences and turn them around to keep people in instead of people out. Well, that made sense.

So I had an amendment on a bill, and it was a bill that I remember was a big punishment bill that became very controversial at that time. But I had that amendment to do that, and they defeated the amendment. The reason they defeated it was they said: We cannot expect our prison population to live in such substandard housing. Then I remembered, wait a minute. I was in the U.S. Army. I lived in that housing. I know a little bit about that. So that was kind of the punishment.

Then at the end of the Cold War—you know, so we do not need the military—a lot of them were saying: We need to cut back. And we did. We actually cut back, and Republicans and Democrats agreed at that time. But now it has changed because what we are doing now—I call it the Obama disarming of America. I can remember—and a lot of times when you talk about people as being liberals or conservatives, you are not name-calling, you are saying: What is the involvement of government? A liberal believes the government should have a greater involvement in our lives. Conservatives believe the government has too much control and, therefore, we do not need to do that.

Anyway, I went to Afghanistan when the first budget 4½ years ago came out.

I stood over there knowing I would get national attention, knowing this would be the first step in what I call the disarming of America by Obama. So I stood over there. I recall in that very first budget he did away with our only fifth-generation fighter, the F–22; he did away with our lift capacity, the C–17; he did away with our future combat system, which would have been the first advancement in ground capability in 50 years; and he did away with the ground-based interceptor in Poland. By the way, we are paying dearly for that now because we realize now, with Iran having the capability they have and our intelligence saying they are going to have a delivery system by 2015, we need to have something to defend that coast. Then we went through, and, of course, if you extend the budget of the President, it took $487 million out of the military.

So I just wanted to say that is true. This is after several years, way back when I was in the House of Representatives. Deficit spending, not bad public policy—that is something we have heard quite often from some of our more liberal friends on the other side.

But the fourth thing is that government can run our lives better than people can. Now, I tell my friend from Texas, this goes all of the way back to the late eighties; this observation was made by me. That is exactly what we are looking at today—a recognition by some people that somehow government can run this system better than people can.

So last night when I was honored to stand with my good friend from Texas—I recall having been here back during the Clinton administration. We had a thing called Hillary health care. That goes right along with the same thing. So a lot of the phone calls I got last night after being on the Floor with you were people saying: Well, I do not even remember that. I did not know we tried that before.

The big point here is that they thought it was over, it was done. They were going to have Hillary health care; as Senator Reid said, yes, a single-payer system. This is what they want. That is what they wanted back in the early and middle nineties. So we had Hillary health care. They thought it was over. They said: It is over; we are not going to win this. Consequently, you know, a lot of people actually believed that.

Last night I talked about after we finally had victory. It happened that there was a full-page ad in the Wall Street Journal by the AMA saying that we embrace Hillary health care because they thought they were going to lose it.

That is kind of where we are today. At that time they thought there was no way in the world we were going to win this. They were going to be able to defeat it because it was a done deal.

That is why I admire our good friend Senator Cruz for having the tenacity to stay in here and recognize that we went through this once before. If we did it once before, we can do it again.

The reason Hillary health care lost way back in the middle nineties was that people realized it as socialized medicine. Again, you ask the question. It does not work anywhere else. It does not work in Sweden, Great Britain. Why would it work here? And the answer? I know they will never say it, but what they are thinking is, well, if I were running it, it would work. It is kind of a mentality that government can run our lives better than people can.

So I want to say one thing before I ask my question; that is, I have had a great blessing in my life, which is getting to know a great American whose name is Rafael Cruz. Rafael Cruz came to this country the tough way. He recognized from his past experience what real freedom is.

I have some quotes here that I wrote down because I use these quite often. He said: "Our lives are under attack. ObamaCare is going to destroy the elderly by denying care, by even perhaps denying treatment to people who are in catastrophic circumstances." I hear people say all the time that this will never happen in America. It is happening in America. It is happening in America, and our rights are being eroded more and more every day.

In one of his speeches he gave not too long ago, he said:

> I think the most ominous words I've heard was in the last two State of the Union addresses, when our President said, "If Congress does not act, I will act unilaterally."

Scarily reminiscent of how things were done in Cuba. A law that no Republican voted for is now the law of the land; governing by decree, by Executive order, just like Cuba, the country he left behind.

This is Rafael Cruz, who happens to be the father of our own Senator TED CRUZ. He is one who came over. He escaped the very overbearing power of government to come here for that reason.

So I look at that, and I remember one of the greatest speeches—I have said this often. I know a lot of people do not agree with it. Probably the greatest speech I have heard in my life was "A Rendezvous With Destiny" by Ronald Reagan. In his speech, he tells the story of someone who could have been Rafael Cruz, someone who was escaping from Communist Castro Cuba to come to this country and risking his life.

In his speech "Rendezvous With Destiny," Ronald Reagan said—this is way back when he was the Governor of California. He said: The boat came up. It washed up on the shore in southern Florida. There was a woman there, and he was telling the woman about the atrocities in Communist Cuba.

When he was through, she said: Well, we do not know how fortunate we are in this country.

He said: No, we are the ones who are fortunate because we had a place to escape to.

Does that not tell the story? That was a government running everything. They escaped that and came to this country, risked their lives, and they are over here.

I know that my kids—Kay and I have 20 kids and grandkids. I was listening last night when the Senator was reading a bedtime story to his little kids. Ours are not little kids anymore, but my grandkids are. The Senator stopped and said: What kind of America, what kind of America are these kids going to be inheriting? Why is it popular now? Why would someone who believes government should have a larger role in our lives be reelected? What has happened to the American people and the values we held for so many years so close to us?

Well, that is a hard thing to answer. But I know there are several of them—people who have experienced that, leaving slavery to come to this country.

By the way, last night when I was reading the various things, I did not have any statements from the people from Oklahoma, so I was reading from LOUIE GOHMERT, who represents the eastern part of Texas. He had a lot of anecdotal stories from people in East Texas—just like Oklahoma. We are not that far apart. But since that time, someone called last night and they said: You should use stories from Oklahoma.

K. Matheson said:

Stand with Senator Ted Cruz. Defund ObamaCare. A single-payer health care system is nothing more than a socialized system.

She is from Bethany, OK. I do not want to give her last name. She did not want it given.

Sue said:

Thank you. What's to protect people from being victims of identity theft with all of these so-called advisors having access to people's financial and health care records? Why aren't members of Congress, the White House and their staffs included?

Well, they should be included. We have been talking about that. The Senator from Texas has been talking about that.

We had a tweet that came in this morning. It said:

What allows the executive branch to pick & choose who must follow ObamaCare & what parts to enforce?

So we have got a lot of that stuff. But the thing I wanted to bring up last night—one of the things—is that something really good is happening. We are talking about the bad things, but there is another opportunity. We have a great guy in Oklahoma by the name of Scott Pruitt. He is our attorney general. In fact, I tell my friend Senator CRUZ that while he was running for attorney general, I flew him around. Aviation is kind of my thing. I was flying him around the State. I got to know him quite well. He told me at that time that he saw this threat coming. So what he has done is he has filed a lawsuit.

I am proud to say that Oklahoma and the attorney general, through the courts, are leading the charge to dismantle ObamaCare and put an end to its onerous taxes. Just last month a judge overseeing the lawsuit ruled against a motion filed by the administration to dismiss the case, which means the case will proceed. Well, that was a major obstacle. No one thought he would be able to overcome this motion to dismiss. So it is still out there.

The law is a train wreck. We know that. There have been several proposals to prevent further damage. We need to defund the law. We need to make sure no additional taxpayer money would be used.

If he is successful, that will affect some 34 States that are in the same situation as Oklahoma. If he is successful, that is going to pull the funding out of ObamaCare, and it could be that just one guy in the State of Oklahoma will be responsible for that. So this is happening.

Yes, there are all of the efforts that are taking place here, primarily by my good friend from Texas, but we are in Oklahoma. We are involved in this too. We are hoping to be able to have that opportunity.

I want to mention one other thing because this came in. I am going to read this. It is a letter. It is not all that long, but I think it is really revealing. It says:

I cannot tell you how distressed I am with regard to the Affordable Health Care Act—

This came from Lynn in Oklahoma. This came in last night—

Obama-care. I am fearful for my kids, now 18 and 20. There is the effect it is having right now—employers are not allowing their workers to have full-time hours. They are hiring more part-time workers to make up the difference for the company so they won't be penalized for not providing health insurance. Both of my kids are unable to get full-time employment. For a year, my daughter was able to work 40-plus hours a week. Then, with the implementation of the ACA, no one can work over 29 hours a week. Instant pay cut. My son, who just graduated from high school, finally found a job at a restaurant, and they give him 4 hours a day. He is still looking.

Additionally, I have adult friends whose hours are being cut at UCO so they don't get penalized for not providing health insurance to their part-time people, adults with families getting their wages cut—

This is just a normal citizen out there. This is not a professional. This is what people are thinking, at least in my State of Oklahoma and I think throughout the Nation.

—adults with families getting their wages cut so the employer does not have to pay for health insurance. Did you not think employers would not find a way out of this at the expense of the American people? Is everyone in Washington so blind or is it selfish?

My husband's employer now wants to penalize us if I choose to stay on his health coverage rather than take the inferior health care package at my employment.

Mr. Inhofe, I dedicated my life to raising my kids and taking care of my family. I currently make $12.25 an hour. I have a bachelor's degree. It would be senseless for me to pay for health care on a salary when my husband's health care is so much better, and I have been on it for the last 13 years.

Thirteen years. She would have to give that up.

He takes care of me as my husband. I should not be penalized for wanting to work full time at this juncture of my life. If his company pushes the issue, I feel as if I will not be able to stay employed full time, which is a violation of my basic human rights. Now that my kids are grown, I need and want to work. At 52 it is highly unlikely that I am going to make a wage that is going to allow me to pay for health insurance. It is against my constitutional right to force me to purchase health insurance I do not need. The law is unconstitutional and un-American. Please tell me what we can do. The American people deserve to be able to work full time without being penalized.

I am tired of Washington and its dirty politics. Everyone in Washington should be held to the same laws it passes for the American people.

Amen.

Each one of you need to have the same health coverage expenses that we have.

I feel as if our country is headed, at lightening speed, for a major breakdown. What are you going to do to stop it and how can I help? I am frightened for the future of my children and the future of America. I am tired of DC politics.

That was Lynn from Oklahoma City. This came in last night. I have several others that just came in overnight.

But I think the thing that people did not realize and that we were able to talk about last night was the fact that this has happened once before, and they came dangerously close to pulling it off back in the middle nineties.

You know, I have to say this. There is a brilliant strategy going on right now. I didn't realize it until yesterday. There are some pro-ObamaCare people who are doing robocalls. I know the occupier of the chair knows what robocalls are, but a lot of people do not. These are automated calls where they call and a voice comes on and it gives a message. People listen to that. Sometimes they believe it, sometimes they do not. Most of the times they do.

So there are robocalls that are going on by the pro-Obama health care people, going to the strongest opponents of ObamaCare and trying to make people think they are supporting it. It is to confuse the electorate. When you stop to think about it, that is pretty brilliant, and they did it.

All day yesterday there were calls going around my State of Oklahoma by someone. The message was something like this: This is Joe Smith. I am with the ABC tea party—these are not tea party people, but nonetheless that is how they identify themselves—your Senator JIM INHOFE is supporting ObamaCare and you have to call his office. This is what his number is.

We started getting calls and people didn't even know there were 14 of us who joined together with Senator CRUZ about 6 weeks ago. I was 1 of the 14 and one of the strongest supporters of his cause. Yet they were trying to make people believe something else just to confuse them. Frankly, it is dishonest, but it is brilliant.

When we are looking and we are seeing what happened, what is going on today, I do applaud my friend. I feel guilty, I have to say to my friend, Senator Cruz, because I left him last night at 10 o'clock.

I went home, had dinner, and went to bed. I got up and he was still talking. That is the depth of his feeling about this. I believe what we learned, a lesson we can remember back in the middle of the 1990s, the lesson we learned there, when it was all over, we had lost, but we didn't lose because the American people came to our aid. We were a minority at the time, but they came to our aid and we turned this whole thing around. That is exactly where we are today.

My question to my good friend, Senator Cruz, is I believe that history could repeat itself. Does the Senator?

Mr. CRUZ. I thank the Senator from Oklahoma for his learned insight for that very good question. The answer, in short, is yes. Yes, yes, absolutely, I think to use the same phrasing majority leader HARRY Reid used when asked if he supported single-payer government socialized health care.

I wish to make three comments in response to Senator INHOFE's question and his thoughts that he has shared with this body. First is simply a word of thanks to the Senator from Oklahoma. Senator INHOFE is an elder statesman of this body. He has served many years. He has earned the respect of his colleagues on the Republican side of the aisle and on the Democratic side of the aisle.

From day one, when Senator MIKE LEE began this fight, Senator INHOFE has been with us on saying ObamaCare is such a train wreck, such a nightmare, such a disaster that we should defund it.

I observed earlier, it is one thing for the young Turks, the so-called wacko birds, to stand in this spot. It is another thing altogether to see elder statesmen, Senator INHOFE, Senator PAT ROBERTS, Senator JEFF SESSIONS, and Senator MIKE ENZI, standing with us.

That is significant, particularly when the leadership of our party is publicly urging Republicans to go the other way. I am grateful for the friendship. I am grateful for your steadfastness. I am grateful for the principled and courageous willingness of the Senator from Oklahoma to fight for the American people.

I will say it makes a real difference. If you trust what is written in the media, this battle is doomed. Indeed, I recall reading a day or two ago an article that purported to be an objective news story—not an editorial—by a reporter allegedly reporting on the news that began with something like: The fight to defund ObamaCare, which is doomed to fail.

That was reported as a fact. There was no editorializing, apparently. That is just an objective fact that it is doomed to fail.

I would say the momentum has been steadily with us. They said this fight was doomed to fail 2 months ago. We saw the American people unite, over 1.6 million Americans, signed a national petition saying defund ObamaCare now because it is a train wreck, it is a disaster, and it is hurting Americans.

They said it was doomed to fail, the House of Representatives would never pass a continuing resolution conditioned on defunding ObamaCare. It wouldn't happen.

Then last Friday the House of Representatives did exactly that because courageous House conservatives stuck their neck out and because House leadership, in an action for which I commend them, listened to the American people.

This week the press says it is doomed to fail that Republicans be united. Yet I would note seeing elder statesman after elder statesman come down and support us, it indicates the momentum that is with this movement. Listen, this is not a movement by any 1, 2, 3 or 100 Senators. This is a movement from the American people.

Why are we seeing momentum move in favor of defunding ObamaCare? Why are we seeing momentum for Republicans in favor of voting against cloture so as to deny HARRY REID the ability to fund ObamaCare on a 51-partisan vote? Because the American people are rising up and their voices are being heard. That is the first point I wished to make in response to the Senator from Oklahoma.

Mr. INHOFE. Before the Senator continues, would he yield for one followup question.

Mr. CRUZ. I yield to the Senator for a question but not the floor.

Mr. INHOFE. It was interesting. I don't think I have ever been referred to as the senior statesman, but I kind of like that. I wondered, when the Senator mentioned the four of us coming down—he put us in that category. We have been here for a while. There is one thing we all four had in common. We all had a career in the real world first.

One of the problems we have that I have observed, I say: What do you want to do?

The reply is: Oh, I want to be a Member of Congress.

So they leave the fraternity house and they move to Congress. They have never been in the real world.

People ask me the question: what should I do if I want to get into politics. I say go out for at least 15 years, live under this system, and learn how tough things are. In my case I spent over 20 years, did a lot of building and developing in the State of Texas where Senator CRUZ is from. I have talked to his father, Raphael, several times about this.

I remember there I was doing things that Americans are supposed to do. I was making money, losing money, expanding the tax base.

Yet the obstacle I had all during those years was the Federal Government, and I was doing what Americans are supposed to be doing. I remember that is when I decided.

The last thing I did down in Texas, a pretty good-sized development, and I had to go to 25 governmental agencies to get a dock permit. I thought, wait a minute, they are supposed to be on our side. I decided I would run to come to Congress and try to save the free enterprise system.

That is what all four of us have in common. We may have been here for a while, but we are here with a cause and here with experience.

How abusive government can be. I have not seen a time when the abuse is greater than it is today on what is happening to us, to think that we have a policy by the President, as he has been able to sell the idea, get the votes, get it through, and it is socializing medicine. It is something that has failed year after year after year in every country where they have tried to do it.

Does my friend from Texas see anything different about the United States of America, how socialized medicine would work here when it hasn't worked anywhere else?

Mr. CRUZ. I think the Senator from Oklahoma raises a very good question. The clear facts are everywhere in the world socialized medicine has been implemented, it hasn't worked. It produces results consistently. We can predict where socialized medicine leads. It leads to scarcity. It leads to waiting periods. It leads to poor quality health care. It leads to government rationing. It leads to government bureaucrats deciding what health care you can get and what health care I can get.

If you go in for a health treatment, a government bureaucrat may say, Mr. INHOFE, you can get that treatment in 6 months or maybe a year. On the other hand, perhaps your mom goes in for a treatment and the government bureaucrat may say: Ma'am, I am afraid you don't get that treatment. We have determined on our schedule we are not allowing it.

That is what happens with socialized medicine. If you want not to be able to pick your doctor, if you want a government bureaucrat making health care decisions for you instead of you and your doctor, then you should welcome what Majority Leader REID says is the inevitable result of ObamaCare. That is single-payer government socialized medicine. That is where this law is headed.

Mr. INHOFE. Would the Senator yield one last time for a question?

Mr. CRUZ. I yield to the Senator for a question without yielding the floor.

Mr. INHOFE. I hope my wife will forgive me, because I know she is watching, or I suspect she is watching because she has an equal interest in this issue for a totally different reason.

Kay and I have been married—our 54th wedding anniversary is coming up. We have 20 kids and grandkids.

She went through an experience, and our whole family went through the experience with her a short while ago, less than 1 year ago. She discovered she had a serious heart problem with the aortic valve. I have to praise her for not telling me anything about it for 4 months. She knew she was going to have to have this very serious operation. She is only 1 year younger than I am. She knew she was going to have the operation and she didn't want to say anything because she didn't want to worry me. She was writing things out about what things would go to what kids because she didn't think she was going to make it. She thought there was a good chance she wouldn't. We went through that experience with her.

I will tell you what is funny. All our grandkids call us—my name is Inhofe, so "I" is for Inhofe so they called us Mom I and Pop I. That is how they have referred to us. Since she had a valve put in her heart that was from a cow, instead of calling her Mom I, they call her Moom I. She went through this very difficult procedure with the best medical care in St. John's Medical Center in Tulsa, Dr. Robert Garrett, all the nurses, all the people all the way down.

I was thinking, that is my first experience at my age, my senior age, of seeing this system work.

Where would she have been in Canada? I have talked to people and they said: No. At her age she would have waited in such a long line that she probably would not have been able to make it.

It is serious things she is going through. I don't think I am the only one who has had this experience, but that was a wakeup call. I would hope and suggest to the Senator that other people speak up, even though it is somewhat uncomfortable. I thank God we had the system that allowed Kay and me to be able to look forward to our next 54 years of marriage.

Mr. CRUZ. I thank the Senator from Oklahoma for that excellent question, and I will make several points in response; first, is hearing that story of your wife and her courage. It reminds me, I will confess, I knew there were many reasons why the Senator and I had become friends, why I like and admire the Senator. I discovered yet another. It sounds as if the Senator and I married very similar women.

If it is anything like our marriage, at least in my marriage, I married way, way, way above myself.

I will tell you a story that your story reminded me of, which is my wife Heidi was taking a car to the airport. The car was hit. It was hit by another car, T-boned. The driver was very upset. Heidi called 911, and an ambulance came and took the driver to the hospital. Heidi proceeded to call a cab and take the cab to the airport, got on a plane and flew to a business meeting she had in New Mexico.

At the end of the meeting she noticed: Gosh, I am kind of hurting. My head hurts and my shoulder hurts. She went to the hospital that afternoon in New Mexico and discovered she had both a concussion and a broken collarbone.

Much like Senator INHOFE relayed, Heidi did not share this news with her husband until that evening. She didn't call me when the accident occurred. She didn't call me even when she got the diagnosis. She called me and was describing her injuries to me. She said: Sweetheart, I wanted to let you know I had a car accident. I am all right, but I do have a broken collarbone. I have a concussion.

Oh, my goodness. It is very disconcerting when your wife tells you that. She was describing where it happened. As she described the street in Houston, I am thinking: Wait, if it happened in Houston, what are you doing in New Mexico if you were in a car wreck in Houston?

She said: I got on a plane and flew, without going to the doctor, with a broken collarbone and concussion and went to the business meeting, completed the business meeting, before bothering to get treated.

Let me say to anyone watching this, I do not commend my wonderful, love of my life, wife's conduct to anyone who has had an accident. I would suggest getting medical treatment immediately. I would strongly suggest not following the path of the wife of the Senator from Oklahoma and my wife and not telling your husband.

I would strongly encourage, call your spouse and let them know. I certainly urge, should that happen again to my wife: Sweetheart, please let me know when it happens and not 12, 14 hours later.

But it is the virtue of marrying strong women who know what they want and are able to tackle the world. I, for one, am blessed and I have no doubt that you feel deeply blessed with 20 kids and grandkids. You know, the psalmist talks about my cup runneth over, bountiful blessings, and 20 kids and grandkids certainly qualifies as that.

Indeed, an additional point I wanted to make is I wanted to thank the Senator from Oklahoma for his very kind comments about my father. As the Senator knows, my father has been my hero my whole life. I have admired him for as long as I can remember.

I also want to note something particularly meaningful the Senator from Oklahoma did. Every week in the Senate there is a prayer breakfast. It is a bipartisan prayer breakfast, which is nice. There are not a lot of bipartisan things we do here in the Senate. There are a number of

Senators who attend regularly, Republicans and Democrats, and they invite a different Senator each week to share his or her testimony, share some thoughts. Some weeks ago I was invited to do so, and I felt honored to have the opportunity. I had attended the prayer breakfast a number of times.

The way it typically works is another Senator is asked to introduce whoever is speaking that day. So at this particular prayer breakfast Senator INHOFE was asked to introduce me. It is really quite interesting to me. Almost anyone, when asked to introduce someone, would do so fairly easily. Maybe they would print out a bio to pick a little biographical fact or two. Most treat introductions as fairly routine efforts, but Senator INHOFE didn't treat it that way. He picked up the phone and he called my dad. He picked up the phone and he called my college roommate. He picked up the phone and called one of my dearest friends here in Washington, for whom Heidi and I are the Godparents of their kids.

The Senator made these calls totally out of the blue and said: Hi, this is JIM INHOFE. I have been asked to introduce Ted and I was wondering if you could share any particular stories, and they shared a few mildly embarrassing stories. Actually, I give them all credit for finding exactly the right balance of stories that were just embarrassing enough but not quite so scandalous that the blood drains from your face when they are told. I would say that showed a personal level of consideration that is unusual in this town and I appreciated that.

I thanked the Senator then, but I wanted to take this opportunity to thank the Senator publicly for putting that degree of personal consideration in trying to tell not just that I went to so-and-so college and did this and this—not just the empty biographical facts—but in trying to put a little color on who this individual is.

The final point I will make is a point that goes to the substance of some of the remarks the Senator from Oklahoma made in the process of asking his first question, which is he talked about the battle of HillaryCare. I think it is quite fitting to the battle we are having right now over defunding ObamaCare. When the battle over HillaryCare was occurring—I remember it well—I was in law school. I wasn't serving in the Senate. If you remember the context at that time, when HillaryCare was playing out, all of the media said this is unstoppable. All of the media said this is going to happen and there is nothing the hapless Republicans can do to stop it. Indeed, there were a number of Republicans who came forth and said: We can't stop this, so we propose, what I derisively referred to at the time as—perhaps due to being a law student—HillaryCare light.

I remember watching that. During the course of that debate, I almost put my boot through the television set. I remember yelling at the TV set a sentiment that perhaps maybe more than a few people watching us feel, where you feel you don't have a voice in the process. Certainly, as a law student I didn't have a voice in the process. But I remember yelling at the TV set: What on Earth do we believe? What are we doing? If we are going to accede to marching down the road to socialized health care, what the heck are we doing? I remember saying: All right. To heck with all of this. I am going to move to an island and fish all my life. Heck, I'm Cuban. I like to fish. That would be a great life.

And Senator INHOFE will remember, because he was part of this effort. At the time I was particularly focused on the Senator from my State of Texas, Senator Phil Gramm. Senator Gramm had been a hero of mine for a long time. Indeed, I am particularly honored that the desk at which I sit used to be Senator Phil Gramm's desk. His name is written on the side drawer.

This is one of the curious traditions of the Senate; that Senators, when they leave the Senate, scrawl their signatures on the drawer of the desk. You are actually encouraged to deface government property, and with some frequency. I hope the next individual fortunate to have this desk appreciates it. I find it an inspiration to sit at the desk that was Senator Phil Gramm's.

But I remember at the time, when it seemed the whole stampede in the Republican conference back then was listening to the media, which was saying: You can't win. You must accede to this. Hillary-Care is unstoppable. I remember Phil Gramm walking out to a microphone and saying, in his inimitable drawl: This will pass over my cold, dead political body.

I have to tell you, when Phil Gramm said that, it was fairly lonely. He didn't have a whole lot of allies when he marched out and did that. Senator INHOFE knows, because he was part of that fight and he bears the scars from that fight. But because of that leadership and standing and fighting—it was very interesting that it ended up where we saw Republicans looking all around, and Gramm was standing there and he didn't get killed. They all essentially ran behind him saying: Yeah, yeah, what he said. But I am convinced if we hadn't had a handful of leaders back then who had the courage to not read the papers and believe all those who were saying: Oh, we have to concede, the papers say they have already won, we are going to HillaryCare, if we hadn't had a handful of leaders willing to buck the conventional wisdom and saying we can win, when they are being told no you can't, ObamaCare would have passed 19 years earlier and it would have been called HillaryCare instead. That is the power of leadership.

So everyone in this body who said 2 months ago and who are saying this morning that we can't win this fight, I point out that history is replete with example after example after example of those who stood up and listened to the American people and fought for the principles, for the values the American people share, fought for the interests of the American people, and who, with the support of the American people, won those fights.

That is what we are fighting for. Listen, it is my hope that by the end of this process we will see all 46 Republicans unite in opposing cloture and saying: No, we are not going to allow HARRY REID and a bare majority of Democrats on a partisan political vote to fund ObamaCare. It is my hope over time, once that happens, we start to get one Democrat after another, after another to come with us.

Now, will that happen now? Probably not. As long as Republicans are publicly divided, no Democrat is going to join us. But if we unite as Republicans, and if particularly those Democrats running for reelection in red States where their citizens passionately oppose ObamaCare and the damage it is doing to the economy, and the damage it is doing to jobs, and the damage it is doing to all of the people who are being hurt—if they hear from more and more and more of their citizens, 5,000, 10,000, 20,000, 50,000—that starts to change the count.

People have asked over and over: What is the end game? How can you possibly win? I can't win. There is no way I can win, nor can any elected official win. The only way we can win is with the American people. That is it. When people ask: What is your end game, it is very simple. I have faith in the American people. And ultimately I have faith, or at least hope, in the 100 Members of the Senate.

I share the frustrations of Americans across this country that politicians on both sides of the aisle don't listen to people, that instead the political establishment in Washington protects itself, maintains its power, entrenches its power and does things like exempt itself from ObamaCare while letting the American people suffer under this train wreck of a disaster—this nightmare. But I also know at the end of the day, if enough people speak up, that every Member of this body at some point is compelled to listen to the constituents he or she represents. It is why I am so encouraged by the outpouring we have seen over the last 19½ hours, with all of the people engaged, all of the people tweeting the hashtag "MakeDCListen."

The citizen activists are transforming this debate. Listen, all of Washington wants to tell you, the citizen, it can't be done. You cannot win. Your view will not be listened to. The disaster, the train wreck, the nightmare—and I have used the word nightmare over and over. Let me be clear, for those who are just tuning in, where nightmare comes from. Nightmare is not my term. Nightmare is the language that James Hoffa, president of the Teamsters, used to describe ObamaCare because it is hurting millions of Americans. So at some point I believe, I hope, Republicans will unite and that Democratic Senators will start listening to their people.

It is striking if we listen to the letter from Mr. Hoffa. With permission I want to share that letter again, because I think it is powerful, it is potent. It is something, frankly, I think every Democrat in this body who is supporting ObamaCare, who is opposing defunding ObamaCare, who is going to vote with the majority leader, should be asked about by reporters. I think the President should be asked about this letter.

Let me just read it. These are not my words, these are the words of the president of the Teamsters.

Dear Leader Reid and Leader Pelosi: When you and the President sought our support for the Affordable Care Act (the ACA), you pledged that if we liked the health plans we have now, we could keep them. Sadly, that promise is under threat. Right now, unless you and the Obama administration enact an equitable fix, the ACA will shatter not only our hard-earned health benefits, but destroy the foundation of the 40-hour work week that is the backbone of the American middle class.

Now, that is not a Republican saying that. That is not a politician saying that. That is the head of the Teamsters, who supported ObamaCare. The letter continues:

Like millions of other Americans, our members are front-line workers in the American economy. We have been strong supporters of the notion that all Americans should have access to quality affordable health care. We have also been strong supporters of you.

I remind you, this letter is addressed to Senate majority leader HARRY REID and House minority leader NANCY PELOSI.

In campaign after campaign we have put boots on the ground, gone door-to-door to get out the vote, run phone banks and raised money to secure this vision.

So it is worth emphasizing the Teamsters are not fair-weather friends. They have been active, aggressive, full-throated members of the Democratic coalition and played a significant part in helping to elect this Democratic majority in the Senate and helping elect this President.

Now this vision has come back to haunt us.

What vision is that? The vision of electing Democrats as a majority in the Senate, electing the President. Why? Because ObamaCare is the law of the land and they are discovering it isn't working. What does Mr. Hoffa say next?

> Since the ACA was enacted, we have been bringing our deep concerns to the Administration, seeking reasonable regulatory interpretations to the statute that would help prevent the destruction of non-profit health plans. As you both know first- hand, our persuasive arguments have been disregarded and met with a stone wall by the White House and the pertinent agencies.

Now, let me stop at this point and make a comment. For all of you at home who are not leaders of powerful unions and who have been major supporters of the President of the United States, major supporters of the Democratic majority in the Senate, my guess is you may not have the same access to the west wing, to the Oval Office, to the office of the majority leader of the Senate as James Hoffa, head of the teamsters does. Yet James Hoffa, head of the teamsters says in writing that he was met with a stone wall by the White House and pertinent agencies.

Listen, if a major union—that in its own words had boots on the ground, went door-to-door to get out the vote, ran phone banks and raised money to secure a democratic vision—was met with a stone wall, what do you think we the citizens will be met with? Do you think this administration listens to a single mom working at a diner who is saying ObamaCare is slamming her and making her life harder? Do you think this administration listens to you even if the politically powerful are lamenting what is happening with them?

Mr. Hoffa continues:

This is especially stinging because other stakeholders have repeatedly received successful interpretations for their respective grievances. Most disconcerting of course is last week's huge accommodation for the employer community—extending the statutorily mandated "December 31, 2013" deadline for the employer mandate and penalties.

Notably, two things are included there. One, Mr. Hoffa on behalf of the Teamsters said that deadline for the employer mandate is statutorily mandated; that the law requires it. What he is saying there is that the President is ignoring the law because it is statutorily mandated. No. 2, it is a gift for big business that is not being given to others.

Mr. Hoffa continues:

Time is running out: Congress wrote this law; we voted for you. We have a problem; you need to fix it. The unintended consequences of the ACA are severe. Perverse incentives are already creating nightmare scenarios:

First, the law creates an incentive for employers to keep employees' work hours below 30 hours a week. Numerous employers have begun to cut workers' hours to avoid this obligation, and many of them are doing so openly. The impact is two-fold: Fewer hours means less pay while also losing our current health benefits.

This is the president of the Teamsters saying ObamaCare is causing workers to have their hours forcibly reduced. That means less pay, and they are losing their current health insurance. Anytime the majority leader of the Senate goes on television and says that ObamaCare is working terrifically, this letter stands in stark contrast to that assertion.

Second, millions of Americans are covered by non-profit health insurance plans like the one in which most of our Members participate. Those non-profit plans are governed jointly by unions and companies under the Taft-Hartley Act. Our health plans have been built over decades by working men and women. Under the ACA as interpreted by the administration, our employees will be treated differently and not eligible for subsidies afforded other citizens. As such, many employees will be relegated to second-class status and shut out of the help the law offers to for-profit insurance plans.

And finally, even though non-profit plans like ours won't receive the same subsidies as for-profit plans, they'll be taxed to pay for those subsidies. Taken together, these restrictions will make non-profit plans like ours unsustainable, and will undermine the health-care market of viable alternatives to the big health insurance companies.

This next paragraph is critical:

On behalf of the millions of working men and women we represent—

Let me note, that is not hundreds, that is not thousands, that is millions of working men and women we represent:

—and the families they support—

So millions more

—we can no longer stand silent in the face of elements of the Affordable Care Act that will destroy—(not weaken, not undermine, not slightly impair but destroy)—the very health and wellbeing of our members along with millions of other hard-working Americans.

We believe that there are commonsense corrections that can be made within the existing statute that will allow our members to keep their current health plans and benefits just as you and the President pledged. Unless changes are made, however, that promise is hollow.

We continue to stand behind real health care reform, but the law as it stands will hurt millions of Americans including members of our respective unions.

We are looking to you to make sure these changes are made.

James P. Hoffa, General President, International Brotherhood of Teamsters.

When you have the Teamsters coming out and saying this is hurting millions of working men and women and their families, it begs the question: If Mr. Hoffa can no longer remain silent, if the Teamsters can no longer remain silent, how long can the Democratic Members of the Senate remain silent?

I have no doubt Mr. Hoffa and the Teamsters received harsh criticism for this letter, because politically this letter was inconvenient for the party they have supported with time, blood, and treasure. Yet Mr. Hoffa said: We can no longer remain silent because of the devastation being inflicted on the working men and women of America.

If that is true, I am hopeful that among the 54 Democrats in this body we will see first one and then maybe two and then maybe three and then maybe a dozen Democrats with the same courage that James Hoffa shows, the courage to say, Listen, I am willing to make a statement that is contrary to the political leadership of the party I belong to and have fought for.

To any Democrats who are contemplating doing so, let me note that bucking your party's leadership inevitably provokes a reaction, inevitably provokes expressions—and often strong expressions—of displeasure. But let me also encourage any Democrats, there are worse things in life than a few harsh words being tossed your way. To be honest, that pales compared to the suffering of the working men and women of this country who are losing their jobs, who are losing their health care, who are being forced into parttime work. Any politician who whines "Someone has said something mean about me" has totally lost perspective compared to the hurt the American people are feeling. So I am hopeful.

I want to appeal to the better angels of our Democratic Senators that they show the same courage Mr. Hoffa showed to be willing to buck party leadership and speak out for the men and women who are your constituents.

I make that same plea to the Republicans, that you show the courage to buck party leadership and stand up to the men and women who are your constituents who are suffering under ObamaCare. Any Republican who votes for cloture, who votes to give HARRY REID the ability to fund ObamaCare on a 51-vote partisan vote is directly participating in and responsible for funding ObamaCare.

If a Republican wants to say openly, I don't think we can defund ObamaCare; I don't agree with this fight, so I am siding with HARRY REID because on principle I think it is right, I don't agree with that, but I respect that view. You are entitled to that view. You are entitled to articulate that view. But I will tell you this, I don't think you are entitled to vote with HARRY REID and the Democrats, give HARRY REID and the Democrats the ability to fund ObamaCare, and then go to your constituents and say, I agree with defunding ObamaCare. You don't get it both ways.

If we are going to listen to the people, we need to be honest with the people and tell them what we are doing. That is what this fight is about, whether Democratic Senators and Republican Senators will listen to the people. We need to make DC listen.

Mr. VITTER. Will the Senator yield for questions and comments without yielding the floor?

Mr. CRUZ. I am happy to yield to my friend from Louisiana for a question without yielding the floor.

Mr. VITTER. I appreciate the Senator's comments, and certainly his correct recitation about what the real impact of ObamaCare is across the country, particularly for hard-working men and women. And the Senator is right. These descriptive phrases such as "nightmare" and another one is "train wreck," are not his words, they are not my words. They are actually words from supporters of the law.

"Nightmare," as the Senator pointed out, comes from the leader of the Teamsters, a very powerful organization on the Democratic side politically that strongly supported the law.

The chairman of the Senate Finance Committee that helped write the law called ObamaCare implementation "train wreck" a few months ago. Not coincidentally, that was right before he announced he wasn't running for reelection.

I appreciate the notation of those descriptions from folks on the Democratic side of the aisle, from folks who helped pass ObamaCare. This is clear proof that this is not ready for prime time, causing real pain and dislocation to hard-working Americans: job loss, folks being moved into part-time work, jobs not being created, folks losing the health care they have now which they enjoy.

But did the Senator know, I think the leader of the Teamsters, James Hoffa, is even more upset today than he was when he wrote that letter because in the intervening time something else has happened, which is that the administration bailed out Congress with a special exemption, with a special subsidy, with a special rule, hasn't helped the working-class Americans Mr. Hoffa represents through the Teamsters, but has bailed out Congress?

That is what I have an amendment on the CR about. It would be a germane amendment. I will present it. Unfortunately, it seems clear that the plan is for the majority leader to block out all amendments, including mine, except the ones he chooses that would take out the defunding language from the House-passed bill.

Again, what I am talking about is a special bailout exemption subsidy for Congress. This goes back to the original ObamaCare debate, and our distinguished colleague Senator GRASSLEY of Iowa proposed language which so many of us strongly supported that said every Member of Congress and all congressional staff would have to go to the same fallback plan under ObamaCare as there is for all Americans. First it was called the public option, then eventually the exchange.

Amazingly, happily—I was pleasantly surprised at the time, that language got in the bill and was passed into law. That became a classic case of what NANCY PELOSI said: We have to pass the bill to figure out what is in it. Because after that language got in the bill and passed into law, then lots of folks around Capitol Hill read that provision and they said, Oh, you know what, they said, Wait a minute. We can't live with this. We can't deal with this, because we are going to be in the same fallback plan as there is for every other American with no special treatment. We can't deal with that.

Then, because of that, furious lobbying started on the Obama administration, folks such as the distinguished majority leader talking directly to President Obama himself, saying, We need a bailout. We need a special fix, a special rule just for us.

Sure enough, that lobbying yielded results. By many press reports, President Obama got personally involved to ensure that a special rule was issued by his administration. The draft version of it was issued conveniently just after Congress left town for the August recess and got away from the scene of the crime. That draft rule is completely improper, completely illegal, because it goes beyond the statute and is inconsistent with the statute, but it is a special exemption for Congress. It essentially does two things:

First, even though the ObamaCare statute explicitly says that every Member of Congress, all congressional official staff have to go to the exchange, the rule basically negates that in a way and says, Well, we don't know what "official staff" means, so we are going to leave it up to each individual Member to decide which of their staff is official and which is not, who has to go to the exchange and who doesn't.

The statute doesn't say that. The statute is very clear: All congressional official staff have to go to the exchange. There is no discretion to individual Members.

Then the second thing that this special rule, this special exemption does is even more egregious. It says, Oh, and by the way, whoever does go to the exchange, whatever Members and whatever congressional staff do go to the exchange, they get a huge taxpayer-funded subsidy that follows them there. That is not in the statute. That is nowhere in ObamaCare. That is nowhere in that Grassley provision as passed into law. In fact, there are other sections of ObamaCare that make it crystal clear that employees who go to the exchange lose their previous subsidy from their large employer that they may have enjoyed previously. That is clear in the law, completely inconsistent with this illegal rule made up out of thin air.

So Washington is getting a special exemption, a special bailout, a special subsidy completely unavailable to other Americans. That is not right, and that is why I have an amendment. I tried to present it last week, was blocked out by the majority leader. I am here again on the CR. It is important, it is necessary we vote, and we should, before October 1, when this illegal rule will otherwise go into effect.

My amendment is simple. It negates that illegal rule. It says, Yes, every Member of Congress, all congressional staff. And, oh, by the way, other Washington policymakers—the President, the Vice President, all of their political appointees—have to go to the exchange with no special treatment, no special exemption, no special subsidy unavailable to other Americans. So if you are a lower paid staff member and you qualify by your income for a subsidy available to every other American who goes to the exchange at that income level, fine. That is certainly available. That is equal treatment. That is Washington being treated like the rest of America, but no special exemption or bailout or subsidy, only those available to all other Americans going to the exchange.

We need a vote on this provision. It is directly relevant to the CR. It is directly relevant to this debate.

This illegal Obama administration rule will go into effect October 1 unless we act. That is why I demanded a timely vote last week. Unfortunately, it was blocked out by the majority leader. After threatening and bullying did not work, he claimed he had no objection to the vote. But still he did not let it happen.

Here we are in the CR debate and that is why we need that debate and that vote now. What the problem is, and it is clearly the plan of the majority leader, it is clear this upcoming cloture vote would block all that out again. The majority leader would get his select amendments to take out of the House bill the provision that defunds ObamaCare but nobody else would get any other amendment. I would not get a vote on my amendment. There are plenty of other relevant and germane amendments. We would not have votes on those. That is the plan being laid out for this week and that is what voting yes on cloture on the bill will enable. So I cannot do that.

I commend the Senator from Texas for helping lead this fight, helping point out the dangers and the tragedies of ObamaCare, particularly for working men and women and also for supporting the broader effort to make sure, however America is treated, Washington should be treated exactly the same. That should be the first rule of democracy.

The Founders talked about that basic principle, Federalist Paper No. 57 by Madison. He specifically talks about this basic principle: Whatever is good for America needs to be good for Washington. Whatever is applied to those who are ruled needs to be applied equally in full force and in the same way to those who make up the rules. That is what this specific part of this debate is all about.

I again thank the Senator from Texas for his leadership on this and the general issue. I ask, does he think, now that that special exemption has come out since the Hoffa letter, would he guess Mr. Hoffa is more or less upset now that Washington has been protected but the working Americans Mr. Hoffa represents are still in the dire straits described in that letter?

Mr. CRUZ. I thank the Senator from Louisiana for that very good question. I thank him also for his support of this effort, his vocal support, his support from day one. I thank him for appearing with us last night, appearing with us today, standing together to defund ObamaCare, standing together to oppose cloture because it would empower HARRY REID and the Democrats to fund ObamaCare with a partisan 51-vote, party-line vote. It would shut out amendments to address and ameliorate the harms that are coming from ObamaCare that are hurting hardworking Americans.

As to the question the Senator from Louisiana asked, I certainly do not want to put words in Mr. Hoffa's mouth. He is quite capable of speaking for himself. But I cannot imagine, given the language of his letter, that the exemption for Congress would be in any way different from the exemption for big business. They are both exemptions for political friends of the administration. According to the language of his letter, he expressed dismay that they and other political friends of the administration did not get an exemption.

I will note part of that letter is asking: Give us a special exemption too. But that did not happen. But I will make a prediction. If the Senate doesn't act now, doesn't defund ObamaCare, if it doesn't stand and stop this, before President Obama leaves the White House he will grant an exemption to those union bosses. It is the trifecta of the privileged classes being excepted. I understand politically it was an inopportune time to grant that now. It would be lawless, it would be contrary to law to grant an exemption to the union bosses but it is also contrary to law to grant an exemption to big business and Members of Congress and that hasn't slowed the President down. If he is willing to disregard the law for them, there is no reason to think he would not be willing to disregard the law for his union boss friends except for the fact right in the middle of the defund debate it is not rocket science that that would not be ideal politics.

The courage of the Senator from Louisiana in introducing his amendment—he has endured vilification that has been beyond the pale and I appreciate his courage standing for the basic principle that Congress should be bound by the same rules as everyone else. The American people, millions of Americans, should not be put onto exchanges subject to pain that Members of Congress are not. We should not operate under the principle one rule for thee, a different one for me.

For all of you who say this fight is not winnable, I would like to share a letter talking about fighting and winning unwinnable fights, because none of us can win this fight but the American people can.

Fans of Rush Limbaugh know that every year he reads something that his father wrote about the true story of the price paid by the signers of the Declaration of Independence. I think it is fitting to read this morning. It is called "The Americans Who Risked Every- thing." [At this point, Senator Cruz reads Rush Limbaugh's father's work, "The Americans Who Risked Everything." The entire text can be found at http://www.freerepublic.com/focus/f-news/2040698/posts.]

That is the story of the Signers of the Declaration of Independence. It is the story of our shared legacy.

I will make this note to my friends on the Republican side of the aisle and the Democratic side of the aisle, as Benjamin Franklin wryly noted: Indeed, we must all hang together, otherwise we should most assuredly hang separately.

That is the message all of us should think about. Are we going to hang separately because we disregarded the will and the view of our constituents and have given in to the Washington establishment or are we going to stand together and say: Let's break the broken pattern of Washington, of empty showboats, of fixed procedures, and ignoring the will of the people? Instead, let's come together—much like James Hoffa, president of the Teamsters, has—and say: We will remain silent no longer. We cannot ignore the suffering of the millions of Americans who have lost their jobs, cannot find jobs, have had their hours forcibly reduced to 29 hours a week, facing skyrocketing health insurance premiums, and are losing or are at risk of losing their health insurance. Our constituents, the American people, are hurting and suffering, and it is the role of Congress to answer their call. All of us must listen to the people. Together we must make DC listen.

Mr. RUBIO. Would the Senator from Texas yield for a question and a comment without yielding the floor?

Mr. CRUZ. I am happy to yield to my friend from Florida for a question without yielding the floor.

Mr. RUBIO. First of all, that is a very inspirational letter that the Senator read, and it reminds us of our shared legacy as a nation. It also makes me appreciate the freedoms we have in this country, and the opportunity to stand here today and have this vibrant debate. I am reminded that around the world people don't have this opportunity. I am reminded that around the world people are still losing not just their freedom but their lives for the purposes of speaking out.

I will confess that I hope we can avoid the hanging part of the situation the Senator have outlined, and I am sure we will because we are so blessed to live in this Republic.

I do something every week where I take letters from my constituents, read them in a video on the air, and then I answer them. I call it the constituent mailbox. I have been doing that since I have gotten here. It is important because it allows us to answer the real questions of real people, and their comments.

They are not always nice letters, by the way, but we address those too because that is important. One of the benefits we have with the advances in technology is that the people we serve and work for can now reach us directly and speak to us in real time as opposed to the days gone by where people had trouble accessing their elected officials.

So, with Senator CRUZ's indulgence—as you have given me time but have not yielded the floor—I would like to read a few e-mails I have received.

The first e-mail is from someone named Luis. He lives in Cutler Bay, FL, which is south Florida down where I live in Miami-Dade County.

Here is what he writes:

There are so many companies with a large number of part time workers. The latest company Trader Joes in which I have a family member will lose her part time health benefits because of ObamaCare. She works as a substitute English teacher in New Jersey and the job does not offer any health benefits to part time substitute teachers. She has to be a full time teacher in order to receive health benefits. She decided not to leave her job at Trader Joes because they offered her health benefits as a part time worker. Put yourselves as present grandparents and parents in her own situation what a hard pill to swallow. What is she supposed to do now?

This letter talks about a family member of hers who is a part-time teacher in New Jersey, but also works at a restaurant called Trader Joe's. The reason why she works there is for the health benefits that she is offered, but now she is losing that. Unfortunately she is not alone.

This is an article from Bloomberg from September 19 of this year. It highlights all these upheavals that are going on by private employers. UPS is dropping coverage for employed spouses; IBM is reworking its retiree benefits. Let me explain that one for a second. They are going to send their retirees to the private exchanges. They said the move was made to help keep premiums low for the rest of their workers that are impacted by ObamaCare.

Walgreens, the largest U.S. drugstore chain, has told 160,000 workers that they must buy insurance through a private exchange rather than continuing to have it offered by the company, by Walgreens. They are not alone. Stanford University researchers voiced concerns in a study last week. They wrote that "the rising premiums can drive workers from employer plans to coverage under the health law, boosting costs for the government by as much as $6.7 billion."

There are other examples of businesses that are doing this. I talked about Trader Joe's. That is a closelyheld supermarket chain. I said a restaurant. I apologize, it is a supermarket chain. It said it would end health benefits next year for part-time workers.

This is the real disruption in real lives. So one thing is to stand here and have people debate about the theory of ObamaCare and what great things it might do for some people, according to the supporters of this law. Another thing is to put a human face on the story. We already know, just from this e-mail alone, of one person in America, living in New Jersey, a part-time teacher and a worker at Trader Joe's who has lost her benefits and will now be thrown into this uncertain world of exchanges, because of this law, because of ObamaCare.

Here is another e-mail. This one comes from Kissimmee, FL. That is in central Florida. My colleagues may know that as the home of Walt Disney World. This is from Patty. She writes:

As mentioned in your letter—(She is referring to a letter I sent to Secretary Sebelius—) urging her to visit Sea World to discuss the impact of ObamaCare that will be enacted in the near future, I—(Patty, the writer of this letter—) am a part-time employee at Valencia College in Orlando.

Valencia is a community college. By the way, I am a big fan of community colleges. They are the backbone of retraining, but also the only access point available to many of our people. So if you are out there trying to work to support your family—let's say you are a single parent trying to raise three kids and you have to work during the day—community college is also one of the few places where you can get an advanced degree and the skills you need for a better job. One of the best ways to improve your pay and your economic security is to get an education. Community colleges are an access point for people all over the country. I am a huge fan of community colleges. We have great ones in Florida. She is a part-time employee of Valencia College in Orlando. She continues:

> My hours too have been cut from 29 hours to 25 hours to avoid any negative impact of the Obamacare health care act. I have numerous e-mails from my supervisor and human resources stating that my hours are being cut specifically because of this.
>
> I have lost the hours that made it possible to live in a severely reduced income and know that I will never get those hours back as positions have been created by the extra hours, so we have more people working and earning less. I am not really asking anything; I'd just like you to know what this government is doing to my ability to survive.

This is not an e-mail from a millionaire or a billionaire. This is not an email from someone who has made it and is making a ton of cash. This is an e-mail from a part-time worker at a community college with desperation that comes out in the e-mail: a parttime worker losing hours. Did we know what those hours mean, 4 hours a week of a pay cut to someone? She writes about it. She says: "I would just like you to know what this government is doing to my ability to survive."

Do we want to know why a growing number of Americans are starting to doubt whether the American dream is still alive? Read this e-mail.

Unfortunately, we are hearing stories about this all the time. Here is an article from CNBC published Monday, September 23, this week. It leads off with this line:

> With open enrollment for Obamacare about to begin, small- and medium-sized businesses are not hiring because of the uncertainty surrounding the implementation of the new law, the CEO of the Nation's fifth-largest staffing company said on Monday.
>
> Companies are really not interested in hiring full-time people. "That's really the issue with Obamacare," Express Employment Professionals boss Bob Funk told CNBC's "Squawk Box" on Monday.

By the way, Mr. Funk is the former chairman of the Kansas City Federal Reserve.

Now, someone—the former auto czar at Treasury, Mr. Steve Rattner—disputes his assertions. He says:

> I don't think with the approach of Obamacare you see in the numbers people suddenly stopping hiring.

Mr. Funk argues—and he counters very persuasively—he says:

> We're out there on Main Street and Obamacare is affecting the job hiring picture. Whether it's in the numbers or not, it is affecting small and medium-sized businesses. They're not going to hire until they know what their costs are going to be.
>
> We don't know what the rules are going to be, but they haven't written half of the rules . . . and it is affecting businesses out there. That's why our industry is growing quite rapidly.

So here we have a person tied to the government basically saying these guys don't know what they are talking about; the numbers

458 STAND WITH TED

don't bear this out. And then we have someone who reminds them that he is on the front lines. That is what Mr. Funk is doing. He is very clear. He says, "We are out there on Main Street and Obamacare is affecting the job hiring picture."

Listen again to what Patty from Kissimmee says in her e-mail. This is what she says:

> I have lost the hours that made it possible to live in a severely reduced income and know that I will never get those hours back as positions have been created by the extra hours.

Do my colleagues know what she is saying? She is saying what they have done is reduced her hours and then just hired additional people to make it up. They have created another part-time job to make up for it. This is the impact of ObamaCare.

By the way, with all due respect to my colleagues, I will tell my colleagues right now in case people are wondering, every single member of the Republican Conference here in the Senate is prepared to repeal ObamaCare right now. The debate we are having in the party is about the tactics, the right way to do it. The one thing I would say, however, is what the last day has provided us, which is an extraordinary opportunity to tell these stories.

There is more. Here is an e-mail from Bill in Panama City, FL. That is in northwest Florida, a great place for spring break if you are in college and can afford to go. Maybe you lost your part-time job so now you can't. Bill says:

> This is just a note to let you know that you can include me as another one of your constituents who has seen my health care cost go up by over $200 a month. I also just learned that my girlfriend, who works for a major corporation, is losing her health care after she retires because of Obamacare. I hope you will continue your fight to defund this disastrous bill.

I wish, Bill, that—I obviously feel terrible for the situation you are facing and certainly for the situation your girlfriend is facing. Unfortunately, you are not alone.

Let me read something to my colleagues that Jim Angle from Fox News published on the 24th of this month, I guess that was yesterday, right? He tells the story of Andy and Amy Mangione of Louisville, KY, and of their two boys. He leads off by saying:

These are just the kind of people who should be helped by ObamaCare, but they recently got a nasty surprise in the mail.

"When I saw the letter when I came home from work," Andy said, describing the large red wording on the envelope from his insurance carrier, (it said) "your action required, benefit changes, act now." Of course I opened it immediately.

Guess what that letter that was in the mail said? It had stunning news. His insurance—the insurance for his family, his two boys, his wife and him—insurance they were buying on the individual marketplace—was going to almost triple next year, from $333 a month to $965 a month. In the letter, the carrier made it clear that the increase was in order to be compliant with the new health care law.

He goes on to say:

This isn't a Cadillac plan, this isn't even a silver plan. This is a high deductible plan where I'm assuming a lot of risk for my health insurance for my family. And nothing has changed, our boys are healthy—they're young—my wife is healthy, I'm healthy. Nothing in our history has changed to warrant a tripling of our premiums.

His wife adds:

Well, I'm the one that does the budget. Eventually, I've got that coming down the pike that I gotta figure out what we're gonna do, to afford a $1,000 a month premium.

The insurance carrier, Humana, declined to comment, but the notice to the Mangiones carried this paragraph: If your policy premium increased, you should know that this isn't unique to Humana—premium increases generally will occur industry-wide.

Increases aren't based on your individual claims or changes in your health status.

(It continued:) Many other factors go into your premium, including: ACA compliance—(which is ObamaCare—) Including the addition of new essential health benefits.

Robert Zirkelbach, who is the spokesman for American Health Insurance Plans, which represents insurers, explains that:

For people who currently choose to purchase a high-deductible, low-premium policy that is more affordable for them, they are now being required to add all of these new benefits to their policy. That, (He says,) is going to add to the cost of their health insurance premiums.

This is a real life story. It is not a letter from a millionaire or billionaire, and this is not the story of a millionaire or billionaire; this is the story of a husband and wife and two children who are buying insurance as individuals from the individual marketplace who will now have to cobble together another $700 a month and they have no idea how they are going to do it. This is the real story of ObamaCare. Here it is. These are the people we are supposed to be helping. These are the people who—when they passed this thing, they went around telling people, We are going to help you get insurance. These are the people it is supposed to be helping, but look what it is doing. I wish that was the only example, but I have an e-mail here from Florida that says that, too. Here is another one from Barbara in Palm Coast, FL:

I am a master's level RN who up until last week held a good job with good benefits. Due to the many new restrictions on employers, I have been reduced to part-time without benefits at age 64.

It is starting to sound like a broken record.

Many healthcare workers are being cut in hours due to Obamacare. My company tried to offer me an insurance plan that I could afford to purchase, but I received a letter stating that it didn't meet the standards of the Affordable Care Act, and so I had until January 1st to purchase more costly insurance or have consequences.

She writes:

This is a terrible, despicable law—(And I agree—) that has damaged many more people than just myself.

Then she closes with this extremely powerful sentence. This is not from a millionaire or a billionaire, from the infamous 1-percenters that we hear these protesters against. This is from a nurse in Florida, and here is what she finishes with:

I just want to live in a free country where I can work hard and support myself. Repeal Obamacare.

Well, one may ask themselves: Is this really happening? People are losing access to their coverage? Let me read something from a conservative, rightwing newspaper, *The New York Times*, dated September 22, 2013:

Federal officials often say that health insurance will cost consumers less than expected under President Obama's health care law. But they rarely mention one big reason: Many insurers are significantly limiting the choices of doctors and hospitals available to consumers.

One more impact of ObamaCare

. . . . They have created smaller networks of doctors and hospitals than are typically found in the commercial insurance plans.

In a new study, the Health Research Institute of PricewaterhouseCoopers, the consulting company, says that "insurers passed over major medical centers" when selecting providers in California, Illinois, Indiana, Kentucky and Tennessee, among other states.

In New Hampshire, Anthem Blue Cross and Blue Shield, a unit of WellPoint, one of the Nation's largest insurers, has touched off a furor by excluding 10 of the state's 26 hospitals from the health plans that it will sell through the insurance exchange.

Anthem is the only commercial carrier offering health plans in the New Hampshire exchange.

What does this mean? Let me tell my colleagues what it means. ObamaCare says if you can't find insurance, we are going to set up these government exchanges. Theoretically, that is not a terrible idea. You go online, you shop between different companies, they compete against each other, you find a price that works for you, you find coverage that works for you, and that is where you are going to be required to go. That is where the people who got cut off from Walgreens insurance plans have to go now. It is where a bunch of other people have to go.

What are these companies doing? There are a couple of things happening. First, in States such as New Hampshire, only one insurance company applies. There is no choice. There is no competition. The exchange is one company: Anthem.

No. 2, what are these companies doing in order to offer these plans? They are basically narrowing the doctors and the hospitals that will see you. One may say, at least I get to go to a hospital or a doctor. Let me tell my colleagues where the problem is. Remember what they said when this passed? If you have health insurance and you like it, if you have a doctor and you are happy with that doctor, you can keep it? Not if you are on the exchange. If they are narrowing the number of people, the number of doctors and providers, that means chances are that you will no longer be able to keep going to the same doctor and the same hospital you were going to before.

So now let's work that out. Let's walk through this for a second. Put yourself in the position of this nurse who wrote to us. Let's say you are chronically ill. Let's say your child has asthma or some other condition. Let's say you have four healthy kids but you have to take them to the doctor at least once a year, right? You love the doctor you go to. They know your family and your history. When you have a problem you can call them on the phone at 2 in the morning and you get a call right back, avoiding emergency room visits, by the way; you can get your doctor on the phone. Now you wake up and all of a sudden your company comes to you and says the insurance plan you are on right now, we are not offering it anymore, go get it on the exchange.

So you go over to the exchange and you find two things: No. 1, it is more expensive, and, No. 2, your doctor ain't on the plan. That is a broken promise. That is specifically what they said this law would not do, and that is what it is doing.

This is the real-life story of what is happening. You want to know why there is passion about this issue? You want to know why every Republican Member of the Senate wants to repeal this thing? You want to know why privately some Democrats wish it would go away? Because of this. This is whom we are fighting for. This is not just a fight against a bad law. This is a fight on behalf of people across this country who are going to get hurt by this.

By the way, I have no idea—these people who have written me or others who are suffering, I do not know whom they voted for in the last election. It does not matter. I do not know if they ever voted for me in 2010. I do not know if they supported the law when it first came out. But I know they are being hurt by this, and I know they are being hurt by this in ways that will hurt all of us, that will hurt every single one of us.

I talked about it earlier this morning. I repeat it today: There is nothing more important than preserving, reclaiming, and restoring the American dream. It is the essence of what makes us special as a country. It separates us from the world.

What is the American dream? It is pretty straightforward. This is a country where if you work hard and you sacrifice, you should be able to get ahead and earn a better life for yourself and for your family. Does this sound like the story of a law that is making it easier for people to get ahead? Does being moved from full-time to part-time work make it easier to get ahead? Of course not. Does losing a doctor whom you are happy with make it easier for you to get ahead? Of course not. Does the fact that businesses are not hiring make it easier to get ahead because they are afraid of ObamaCare? Does it make it easier to get ahead? Of course not. Does having your hours reduced from 29 to 26—or whatever the figure was I read a moment ago—does that make it easier to get ahead? Of course not.

If for no other reason, this law needs to be repealed because of the impact it is having on the American dream. I will reiterate what I have said time and again on this floor and here as part of this process: You lose the American dream, you lose the country. What you have then—what you have then—is just another rich and powerful country but no longer an exceptional one.

The American dream is at the cornerstone of what makes us different and special, and it is being threatened by this. That is why I feel so passionately that we must do everything we can—everything we can—to call attention to what this is doing and try to change it.

I think if nothing else, Senator, the great service of these last—what is it now? 19 hours, as your tie continues to loosen—if nothing else, I think people today across this country know more about this law and its impacts than they did 1 day ago. If nothing else, the people in this country are now increasingly aware of all the implications of this law on their lives, on their dreams, on their hopes, and on their families.

I believe this is just the beginning, and I hope we can prevent these harmful effects from happening. But it does not sound like it. It sounds like there are still people here who are willing to shut down the government unless this thing is fully funded, unless we continue to pour your hard-earned taxpayer dollars. The irony of it is, for Luis in Cutler Bay, for Patty in Kissimmee, for Bill in Panama City, for Barbara in Palm Coast, FL, for all the people who were cited in these articles, for the Mangione family in Louisville, KY, guess whose money is paying for this disaster. Yours. Your taxpayer dollars are paying for this catastrophe because of the stubbornness of saying: This is our law, and we are going to go through with it, no matter all these anecdotal things that are coming out.

By the way, the only way you can get relief from the negative impacts of this law is if you can afford to hire a lobbyist to come up here and get you a waiver. The only way you can avoid some of the disastrous impacts of this law is if you can somehow figure out a way to influence this administration to write the rules in a way that benefits you.

That is wrong. That is wrong. I hope we will do something about this. I think the last 19-some-odd hours have been a huge step in that direction.

I guess my question to Senator Cruz would be: I am sure he is getting letters such as these from Texas and across the country given the events of the last day. This is what this is all about, isn't it? This is not a fight just against a law; this is a fight on behalf of the people who are being hurt by it in the most fundamental way possible. It is hurting their hopes and dreams they have for themselves, for their families. It is undermining the American dream. Is that not what this is all about?

Mr. CRUZ. I thank the junior Senator from Florida, and I would note that is precisely what this is about. This is a fight for the millions of men and women who are facing a stagnant economy, who are facing jobs that are drying up or disappearing altogether, who are finding themselves being forcibly put in part-time work, being forced to work 29 hours a week or less, who are finding their health insurance premiums skyrocketing, and who are being threatened or facing already their health insurance being taken away. All of these are the very real consequences of ObamaCare right now for millions of Americans.

Listen, there are people in this body who in good faith 3½ years ago could have believed this was a good idea, it might work. I did not think it at the time, but I understand that people in this body did.

At this point, with all the evidence, I would suggest that case can no longer be made, that the evidence is abundantly clear. It is why the unions are jumping ship. It is why Members of Congress have asked for an exemption. It is why it is now abundantly clear that this train wreck, this nightmare, is hurting Americans all over this country.

I will note a couple of things. First of all, I note that my assistant majority leader is on the floor, and I would make a request that either—I do not know if the assistant majority leader is in a position to speak for the majority leader or, if he is not, I would make a request, if the majority leader is monitoring this proceeding, that he come to the floor because I would like to promulgate a series of unanimous consent requests. I do not want to surprise the majority leader or the assistant majority leader, so I would like the opportunity to explain those requests before promulgating them, to give Democratic Party leadership an opportunity to think about it, to spend a little bit of time contemplating it, to make a decision whether they would consent.

So I would make a request, unless the assistant majority leader is prepared to speak for the majority leader, that I would ask that the majority leader, if he can—I know his schedule is certainly very busy—but I would ask if he can come to the floor so I may lay out the unanimous consent requests that I would like to promulgate.

I would also note that for some time Senator GRASSLEY from Iowa has been waiting, and he has requested time to raise a question. So if Senator GRASSLEY at this point would like to ask a question——

Mr. DURBIN. Mr. President, I would like to enter into a dialog with the Senator from Texas without jeopardizing his control of the floor, if I could have consent for that purpose.

The ACTING PRESIDENT pro tempore. Without objection, it is so ordered.

Mr. CRUZ. On the condition that it does not jeopardize in any way my full control of the floor, I am amenable to that request.

Mr. DURBIN. First, I do not come in the place of the majority leader. He will speak for himself. We do not know what the Senator's unanimous consent requests might be. If the Senator would articulate it, describe it, I am sure we will take it under consideration, as we do with any request from any Senator. But this comes as a surprise at this moment, as the Senator can understand.

I just wished to come to the floor and continue the dialog we started last night. After listening to my friend and colleague Senator RUBIO describe a situation, I wanted to ask the Senator from Texas, if I could, a question about the situation he described.

Senator RUBIO talked about the insurance exchanges and the insurance marketplaces and the fact that some of the lowest cost health insurance plans that are being offered have limitations as to doctors and hospitals that a person can use under those low-cost plans.

I would ask the Senator from Texas—I talked to him last night about Judy, who is a housekeeper at a motel in southern Illinois. She is 62 years of age. She has worked her entire life, has never had health insurance one day in her life—not once—never had it offered by an employer, never could afford it, and now will be able to have health insurance for the first time in her life, and she qualifies under Medicaid in the State of Illinois. She will not pay for it. It is going to be coverage. In her case, even a limitation on doctors and hospitals is a dramatic improvement over no doctor, no hospital, and relying on emergency rooms for her diabetes.

So I would ask the Senator from Texas, try to put yourself in the shoes of this woman who has worked her entire life. If you are being told you have a limitation on doctors and hospitals you can use, but you have health insurance, isn't that a dramatic improvement over a lifetime of no health insurance?

That is what ObamaCare is going to offer to her for the first time in her life. To say that we should not give her that opportunity is akin to someone saying: If you can't fly first class, you can't get on the airplane. Listen, a lot of people would be glad to sit back in economy if they could just make the trip that the Senator and I can make because we are blessed with health insurance.

I would say to the Senator, as you condemn ObamaCare, I go back to the question I asked you last night: Judy, 62 years old, a lifetime of work, diabetes, first chance to get health insurance—do you want to abolish the ObamaCare program that will give Judy that first chance?

Mr. CRUZ. I thank the Senator from Illinois for that question, and I would respond threefold.

No. 1, for Judy, as the Senator describes her circumstances, I would certainly support health care reform that increases competition and increases free market alternatives that lower the rate of health insurance that is available to people by allowing interstate competition, creating a national marketplace. But, in my view, any health care reform should empower individuals and patients to make health care decisions in consultation with their physicians—not having a government bureaucrat get in between them and their doctor.

If I may finish the remainder of my points, concomitantly, the Senator has told the story of Judy, and I do think we should have reforms to address her circumstance, but over the course of the last many hours we have read scores, if not hundreds, of stories that are a small representation of the thousands or millions of people who are losing or are in jeopardy of losing their health insurance right now. They have to be balanced in this equation as well.

ObamaCare is causing people all over this country to lose their health insurance or be at risk of losing their health insurance, and I am sure if I were to promulgate the question to the Senator from Illinois: Do you want all of these people who are losing their health insurance to lose their health insurance—all of the names I read—I am sure the Senator would say no. But to date, no one on the Democratic side of the aisle has proposed any way to fix that.

Let me make a second point, and then I am going to have a third point. Then, if the Senator would care for another question, I am happy to do my best to respond.

The second point: The Senator from Illinois made a reference to Judy not needing to be in first class but being content to be in coach. I think that analogy is a powerful one, but what it highlights is the special exemption that has been put in place for Members of Congress. Because President Obama has put an exemption in place for Members of Congress that says: Members of Congress will fly first class, to use the Senator's airline analogy, but average Americans who are being forced onto exchanges, where their employers cannot subsidize their premiums, are not even flying coach. They are being put in the baggage department.

I will say I agree with the intent and the spirit of Senator GRASSLEY's amendment to ObamaCare that was adopted, that is part of the law that the President is disregarding, which is that if we are going to force millions of people to lose their health insurance, be forced into these exchanges, then we should have skin in the game. Congress should not be treated any better than the millions of Americans we are forcing onto the exchanges.

Mr. DURBIN. Will the Senator yield on that point?

Mr. CRUZ. Let me make my third point, and then I am happy to yield at that point for a question.

The third point is twice I have read in the course of this debate the letter from Mr. Hoffa, the head of the Teamsters.

I assume the Senator from Illinois has read that letter. In fact, I expect the Senator from Illinois has had direct conversations with the author of that letter. I do not know that.

I would ask the Senator from Illinois, No. 1, has he read that letter; No. 2, does he think Mr. Hoffa is telling the truth; and No. 3, in particular, does he agree with the following paragraph?

> On behalf of the millions of working men and women we represent and the families they support, we can no longer stand silent in the face of elements of the Affordable Care Act that will destroy the very health and wellbeing of our members along with millions of other hardworking Americans.

So my question is, does the Senator believe Mr. Hoffa is telling the truth when he says that? If so, does the Democratic majority in this body have any plans, any proposals, any amendments to fix that problem for what Mr. Hoffa describes as "millions of working men and women" whose health care will be—the word he uses—destroyed.

I am happy to hear the Senator from Illinois.

Mr. DURBIN. I thank the Senator from Texas for this dialog. First class health care. Let me tell you who has first-class health care. The Senator from Texas has first-class health care. The Senator from Illinois has first-class health care. You see, Members of Congress, Members of the Senate and the House, under the Federal Employees Health Benefits Program, have the best health insurance in America. We fly first class. Our employer, the Federal Government, as it does for every other employee, pays 72 percent of the monthly premium. Some 150 million Americans have that benefit where an employer pays some share of it. Ours pays 72 percent. We are lucky. We are fortunate. So are our families and so are our staff.

But what the Senator is saying in abolishing ObamaCare, you not only want to fly first class, you do not want other people to get on the plane. Fifty million Americans have no health insurance. You want to abolish the opportunity through the marketplace for them to buy affordable health insurance for the first time in their lives for many people. That is what it comes down to.

Don't say you want Members of Congress treated like everybody else if you are currently under the Federal Employees Health Benefits Program. May I ask Senator CRUZ, are you currently—you and your family—covered by the Federal Employees Health Benefits Program, which includes a 72-percent employer contribution from the Federal Government for your family's health care protection?

Mr. CRUZ. I appreciate the Senator's question, but I will answer the Senator's question when the Senator first answers the three questions I asked him, none of which the Senator has chosen to answer, namely: Have you read Mr. Hoffa's letter? Do you agree with that paragraph? Do you think he is telling the truth? What, if anything, does the Democratic majority purport to do about millions of working men and women whose health care, according to Mr. Hoffa, is being destroyed?

I would note that the Senator from Illinois made an allegation impugning my motive, saying that I wanted 50 million people to be denied health care. Let me be very clear. That statement is categorically false. I want a competitive marketplace where health care is accessible, it is affordable, where it is purchased across States lines, where it is personal, where it is portable, and where people have jobs so they can get health insurance. ObamaCare is what is denying health insurance to millions of Americans. If you do not take my word for it, I assume you do not contend that Mr. Hoffa is being less than truthful?

Mr. DURBIN. I would like to respond to that. If this were a courtroom—and you are an attorney, and I once practiced law myself—I would say: Your Honor, the witness refused to answer the question about his very own health insurance policy.

Now let me address the issue about Mr. Hoffa. I have been approached by many labor unions. Some of them have Taft-Hartley plans, some of them have trust fund plans, some have multistate plans. They need provisions made in the ObamaCare law to deal with their specific circumstances.

Under the ordinary course of legislative and congressional business, over the last 3 years we would have addressed these anomalies in the ObamaCare program. Sadly, we cannot get anyone to come to the table from the Senator's political party. Now 42 or 43 times the House Republicans have voted to abolish ObamaCare. Not once have they proposed sitting down to work out any differences, work out any problems within the law. I am prepared to do that. I have told the labor unions, including Mr. Hoffa, the same. I know the administration feels the same. But, unfortunately, those who are opposed to this plan want it to descend into chaos. They want as much confusion, as many problems as possible. They do not want to work to cover the 50 million uninsured in America.

What the Senator just described and said he could sign up for, frankly, is ObamaCare. We are talking about a marketplace. Do you know how many companies will be offering health insurance in the State of Texas under the ObamaCare plan? Let me make sure I get this correct. My understanding is that at least 54 plans are going to be offered in the State of Texas—54. There will be choice and a marketplace for the first time ever for many people who were stuck with one plan or who could not get into any plan.

Let me ask you this question as we get back to this point. Does the Senator still believe we should abolish the provision in ObamaCare that says you cannot discriminate against people with preexisting conditions who apply for health insurance?

Mr. CRUZ. I will answer that question. Since I have not yielded the floor, I would like to make a broader point after that and have a colloquy. I will point out why, which is that we are operating under some time constraints. So I want to do what the Senator asked of detailing the unanimous consent requests that I want to promulgate so he and the majority leader may consider them. I also want to be respectful of Senator GRASSLEY and Senator SESSIONS, who have been waiting to speak. The Senator and I have engaged in multiple exchanges, both now and earlier, and so I want to be respectful of the other Senators on the floor.

But let me answer the question. I believe we should repeal every word of ObamaCare. I think it has failed. I agree with James Hoffa that on behalf of millions of working men and women and the families they support, that "the Affordable Care Act will destroy the very health and well being of our members, along with millions of other hard-working Americans." So I think we should repeal it. I think we should defund it in the interim. This is not a fight over repealing, it is a fight over defunding it. Then I think we should adopt free market plans to lower prices, make health care more affordable, make it portable, and allow it to go with individuals.

Mr. DURBIN. Now will the Senator answer my question of whether his family is protected by the government-administered Federal Employees Health Benefits Program—the best health insurance in America—where his employer, the Federal Government, pays 72 percent of his monthly premium? Will the Senator from Texas for the record tell us—and those who watch this debate—whether he is protected.

Mr. CRUZ. I am happy to tell the Senator. I am eligible for it. I am not currently covered under it.

Let me note that the Senator from Illinois embraced the analogy and said: Yes, we in Congress have first-class health care. Under his analogy, he wants to stick Judy in coach class. What Senator GRASSLEY's amendment was all about is, you know what, if you stick Judy in coach class, guess what. Members of Congress are going back in coach class. The Senator and I may disagree. I do not think Judy is in coach class, I think she is down in the baggage claim.

Regardless, in his hypothetical the Senator is conceding that the congressional health care plan right now is better than Judy's under ObamaCare, and he is saying that he supports a special exemption for Members of Congress that Judy does not get.

I agree with Senator GRASSLEY's amendment that we should not be forcing millions of Americans into coverage we are not willing to experience. I recognize the passion of the Senator, but I would note that I have not yielded the floor.

I would like to describe the unanimous consent requests that I would like to promulgate. I would ask the assistant majority leader and the majority leader to confer with my staff and simply let me know if these requests would be amenable. I am not promulgating them at this time because I do not want to surprise leadership staff without giving you time to consider them.

The first unanimous consent request that I would propose to promulgate is a request that we vitiate the cloture on the motion to proceed that is scheduled this afternoon and agree by unanimous consent to proceed to this bill. To my knowledge, I am not aware of any Senator in this body who opposes proceeding to this bill. I think all of us agree that we should proceed to this bill, we should keep the government open. Some of us think we should keep the government open and defund ObamaCare, others think we should fund it, but to the best of my knowledge, no one disagrees. So if the majority is amenable, I would propose vitiating the cloture motion and simply agreeing to the motion to proceed. That would be the first unanimous consent request I would promulgate if it is agreeable to the majority.

The second unanimous consent request that I would promulgate is, if it is agreeable to the majority, as I understand in the timing, all of the delays are put in place. Cloture on the bill would be scheduled to occur on Saturday. In my view, in order to defeat cloture on the bill—you know I want to defeat cloture on the bill. That is no secret. I think the best chance to defeat cloture on the bill is for this bill to be visible to the American people—highly visible. So accordingly, I would be amenable to shortening the time for postcloture debate such that that vote on cloture on the bill occurs on Friday afternoon rather than Saturday. Why is that? Because I think that on a Friday afternoon, a lot more American people are going to pay attention to what we are doing than a vote on Saturday during football games and when people are paying attention to other things. That may or may not be amenable to the majority, but if it is, we can shorten this time by a period because I think we have a better chance in prevailing in this fight if that vote—I note the majority leader is here. I do not know if he heard the initial unanimous consent, which, if it is amenable to the majority leader, we would negotiate the language with him and promulgate.

So the first one I offered, Mr. Leader—and I have not yielded the floor, but I am describing during my time on the floor the unanimous consent requests I would promulgate if the majority would be amenable. The first would be to vitiate the cloture request and simply agree on the motion to proceed because to my knowledge everyone in this body agrees we should proceed to this bill, although we have sharp disagreements on what we should do.

The second unanimous consent request, if it is amenable to the majority, that I would suggest—and I think the majority leader heard this as he was walking in—is to agree to shorten the time of postcloture debate such that cloture on the bill would occur Friday afternoon rather than Saturday. The reason is—I am being very transparent about my reasoning. I think it is better for this country if this vote is at a time that is visible for the whole country so that the American people have a voice in it. I think sticking it in Saturday in the middle of football games disserves that objective.

Then the third request—if the majority leader would be amenable—I would put forward is, as I understand it, under the rules of the Senate, in some 35 minutes, my time will be automatically cut off as the new legislative day begins and it begins with a prayer. When I started this filibuster yesterday afternoon, I told the American people that I intended to stand until I could stand no more. I will observe to the majority leader that although I am weary, there is still at least strength in my legs to stand a little longer. So the third thing I would simply ask is if the majority would consent to allow me to speak until the conclusion of my remarks and then begin the next legislative day and have the prayer at the conclusion of those remarks. If the majority says no, then my time will end at noon under the rules of the Senate. So it is entirely up to the majority whether to let me continue to speak. But given that I began by saying I will speak until I can stand no more, I believe I should at least ask if those consents are amenable.

I would note that under the rules of the Senate, if the majority leader cares to ask a question, I can yield for a question in which he might share his views or, if the majority leader wants to think about it, to discuss it with his staff, then I would note that the majority leader could simply convey to my staff if any or none of those unanimous consent requests are amenable. If none of them are, that is fine and we will conclude at noon.

The PRESIDING OFFICER. The majority leader.

Mr. REID. Madam President, is there a consent?

Mr. CRUZ. I want to clarify. I have the floor. I have not yielded the floor to anyone. Neither the majority leader nor any other Member has the right of recognition right now. If the majority leader wishes, he may ask me to yield for a question. I might yield for that limited purpose. But other than that, no one has the floor, if I understand the rules of this body correctly.

The PRESIDING OFFICER. The Senator is correct.

Mr. CRUZ. So I make that note. If the majority would care to ask a question, I would be amenable to yielding for a question. If the majority leader would not, that is certainly his prerogative, and I am happy to continue talking about the issues this debate has focused the country on because they are issues of vital importance.

Mr. REID. I am without a question.

Mr. CRUZ. Mr. President, I would simply note to the majority leader that if those unanimous consent requests are amenable, I would ask that his staff convey that to my staff. If they are not, I would ask that his staff convey that to my staff simply so we know which way to proceed. Regardless, I want to make sure before we wrap up because I assume now in 31 minutes we will be concluded. I want to yield to Senator GRASSLEY in just a moment because I do not want to miss—I apologize to Senator GRASSLEY, but I do not want to miss the opportunity within the limited time to do something that is imperative that I do, which is to thank the men and women who have endured this Bataan Death March. I want to take a little bit of time to thank them by name.

I would like to start by thanking the Republican floor staff and cloakroom. I thank Laura Dove for her fairness, for her dealing with crises and passion on all sides, and for her effectiveness in the job. This is an interesting occurrence to occur so early in her job. I thank her for her service.

I wish to thank Robert Duncan, Patrick Kilcur, Chris Tuck, Megan Mercer, Mary-Elizabeth Taylor, and Amanda Faulkner.

I wish to thank Democratic floor staff and cloakroom: Gary Myrick, Tim Mitchell, Trish Engle, Meredith Mellody, Dan Tinsley, Tequia Delgado, Brad Watt, and Stephanie Paone. I wish to thank the clerks and Parliamentarians. I wish to thank the Capitol Police, the Sergeant at Arms, and the Secretary of Senate employees.

The Parliamentarians are Elizabeth MacDonough, Leigh Hildebrand, Mike Beaver; the Legislative Clerk, Kathie Alvarez; the Journal Clerk, Scott Sanborn; the Bill Clerk, Mary Anne Clarkson; the Daily Digest, Elizabeth Tratos; the Enrolling Clerk, Cassie Byrd; the chief reporter, Jerry Linnell; CONGRESSIONAL RECORD, Sylvia Oliver, Val Mihalache, Pam Garland, Desi Jura, Joel Breitner, Doreen Chendorain, Julie Bryan, Patrick Renzi, Mark Stewart, Wendy Caswell, Ann Riley, Patrice Boyd, Mary Carpenter, Octavio Colominas; captioning, JoEllen Dicken, Jim Hall, Sandy Schumm; Sergeant at Arms and Secretary of the Senate employees; the Senate pages, many of whom I caused to miss school. I appreciate you all for enduring this, and all those who work in the Capitol complex.

I wish to thank my entire staff, many of whom have been here all night.

I ask unanimous consent to have printed in the RECORD a note of sincere gratitude to my staff, who worked tirelessly to help me prepare and sustain extended floor remarks. I especially appreciate their appearance in the Chamber throughout the night, which was a great source of encouragement. I extend my appreciation to each of the following individuals:

Chip Roy, Chief of Staff; Sean Rushton, Communications Director; Amanda Carpenter, Speechwriter & Senior Communications Advisor; Catherine Frazier, Press Secretary; Josh Perry, Digital Director; Brooke Bacak, Legislative Director; Jeff Murray, Deputy Legislative Director; Scott Keller, Chief Counsel; John Ellis, Senior Counsel; Bernie McNamee, Senior Domestic Policy Advisor and Counsel; Kenny Stein, Legislative Counsel; Alec Aramanda, Legislative Assistant; Max Pappas, Director of Outreach & Senior Economist; Victoria Coates, Senior Advisor of National Security.

Jeremy Hayes, Military Legislative Assistant; David Milstein, Research Assistant; Dougie Simmons, Director of Scheduling; Christine Shafer, Deputy Director of Scheduling; Kimberly Henderson, Administrative Director; Dan Soto, IT Director; Amy Herod, Scheduling Assistant & Assistant to the Chief of Staff; Hunter Rome, Legislative Correspondent; Samantha Leahy, Legislative Correspondent; Martin Martinez, Legal Assistant; Melanie Schwartz, Legislative Correspondent; Caitlin Thompson, Legislative Correspondent; Ben Murrey, Legislative Correspondent; Brittany Baldwin, Press Assistant; Nico Rios, Staff Assistant; John Landes, Staff Assistant.

I wish to thank Democratic Senators who have presided: Senator BALDWIN, Senator MANCHIN, Senator WARREN, Senator DONNELLY, Senator KAINE, Senator MURPHY, Senator SCHATZ, Senator BALDWIN again, Senator DONNELLY, Senator DURBIN, Senator HEITKAMP, and Senator MARKEY.

I wish to thank the Republican Senators who have spoken in support of our efforts: Senator SESSIONS, Senator RUBIO, Senator PAUL, Senator INHOFE, Senator ENZI, Senator ROBERTS, Senator VITTER, and very soon, Senator GRASSLEY.

I wish to thank the House Members who have come over. Representative AMASH, Representative BROUN, Representative HUDSON. I wish to make a special note of Representative GOHMERT who was here the entire night enduring this.

I wish to make a point, particularly to the floor staff and to everyone: You all didn't choose this. I appreciate the hard work and diligence going through the night. That is not part of your typical job responsibility. I would not have imposed on your time and energy if I did not believe this was an issue of vital importance to the American people. I wish to thank you for your hard work, diligence, and cheerfulness through what has been a very long night.

I wish to thank, second to last, Senator MIKE LEE. Senator MIKE LEE began this fight. Senator MIKE LEE has been here throughout the course of this battle. Senator MIKE LEE has been always cheerful, always focused, always ready to march into battle and always ready to focus on the ultimate objective, which is serving the American people by standing and fighting to stop the train wreck, the nightmare, the disaster that is ObamaCare.

We wouldn't be here if it weren't for Senator LEE's principle, for his courage, for his bravery under fire. I feel particularly honored to serve as his colleague and consider him a friend.

Last, I wish to thank the American people. I want to thank people all across the country who watched on C–SPAN, tweeted, engaged, and have been involved in this process. This is ultimately about the American people. What this whole fight is about is whether this body, the Democratic Senators and the Republican Senators, will change the broken ways of Washington and start listening to the people. That is what this fight is all about.

With those thank yous, I apologize, but I felt obliged to conclude before 12 o'clock when my time will be cut off by force. I will note at this point Senator GRASSLEY had wished to ask a question.

I am prepared to yield for a question if Senator GRASSLEY wishes to ask me a question.

The PRESIDING OFFICER (Ms. BALDWIN). The majority leader.

Mr. REID. I ask my friend from Texas to yield to me, without losing his right to the floor, for a colloquy.

The PRESIDING OFFICER. Will the Senator so yield?

Mr. CRUZ. With the reservation that I do not lose the right to the floor, I am pleased to engage in a colloquy with the majority leader.

Mr. REID. Madam President, first, this is not a filibuster. This is an agreement that he and I made that he could talk.

Let me say this: We are going to have a vote about 1 o'clock today. After that is over, we will follow the rules of the Senate. My goal is to get this to the House of Representatives as quickly as possible.

I think a lot of this time has been—without talking about what has transpired at this point—I would hope that we could collapse the time dramatically and move forward so the House of Representatives can get what we are going to send back to them.

There is a possibility they may not accept what we send them. They may want to send us something back. If we use all this time under the rules as they now exist——

Mr. CRUZ. I have decided to not yield my right to the floor. I was amenable to a colloquy. The majority leader is giving a speech.

Given that, as I understand, the majority leader is not going to consent to extend the time, I have 24 minutes, I am going to reassert my time on the floor since I have not yielded my time on the floor.

Mr. REID. If I could ask for a unanimous consent agreement with my friend.

The PRESIDING OFFICER. Is there objection?

Mr. CRUZ. There is objection. I am sorry. I cannot be asked to consent to an unnamed consent agreement.

Given that the majority leader, as I understand, is not going to consent to extend my time, then let me say quite simply to the majority leader that I will yield time to him for a question when the majority leader is prepared to yield to the American people. But I am not prepared to yield prior to that because Senator GRASSLEY, Senator SESSIONS, and Senator INHOFE are waiting to speak. I believe they are endeavoring to listen to the American people. If the majority is going to cut off and muzzle us in another 24 minutes, then at this point I don't feel it is appropriate to allow the majority leader to consume that time.

I will note to any Senators who were here—if anyone would care, I know a number of Senators are waiting to ask questions, I am prepared to yield to a question from any of them.

Mr. REID. I have a question I wish to ask my friend from Texas.

The PRESIDING OFFICER. Will the Senator from Texas yield for a question without losing the floor?

Mr. CRUZ. I yield for a question without yielding the floor.

Mr. REID. Between 12 and 1 o'clock, would my friend yield to Senator McCAIN for 15 minutes of that time?

Mr. CRUZ. That question is asked, but it will not prove necessary, absent the consent that I promulgated. I am assuming it would not be acceptable to the majority because my time will end at noon. There is nothing left to yield because, as I understand it under the Senate rules, when the new legislative day begins and the prayer begins, my time yields.

Mr. REID. Madam President, he has the right to speak from 12 o'clock to 1 o'clock. What I am asking the consent for is would he allow, during that period of time, Senator McCAIN to speak for 15 minutes.

Mr. CRUZ. It is my understanding my time expires at noon. Absent a consent to extend it, I will honor the Senate rules and allow my time to expire at noon, so there is nothing to yield.

I will note Senator SESSIONS is standing.

Mr. SESSIONS. Will the Senator yield for a question?

Mr. CRUZ. I yield for a question without yielding the floor.

The PRESIDING OFFICER. The majority leader.

Mr. REID. Parliamentary inquiry, Madam President.

The PRESIDING OFFICER. Does the Senator from Texas yield for a parliamentary inquiry?

Mr. CRUZ. Given the majority leader has cut off our time in 20 minutes, no, I am sorry, I do not. The majority leader was welcome to come down any time in the last 20 hours and ask parliamentary inquiries or questions. I would note Senator DURBIN did so, Senator KAINE did so, others Senators did so.

At this point, our time is expiring and I wish to allow other Republican Senators who appeared and asked questions to ask questions to have the opportunity to do so.

The PRESIDING OFFICER. The majority leader.

Mr. REID. May I direct a question to my friend from Texas?

The PRESIDING OFFICER. Does the Senator yield for a question?

Mr. CRUZ. I yield for one more question without yielding the floor.

Mr. REID. The question is the Senator seems to not understand that he has time, after the prayer is given at 12 o'clock, time until 1 o'clock. During that period of time my question was, because the Senator still has the floor, would the Senator yield 15 minutes to JOHN McCAIN.

Mr. CRUZ. It is my intention, if the consent request that I asked is not agreed to, to accept the end of this at noon under the Senate rules.

Mr. REID. I understand.

The PRESIDING OFFICER. Does the Senator from Texas yield for a question?

Mr. CRUZ. I yield for a question without yielding the floor.

Mr. SESSIONS. I thought that a very gracious question of the author of unanimous consent, that we would vitiate the vote and 30 hours of debate. The Senator asked very little in exchange for it, other than to continue to talk.

Mr. CRUZ. Let me briefly clarify, I asked nothing in exchange for that. None of those were contingent on each other. Those were three independent unanimous consent requests—which the majority leader wanted consent to any of those. It wasn't an offer of horse trade, it was simply—I think all three of those make sense. I think any one of the three of them makes sense. If he chooses to reject them all, that is his prerogative and that is fine. I was only suggesting we not waste this body's time by doing so.

Mr. SESSIONS. To follow up on that then, it seems to me that what the Senator was saying would be an offer that most everyone here would be pleased to receive and accept, unless they have some surreptitious motive.

In addition, I think the Senator's continued request to be allowed to continue to speak is reasonable. I think the Senator has earned the right to ask that. The Senator has now spoken. The American people are watching the fourth longest time any filibuster or floor time has been held by a Senator. I think that is a perfectly reasonable request. It will allow the Senator to continue to express the concerns that he has expressed. I am somewhat taken aback that it wasn't agreed to.

Again, to make clear, it would seem to me little if any reason that they would object to that, the majority would object to that.

Mr. CRUZ. I thank my friend from Alabama.

I would note that unfortunately I am not surprised that none of the consents were taken. I note the first two consents, one would think, would be quite amenable. Yet, look, throughout this debate, the problem has been the majority does not wish to listen to the American people and doesn't want a debate in front of the American people, particularly about the merits of ObamaCare. They don't want to talk about how ObamaCare is failing millions of Americans. They don't want to talk about how millions of Americans are losing their jobs and how they are not being hired. They don't want to talk about how millions of Americans are facing being pushed into part-time work. They don't want to talk about how millions of Americans are either losing their health insurance or are at risk of losing their health insurance.

This process is all about, sadly, the Democratic majority not listening to the American people. The whole purpose of this filibuster was to do everything we could to draw this issue to the attention of the American people so the American people could be heard.

If the American people speak with sufficient volume, I continue to have confidence that this body, that the Senators on both sides of the aisle, will have no choice but to listen.

Given that we have 16 minutes remaining, I inadvertently omitted in my thank yous the doorkeepers by accident.

The doorkeepers were: Tucker Eagleson, Dawn Gazunis, Elizabeth Garcia, Rocketa Gillis, Marc O'Connor, Laverne Allen, Daniel Benedix, Cindy Kesler, Scott Muschette, Tony Goldsmith, Jim Jordan, Megan Sheffield, David West, Denis Houlihan, and Bob Shelton.

Let me say for any of the floor staff or others, if I inadvertently omitted someone, please accept my apology. It was my intention to endeavor to thank anyone. If I have made an inadvertent omission, that is my fault and I take responsibility for it.

I wish to note also that an additional Member of Congress, Congressman STEVE KING, has joined us. I wish to thank Congressman KING for joining us.

I would note, as we are in the last 15 minutes, that if my friend and colleague Senator MIKE LEE wished to ask a question, I would be prepared to yield as we are wrapping up.

Mr. LEE. Will the Senator from Texas yield for a question?

Mr. CRUZ. I yield for a question without yielding the floor.

Mr. LEE. From day 1, there have been those in the Washington establishment who have been working against this, and it was the American people who stood up in strong support of us. It was the American people who served as the heroes of this story who spoke overwhelmingly to the Congress and spoke overwhelmingly to the House of Representatives and convinced the House of Representatives to pass this great continuing resolution—one that keeps government funded and allows it to avoid a shutdown while defunding ObamaCare. That is what this effort has been all about. It has been all about the people we are trying to protect from this horrible law.

Across the country Americans stayed up with us overnight forging this argument, helping us distribute this argument, choosing to forego sleep and to show their support of this effort, and we greatly appreciate that. I want to take a moment to reflect on how all of us who have been up all night feel right now—with dry eyes, with a certain amount of grogginess, and yet ultimately this is an exhilarating moment. It is exhilarating because we are inspired by the American people who have informed this message and who have expressed their views so well and so forcefully, and I am grateful to have been part of this effort.

I ask the Senator from Texas: As we come to the end of this uphill climb we have experienced over the past 24 hours, give or take, we see the cards are somewhat stacked against us. Today, although Washington may appear to have the upper hand, in our hearts don't we know the American people are with us, and don't we know the American people will have the final word, and that as George Washington predicted a couple of centuries ago, this country will always remain in good hands—in the hands of its people?

Mr. CRUZ. I thank my friend Senator LEE from Utah, and I think that is exactly right. At the end of the day it is the United States of America—"we the people"—who are sovereign. Ultimately every Member of this body works for "we the people." The reason there is such profound frustration across this country, the reason this body is held in such abysmally low esteem is that for too long Washington has not listened to the American people. Every survey of the American people, no matter what State, no matter whether you are talking Republicans, Democrats, Independents or Libertarians, the answer is always the same: The top priority for the American people is jobs and the economy.

The Presiding Officer and I both began serving 9 months ago as freshmen in this body. I will tell you my greatest frustration in this body during those 9 months is that we have spent virtually zero time talking about jobs and the economy. We spent 6 weeks talking about guns and taking away people's Second Amendment rights. But when it comes to jobs and the economy in this Senate, it doesn't even make the agenda.

We spend no time talking about fundamental tax reform. We spend no time or virtually no time talking about regulatory reform. When it comes to defunding ObamaCare, the single biggest thing we could do to restore jobs in the economy, the Democratic majority is not interested in that conversation. Indeed, for the bulk of this conversation, with a couple of exceptions, the Democratic majority chose not to engage in the debate. Why? I would submit it is because on the merits, on the substance, the defense of ObamaCare is now indefensible.

There may have been some, even many, who 3½ years ago, when ObamaCare was adopted, believed in good faith it was going to work. But at this point the facts are evident that it is not. At this point we have seen small businesses all over this country who are losing the ability to compete, who are not expanding, who are staying under 50 employees, who are not hiring, and who are forcing employees to move to part-time work.

According to the Chamber of Commerce survey of small businesses, half of small businesses eligible for the employee mandate are either moving to part-time workers or forcing full-time workers to go part time. This is not a small problem. This is not a marginal problem. This is a problem all over the country. We are talking to millions of small businesses. Another 24 percent, I believe is the number, are simply not growing, are staying under 50 employees, which means they are not hiring people.

So anyone in America right now who is struggling to find a job—and small businesses provide two-thirds of all new jobs—small businesses are crying out that ObamaCare is killing them. Unfortunately, the Senate is not hearing their cries. For the millions of Americans who are facing the threat of being forced into part-time work, unfortunately, the Senate is not hearing their cries. For the millions of Americans who are facing skyrocketing health insurance premiums and facing the reality or the risk of losing their health insurance, the Senate is not hearing their cries.

The people who are facing this are not the wealthy, they are not the powerful, they are not, as the President likes to say, the millionaires and billionaires. They are the most vulnerable among us. They are young people who are being absolutely decimated by ObamaCare. They are single moms who are working in diners, struggling and suddenly finding their hours reduced to 29 hours a week. The problem is 29 hours a week is not enough to feed your kids. Single moms are crying out to the Senate to fix this train wreck, to fix this disaster. And for the struggling single moms, for young people, unfortunately, the Senate is closed for business.

Mr. RISCH. Madam President, will the good Senator yield for a question without yielding the floor?

Mr. CRUZ. I am happy to yield for a question without yielding the floor, although I would note we have all of 6½ minutes until the time will expire.

Mr. RISCH. I will be brief. I want to talk briefly and ask a question about the area the Senator was just talking about. My good friend Senator RUBIO made reference to the story I am going to tell. My good friends on the other side of the aisle are good about bringing out pictures of people with sad faces. My only regret is I don't have a picture of somebody with a sad face, but I can assure you these people are greatly saddened by this.

We had a hearing in the Small Business Committee and we brought in people from around the country, small businesses who are suffering under this terrible burden. The Senator was not here in the middle of the night when this abomination was shoved down the throat of the American people on a straight party-line vote. I can assure him that we fought it tooth and nail, but now the American people are having to live with this, and so it is good to be reminded again of what we have here.

But this gentleman operated a business called Dot's Diner in Louisiana. He had, I forget whether it was six or seven diners, and this man was living the all-American dream. He had quit a very good job, cashed in his retirement, borrowed money and he and his wife opened this diner. The diner did well because they worked hard. Like the Senator did all night tonight, sometimes they worked that hard. They opened more diners and were just about to open another one when the Senate announced they were going to force ObamaCare on the American people and on the small businesses of this country.

They immediately stopped their plans to open a new diner and then looked at what ObamaCare was going to cost them. The cost of ObamaCare was substantially higher than the profits they were making in the business every year. So what they did, they went and got counsel and said: How can we get around ObamaCare? What they were told is, if you have 49 employees, you are outside of ObamaCare. So given that, what they did is they closed the diners and got down to 49 employees and that is where they are.

Will the Senator tell me, because I would like to hear his thoughts on that and whether he believes the American government that our Founding Fathers fought for and died for should be visiting this on the American people, particularly on small businessmen who are the backbone of this economy?

Mr. CRUZ. I thank the Senator from Idaho for his question and for his steadfast leadership and willingness to stand and fight for the American people to stop this train wreck that is ObamaCare. And the answer to my friend's question is: Of course not. Small businesses all over this country are getting hammered by ObamaCare, and the real loses are not even to the small business owners. The real losers are the people, the teenaged kids who would get hired, the single moms who would get hired, the African Americans, the Hispanics who are suddenly finding themselves without a job or are being forcibly reduced to 29 hours a week and denied the opportunity to get to that first rung of the economic ladder, which would then get them to the second, the third, and the fourth.

Millions of Americans are hurting under ObamaCare. It is my plea to this body, to the Democrats, that they listen to the unions that are asking on behalf of millions of Americans who are struggling to repeal ObamaCare, that we not have a system where the rich and powerful or big corporations and Members of Congress are treated to a different set of rules than hard-working Americans. President Obama has granted illegal exemptions to big businesses and Members of Congress. I don't think the American people should be subject to harsher rules.

So my plea to this body is that we listen to the American people, because if we listen to our constituents, the answer is: Defund this bill that isn't working, that is hurting the American people, that is killing jobs and forcing people into part-time work, that is driving up health insurance premiums and that is causing millions to lose or to fear they will lose their health insurance.

As the time is wrapping up, I will close by noting that at noon we will have a prayer. I think it is fitting this debate conclude with prayer, because I would ask that everyone in this body ask for the Lord's guidance on how we best listen to our constituents, listen to the pleas for help that are coming from our constituents.

The final thing I will do is to make two unanimous consent requests I mentioned, and the majority leader may or may not agree to them. The first is:

I ask unanimous consent that the cloture vote at 1 p.m. be vitiated and that at the conclusion of my remarks the motion to proceed to the resolution be agreed to.

The PRESIDENT pro tempore. Is there objection?

Mr. REID. Reserving the right to object, my friend has had an opportunity to speak. I will speak for a longer time period in a few minutes about statements he has made in the last several hours. But he has spoken.

At 1 p.m. the Senate will speak, and we will follow the rules of the Senate. I have said very clearly on a number of occasions that we should be moving quickly to get this to the House as soon as we can.

I object.

The PRESIDENT pro tempore. Objection is heard.

Mr. CRUZ. Mr. President, my second request is:

I ask unanimous consent that if a cloture motion is filed on the underlying measure, that cloture vote occur during Friday's session of the Senate, notwithstanding the provisions of rule XXII.

The PRESIDENT pro tempore. Is there objection?

Mr. REID. Reserving the right to object, we are going to have a cloture vote at 1 o'clock and any consent agreements after that I will be happy to listen to them. At this stage, I object.

The PRESIDENT pro tempore. Objection is heard.

Mr. CRUZ. Well then, it appears I have the floor for another 90 seconds or so, and so I simply will note for the American people who have been so engaged that this debate is in their hands. Ultimately, all 100 Senators—all 46 Republicans, all 54 Democrats—work for you. The pleas from the American people—certainly those in Texas—are deafening. The frustration that the United States Senate doesn't listen to the people is deafening. So I call on all 46 Republicans to unite, to stand together and to vote against cloture on the bill on Friday or Saturday; otherwise, if we vote with the majority leader and with the Senate Democrats, we will be voting to allow the majority leader to fund ObamaCare on a straight party-line vote of 51 partisan votes.

The American people will understand that. Voting to give that power to the majority leader, I would suggest, is not consistent with, I believe, the heartfelt commitment of all 46 members of this conference who oppose ObamaCare. The only path, if we are to oppose ObamaCare, is to stand together and oppose cloture. I ask my friends on the Democratic side of the aisle to listen to this plea.

The PRESIDENT pro tempore. Pursuant to the order of February 29, 1960, the hour of 12 noon having arrived, the Senate having been in continuous session since convening yesterday, the Senate will suspend for a prayer from the chaplain.